Fodor's 2010

D0827910

CHICAGO

Where to Stay and Eat
for ALL Budgets

Must-See Sights
and Local Secrets

Ratings You Can Trust

Fodor's Travel Publications   New York, Toronto, London, Sydney, Auckland
www.fodors.com

FODOR'S CHICAGO 2010

Editors: Stephanie Butler, Kelly Kealy (coordinating editor), Alexis Kelly, Margaret Kelly

Editorial Contributors: Erica Duecy, Carolyn Galgano
Writers: Kelly Aiglon, Kate Leahy, Heidi Moore, Jo Napolitano, Roberta Sotonoff

Production Editor: Astrid deRidder
Maps & Illustrations: David Lindroth, Mark Stroud, *cartographers*; Bob Blake, Rebecca Baer, *map editors*; William Wu, *information graphics*
Design: Fabrizio La Rocca, *creative director*; Guido Caroti, Siobhan O'Hare, *art directors*; Tina Malaney, Chie Ushio, Ann McBride, Jessica Walsh, *designers*; Melanie Marin, *senior picture editor*
Cover Photo: (Chicago Theater marquee, North State Street, The Loop): age fotostock/ SuperStock, with permission from MSG, a division of Madison Square Garden
Production Manager: Angela L. McLean

ISBN 978–1–4000–0860–5

ISSN 0743–9326

SPECIAL SALES

This book is available at special discounts for bulk purchases for sales promotions or premiums. Special editions, including personalized covers, excerpts of existing books, and corporate imprints, can be created in large quantities for special needs. For more information, write to Special Markets/Premium Sales, 1745 Broadway, MD 6-2, New York, New York 10019, or e-mail specialmarkets@randomhouse.com.

AN IMPORTANT TIP & AN INVITATION

Although all prices, opening times, and other details in this book are based on information supplied to us at press time, changes occur all the time in the travel world, and Fodor's cannot accept responsibility for facts that become outdated or for inadvertent errors or omissions. So **always confirm information when it matters,** especially if you're making a detour to visit a specific place. Your experiences—positive and negative— matter to us. If we have missed or misstated something, **please write to us.** We follow up on all suggestions. Contact the Chicago editor at editors@fodors.com or c/o Fodor's at 1745 Broadway, New York, NY 10019.

PRINTED IN THE UNITED STATES OF AMERICA

10 9 8 7 6 5 4 3 2 1

Be a Fodor's Correspondent

Your opinion matters. It matters to us. It matters to your fellow Fodor's travelers, too. And we'd like to hear it. In fact, we need to hear it.

When you share your experiences and opinions, you become an active member of the Fodor's community. That means we'll not only use your feedback to make our books better, but we'll publish your names and comments whenever possible. Throughout our guides, look for "Word of Mouth," excerpts of your unvarnished feedback.

Here's how you can help improve Fodor's for all of us.

Tell us when we're right. We rely on local writers to give you an insider's perspective. But our writers and staff editors—who are the best in the business—depend on you. Your positive feedback is a vote to renew our recommendations for the next edition.

Tell us when we're wrong. We're proud that we update most of our guides every year. But we're not perfect. Things change. Hotels cut services. Museums change hours. Charming cafés lose charm. If our writer didn't quite capture the essence of a place, tell us how you'd do it differently. If any of our descriptions are inaccurate or inadequate, we'll incorporate your changes in the next edition and will correct factual errors at fodors.com immediately.

Tell us what to include. You probably have had fantastic travel experiences that aren't yet in Fodor's. Why not share them with a community of like-minded travelers? Maybe you chanced upon a beach or bistro or B&B that you don't want to keep to yourself. Tell us why we should include it. And share your discoveries and experiences with everyone directly at fodors.com. Your input may lead us to add a new listing or highlight a place we cover with a "Highly Recommended" star or with our highest rating, "Fodor's Choice."

Give us your opinion instantly at our feedback center at www.fodors.com/feedback. You may also e-mail editors@fodors.com with the subject line "Chicago Editor." Or send your nominations, comments, and complaints by mail to Chicago Editor, Fodor's, 1745 Broadway, New York, NY 10019.

You and travelers like you are the heart of the Fodor's community. Make our community richer by sharing your experiences. Be a Fodor's correspondent.

Happy traveling!

Tim Jarrell, Publisher

CONTENTS

Fodor's Features

ABOUT
THIS BOOK

Our Ratings

Sometimes you find terrific travel experiences and sometimes they just find you. But usually the burden is on you to select the right combination of experiences. That's where our ratings come in.

As travelers we've all discovered a place so wonderful that its worthiness is obvious. And sometimes that place is so experiential that superlatives don't do it justice: you just have to be there to know. These sights, properties, and experiences get our highest rating, **Fodor's Choice,** indicated by orange stars throughout this book.

Black stars highlight sights and properties we deem **Highly Recommended,** places that our writers, editors, and readers praise again and again for consistency and excellence.

By default, there's another category: any place we include in this book is by definition worth your time unless we say otherwise. And we will.

Disagree with any of our choices? Care to nominate a place or suggest that we rate one more highly? Visit our feedback center at www.fodors.com/feedback.

Budget Well

Hotel and restaurant price categories from ¢ to $$$$ are defined in the opening pages of each chapter. For attractions, we always give standard adult admission fees; reductions are usually available for children, students, and senior citizens. Want to pay with plastic? **AE, D, DC, MC, V** following restaurant and hotel listings indicate if American Express, Discover, Diners Club, MasterCard, and Visa are accepted.

Restaurants

Unless we state otherwise, restaurants are open for lunch and dinner daily. We mention dress only when there's a specific requirement and reservations only when they're essential or not accepted—it's always best to book ahead.

Hotels

Hotels have private bath, phone, TV, and air-conditioning and operate on the European Plan (aka EP, meaning without meals), unless we specify that they use the Continental Plan (CP, with a continental breakfast), Breakfast Plan (BP, with a full breakfast), or Modified American Plan (MAP, with breakfast and dinner), or are all-inclusive (AI, including all meals and most activities). We always list facilities but not whether you'll be charged an extra fee to use them, so when pricing accommodations, find out what's included.

Many Listings	
★	Fodor's Choice
★	Highly recommended
⊠	Physical address
⊹	Directions
⌂	Mailing address
☎	Telephone
🖶	Fax
⊕	On the Web
✉	E-mail
🎟	Admission fee
☉	Open/closed times
Ⓜ	Metro stations
▭	Credit cards
Hotels & Restaurants	
🏨	Hotel
⌁	Number of rooms
⚲	Facilities
⦿|	Meal plans
✕	Restaurant
⟰	Reservations
⤵	Smoking
⚟	BYOB
✕🏨	Hotel with restaurant that warrants a visit
Outdoors	
🏌	Golf
⛺	Camping
Other	
☾	Family-friendly
⇨	See also
⊠	Branch address
☞	Take note

1

Experience Chicago

WORD OF MOUTH

"Take the architectural boat tour; it's a wonderful way to see the city. [Plan to see the] Museum of Natural History together with the Shedd Aquarium and Adler Planetarium (all located within walking distance to each other). The ethnic neighborhoods (German, Polish, Italian, Russian, Jewish, etc.) have wonderful, fun, different restaurants. For lunch one day try Al's Beef for an Italian beef sandwich; it's a Chicago tradition. Lakefront, Millennium Park, Lincoln Park Zoo are always free and easily accessible."

—AAFrequentFlyer

www.fodors.com/community

CHICAGO PLANNER

The Second City?

New Yorkers will tell you theirs is the greatest city in the world. But Chicagoans beg to differ. Chicago's charm is indisputable—the impeccably clean streets; the friendly Midwestern vibe; the alluring mixture of lush parks, Lake Michigan, and sleek skyscrapers. It's what keeps the debate going (log onto the Fodors.com "Talk" forum and check out one of the "favorite city" debates!), and what keeps everyone coming back.

My Name Is . . .

Much to locals' chagrin, a number of Chicago's storied institutions have undergone recent name changes. In the summer of 2009 the Sears Tower, once the world's tallest building, was renamed the Willis Tower after its new tenant, Willis Group Holdings, a London-based insurance broker. Macy's renamed the famed Marshall Field's department stores in 2006, and the departure of Carson Pirie Scott from its landmark Louis Sullivan building led to its new moniker, the Sullivan Center. Chicagoans still frequently refer to these three popular sights by their original names.

Getting Around

Chicago has an excellent network of buses as well as trains, which are collectively called the El (for "elevated," which many of them are). The combination should bring you within ¼ mile of any place you'd like to go. Those with city smarts will find it safe to take any train, any time. Others may want to take extra caution after 11 PM. Buses are almost always safe; there are several express buses running from downtown to destinations like the Museum of Science and Industry.

As of this writing, the fare for the bus is $2 and the train is $2.25 and a transfer is 25¢ with a Transit Card; if you're paying cash, all rides are $2.25. Travelers may want to get a Visitor Pass at their hotel, airport CTA stations, or any visitor center. These passes allow unlimited rides for a small fee and are worth it as long as you take three trips a day.

For directions to specific places via public transportation, for public transportation maps, and for places to buy Transit Cards, see ⊕ www.transitchicago.com.

Free trolley service runs from State Street to Navy Pier via Grand Avenue and Illinois Street.

If you drive downtown, park in one of the giant city-owned parking lots underneath Millennium Park or by the Museum Campus, which charge a flat fee. Private lots usually cost double.

A Few of Our Favorite Things

What do Fodor's editors do when they head to Chicago? Here are a few of our personal picks. We love walking along the Chicago River and watching the boats ply the water, then strolling down State Street to the old Carson Pirie Scott building, just to admire the iron scrollwork outside. We gallery-hop in River North, and duck into cute boutiques along Oak Street. We head to Hyde Park to gawk at the colorful, noisy monk parakeets. We never leave without indulging in deep-dish pizza. We won't tell you which baseball team we cheer for, but we do love going to the games. And at night? You can find us catching the blues at B.L.U.E.S., going to an outdoor concert (we've heard great ones at Grant Park), howling at Second City improvisers, or having drinks at the Signature Room at the John Hancock.

Visitor Centers

Chicago Cultural Center (✉ 78 E. Washington St. ☎ 312/744–6630 ⊕ www.chicagoculturalcenter.org ⊙ Mon.–Thurs. 8–7, Fri. 8–6, Sat. 9–6, Sun. 10–6).

Chicago Water Works (✉ 163 E. Pearson St., at Michigan Ave. ☎ 877/244–2246 ⊕ www.explorechicago.org ⊙ Daily 7:30–7).

Millennium Park Welcome Center (✉ 201 E. Randolph St., in the Northwest Exelon Pavilion ☎ 312/742–1168 ⊕ www.millenniumpark.org ⊙ Daily 6 AM–11 PM).

Chicago Greeters (☎ 312/744–8000 ⊕ www.chicago greeter.com). This free service, offered by the Chicago Office of Tourism, pairs visitors with a city-smart volunteer guide for an informal two- to four-hour walking tour. Register two weeks in advance. Chicago Greeter tours step off from the Chicago Cultural Center).

When to Go

June, September, and October are mild and sunny. November through March the temperature ranges from crisp to bitter, April and May can fluctuate between cold/soggy and bright/warm, and July and August can either be perfect or serve up the deadly combo of high heat and high humidity. That said, the only thing certain about Chicago's weather, according to locals, is that it can change in an instant. If you head to Chicago in warmer months, you'll be able to catch some of the fantastic outdoor festivals; during the holiday season the city's decked out in lights.

Local Know-How

Most businesses in Chicago are open 10 to 6. Some shops stay open as late as 9. Restaurants can be closed on Monday and usually stop serving around 10 PM on weeknights, 11 PM on weekends. There are a few 24-hour diners, but they are rarer than you might expect. Bars close at 2 AM or 4 AM.

You can avoid the long lines at Chicago museums by buying tickets online at least a day in advance. The most popular architecture tour, led by the Chicago Architecture Foundation, always sells out—be sure to buy tickets in advance.

CHICAGO
TOP ATTRACTIONS

Willis (Sears) Tower Skydeck

(A) Take the ear-popping ride to the 103rd-floor observatory, where on a clear day you can see as far as Michigan, Wisconsin, and Indiana. At the top, interactive exhibits tell all about Chicago's dreamers, schemers, architects, musicians, writers, and sports stars. Kids love Knee-High Chicago, a 4-foot-high exhibit that has cutouts of Chicago sports, history, and cultural icons at a child's eye-level. Security is very tight, so figure in a little extra time for your visit to the Skydeck.

John Hancock Center Observatory

(B) The third-tallest building in Chicago has the most impressive panoramic views of the lake and surrounding skyline—it's high enough to see the tops of neighboring buildings in vivid 3-D, but not so remote that you feel like you're looking out from a plane. Our tip? Skip the observatory and head to the bar that adjoins the Signature Room restaurant on the 95th floor—you'll spend your money on an exorbitantly priced cocktail instead of the entrance fee and enjoy the same view. Women can head to the 95th-floor ladies' room for the best view in the whole building.

Shopping on the Magnificent Mile

(C) Exclusive shops, department stores, and boutiques line the northern half of swanky Michigan Avenue. Even better, the concentration of prestigious stores in vertical malls means you can get a lot of shopping done in winter without venturing into the bluster outside.

The Blues Scene

(D) Explore jumping North Side clubs, like Kingston Mines, or South Side venues like the Checkerboard or Lee's Unleaded Blues (where greats like Muddy Waters and Buddy Guy first honed their talent) for the sound Chicago gave birth to—the scintillating electric blues. If you're here in June, don't miss the Chicago Blues Festival, which packs in fans every summer.

Navy Pier

(E) Yes, it's a little schlocky, but Navy Pier is fun, especially for families. Everyone can fan out to shop in the mall, play 18-hole minigolf in Pier Park in the summer, see a movie at the IMAX Theater, or explore the Chicago Children's Museum. Plus, there's a stained-glass museum, a funhouse maze with scenes of Chicago landmarks, and an old-fashioned swing ride. Meet up later at the Ferris wheel for a photo op or just settle on the pier with a drink and enjoy the view.

Art Institute of Chicago

(F) This Chicago cultural gem has the country's best collection of Impressionist and Postimpressionist art, as well as the brand-new Renzo Piano–designed modern wing. It's also a great place to see all those paintings you've only seen on postcards, like *American Gothic* and *Nighthawks*.

Adler Planetarium and Astronomy Museum

(G) How can you not enjoy getting up close with the cosmos at the country's oldest planetarium? Older children and astronomy fanatics get geeked about the interactive science exhibits and the high-tech Sky Pavilion, while younger visitors set their sights on virtual-reality shows in the StarRider Theater.

Field Museum

(H) Say hello to Sue, the Field's beloved gigantic T. rex, before immersing yourself in this extraordinary museum's collection of anthropological and paleontological artifacts and animal dioramas. The dinosaurs are the thing here, but surprising collections like Tibetan Buddhist altars, mummies, and re-creations of famous gems may entice you to linger for hours.

Museum of Science and Industry

(I) Travel down an elevator shaft to a "working" coal mine, stroll the cobblestone streets of Chicago circa 1910, explore the caves of a human heart, or watch quietly as a baby chick pecks its way out of its shell at this endlessly interactive museum.

Shedd Aquarium

(J) We find the experience of watching entire universities—not just schools—of fantastically colored fish, as well as dolphins and whales, completely mesmerizing. Don't miss the Wild Reef exhibit, where stingrays slide quietly under the Plexiglas at your feet.

Frank Lloyd Wright Architecture

(K) Frank Lloyd Wright's Prairie School captured the flat, expansive Midwestern plains he saw around him. Oak Park, a Chicago suburb, has many fine examples, though one of the best is Robie House in Hyde Park, which is open for tours.

Millennium Park

Make a beeline for Frank Gehry's **Jay Pritzker Pavilion,** where an incredible sound system allows audiences to enjoy concert-hall sound in the great outdoors. The *Bean* is a luminous polished-steel sculpture that plays tricks with the reflection of Chicago's skyline. In warmer months children of all ages can't resist a splash in the Crown Fountain, twin 50-foot towers that project close-up video images of Chicagoans "spitting" jets of water.

SOAKING IT ALL IN: RIVER AND LAKE TOURS

Coursing through the heart of the Windy City is the majestic Chicago River, lined with some of the city's finest architecture and dotted with river walks and restaurants. Hop in a boat, kayak, canoe, or gondola and sail down for some of the prettiest views of the city. Some tours even head out to the lake for a skyscraper-studded panorama.

Best Tour Companies

The **ArchiCenter of the Chicago Architecture Foundation** (⊠ *224 S. Michigan Ave., Loop* ☎ *312/922–3432* ⊕ *www.architecture. org* ⊗ *Daily 9–6:30*) conducts excellent, docent-led boat, walking, and bus tours of the Loop and beyond. Our favorite walking tours spotlight "Historic Skyscrapers" and "Modern Skyscrapers." The Archi-Center also hosts exhibitions, lectures, and discussions.

Watch the panoply of Chicago's magnificent skyline from the decks of *Chicago's First Lady, Chicago's Little Lady,* and *Chicago's Fair Lady,* the fleet of the **Chicago Architecture Foundation River Cruise.** Make reservations in advance for the popular 90-minute tours. **Ticketmaster** (☎ *800/982-2787* ⊕ *www. ticketmaster.com/illinois*) sells tickets by phone, online, and at the Hot Tix booth in the Chicago Water Works Visitor Center. You can also purchase tickets at the *Chicago's First Lady* ticket window or at the Chicago ArchiCenter (224 S. Michigan Ave.). ⊠ *Southeast corner of Michigan Ave. Bridge* ☎ *847/358–1330* ⊕ *www.cruisechicago. com* ✉ *$28 Mon.-Fri., $32 weekend* ⊗ *May-Oct., daily; Nov., weekends.*

Other Recommended Companies

Shoreline Sightseeing. Shoreline's been plying these waters since 1939, and has tours of both the river and Lake Michigan. ⊠ *West end of Navy Pier* ☎ *312/222–9328* ⊕ *www.*

TOUR ALTERNATIVES

Hop on a Shoreline water taxi and cruise down the river. You won't get running narration, but it's affordable (single rides range from $2 to $6 from Michigan Aveue with stops on LaSalle/Clark, Madison Street and Chinatown) and not crowded.

For a more adventurous spin down the river, rent a canoe or a kayak. Just beware of large boats and crew shells. **Chicago River Canoe and Kayak** (⊠ *3400 N. Rockwell St.* ☎ *773/704-2663* ⊕ *www. chicagoriverpaddle.com*). **Chicagoland Canoe Base** (⊠ *4019 N. Narragansett Ave.* ☎ *773/777–1489* ⊕ *www.chicagoland canoebase.com*). **Wateriders** (⊠ *900 N. Kingsbury Ave.* ☎ *312/953–9287* ⊕ *www. wateriders.com*).

shorelinesightseeing.com ⊗ *Apr.–Oct., daily; Nov., weekends only.*

Wendella Sightseeing. See the city as the sun sets on the Chicago at Sunset tour. There's a river architecture tour, a combined river and lake tour, and a pirate tour. ⊠ *400 N. Michigan Ave., at the Wrigley Building* ☎ *312/337–1446* ⊕ *www.wendellaboats. com* ⊗ *Apr.–Nov., daily.*

Mercury Cruises. Mercury does Canine Cruises, where dogs are welcome, and a City Lights tour that glides past Buckingham Fountain's lights. ⊠ *112 E. Wacker Dr.* ☎ *312/332–1353* ⊕ *mercuryskyline cruiseline.com* ⊗ *May–Oct., daily.*

CITY ITINERARIES

Two Hours in Town

If you've only got a bit of time, go to a museum. Although you could spend days in any of the city's major museums, two hours will give you a quick taste of Chicago's cultural riches. Take a brisk walk around the **Art Institute** to see Grant Wood's *American Gothic,* Edward Hopper's *Nighthawks,* and one of the finest Impressionist collections in the country. Or check out the major dinosaur collection or the gorgeous Native American regalia at the **Field Museum.** Take a close look at the sharks at the **Shedd Aquarium.** If the weather's nice, stroll along the lakefront outside the **Adler Planetarium**—you'll see one of the nicest skyline views in the city. Wander down State Street, the Magnificent Mile, or around Millennium Park. If you're hungry, indulge in one of Chicago's three famous culinary treats—deep-dish pizza (head to **Pizzeria Due** to avoid the lines at **Giordano's, Gino's,** and **Pizzeria Uno**); garden-style hot dogs; or Italian beef sandwiches. After dark? Hear some music at a local club. Catch some blues at **Blue Chicago** to get a taste of authentic Chicago.

■TIP➜ Remember that many of the smaller museums are closed on Monday.

A Perfect Afternoon

Do the zoo. Spend some time at the free **Lincoln Park Zoo and Conservatory** (the tropical plants will warm you up in winter), take a ride on the exotic animal-themed carousel, and then spend a couple of hours at the nearby **Chicago History Museum** for a quirky look at the city's past. If you'd like to stay in the Lincoln Park neighborhood a bit longer, have dinner at one of many great local restaurants and then head to **The Second City,** the sketch comedy troupe that was the precursor to *Saturday Night Live.*

■TIP➜ The Second City offers free improvisation following the last performance every night but Friday.

Sightseeing in the Loop

State Street, that Great Street, is home to the old **Marshall Fields,** which has been reborn as Macy's; Louis Sullivan's ornate iron entrance to the former department store **Carson Pirie Scott;** a nascent theater district; as well as great people-watching. Start at Harold Washington Library at Van Buren Street and State Street and walk north, venturing a block east to the beautiful **Chicago Cultural Center** when you hit Randolph Street. Grab lunch at the Museum of Contemporary Art's serene Wolfgang Puck café, **Puck's at the MCA,** and then spend a couple of hours with in-your-face art. Go for steak at Morton's or the Palm before a night of Chicago theater. Broadway touring shows are on Randolph Street at the Oriental or the Cadillac Palace, or head elsewhere downtown for excellent local theater—the Goodman, Steppenwolf, Lookingglass, and Chicago Shakespeare will each give you a night to remember.

Get Outdoors

Begin with a long walk (or run) along the lakefront, or rent a bike or inline skates and watch the waves on wheels. Then catch an El train north to **Wrigley Field** for Cubs baseball; grab a dog at the seventh-inning stretch, and sing your heart out to "Take Me Out to the Ball Game." Afterward, soak up a little beer and atmosphere on the patio at one of the local sports bars. Finish up with an outdoor concert in **Grant or Millennium park.**

Family Time

Start at **Navy Pier**—or heck, spend all day there. The **Chicago Children's Museum** is a main attraction, but there's also an IMAX theater, a Ferris wheel, a swing ride, a fun house, a stained-glass museum, and, in summer, Chicago-themed miniature golf in Pier Park. If the crowds at the Pier get to be too much, walk to **Millennium Park,** where kids of all ages can ice-skate in winter and play in the fountain in summer, and where giant digital portraits of Chicagoans spit streams of water to help cool you off. Whatever the weather, make sure to get your picture taken in the mirrored center of the *Bean*—the sculpture that's formally known as *Cloud Gate.* At night in summertime, take a stroll by Buckingham Fountain, where the dancing sprays jump to music and are lit by computer-controlled colored lights, or take a turn on the dance floor during Chicago's nightly SummerDance celebration.

■ TIP➔ Fireworks explode near Navy Pier every Wednesday and Saturday night at 9 PM Memorial Day through Labor Day.

Cityscapes

Start at the top. Hit the heights of the **John Hancock Center** or the **Willis (Sears) Tower Skydeck** for a grand view of the city and the lake. Then take a walking tour of downtown with a well-informed docent from the **Chicago Architecture Foundation.** In the afternoon, wander north to the **Michigan Avenue Bridge,** where you can take an informative boat tour of the Chicago River. Enjoy the architecture as you float by, resting your weary feet.

Shop Chicago

Grab your bankroll and stroll the **Magnificent Mile** in search of great buys and souvenirs. Walking north from around the Michigan Avenue Bridge, window-shop your way along the many upscale stores. Hang a left on **Oak Street** for the most elite boutiques. **Accent Chicago** (875 North Michigan Ave.) or **City of Chicago Store** at the Chicago Waterworks Visitors Center are where serious souvenir hunters spent their cash. Dedicated shoppers will want to detour a little farther south to **State Street** in the Loop for a walk through the landmark Marshall Field's building, now Macy's. For a culture buzz, check out the **Museum of Contemporary Art** (closed Monday). After making a tough restaurant choice (Prime rib at Smith & Wollensky's or Lawry's? or deep-dish pizza at Giordano's?), consider a nightcap at the **Signature Room** at the 95th-floor bar on top of the John Hancock Center—the city will be spread beneath your feet.

GETTING OUTSIDE: PARKS AND ZOOS

Chicago may not be the country's biggest city, but it's arguably the prettiest. Architect Daniel Burnham designed the city to have plenty of green space so city dwellers could relax, and even the tiniest green outpost usually has some sort of public art. With winter never too far from thought, Chicagoans pour into the city's parks and zoos at the first hint of summer, or take to conservatories when the weather's less than ideal. The following are our favorite city parks and zoos.

Parks

Garfield Park Conservatory. Escape winter's cold or revel in summer sunshine inside this huge Victorian glass structure housing tropical palms, spiny cacti, and showy blooms. A children's garden delights with climbable leaf sculptures and a tube slide that winds through trees. The Sweet House now houses a permanent Sugar from the Sun exhibit focused on the elements of photosynthesis—sunlight, air, water, and sugar—in a full-sensory environment filled with spewing steam, trickling water, and chirping sounds. And don't miss the historic Jens Jensen–designed fern house with its lagoon, waterfalls, and profusion of ferns. Events include botanical-theme fashion shows, flower shows, and the annual Chocolate Fest in February, which pays homage to the conservatory's fruiting cacao trees with chef demonstrations and free samples from area chocolate shops. ⊠ *300 N. Central Park Ave., Garfield Park* .

★ Fodor's Choice **Grant Park & Buckingham Fountain.** Two of Chicago's greatest treasures reside in Grant Park—the Art Institute and Buckingham Fountain. Bordered by Lake Michigan to the east, a spectacular skyline to the west, and the Museum Campus to the south, the ever-popular Grant Park serves as the city's front yard and unofficial gathering place. This pristine open space is decked out with walking paths, a stand of stately elm trees, and formal rose gardens, where Loop dwellers and 9-to-5-ers take refuge from the concrete and steel. The park also hosts many of the city's largest outdoor events, including the annual Taste of Chicago, a vast picnic featuring foods from more than 70 restaurants. The event precedes a fireworks show around July Fourth. The fountain is a wonderful place to people-watch.

The centerpiece of Grant Park is the gorgeous, tiered **Buckingham Fountain** (⊠ *Between Columbus and Lake Shore Drs. east of Congress Plaza*), which has intricate designs of pink-marble seashells, water-spouting fish, and bronze sculptures of sea horses. Built in 1927, it was patterned after a fountain at Versailles but is about twice the size of its model. See it in all its glory between May 1 and October 1, when it's elaborately illuminated at night and sprays colorfully lighted waters. Linger long enough to experience the spectacular water display that takes place every hour on the hour, and you'll see the center jet of water shoot 150 feet into the air. ⊠ *South Loop* ☎ *312/742–7529.*

Lincoln Park Conservatory. Green grows on green in the lush tropical main room of this refreshing city greenhouse. Stroll through permanent displays in the Palm House, Fern Room, and Orchid House, or catch one of the special shows, like the fragrant Easter Lily show in March or April and the festive Chrysanthemum Show in November. The peacefulness and abundant greenery inside the 1892 conservatory offer a refreshing respite in the heart of this bustling neighborhood.

✉ *2391 N. Stockton Dr., Lincoln Park* 🏠 *312/742–7736* ✍ *Free* ⊙ *Daily 9–5.*

★ **Millennium Park.** The Bean, the fountains, the Disney-esque music pavilion—all the pieces of this new park quickly stole the hearts of Chicagoans and visitors alike. This is one of our favorite places to spend a sunny day.

The showstopper here is Frank Gehry's stunning **Jay Pritzker Pavilion.** Dramatic ribbons of stainless steel stretching 40 feet into the sky look like petals wrapping the music stage. The sound system, suspended by a trellis that spans the great lawn, provides concert-hall sound outside. So what can you see on this beautiful stage? Take your pick. There's the Grant Park Music Festival—a free classical-music series—as well as the city's popular free summer concerts, including the jam-packed Chicago Blues and Chicago Jazz festivals.

Hot town? Summer in the city? Cool off by letting a local resident spit on you. Okay, it's just a giant image of a Chicagoan's face—actually, dozens of Chicagoans' faces rotating through on two huge (read 50-foot-high) glass block–tower fountains. The genius behind the **Crown Fountain,** Spanish sculptor Jaume Plensa, lined up the mouths on the digital photos with an opening in the fountain. When a face purses its lips, water shoots out its "mouth." Kids love it, and we feel like kids watching it. It's at the southwest corner of the park.

You've seen the pictures. Now go, take your own. The **Cloud Gate sculpture,** otherwise known as "the Bean," awaits your delighted *ooohs* and *aaahs* as you stand beneath its gleaming seamless polished steel. It's between Washington and Madison streets. Go on, get camera happy.

If you're feeling artsy, you can find out if there's a show playing at the indoor, underground **Harris Theater for Music and Dance,** behind the Jay Pritzker Pavilion.

In summer the carefully manicured plantings in the **Lurie Garden** bloom; in winter the **McCormick Tribune Ice Rink** is open for public skating. ✉ *Bounded by Michigan Ave., Columbus Dr., Randolph Dr., and Monroe St., Loop* ⊕ *www.millenniumpark. org* ✍ *Free* ⊙ *Daily 6 AM–11 PM.*

Zoos

★ **Brookfield Zoo.** Spend the day among nearly 3,000 animals at this gigantic zoo. The highlights? First, there's the popular **Tropic World,** a simulated tropical rain forest where monkeys, otters, birds, and other rain-forest fauna cavort in a carefully constructed setting of rocks, trees, shrubs, pools, and waterfalls. Next, test your "flying strength" in the **Be a Bird House** by flapping your "wings" on a machine that decides what kind of bird you would be, based on how you flap. We also like the **Living Coast,** where you can venture through huge glassed-in passageways to see sharks, rays, jellyfish, and turtles swimming by. Daily dolphin shows are a favorite even for adults. Walruses, seals, and sea lions inhabit a rocky seascape exhibit. Don't worry if you don't want to trek around the grounds—you can hop aboard a motorized safari tram in warm weather ($4) or the heated *Snowball Express* tram in the cold (free).

The two best educational exhibits are Habitat Africa and Swamp. In **Habitat Africa** you can explore two very different environments. See such tiny animals as klipspringer antelope, which are only 22 inches tall, and rock hyraxes, which resemble prairie dogs, in the savanna exhibit, which also has a water hole, rock formations characteristic of the African savanna, and termite mounds. If you look closely in the dense forest exhibit, you might be able to find animals like the okapi. The **Swamp** is about as realistic as you would want an exhibit on swamps to be, with a springy floor, push-button alligator bellows, and open habitats with low-flying birds vividly demonstrating the complex ecosystems of both southern and Illinois wetlands.

For hands-on family activities, check out the **Hamill Family Play Zoo** (⊠*$3.50, children $2.50*), where kids can learn to care for nature by playing zookeeper, gardener, or veterinarian. The **Children's Zoo** (⊠*$2, children $1*) includes a petting farm, excellent animal shows, and the Big Barn with its daily cow and goat milking and weekly wool-spinning demonstrations. Watch the dolphins show off and act silly at the **Seven Seas Dolphin Show** (⊠*adults $4, children $2.50*). ⊠*1st Ave. and 31st St.* ☎*708/485–0263 or 800/201–0784* ⊕*www.brookfieldzoo.org* ⊠*Zoo $12 ($8 children), free on Tues. and Thurs. Oct.–Feb.; parking $8* ☉*Oct.– Mar., daily 10–5; Apr. and Sept., weekdays 10–5, weekends 10–6; May–Aug., daily 9:30–6; Oct.–Dec., daily 10–5.*

★ **Fodor's Choice** | **Lincoln Park Zoo.** Lions, gorillas, and bears—oh my! At this urban zoo you can face-off with lions (separated by a window, of course) outside the Lion House; watch about two-dozen gorillas go ape in the sprawling, state-of-the-art Regenstein Center for African Apes, with three separate habitats featuring real bamboo stands, 5,000 feet of swinging vines, and termite mounds for chimpanzee snacking; or watch some rare and endangered species of bears, such as

the spectacle bear (named for the eyeglass-like markings around its eyes).

Animals both slithery (pythons) and cuddly (koalas) reside in the glass-dome Regenstein Small Mammal and Reptile House; if you're looking for the big guys (elephants, giraffes, black rhinos), they're in the large-mammal house. Bird lovers should make a beeline for the Kovler Penguin and Seabird House, where you can watch razorbills and tufted puffins frolicking on a simulated North Atlantic coast and king penguins splashing in an 18,000-gallon pool. For youngsters, there are the children's zoo, the Farm-in-the-Zoo (farm animals and a learning center with films and demonstrations), and the Conservation Station, with hands-on activities. Be sure to leave time for a ride (or two) on the Endangered Species Carousel, featuring a menagerie of 48 rare and endangered animals. ⊠*2200 N. Cannon Dr., Lincoln Park* ☎*312/742–2000* ⊕*www.lpzoo.com* ⊠*Free* ☉*Apr.–May, daily 10–5; late May–early Sept., weekdays 10–5, weekends 10–6:30; Sept.–Oct., daily 10–5; Nov.–Mar., daily 10–4:30.*

AUTHENTIC CHICAGO

So you've done the Art Institute and the Willis (Sears) Tower—now it's time to put away your tourist hat and make like a local. Luckily, it's not hard to figure out what Chicagoans like to do in their spare time. Here's how to follow in their footsteps.

Visit an Ethnic Neighborhood

Chicago is a city of neighborhoods, and in many of them you can see traces of each successive immigrant group. Each neighborhood in the city has its own flavor, reflected in its architecture, public art, restaurants, and businesses, and most have their own summer or holiday festivals. Here are a few stand-out 'hoods.

Little Italy. Though most Italians moved to the West Side a couple of generations ago, Little Italy's Italian restaurants and lemonade stands still draw them back.

Andersonville. The charming diversity of the Swedish/Middle Eastern/gay mecca of Andersonville means you can have lingonberry pancakes for breakfast, hummus for lunch, and drinks at a gay-friendly bar after dinner.

Chinatown. The Chinese New Year dragon parade is just one reason to visit Chinatown, which has dozens of restaurants and shops and a quiet riverfront park.

Devon Avenue. Devon Avenue turns from Indian to Pakistani to Russian Orthodox to Jewish within a few blocks. Try on a sari, buy a bagel or electronics, or just people-watch—it's an excellent place to spend the afternoon.

Pilsen/Little Village. The best Mexican restaurants are alongside Pilsen's famous murals. Be sure to stop into the National Museum of Mexican Art, which will give you an even deeper appreciation of the culture.

Bronzeville. Bronzeville's famous local historic figures include Ida B. Wells—a women's-rights and African-American civil-rights crusader—the trumpeter Louis Armstrong, and Bessie Coleman, the first African-American woman pilot. The area has nine landmark buildings and is rapidly gentrifying.

Enjoy the Lake

San Diego and L.A. may have the ocean, and New York its Central Park, but Chicago has the peaceful waters of Lake Michigan at its doorstep. Bikers, dog walkers, boaters, and runners crowd the lakefront paths on warm days; in winter the lake is equally beautiful, with icy towers formed from frozen sheets of water.

Bike Along the Lakeshore

To bike any part of the gentle dips and swells of Chicago's 20 mi **lakefront bicycle path** is to see the city: the skyline, the people, the water. The breeze from the lake mixes with the sounds of the city at play as you zoom by, carefree, whiling away an afternoon.

The **Chicago Park District** (☎ *312/742–7529* ⊕*www.chicagoparkdistrict.com*) is a good source for bike maps.

For information on biking in the city, contact the **Chicagoland Bicycle Federation** (✉ *9 W. Hubbard St., South Loop* ☎ *312/427–3325* ⊕*www.chibikefed.org*).

Bike Chicago (✉ *600 E. Grand Ave., Near North* ☎ *312/595–9600 or 773/327–2706* ⊕*www.bikechicago.com*) can deliver a bike to your hotel and pick it up after your ride. Fees start at $10 per hour and $49 a day. It also offers lakefront, neighborhood, and nighttime bike tours for $25 to $49 (bike rental included), weather permitting.

You can rent a bike for the day or by the hour from **On the Route** (✉ *3146 N. Lincoln Ave., Lakeview* ☎ *773/477–5066* ⊕*www. ontheroute.com*), which stocks a large

Beaches

inventory of bicycles, including children's bikes. They also supply helmets and other safety equipment.

Boating

Nothing beats the view of the Chicago skyline from the water, especially when the sun sets behind the sparkling skyscrapers. Plenty of boats are available to rent or charter, though you might want to leave the skippering to others if you're not familiar with Great Lakes navigation.

Sailboat lessons, rentals, and charters are available from **Chicago Sailing** (⊠*Belmont Harbor, Lakeview* ☎*773/871–7245* ⊕*www.chicagosailing.com*). Chicago Sailing focuses on sailing instruction for all levels and includes a program on keeping your boat in tip-top shape.

Sailboats, Inc. (⊠*Monroe Harbor, Loop* ☎*312/861–1757 or 800/826–7010* ⊕*www.sailboats-inc.com*), one of the oldest charter-certification schools in the country, prepares its students to charter any type of boat.

For a more placid water outing, paddle boats, including swan-shaped two-seaters, are available for rent at **Lincoln Park's South Lagoon** (⊠*2021 N. Stockton Dr., Lincoln Park* ☎*312/742–2038*), just north of Farm-in-the-Zoo.

Beaches

One of the greatest surprises in the city is the miles of sandy beaches that Chicagoans flock to in summer. The water becomes warm enough to swim in toward the end of June, though the brave will take an icy dip through the end of October. Chicago has about 30 mi of shoreline, most of it sand or rock beach. Beaches are open to the public daily from 9 AM to 9:30 PM, Memorial Day through Labor Day, and many beaches have changing facilities; all are handicap accessible.

BEACHES	Block	Best For	Bathrooms	Changing Facilities	Showers	Lifeguard
Far North Side						
Foster Beach	5200 N	Families	yes	no	no	yes
Montrose Beach	4400 N	Learning to sail	yes	no	yes	yes
Osterman Beach	5800 N	Quiet conversations	yes	no	yes	yes
Hyde Park						
South Shore Country Club	7100 S	Quieter beach	yes	yes	yes	yes
Jackson Beach Central	5700–5900 S	Beach trip after the Museum of Science and Industry	yes	no	no	yes
Lincoln Park						
North Avenue Beach	1600–2400 N	Margaritas at the upstairs concession	yes	yes	yes	yes
Near North						
Oak Street Beach	600–1600 N	Singles scene	yes	no	no	yes
South Loop						
12th Street Beach	1200 S at 900 E	Post museum-hopping break	yes	no	yes	yes

The **Chicago Park District** (☎312/742–7529 ⊕*www.chicagoparkdistrict.com*) provides lifeguard protection during daylight hours throughout the swimming season.

All references to north and south in beach listings refer to how far north or south of the Loop each beach is. In other words, 1600 to 2400 north means the beach begins 16 blocks north of the Loop (at Madison Street, which is the 100 block) and extends for eight blocks.

⚠ Along the lakefront you'll see plenty of broken-rock breakwaters with signs that warn NO SWIMMING OR DIVING. Although Chicagoans frequently ignore these signs, you shouldn't. The boulders below the water are slippery with seaweed and may hide sharp, rusty scraps of metal, and the water beyond is very deep. It can be dangerous even if you know the territory.

Brave the Cold

The city's brutal windy winters are infamous, but that doesn't keep Chicagoans from making the best out of the long cold months. Throw on lots of layers, lace up your ice skates, and show those city dwellers what you're made of.

★ The rink at **Millennium Park** (⊠55 N. Michigan Ave., Loop ☎312/742–1168 ⊕*www.millenniumpark.org*) has free skating seven days a week and a dazzling view of the Chicago skyline. Skate rentals are $10 a session.

On the snowiest days some hardy souls **cross-country ski** and snowshoe on the lakeshore—bring your own equipment.

Loosen up by playing outdoor paddle tennis at **Midtown Tennis Club** (⊠2020 W. Fullerton Ave. ☎773/235–2300 ⊕*www. midtowntennisclub.com*). If it's snowing, they turn on the heated floors.

Holiday-walk Chicago's windows during the **Magnificent Mile Lights Festival,** in November, the Saturday before Thanksgiving. The celebration includes music, ice-carving contests, and stage shows, and ends in a parade and the illumination of more than one million lights.

FREE THINGS TO DO

It's easy to spend money in the big city: think shopping, museum-entrance fees, restaurants, theater. But if you'd like to put your wallet away for a while, here are some of our favorite options.

Free Art

Chicago has some of the most famous public art in the country, including a **Picasso** piece in Daley Plaza, **Alexander Calder's** *Flamingo* in Federal Plaza, and the *Cloud Gate* sculpture in Millennium Park. For a fairly comprehensive list, see ⊕*egov.cityofchicago/publicart* or pick up a *Free Public Art* guide at a visitor center.

The **City Gallery** (⊠*806 N. Michigan Ave.* ☎*312/742–0808*) in the Historic Water Tower hosts rotating exhibits of Chicago-theme photography.

Five different galleries showcase contemporary visual art by local artists at the **Chicago Cultural Center** (⊠*78 E. Washington St.* ☎*312/744–6630* ⊕*www.chicagoculturalcenter.org*).

Free Concerts

Grant Park and Millennium Park host regular classical and pop concerts in summer. For a schedule, pick up the *Chicago Reader* or buy a copy of *TimeOut Chicago*.

Chicago is a festival town, celebrating blues, jazz, country, gospel, Celtic, and world music during the warm months. For a schedule, see ⊕*www.explorechicago.org*.

Free jazz and classical concerts are performed Monday through Wednesday and Friday at 12:15 in the **Chicago Cultural Center** (⊠*78 E. Washington St.* ☎*312/744–6630* ⊕*www.chicagoculturalcenter.org*).

Free Movies

Every Tuesday night in summer Grant Park shows classic films at sundown on a giant screen. The films tend to be popular, so go early, spread out a blanket, and have a picnic a couple of hours beforehand. There's even a free bike valet. Local library branches and parks also have free movies—check the city's Web site for details.

Free Dance Lessons

Learn to swing, polka, step, waltz, and salsa to the beat of a live band in Grant Park during the summer-long Chicago SummerDance Festival. Chicagoans of all ages and abilities sashay around the dance floor during the lessons and the free dancing afterward. For more information, see ⊕*www.explorechicago.org*.

Free Fireworks

Every Wednesday and Saturday night in summer Navy Pier puts on a showy display of colorful explosives. Watch from the pier or along the waterfront opposite Buckingham Fountain.

Free Trolley Rides

A free trolley runs from State Street to Navy Pier via Grand Avenue and Illinois Street every 20 minutes until 9 PM on weekdays and 11 PM on weekends. For more information, call ☎*312/595–7437*.

Free Improv

The world-famous Second City comedy troupe has a free improv set following the last performance every night but Friday. For more information, go to ⊕*www.secondcity.com* or call ☎*312/664–4032*.

Free Museum Days

Always Free
Jane Addams Hull-House Museum
Museum of Contemporary Photography
National Museum of Mexican Art

Oriental Institute

Smart Museum

Sunday:

DuSable Museum of African American History

Chicago Children's Museum (for those 15 and younger the first Sunday of each month)

Monday:

Adler Planetarium & Astronomy Museum (selected months only)

Tuesday:

Adler Planetarium & Astronomy Museum (selected months only)

Museum of Contemporary Art

Swedish American Museum Center (second Tuesday each month)

Thursday:

Art Institute of Chicago (after 5 PM)

Chicago Children's Museum (5–8 PM only)

Peggy Notebaert Nature Museum

Free TV-Show Tickets

Oprah Winfrey and Jerry Springer tape their shows in front of live audiences in Chicago. Though tickets are free, they are at a premium and must be reserved far in advance. Oprah's shows are filmed at **Harpo Studios** (⊠ *1058 Washington St.* ☎*312/591–9222 for tickets* ⊕*www. oprah.com*). *The Jerry Springer Show* is filmed at **NBC Tower** (⊠ *454 N. Columbus Dr.* ☎*312/321–5365* ⊕*www.jerryspringer tv.com*).

Sightseeing Walks

That Great Street

The Loop—defined by the rectangle created by the El tracks—is the heart of downtown, and the heart of downtown is State Street. Begin at the south end of the Michigan Avenue Bridge, with your back to the Chicago Tribune's Gothic tower.

Walk west along the river past Marina City's iconic corncob towers, perhaps taking the stairs down to the Riverwalk for a drink at one of the cafés. Once you're back at street level, make a left on State Street, cruising by the famous Chicago Theatre sign that marks the beginning of the theater district. Window-shop at the local landmark Marshall Field's, which is now Macy's, or just enjoy the facade of the old Carson Pirie Scott Building (store is closed). Heading south toward Congress Parkway, gaze up at the dramatic facade of the neoclassical Harold Washington Library, with its gigantic gargoyle-like owls—then head inside to admire the airy, glass-roofed Winter Garden on the ninth (and top) floor.

Zootopia

In two hours on a beautiful day you can breeze through the Lincoln Park Zoo, stroll beside the park's lagoons, and discover the quaint, upscale neighborhood of Old Town. Beginning on North Avenue and Lake Shore Drive, walk north through the park alongside the lagoons. Watch the crew shells try to navigate past the fishing lines, or throw a line into the stocked lagoon yourself. Take your time exploring the zoo or continue north to the Lincoln Park Conservatory, pausing to admire North Pond with its lush greenery and the skyline reflected in its water. Then circle back south and slightly west to Wells Street, where the Second City improv troupe's theater and a host of tony shops and restaurants line brick streets.

CHICAGO WITH KIDS

Chicago sometimes seems to have been designed with kids in mind. There are many places to play and things to do, from building sand castles at one of the lakefront's many beaches to playing 18-hole minigolf at Navy Pier in summer. Here are some suggestions for ways to show kids the sights.

Museums

Several area museums are specifically designed for kids. At the **Chicago Children's Museum** (⊠ *700 E. Grand Ave., Navy Pier*) three floors of exhibits cast off with a play structure in the shape of a schooner, where kids can walk the gangplank and slide down to the lower level, and make a splash with a water playground, featuring a scaled-down river and a water wheel. Also at **Navy Pier** you'll find a Ferris wheel and Viennese swings (the kind that go around in a circle like a merry-go-round). In the summer, crowds of kids make the most of Pier Park's 18-hole minigolf course, musical carousel, and remote-control boats.

Many other Chicago museums are also kid-friendly, especially the butterfly haven and the animal habitat exhibit with its climbable treehouse at the **Peggy Notebaert Nature Museum,** the replica coal mine and hands-on Idea Factory at the **Museum of Science and Industry,** the dinosaur exhibits at the **Field Museum,** and the sharks and dolphins at the **John G. Shedd Aquarium.**

Parks, Zoos and Outside Activities

Chicago's neighborhoods are dotted with area play lots that have playground equipment as well as several ice-skating rinks for winter months. On scorching days, visit the **63rd Street Beach House,** at 63rd Street and Lake Shore Drive in Woodlawn. The interactive spiral fountain in the courtyard jumps and splashes,

---

MORE IDEAS FROM FODORS.COM FORUMS

- Holiday Lights Festival on Michigan Ave.
- Bulls, Cubs, or White Sox Game
- Day trip to Oak Park
- Gospel Brunch at House of Blues (call 312/923–2000)
- Chicago Architecture Foundation Cruise (visit www.architecture.org)

---

leaving kids giggling and jumping. The **North Park Village Nature Center** on the far northwest side (on Pulaski Road north of Bryn Mawr Avenue) is a wilderness oasis, serving up 46 acres of trails and a kid-oriented Nature Center with hands-on activities and fun educational programs. Deer sightings are common here. **Millennium Park** (⊠ *55 N. Michigan Ave.*) has a 16,000-square-foot ice-skating rink. Skaters have an unparalleled view of downtown as they whiz around the ice.

For more structured fun, there are two zoos: the free **Lincoln Park Zoo** (⊠ *2200 N. Cannon Dr. at Lake Shore Dr. and Fullerton Pkwy.*) and the large, suburban **Brookfield Zoo** (⊠ *1st Ave. and 31st St., Brookfield*), which has such surprising exhibits as a wall of pulsing jellyfish. The **Buccaneer Pirate Adventure Cruise** (Wagner Charter Cruise Co. Dock, Lower Wacker Dr. between Wells St. and Franklin/Orleans St. bridges) sets sail with wannabe pirates, teaching them about the river's locks and entertaining kids with magic tricks.

FABULOUS FESTIVALS

Chicago festivals range from local neighborhood get-togethers to citywide extravaganzas. Try to catch a neighborhood street fair for some great people-watching if you're in town between June and September. On some weekends there are several festivals at once. For details, see ⊕*www.chicagoreader.com.*

The **St. Patrick's Day parade** (☎*312/942–9188* ⊕*www.chicagostpatsparade.com*) turns the city on its head: the Chicago River is dyed green, shamrocks decorate the street, and the center stripe of Dearborn Street is painted the color of the Irish from Wacker Drive to Van Buren Street. This is your chance to get your fill of bagpipes, green beer, and green kneesocks. It's over 4 hours, so you probably won't see the whole thing.

The **Chicago Blues Festival** (☎*312/744–3315* ⊕*www.chicagobluesfestival.org*), in Grant Park, is a popular four-day, three-stage event in June starring blues greats from Chicago and around the country. If you see only one festival in Chicago, this is the one.

The medium-size **Chicago Gospel Fest** (☎*312/744–3315*) brings its joyful sounds to Grant Park in early June.

Taste of Chicago (✉*Grant Park, Columbus Dr. between Jackson and Randolph Sts.* ☎*312/744–3315*) dishes out pizza, cheesecake, and other Chicago specialties to 3.5 million people over a 10-day period before the July Fourth holiday that includes top pop and novelty acts.

Thrill-seekers and families flock to the **Chicago Air & Water Show** (✉*Lakeshore, Fullerton Ave. to Oak St.; focal point at North Ave. Beach* ☎*312/744–3315*), a lakefront spectacle featuring aerial acrobatics and daredevil water acts. See the U.S. Navy Blue Angels perform precision flying maneuvers at the three-day event in mid-August.

The **Chicago Jazz Festival** (☎*312/744–3315*) holds sway for four days during Labor Day weekend in Grant Park.

At the **Celtic Fest,** Celtic food, art, storytelling, dance, and a bagpiper's circle celebrate everything Irish. It's held in Grant Park during the month of September.

At the weeklong **World Music Festival,** international artists play traditional and contemporary music at venues across the city in September.

Street fairs are held every week in summer, but two stand out as the best. **Halsted Market Days,** in August, is the city's largest street festival. It's held in the heart of the gay community of Lakeview and has blocks and blocks of vendors as well as some wild entertainment such as zany drag queens and radical cheerleaders. The **Taste of Randolph, in June,** is more sedate, featuring dishes from the fine restaurants lining the western end of Randolph Street.

The holiday season officially starts with the **Magnificent Mile Lights Festival** (⊕*www.themagnificentmile.com*), a weekend-long event at the end of every November with tons of family-friendly activities including musical performances, ice-carving contests, and stage shows. The fanfare culminates in a parade and the illumination of more than one million lights along Michigan Avenue.

GET OUT OF TOWN

You could spend a month or two just exploring the city of Chicago, but the surrounding towns are likewise rich in history, culture, and activities. The closest suburbs offer theaters and museums; the farther out you go, the more likely you are to find wooded parks and quiet places.

Brush Up on Your Ernest Hemingway

Ernest Hemingway Birthplace. Part of the literary legacy of Oak Park, this three-story, turreted Queen Anne Victorian, which stands in frilly contrast to the many streamlined Prairie-style homes elsewhere in the neighborhood, contains period-furnished rooms and many photos and artifacts pertaining to the writer's early life. Museum curators have redecorated rooms to faithfully depict the house as it looked at the turn of the 20th century; you can poke your head inside the room in which the author was born on July 21, 1899. ⌧ *339 N. Oak Park Ave.* ☎ *708/848–2222* ⊕ *www.hemingway.org* 🎟 *Joint ticket with Hemingway Museum $8* ☽ *Sun.–Fri. 1–5, Sat. 10–5.*

Ernest Hemingway Museum. How did the author's first 20 years in Oak Park impact his later work? Check out the exhibits and videos here to find out. Don't miss his first "book," a set of drawings with captions written by his mother, Grace. Holdings include reproduced manuscripts and letters. ⌧ *200 N. Oak Park Ave.* ☎ *708/848–2222* ⊕ *www.hemingway.org* 🎟 *Joint ticket with Hemingway Birthplace $8* ☽ *Sun.–Fri. 1–5, Sat. 10–5.*

Follow the Chicago Symphony Orchestra

If you enjoy music under the stars, the outdoor concerts at **Ravinia Park** are a stellar treat. The **Ravinia Festival** is the summer home of the Chicago Symphony Orchestra. Come for jazz, chamber music, pop, and dance performances. Pack a picnic and blanket and sit on the lawn for a little more than the cost of a movie ($10 to $27). Seats are also available in the pavilion for a significantly higher price ($20 to $100). Restaurants and snack bars are on park grounds. Concerts usually start at 8 PM; be at the park at 6:30 to park and get settled. ⌧ *Green Bay and Lake Cook Rds., in Highland Park, 26 mi north of downtown Chicago* ☎ *847/266–5100* ⊕ *www.ravinia.org.*

ERNEST HEMINGWAY: OAK PARK PROTÉGÉ

It seems unlikely that the rough-and-tumble adventurer and writer Ernest Hemingway was born in 1899 amid the manicured suburb of Oak Park, Illinois, a town he described as having "wide lawns and narrow minds." He excelled at writing for the high school paper—a skill that turned into his life's work. A volunteer stint as an ambulance driver introduced him to World War I and its visceral horrors—he used that experience and the lessons he learned as a reporter for the *Kansas City Star* to craft emotionally complex novels built from deceptively simple sentences, like his master work, *A Farewell to Arms.* Hemingway later lived in Toronto and Chicago. Though his return visits to Oak Park were infrequent, the residents celebrate him there to this day.

Unwind Outdoors

Fodor's Choice See the spectacular spring blooming season or the beautiful display of mid-June roses at the **Chicago Botanic Garden**. Among the 23 different gardens are a three-island Japanese garden, a waterfall garden, a sensory garden, and a 4-acre fruit-and-vegetable garden. Three big greenhouses showcase a desert, a rain forest, and a formal garden with flowers that bloom all winter long. ⊠*Lake Cook Rd. and U.S. 41* ☎*847/835-5440* ⊕*www. chicagobotanic.org* ✉*Free; parking $20, tram tour $5* ⊙*Daily 8 AM–sunset; 45-min summer tours through Oct., daily 10–3, weather permitting.*

Take a quiet hike around the **Morton Arboretum**, full of woodlands, wetlands, and display gardens. Trees, shrubs, and vines flower year-round, but in spring the flowering trees are particularly spectacular. You can drive your car through some of the grounds, but we think it's much nicer to walk. There are lots of trails to take, and most take about 15 to 30 minutes. Don't miss the Daffodil Glade in early spring. Tours are scheduled most Sunday afternoons. ⊠*4100 Illinois Rte. 53, 25 mi southwest of downtown Chicago* ☎*630/968-0074* ⊕*www.mortonarb.org* ✉*$11, Wed. $7; tram tours $5* ⊙*Daily 7–7 (or at sunset, whichever is earlier).*

The 500-acre estate at **Cantigny Park** offers multiple attractions in one: an impressive military history museum with immersive exhibits (think touchscreen videos and re-created battle scenes), sprawling grounds with formal gardens, and its own 27-hole public golf course with separate youth links. But the centerpiece is probably the Beaux Arts–style Col. Robert R. McCormick Museum. Built for the former Chicago Tribune owner, the 35-room mansion features the Joseph Medill Library, the stately wood-paneled Freedom Hall, and an Art Deco movie theater in the basement. The hidden Prohibition-era bar alone is worth a visit—we won't ruin the surprise by revealing where it is. ⊠*1S151 Winfield Rd., 30 mi west of downtown Chicago* ☎*630/668-5161* ⊕*www.cantigny.org* ✉*$5 per car, $2 per car after 5, May 1–Oct. 31, and after 4, Nov. 1 Apr. 30; grounds and museum tours free* ⊙*Grounds and gardens: Nov.–Apr., Mon.– Sun. 9 AM–sunset; May–Oct., Mon.–Sun. 7 AM–sunset; museums: Labor Day–Dec. 31 and Feb. 1–Memorial Day, Tues.–Sun. 10–4; Memorial Day–Labor Day, Tues.– Sun. 10–5; closed Jan.*

Samuel Insull, partner of Thomas Edison and founder of Commonwealth Edison, built the mansion at the **Cuneo Museum and Gardens** in 1916 as a country home. After Insull lost his fortune, John Cuneo Sr., the printing-press magnate, bought the estate and fashioned it into something far more spectacular. The skylighted great hall in the main house resembles the open central courtyard of an Italian palazzo; the private family chapel has stained-glass windows; and a gilded grand piano graces the ballroom. The house is filled with antiques, porcelains, 17th-century Flemish tapestries, and Italian paintings. ⊠*1350 N. Milwaukee Ave., 15 mi west of Lake Forest, 40 mi northwest of downtown Chicago* ☎*847/362-3042* ⊕*www. cuneomuseum.org* ✉*$7 per car; $12 per person for mansion tours* ⊙*Tues.–Sun. 10–4; beginning in mid-May, guided mansion tours are Tues.–Fri. at 11, 1, and 3, self-guided tours are Tues.–Sun. 11–4.*

CHICAGO THEN AND NOW

The Early Days

Before Chicago was officially "discovered" by the team of Father Jacques Marquette, a French missionary, and Louis Jolliet, a French–Canadian mapmaker and trader, in 1673, the area served as a center of trade and seasonal hunting grounds for several Native American tribes, including the Miamis, Illinois, and Pottawattomie. Villages kept close trading ties with the French, though scuffles with the Fox tribe kept the French influence at bay until 1779. That year, black French trader Jean Baptiste Point du Sable built a five-room "mansion" by the mouth of the Chicago River on the shore of Lake Michigan.

The Great Fire

The city grew until 1871, when a fire in the barn of Catherine and Patrick O'Leary spread across the city, killing hundreds. (Contrary to the legend, it was probably not started by a cow kicking over a lantern.) A recent drought coupled with crowded wooden buildings and wood-brick streets allowed the blaze to take hold quickly, destroying 18,000 structures within 36 hours.

Gangsters to the Great Migration

World War I (aka the Great War) changed the face of Chicago. Postwar—and especially during Prohibition (1920–33)—the Torrio–Capone organization expanded its gambling and liquor distribution operations, consolidating its power during the violent "beer wars" from 1924 to 1930. Hundreds of casualties include the seven victims of the infamous 1929 St. Valentine's Day Massacre. In 1934 the FBI gunned down bankrobber and "Public Enemy No. 1" John Dillinger outside the Biograph Theater on the North Side, now a theater venue and a Chicago landmark.

The Great War also led to the Great Migration, when African-Americans from the South moved to the northern cities between 1916 and 1970. World War I slowed immigration from Europe, but increased jobs in Chicago's manufacturing industry. More than 500,000 African-Americans came to the city to find work, and by the mid-20th century African-Americans were a strong force in Chicago's political, economic, and cultural life.

IMPORTANT DATES IN CHICAGO HISTORY

1673	Chicago discovered by Marquette and Jolliet
1779	Jean Baptiste Point du Sable, a "free Negro," and his wife Catherine, a Pottawattamie Indian, are the first Chicago settlers.
1837	Chicago incorporated as a city
1860	First national political convention. Abraham Lincoln nominated as the Republican candidate for president
1871	Great Chicago Fire

Mayor Daley and the Notorious 1968 Democratic Convention

The Daley dynasty began when Richard J. Daley became mayor in 1955. He was reelected five times and his son, Richard M. Daley, currently runs the city.

The first Mayor Daley redrew Chicago's landscape, overseeing the construction of O'Hare International Airport, the expressway system, the University of Illinois at Chicago, and a towering skyline. He also helped John F. Kennedy get elected, thanks to his control of Chicago's Democratic party.

Despite these advances, Mayor Richard J. Daley is perhaps best known for his crackdown on student protesters during the 1968 Democratic National Convention. Americans watched on their televisions as the Chicago police beat the city's youth with sticks and blinded them with tear gas. That incident, plus his "shoot to kill" order during the riots that followed the assassination of Dr. Martin Luther King Jr., and his use of public funds to build giant, disastrous public housing projects like Cabrini–Green, eventually led to the temporary dissolution of the Democratic machine in Chicago. After Daley's death, Chicago's first black—and beloved—mayor, Harold Washington, took office in 1983.

Chicago Today

The thriving commercial and financial "City of Broad Shoulders" is spiked with gorgeous architecture and set with cultural and recreational gems, including the Art Institute, Millennium Park, 250 theater companies, and 30 mi of shoreline. 2.8 million residents live within the city limits, and tens of thousands commute in from the surrounding (and ever-sprawling) suburbs to work downtown during the week. The current Mayor Daley gave downtown a makeover, adding wrought-iron street furniture, regular fireworks, planters of flowers, and Millennium Park. Daley's focus on eco-friendly building initiatives led to a green roof installed on City Hall, and his advocacy of bicycling has brought new bike paths and bike racks. And spectacular lights now brighten buildings along Michigan Avenue after dark. There are always controversies (recent updates to the El system have caused some delays and lots of grumbling), but most Chicagoans are proud to call the city home.

1885	First skyscraper in the country, Home Insurance Building (no longer standing), is built
1886	Haymarket Riot
1893	World's Columbian Exposition
1929	St. Valentine's Day Massacre
1968	Democratic National convention
1973	Sears (now Willis) Tower, tallest building in North America, completed
2005	Chicago White Sox win the World Series

FOR "'DA FANS"

Michael Jordan, Scottie Pippin, Walter Payton, William "the Refrigerator" Perry, Ernie Banks, Sammy Sosa, Shoeless Joe Jackson. You can't mention Chicago without talking about sports. Chicagoans are fiercely devoted to their teams, whether it's baseball, basketball, or football—and whether their team's winning or losing. Come opening day for baseball season, die-hard Cubs and Sox fans take the day off work to cheer on their teams; during football season ticketed tailgaters can go to designated areas and chow down in the parking lot before kickoff, even if it's snowy and in the single digits. One of the most fun ways to get into the Chicago spirit is to go to a game, so throw on your team's colors and join the screaming fans.

Chicago Bears

Chicago football is messy and dirty and sometimes even exciting. Don't expect to be wowed by star quarterbacks and amazing passing, but do get ready for the team's smash-mouth style that reflects the city's blue-collar persona. Legends like Walter Payton have come and gone, but after several mediocre seasons things have started to look up: they made it to the Super Bowl in 2006 but did not come away the champs.

Where They Play: *Soldier Field, 425 E. McFetridge Dr., South Loop*

Season: August–December

How to Buy Tickets: Through Ticketmaster, at ☎*312/559–1212 or* ⊕*www.chicago bears.com*

Most Notable Players: Dick Butkas, Mike Ditka, Walter Payton, William "the Refrigerator" Perry, Jim McMahon

Past Highlights: Although the Bears didn't win the 2007 Super Bowl, they won it in 1986. During that game, defensive tackle William "the Refrigerator" Perry scored a touchdown, highly rare for a defensive player.

Chicago Bulls

It's been years since Michael Jordan and Phil Jackson's "dynasty" teams played in the United Center, but the Bulls' six championships are still revered here. After Jordan's departure in 1998 the franchise became a shadow of its former self—but a new squad of fresh faces is starting to turn things around. Coach Vinny Del Negro and the "Baby Bulls" are back in the playoffs (2005, 2006, 2007, and 2009), and the United Center is starting to rock again.

Where They Play: *United Center, 1901 W. Madison St., Near West Side*

Season: November–April

How to Buy Tickets: From the ticket office, ☎*312/455–4000 or* ⊕*www.bulls.com*

Most Notable Players: Michael Jordan, Dennis Rodman, Scottie Pippen, Toni Kukoc

Past Highlights: The Bulls won six NBA Championship Trophies: 1991, 1992, 1993, 1996, 1997, 1998

Note: Avoid leaving the game early or wandering around this neighborhood at night.

TAKE ME OUT TO THE BALLGAME

In a city where you can get a debate going about all sorts of things—best deep-dish pizza, best blues bar, best big city (Chicago or New York?)—nothing can inspire a passionate discussion quite like Chicago baseball, an argument that's been going strong since 1901.

Your favorite team says more about you than just whether you prefer the National or American League. The rivalry plays out along geographical and class lines. South Siders, who include everyone living south of the Loop, are die-hard Sox fans. North Siders sell out afternoon Cubbies games even when the team is losing—as they do most years.

There's a legendary rivalry between Sox fans and Cubs fans. When the Sox won the World Series in 2005 for the first time in 88 years, most Cubs fans didn't even watch the games. The traitors who did were called "BiSoxual." When the Cubs made the playoffs in 2007, Sox fans actively rooted for the other team

(as the song "Ballad of the South Side Irish" goes, "When it comes to baseball there are two teams that I love, it's the go-go White Sox and whoever plays the Cubs.") One reason that the division has lasted so long is class tension. South Siders, besides the intellectual Hyde Park pocket, tend to be blue collar. North Siders tend to be professionals.

The teams have only played against each other once post-season: the 1906 World Series. The Cubs were favored, but the White Sox won. Fans on both the North and South sides agree on one thing: it would be "an El of a series" if the teams ever faced each other postseason again. As Cubs fans say, "You Gotta Believe."

Photo caption (team photo labels):
CHICAGO
NATIONAL LEAGUE CHAMP... 1907

SCHULTE ZIMMERMAN REULBACH LUNDGREN PFEISTER HOWARD CHANCE mgr. STEINFELDT SLAGLE McCORMICK SHECKARD BROWN KLING ...NKER DRUGS

CHICAGO CUBS

Just the Facts

Nickname: Cubbies

Mascot: None

Founded: 1870

Last World Series appearance: 1945

World Series wins: 1907 and 1908

Most famous players: Sammy Sosa, Ron Santo, Ryne Sandberg, Ernie Banks, Billy Williams

Original name: White Stockings

Did you know?

Most hated fan: Steve Bartman, who, in the eighth inning of Game 6 in the 2003 play-offs, reached for—and caught—a foul ball at the same time as left fielder Moises Alou. Before Bartman, the Cubs were five outs away from advancing to the World Series. After Bartman's catch, the Cubs fell apart, giving up eight runs.

Lifelong Chicagoans: The Cubs are the only team to play continually in the same city since the founding of the National League in 1876.

Curse: William Sianis, the old owner of the Billy Goat Tavern, bought two tickets for one of the 1945 Cubs–Tigers World Series games: one for himself, and one for his goat. The goat was turned away, and Sianis vowed that the Cubs would never again win a World Series.

HARRY CARAY: "HOLY COW!"

Beloved for his hoarse, off-key rendition of "Take Me Out to the Ballgame," the way he mashed up players names, and his infamous "Holy Cow!", the Cubs' exuberant play-by-play broadcaster, Harry Caray (1914–1998), was as much a fixture of Wrigley Field as the bleacher bums.

Caray broadcast 8,300 games in his 53-year career. (Don't tell Cubs fans—before he came to Wrigley field, he was the voice of the St. Louis Cardinals for 25 years, the White Sox for 10.) After his death in 1998, every single player wore a caricature of Caray—with his infectious smile and goggle glasses—on their sleeves.

The curse persists, it seems, even though the current Billy Goat owner, son Sam Sianis, occasionally drags a goat back onto the field.

Best seat in the house: The bleachers. Tradition has it that the most serious fans (known as bleacher bums) sit here, on either side of the ivy covered, hand-operated scoreboard. When rival teams hit a ball into the bleachers, the fans throw it back. After the 2005 season, the Cubs' owners, the Chicago Tribune Company, expanded the bleachers for the first time since 1938.

CHICAGO WHITE SOX

Just the Facts

Mascot: Southpaw, a fuzzy, green character of indeterminate origin. He appeared in 2004.

Founded: 1893 in Sioux City, Iowa. Moved to Chicago in 1900.

Last World Series appearance: 2005

World Series wins: 1906, 1917, 2005

Notable players: "Shoeless" Joe Jackson, Roberto Hernandez, Roberto Alomar, Johnny Mostil, Frank Thomas, Germaine Dye.

Original name: White Stockings, which was also the first name of the Chicago Cubs. Charles Comiskey hoped to buy some goodwill for the new team by taking on the Cubs' former name.

Did you know?

Theme song: "Na Na Hey Hey (Kiss Him Goodbye)," is played every home game by organist Nancy Faust.

From White Sox to Black: Eight players—outfielder "Shoeless Joe" Jackson, outfielder Oscar "Happy" Felsch, pitchers Eddie Cicotte and Claude "Lefty" Williams, third baseman Buck Weaver, shortstop "Swede" Risberg, and infielders Fred McMullen and Arnold "Chick" Gandi—were accused of throwing the 1919 World Series on behalf of a group of gamblers. They were never convicted, though they were banned from baseball for life. That season's team has been known as the Black Sox ever since.

Most Famous Quote: As Shoeless Joe Jackson was leaving a Black Sox scandal hearing, a newsboy supposedly shouted out, "Say it ain't so, Joe!" This inspired headline writers after the 2005 World Series win to write: "Say it IS so!"

Strangest promotional event: Disco Demolition Night, July 12, 1979, at the old Comiskey Park. Fans were asked to bring unwanted disco records to the park for a Sox–Tigers double header; in return, the admission was lowered to a mere 98 cents. After the first game, chaos erupted—fans threw their records like Frisbees and ran onto the field where they started bonfires and mini-riots.

Fireworks: After every home run and every win, the Sox shoot fireworks into the sky from U.S. Cellular Field. They can be heard across the South Side.

WRIGLEY FIELD

Getting There

Address: 1060 West Addison St., at the corner of Addison St. and Clark St.

Phone: 773/404–CUBS

Public transportation: The Red Line's Addison stop is right outside the park. The #22 Clark bus stops at the entrance.

Driving directions: Try not to drive, but if you do, take Lake Shore Drive north to Belmont Avenue. Travel west on Belmont to North Clark Street, and north on Clark to Wrigley Field.

Parking: Parking is difficult to find around Wrigley, though business owners tend to open up their lots for exorbitant prices, as do lucky home owners with garages.

The Park: The Friendly Confines, as it's known, was built in 1914, which makes it the second-oldest ballpark in the country.

Tours: The Cubs offer 90-minute tours that provide an insider's look at 90 years of Wrigley history. Tickets are $25 per person and you must buy tickets in advance.

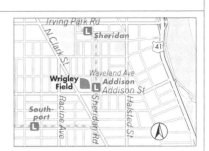

Box Office Hours: Mon.–Fri. 8–6. Sat. 9–4. On game days, box office opens at 9 AM.

What to bring: Don't forget your sunscreen and umbrella/rain gear if you're in the bleachers. Bring water—the container must be one liter or less. Don't bring hard-sided coolers, large bags, thermoses, bottles, cans, or alcoholic beverages.

PLAY BALL

Tickets: Prices can range between $20 to $100. Don't expect to score tickets on short notice—games sell out early in the season.

Wrigley Field Alternatives:

- Join the crowd at Harry Caray's Restaurant in River North (⇨ see Where to Eat chapter, pg. 222).
- Check out the ticketless fans in their lawnchairs on Sheffield Avenue.
- Opt for a White Sox game (tickets are easier to come by).

THE CELL

Getting There

Address: 333 W. 35th St.

Phone: 312/674–1000

Public transportation: Take the CTA Red Line to the 35th Street/Sox Park station of the CTA Red Line.

Driving directions: I-94 West to 35th Street; follow signs to "Sox Parking".

Parking: Parking is $20 in the lots surrounding the park. The lots open two hours prior to game time and close one hour after the game. There is no street parking.

About the name: Now it's "The Cell." But until 2003, when the White Sox made a deal to call it U.S. Cellular Field, it was Comiskey Park, named for former White Sox owner Charles A. Comiskey.

What to bring: Sunscreen and hats on hot days; jackets and small umbrellas if it looks like rain. Food in small, clear, see-through plastic bags and one sealed plastic bottle of water per person is OK–all other beverages, coolers, and large bags are not. Leave beach balls and large radios at home. The area around The Cell is sketchy—don't leave valuables in your car.

Tickets: Prices for tickets can range between $9.50 for a nosebleed seat to $67 for a box seat. Kids who are shorter than the turnstiles—about 36"—get in free but must sit in someone's lap. Monday home games are half price; get a second ticket free when you redeem an empty Pepsi product at ticket windows on the day of the game.

Box Office Hours:
Non-game days: Mon.–Fri., 10–6, Sat. and Sun., 10–4.
Game days: Mon.–Fri. 9–6; 9–6
Sat. 9–6 (day games); 9–8 (night games)
Sun. 9–4 (day games); 9–9 (night games).

Kids: Pontiac FUNdamentals, huge play area for kids, includes baseball and softball clinics, batting cages, and places to practice base running and pitching. It's above the left field concourse, opens 90 minutes before the game, and stays open throughout the game.

Speed pitch machine: Test your pitching speed and accuracy near section 164.

Fan Deck: Get a panoramic view of the field from a two-tiered deck. It's atop the center field concession stands. Free for all fans holding a main level ticket.

Baggage Check: Outside Gate 5 between parking lots A and B. $2 fee per bag.

Pet Check: Between Gates 2 and 3 guests can check their pets. The fee goes to a not-for-profit organization.

ATMs: Sections 139, 531, centerfield, outside the Bullpen Sports Bar, and outside Gate 4.

Concessions: Burgers and veggie burgers, hot dogs and veggie hotdogs, and ice cream are available throughout the park. The Bullpen Sports Bar, offering more substantial food, is near ramp 2. For a small charge, you can sit in the two-tiered, open-air section. Ages 21 and over only.

FIRST GAME CERTIFICATE
The White Sox offer a certificate for guests to commemorate their first time at U.S. Cellular Field. Visit any Guest Relations Booth behind home plate to pick one up.

BEHIND THE SCENES

For a look at what (or who) makes the city tick, check out the following activities.

Black and White and Read All Over

Chicago Tribune Freedom Center. Tour the Chicago Tribune's printing plant and the *New York Times'* Midwest distribution center. ✉ *777 W. Chicago Ave., West Loop* ☎ *312/222–3040* 🎫 *Free, but there are no regular tours and you must call ahead.*

McCormick Tribune Freedom Museum. Take a peek inside the historic Tribune Tower at this two-story museum dedicated to the First Amendment. Engaging interactive exhibits examine the meaning of freedom in the U.S. and abroad. Discover democracy's ancient roots, brush up on your First Amendment rights, and listen to banned music. ✉ *445 N. Michigan Ave., inside Tribune Tower., Near North* ☎ *312/222–4860* ⊕ *www.freedommuseum.us* 🎫 *Free.*

Movers & Shakers

Graceland Cemetery. A comprehensive guide available at the entrance walks you by the graves and tombs of the people who made Chicago great, including merchandiser Marshall Field and railroad-car magnate George Pullman. ✉ *4001 N. Clark St., Far North Side* ☎ *773/525–1105* ⊕ *www.gracelandcemetery.org* 🎫 *Free.*

See Green

Federal Reserve Bank. Though they don't hand out money here, they sure do handle a lot of the green stuff. The facility processes currency and checks, scanning bills for counterfeits, destroying unfit currency, and repackaging fit currency. A visitor center in the lobby has permanent exhibits of old bills, counterfeit money, and a million dollars in $1 bills. One-hour tours explain how money travels and show a high-speed currency-processing machine.

Call in advance for tour reservations, since it's often booked in spring and fall with school groups. ✉ *230 S. LaSalle St., Loop* ☎ *312/322–2400* ⊕ *www.chicago-fed.org* 🎫 *Free.*

Tour a Factory

Though Chicago isn't the industrial center it once was, you can still watch all sorts of things being made in the Chicago area, from cheesecakes to harps (Log on to ⊕ *www.factorytoursusa.com* for a complete list of tours). One of the most popular tours takes you behind the scenes at **Eli's Cheesecake World**, where visitors learn the company's history, tour the bakery facility, and watch cheesecake decorators at work. Of course, the tour ends with a slice of the decadent cheesecake. ✉ *6701 W. Forest Preserve Dr., at Montrose Ave.* ☎ *773/736–3417 or 773/308–7000* ⊕ *www.elicheesecake.com* ☉ *Walk-in tours weekdays at 1* PM; *other times by reservation only.*

Neighborhoods

WORD OF MOUTH

Some of the neighborhoods are very compact and don't take a lot of time to explore. For example, the Gold Coast (Astor Street being voted consistently as one of the most beautiful in our fair city) and Old Town (this is where Second City and Zanies are located, at Piper's Alley). If you want to make a full day of it in a particular neighborhood, pick one that meets all of your needs. And go on the weekend. Much, much more activity in them then.

—exiledprincess

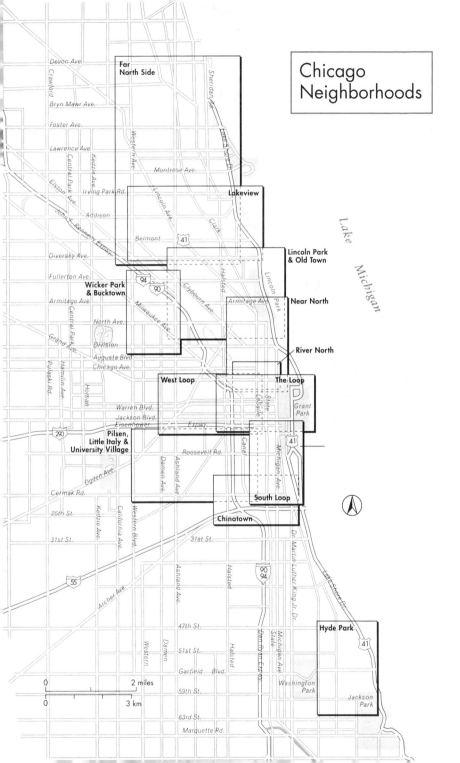

Chicago
Neighborhoods

THE LOOP

Sightseeing
★★★★☆

Dining
★★★☆☆

Lodging
★★★☆☆

Shopping
★★☆☆☆

Nightlife
★★★☆☆

The Loop is a living architectural museum, where shimmering modern towers stand side by side with 19th-century buildings. Striking sculptures by Picasso, Miró, and Chagall watch over plazas alive with music and farmers' markets in summer.

The Loop has noisy, mesmerizing trading centers, gigantic department stores, internationally known landmarks like the Sears Tower (a company has acquired naming rights and, at the time of this writing, plans to rename it Willis Tower—a controversial move that has angered many Chicagoans and architecture buffs) and the Art Institute, and the city's newest playground, Millennium Park. Rattling overhead, encircling it all, is the train system Chicagoans call the El.

Known as the Loop since the cable cars of the 1880s looped around the central business district, downtown Chicago comprises the area south of the Chicago River, west of Lake Michigan, and north of Congress Parkway/Eisenhower Expressway. The western boundary used to be the Chicago River, but the frontier continues to push westward. Handsome skyscrapers line every foot of South Wacker Drive east of the river, and new construction across the bridges is now a near constant.

WHAT'S HERE

Getting around the Loop is easy. It's laid out like a grid: State Street intersects north–south blocks, and Madison Street intersects east–west blocks. Where State and Madison converge is the zero point from where the rest of the city fans out. It's also where you find the building that once housed the department store **Carson Pirie Scott & Co.**, with its breathtaking decorative cast-iron facade—an outstanding example of Louis Sullivan's work. (The company closed the downtown location of the department store in early 2007; the building is now called the Sullivan Center.) Farther north on State Street—the Loop's most famous thoroughfare—is a **Macy's** department store that until 2006 had been

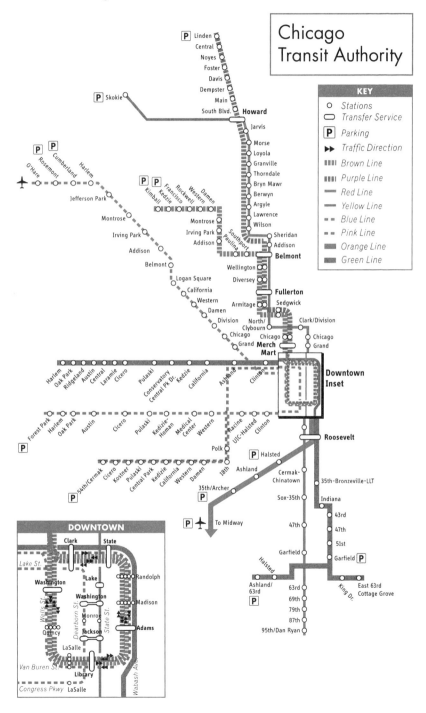

the flagship location for the much-mourned Marshall Field's. Despite the name change, the landmark turn-of-the-20th-century building is still beguiling.

Continuing on State, just north of Randolph Street is the old theater district. First is the ornate 1921 Beaux Arts **Chicago Theatre,** a former movie palace that now hosts live performances. Across the street is the **Gene Siskel Film Center,** which screens art, foreign, and classic movies. West on Randolph Street is the **Ford Center for the Performing Arts–Oriental Theatre,** with its long, glitzy neon sign. On Dearborn is the **Goodman Theatre,** wrapped in the 1923 Art Deco facades of the landmark Harris & Selwyn Twin Theaters. One more block west is the **Cadillac Palace Theatre,** a renovated 1926 vaudeville house that still has its original marble lobby.

On Washington Street is the **Daley Center,** an outdoor plaza that has concerts and holiday and farmers' markets. Check out the unnamed Picasso sculpture, referred to simply as the *Picasso.* Opposite the Daley Center is the **Chicago Temple,** a Methodist church whose beautiful spire is so tall that it's best seen at some distance. Also on the south side of the street is Joan Miró's giant figure *Chicago.*

To the west, following the bend of Wacker Drive, are the Art Deco **Civic Opera House,** where Chicago's Lyric Opera gives its performances, and the pale-grape-color twin towers of the **Chicago Mercantile Exchange.** East on Monroe Street, the sunken, bi-level **Chase Plaza** has room to rest in the shadow of the sweeping Chase Tower building that curves skyward. The Chagall mosaic *The Four Seasons* is at the northeast end of the plaza. Just before you get to State Street is the **LaSalle Bank Theatre** (until recently known as the Shubert Theatre). It was the tallest building in Chicago when it opened in 1906.

Back on Michigan Avenue, just south of Wacker Drive, is the Art Deco **Carbide & Carbon Building,** a polished black granite structure with a dark green terra-cotta tower accented by gold leaf. Local lore has it the building was designed to resemble a champagne bottle with gold foil. Heading south on Michigan, between Monroe and Randolph streets, is **Millennium Park,** anchored by the immensely popular *Cloud Gate* sculpture (also known as the *Bean*) and the sweeping stainless steel Frank Gehry–designed **Jay Pritzker Pavilion.** On the west side of the intersection of Randolph Street and Michigan Avenue is the **Chicago Cultural Center,** home to the **Chicago Office of Tourism Visitor Information Center.** At 200 East Randolph is the soaring **Aon Center.** Directly west of the Aon Center is the **Prudential Building,** Chicago's tallest building until the late 1960s. Behind it rises the rocket ship–like **Two Prudential Plaza,** affectionately nicknamed "Pru Two."

The southern part of the Loop balances the hub of the financial district with the fine arts. On one block are the **Art Institute of Chicago,** the grand-looking **Symphony Center** (home to the internationally acclaimed Chicago Symphony Orchestra), and the **Santa Fe Building.** Farther south on Michigan Avenue is the **Fine Arts Building.**

GETTING ORIENTED

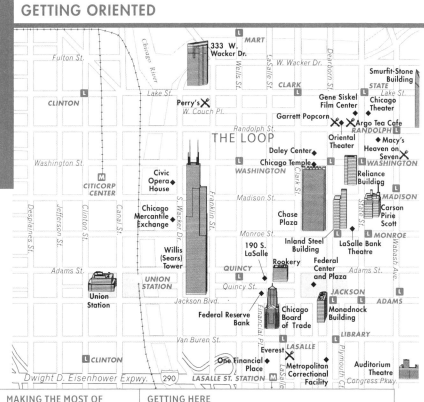

MAKING THE MOST OF YOUR TIME

If you have the time, give yourself a whole day to explore the Loop. You can easily spend half a day at the Art Institute. The rest of your day you can spend sunning yourself in Millennium Park, shopping up and down State Street, taking a trip to the top of the Willis (Sears) Tower, or meandering among the architectural masterpieces and sculptures. And, of course, you'll want to allow yourself time to stand in line for Garrett Popcorn. When night falls, take in a play in the theater district.

GETTING HERE

Take a bus to Michigan Avenue and Wacker Drive. From the north, you can take Bus 3, 145, 147, or 151. Coming from the south, you can take Bus 3, 6, 145, 146, 147, or 151.

The Lake stop on the El's Red Line will put you at State and Lake streets. The Washington, Monroe, and Jackson stops are also in the Loop, just blocks from one another. The Brown, Green, Orange, Pink, and Purple lines stop at State, above ground, at Lake Street. These lines also stop at Randolph, Madison, and Adams in the Loop. If you arrive by car, you can park in the subterranean Grant Park North Garage, with an entrance on Michigan Avenue. Many side streets off Michigan Avenue also have parking garages. But be aware that parking in downtown lots can be pricey—up to $24 for five or more hours. Most streets in the Loop prohibit parking weekdays from 7 AM to 6 PM.

2

KEY

L CTA lines
M Metra lines
✗ Restaurant/Cafe

NEIGHBORHOOD TOP 7

1. Spend an afternoon with Georges Seurat's *A Sunday on la Grande Jatte* at the **Art Institute**.

2. Stand between the 50-foot faces screened onto the two towers of the **Crown Fountain in Millennium Park** and wait for them to spit.

3. Jump in a car and get lost in the underground world of **Lower Wacker Drive**.

4. Spend an afternoon strolling among architectural gems throughout the Loop.

5. Follow your nose and line up at one of the Loop locations of **Garret Popcorn** for a tub or two of the good stuff.

6. Explore **Grant Park** and stay for the spray at **Buckingham Fountain**.

7. Ponder the **Picasso** in Daley Plaza and decide for yourself what it resembles.

QUICK BITES

Choose from dozens of exotic varieties of tea at **Argo Tea Cafe** (✉16 W. Randolph St., Loop ☎312/553-1551). Light lunch fare and sweet treats round out the menu.

The lines form early and stay long throughout the day at **Garrett Popcorn** (✉26 W. Randolph St., Loop, ☎312/201-0455).

Heaven on Seven (✉111 N. Wabash Ave., 7th fl., Loop ☎312/263-6443) is a Loop legend, famous for casual Cajun breakfasts and lunches that have area office workers gladly lining up to be served.

Perry's (✉180 N. Franklin St., Loop ☎312/372-7557) is a hit as much for the trivia questions Perry announces over his deli's PA system as it is for the overstuffed sandwiches.

SOUTH LOOP INCLUDING PRINTERS ROW, MUSEUM CAMPUS AND BRONZEVILLE

Sightseeing
★★★★☆

Dining
★★★☆☆

Lodging
★★☆☆☆

Shopping
★☆☆☆☆

Nightlife
★★☆☆☆

The South Loop, bounded by Congress Parkway/Eisenhower Expressway on the north, Michigan Avenue on the east, Cermak Avenue on the south, and the Chicago River on the west, presents a striking contrast to the Loop, with its less-trafficked streets and more subdued—and, in some spots, grittier—vibe.

Start at the northern edge, where the Loop transitions into the South Loop, for an up-close peek at the looming **Harold Washington Library** on State Street between Van Buren and Congress. The giant gargoyles perched atop the neoclassical building's redbrick facade are actually owls. Inside, the airy ninth-floor **Winter Garden** is well worth a visit. East on Congress at Michigan Avenue is the national landmark **Auditorium Building.** This Romanesque Revival building and opera house was designed by architects Louis Sullivan and Dankmar Adler.

Trips farther south to the Museum Campus and Printer's Row district here are musts. Perched on the lakefront, Museum Campus is a glorious spot to take in the skyline. It's home to the **Field Museum,** the **John G. Shedd Aquarium,** and the **Adler Planetarium & Astronomy Museum.** Printers Row, a small enclave to the west, was once a thriving commercial area and the center of the printing trades in Chicago. Today it stands as a good example of the South Loop renaissance, with coffeehouses, shops, and restaurants. Farther afield, but worth a visit if there's time, is the Bronzeville area, a historic community originally settled by waves of African-Americans fleeing the South after World War I.

WHAT'S HERE

The 57-acre Museum Campus is home to the Big Three—the **Field Museum,** the **John G. Shedd Aquarium,** and the **Adler Planetarium & Astronomy Museum,** all united in one pedestrian-friendly, parklike setting. Park your car in one of the lots just past the Field Museum on McFetridge Drive, or ride the free Museum Campus trolley (☎877/244–2246), which connects the three museums with other downtown tourist attractions and train stations. It operates daily from Memorial Day to Labor Day and on holidays, and runs only on weekends the rest of the year. On the west side of the campus is the Field Museum, which houses a staggering array of culture- and nature-focused exhibits. It's most famous is Sue, the largest and most complete *T. rex* skeleton in the world.

The Shedd Aquarium, on the lakefront just past the Field Museum, has bizarre and fantastically beautiful fish, plus dolphins and beluga whales. On the east side of the campus, at the far end of a peninsula that juts out into Lake Michigan, is the Adler Planetarium & Astronomy Museum— the first modern planetarium in the Western Hemisphere.

FRUGAL FUN

If you're visiting all three museums, plus some of the city's other big attractions, buy a Chicago CityPass (adults $69, kids 3–11 $59). You'll avoid long lines and get access to the Field, the Shedd, and the Adler, plus the Hancock Observatory or Sears Tower Skydeck and the Museum of Science and Industry.

Just south of the Museum Campus is **Soldier Field,** the building with the massive columns reminiscent of ancient Greece and the home of the Chicago Bears. A controversial modern glass expansion was completed in 2003.

The Printers Row district is bounded by Congress Parkway on the north, Polk Street on the south, Plymouth Court to the east, and the Chicago River to the west. It fell into disrepair in the 1960s, but a neighborhood resurgence began in the late 1970s. You can still see examples here of buildings by the group that represented the First Chicago School of Architecture (including Louis Sullivan), as well as **Dearborn Station,** a Romanesque Revival–style structure that was once the city's main passenger train hub. Today the red sandstone building houses everything from banks and law offices to a sprawling Bar Louie restaurant, and the structure's intact 12-story clock tower remains visible from several blocks in any direction. These days this section of town is best known for the annual **Printers Row Book Fair,** a weekend-long literary celebration held each June.

The historic **Bronzeville** neighborhood roughly covers the area south of McCormick Place and north of Hyde Park between State Street and Cottage Grove Avenue. Following World War I, African-Americans moved to this neighborhood to escape race restrictions prevalent in other parts of the city. Landmarks include the symbolic entrance, a tall statue at 26th Place and Martin Luther King Jr. Drive that depicts a new arrival from the South bearing a suitcase held together with string. Walk along Martin Luther King Jr. Drive between 25th and 35th streets to follow a commemorative trail of more than 90 sidewalk plaques honoring the best and brightest of the community, including Pulitzer Prize–winner Gwendolyn Brooks, whose first book of poetry was called *A Street in Bronzeville.*

GETTING ORIENTED

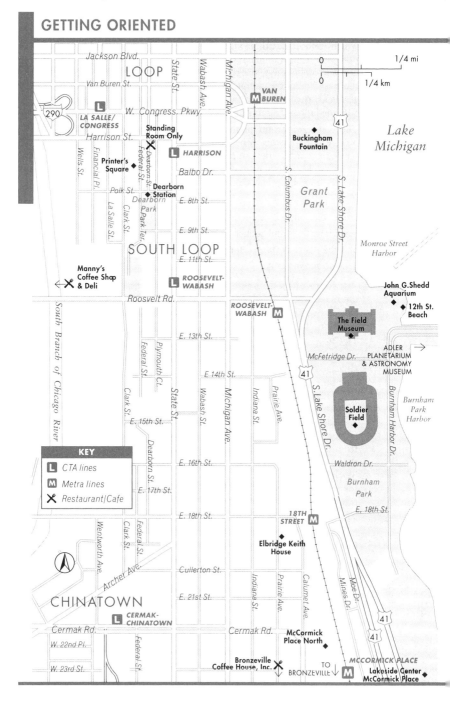

GETTING HERE

Buses 6, 12, and 146 take you to Museum Campus. If you drive, take Lake Shore Drive to the Museum Campus exit. There's some coveted meter parking as well as pricier lots adjacent to the museums. For Printers Row, take the El's Brown, Orange, Pink, or Purple line to the library stop, or the Red Line to Harrison. Buses 6, 22, 36, and 145 will also get you there. Drivers can take Congress Parkway to Dearborn Street. Bronzeville can be easily accessed by buses 49 and 95. To get there by car, take Lake Shore Drive to 31st Street, then travel west to Martin Luther King Jr. Drive.

MAKING THE MOST OF YOUR TIME

Plan on at least a day for a visit to the three museums (you could spend a day at the mammoth Field Museum alone). Allow extra time to enjoy the spectacular skyline and lake views from Museum Campus and to stroll along the harbor. Note that traffic can get snarled and special parking rules go into effect around Museum Campus when the Chicago Bears are playing at neighboring Soldier Field. Prairie Avenue is a quick hit, taking a couple of hours at most. A trip to Bronzeville can take from an hour or two to a half day, depending on whether you opt for one of the longer organized tours.

QUICK BITES

Bronzeville Coffee House, Inc. (✉ 538 E. 43rd St., South Loop ☎ 773/536–0494) is a comfy choice for coffee and pastries.

Have a corned-beef sandwich all the other delis in town aim to beat at **Manny's Coffee Shop & Deli** (✉ 1141 S. Jefferson St., South Loop ☎ 312/939–2855).

"Da Mare" himself, Richard M. Daley, has stood up for the turkey burgers at **Standing Room Only (SRO Chicago)** (✉ 610 S. Dearborn St., South Loop ☎ 312/360–1776).

2

SAFETY

Some parts of the South Loop can feel sketchy, so exercise caution at night by sticking to well-lighted streets. Group tours of Bronzeville are recommended for those unfamiliar with the area.

TOURS

The **Chicago Office of Tourism** (☎ 312/742–1190) offers a half-day bus tour of Bronzeville. Other tours are offered by the **Black Metropolis Convention and Tourism Council** (☎ 773/373–2842) and **Tour Black Chicago** (☎ 773/684–9034). **Black CouTours** (☎ 773/233–8907) offers a 2½-hour excursion of black culture including Bronzeville and other highlights.

NEIGHBORHOOD TOP 5

1. Spot your favorite fish at the **John G. Shedd Aquarium**, then stand next to Sue the *T. rex* at the **Field Museum.**

2. See the stars at the **Adler Planetarium & Astronomy Museum.**

3. Tailgate in the parking lot before a Chicago Bears game at **Soldier Field.**

4. Grab a corned-beef sandwich and potato pancake with a cross-section of Chicago at **Manny's Coffee Shop & Deli.**

5. Take a step back into Chicago's rich African-American history with a guided tour of **Bronzeville.**

WEST LOOP INCLUDING GREEKTOWN

Sightseeing
★☆☆☆☆

Dining
★★★★☆

Lodging
★☆☆☆☆

Shopping
★★☆☆☆

Nightlife
★★★★☆

Most of the West Loop languished for years as a waste-land peppered with warehouses and meatpacking plants. But nowadays many of the warehouses have been con-verted to lofts, and a thriving art scene has emerged around Fulton Market.

Eco-friendly fashion and design showrooms have transformed the area into the heart of Chicago's burgeoning green scene. Harpo Studios, the production house of Oprah Winfrey, is here, and there's also an ultra-hip dining and nightclub scene. By day the neighborhood is a relatively quiet, concrete-heavy area where plant workers, white-collar business types, and stroller-pushing parents share the sidewalks.

WHAT'S HERE

The West Loop is bound by Ashland Avenue on the west, the Chicago River on the east, Grand Avenue on the north, and the Eisenhower Expressway on the south. Randolph Street is the neighborhood's res-taurant row and home to some of the city's most notable dining spots, including French-inspired **Marché,** which many credit with jump-start-ing the neighborhood's turnaround in the early 1990s, and **Blackbird,** a nouveau-American hot spot lauded by critics worldwide. Many of the restaurants offer outdoor seating in warmer months—grab a table and watch the city saunter past. Every June the **Taste of Randolph Street** festival brings entertainment and food stalls operated by dozens of nearby restaurants.

On Carpenter Street between Randolph Street and Washington Bou-levard is **Harpo Studios** (✉*1058 W. Washington Blvd., West Loop* ☎*312/591–9222* ⊕*www.oprah.com*), the taping site for Oprah Win-frey's talk show. The studio isn't open to tours, and tickets to the show can be nearly impossible to score, so a stop here isn't much more than a fun photo op. However, if you're a die-hard Oprah fan and want to attempt to get tickets, here's what you need to know: The show books audiences only for the current and following month. When you call—if you're lucky enough to get through—a staffer will give you the taping schedule and a list of available dates. You can reserve up to four seats for any one taping (all attendees must be at least 18). If you can't get tickets in advance, check the Web site for occasional last-minute tickets via e-mail.

Just to the west of Harpo on Washington is the **Museum of Holography,** where 10,000 square feet of exhibit space are dedicated to the advancement of—you guessed it—holography as an art form. The stylish **Fulton Market** district runs along Fulton Market and Lake Street between Des Plaines Street and Ashland Avenue. The trendsetting galleries, shops, and interior design showrooms that now occupy former meatpacking warehouses have transformed the area into a mecca for cutting-edge design and green living. **Pivot** boutique at 1101 W. Fulton Market showcases earth-friendly fashions made from bamboo and recycled materials. Eco-minded folks also flock to **Green Home Chicago** at 213 N. Morgan Street for sustainably made home furnishings. The art scene draws attention as well—here you'll find everything from printmaking and sculpture to photography, paintings, and glass and metalwork. One of the pioneering forces in the art community, **Mars Gallery,** has showcased contemporary pop and outsider art since 1988 at 1139 W. Fulton Market. Another contemporary art gallery worth a visit is **FLAT-FILEgalleries** at 217 N. Carpenter Street. Be aware, though, that the area remains a bustling commercial district. During the day the seafood and meatpacking plants are swarming with heavy vehicles helmed by harried drivers. Exercise caution while driving or, better yet, cab it to your destination.

The **Chicago Antique Market,** a seasonal indoor-outdoor flea market held May through October on the last Saturday of the month, has established itself as this city's answer to London's famed Portobello Road market. Centered around Randolph Street and Ogden Avenue, the market offers everything from mid-century furniture to vintage handbags. Antiques hunters with fat wallets may want to check the schedule at **Leslie Hindman Auctioneers** (✉ *1338 W. Lake St., West Loop* ☎ *312/280–1212*), a fine-art auctioneer on Lake Street that's the fifth-largest auction house in the country. Auctions run the gamut from 20th-century decorative arts to American and European works of art to fine jewelry and timepieces.

Back on Halsted Street between Madison and Van Buren streets is **Greektown,** a small strip of the West Loop that may as well be half a world away. Greek restaurants are the main draw here. Continue west on Madison, past the slew of new condo developments and vintage conversions in progress, and you'll come to one of Chicago's latest dining and nightlife destinations. On a stretch of Madison roughly between Sangamon and Elizabeth streets you'll find up-to-the-minute boutiques, trendy bars and lounges, and popular restaurants.

GETTING ORIENTED

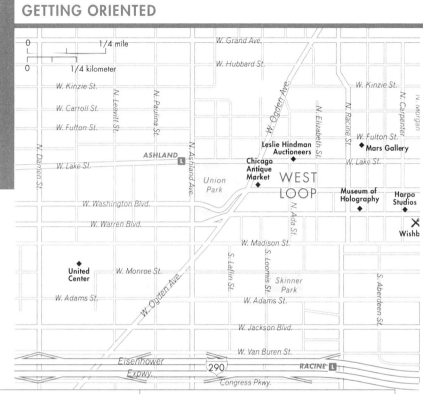

GETTING HERE

By car, take the Kennedy Express-way to the Randolph Street exit. You can also get here by taking the 8 Halsted and 20 Madison buses, or the El's Green Line to Clinton. Note that the Green Line has two branches—take the Harlem/Lake branch heading west, not the Ashland/63rd branch.

For Greektown, take the Blue Line Forest Park branch (not the O'Hare branch) to UIC—Halsted. The 8 Halsted and 20 Madison buses get you here, too. If you're driving to Greektown, exit the Kennedy Expressway at Randolph or Madison streets.

MAKING THE MOST OF YOUR TIME

Oprah fans should start their West Loop visit early with a photo op outside Harpo Studios. If you're lucky, you might catch a glimpse of a VIP guest heading into the building for a taping session. Around midday or early afternoon take a few hours to browse the galleries before heading to one of the trendy neighborhood restaurants for dinner (plan to eat early if you don't have reservations). Randolph Street offers a variety of options within easy walking distance. Then cap off the evening with a visit to a late-night club or lounge.

If your visit to Chicago happens to coincide with the last Saturday of the month (May–October), check out the Chicago Antique Market around Randolph Street and Ogden Avenue for one-of-a-kind souvenirs, including vintage dishware, clothing, handbags, and jewelry. Afterward, stroll east toward Greektown for a delicious lunch or snack—feta and olives, anyone?

2

NEIGHBORHOOD TOP 5

1. Take a picture outside **Harpo Studios,** where Oprah films her talk show.

2. Check out the funky contemporary art and design along **Fulton Market.**

3. Order the *saganaki* (flaming cheese) and shout *Opaaa!* along with waiters who set it ablaze for you tableside in **Greektown.**

4. Experience the vibrant **Randolph Street** dining and nightlife scene.

5. Bone up on Chicago history with a visit to the site of the **Haymarket Riot** at the corner of Randolph and Des Plaines streets.

SAFETY

As you reach the western part of the neighborhood around Ashland Avenue, just a stone's throw from the United Center, the gentrification comes to a halt; the streets around the Fulton Market area are deserted during off times. Exercise caution in both areas.

QUICK BITES

Artopolis Bakery, Café & Agora (✉ 306 S. Halsted St., West Loop ☎ 312/559-9000) has a light menu of salads, soups, and sandwiches, and some of the best bread in the city.

For a quick and authentic taste of Greektown, or just a plain old burger and fries anytime day or night, stop in at **Greektown Gyros** (✉ 239 S. Halsted St., West Loop ☎ 312/236-9310), open 24 hours a day, 7 days a week.

Smoothies and salads will fuel you up without weighing you down at the tiny **Jubilee Juice** (✉ 140 N. Halsted St., West Loop ☎ 312/491-8500).

They come from all over town for the cheese grits, blue claw-crab cakes, and other examples of "Southern Reconstructionist" cooking at **Wishbone** (✉ 1001 W. Washington Blvd., West Loop ☎ 312/850-2663). At breakfast and lunch you can opt for a cafeteria line.

NEAR NORTH INCLUDING THE GOLD COAST, MAGNIFICENT MILE AND STREETERVILLE

Sightseeing
★★★★★
Dining
★★★★☆
Lodging
★★★★☆
Shopping
★★★★☆
Nightlife
★★★★☆

The city's greatest tourist magnet reads like a to-do checklist: Navy Pier, the John Hancock Building, art museums and galleries, lakefront activities, and countless shops where you could spend a few dollars or thousands.

The Magnificent Mile, a stretch of Michigan Avenue between the Chicago River and Oak Street, owes its name to the swanky shops that line both sides of the street. Shoppers cram the sidewalks in summer and keep the street bustling even in winter, when the trees are twined with thousands of white lights and the buildings are aglow with colored floodlights.

East of the Magnificent Mile is upscale Streeterville, which began as a disreputable landfill that the notorious George Wellington "Cap" Streeter and his wife Maria claimed as their own. Along the Lake Michigan shoreline, from North Avenue on the north, Oak Street on the south, and LaSalle Street on the west, is the posh Gold Coast area. Made fashionable after the Great Chicago Fire of 1871 by the social-climbing industrialists of the day, today's Gold Coast neighborhood is still a ritzy place to live, work, shop, and mingle. Architectural styles along the East Lake Shore Drive Historic District include baroque, Renaissance, Georgian, and Beaux-Arts—though varied, they blend together beautifully.

WHAT'S HERE

The **Michigan Avenue Bridge** spans the Chicago River as a gateway to North Michigan Avenue from the south. On the east side of the river is the headquarters of the *Chicago Tribune*, in the crenellated **Tribune Tower,** behind which resides the **NBC Tower.**

The base of Tribune Tower is studded with pieces from more than 120 famous sites and structures around the world, including the Parthenon, the Taj Mahal, and Bunker Hill.

Across the water is the much-hyped Trump International Hotel & Tower, a 92-story mixed-use behemoth on the site of the old *Chicago Sun-Times* headquarters. When completed in early 2009 it became the second-tallest building in Chicago—and the country. The glass and steel structure also houses a spa and acclaimed restaurant **Sixteen**. North of the bridge on the west side of Michigan Avenue is the **Wrigley Building,** with its striking wedding-cake embellishments and clock tower. They mark the beginning of the **Magnificent Mile,** the famous stretch of shops. The tapering **John Hancock Center,** the third-tallest building in Chicago, and the elegant Fourth Presbyterian Church, with its peaceful courtyard, are near the north end of the Mile.

This stretch of Michigan Avenue was originally called the Magnificent Mile because of the architecture. Most of those elegant, small buildings are long gone, however, and the moniker now refers to the excellent shopping that attracts visitors and residents alike.

West of the Mag Mile, at Pearson and Rush streets, is **Water Tower Park**, a Chicago icon. The Water Tower and the matching Water Works Pumping Station across the street are among the few buildings to have survived the Great Chicago Fire of 1871. Since 2003 a new theater space within the historic structure has been home to the renowned Lookingglass Theatre Company. One block east is the imposing **Museum of Contemporary Art,** which concentrates on 20th-century art, principally works created after 1945.

East of the Mag Mile, on Illinois Street and Lake Michigan, is **Navy Pier,** a wonderful place to enjoy lake breezes, hop on an afternoon or evening boat cruise, catch a concert or play, or ride on the giant Ferris wheel. The **Chicago Children's Museum** is part of the Navy Pier complex. North of Navy Pier, hugging Lake Shore Drive, is the Gold Coast neighborhood. Astor Street is the grande dame of Gold Coast promenades. On the northwest corner of Astor and Burton streets you'll find the Georgian **Patterson-McCormick Mansion** (⊠*20 E. Burton Pl.*), commissioned in 1891 by *Chicago Tribune* chief Joseph Medill. Where Astor Street jogs to meet Schiller Street stands the 1892 **Charnley–Persky House,** designed in part by Frank Lloyd Wright. On Goethe Street is the Ambassador East Hotel, home of the famous **Pump Room** restaurant. In its glory days celebrities like Frank Sinatra, Humphrey Bogart, and Lauren Bacall held court in the famed Booth One. Where Dearborn Street meets Oak Street is the Gold Coast's famous shopping district. Past the former **Playboy Mansion** (⊠*1340 N. State St.*), all the way to North Avenue, is a beautiful view of Lincoln Park.

GETTING ORIENTED

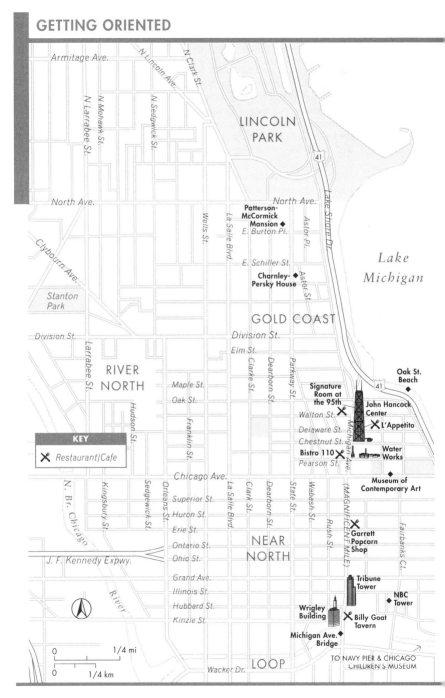

GETTING HERE

If you're arriving from the north by car, take Lake Shore Drive south to the Michigan Avenue exit. From the south, you can start your exploring by exiting at Grand Avenue, the exit for Navy Pier. Numerous buses run along Michigan Avenue, including the 3, 4, 144, 145, 146, 167, and 151. Buses 29, 65, and 66 all service Navy Pier. If you're using the El, take the Red Line to Chicago Avenue or Clark and Division to get closest to the action.

MAKING THE MOST OF YOUR TIME

You can spend a day at a number of the attractions (or just shopping), depending on your interests. Navy Pier takes at least a couple of hours (especially if you have children); you could spend a few hours in the Chicago Children's Museum alone. Art lovers will want to set aside at least one or two hours for the Museum of Contemporary Art. A stroll through the Gold Coast can be done in an hour, but what's the hurry? Make an afternoon of it. Our favorite times are weekend afternoons in spring or fall or just before dusk any day in summer, when the neighborhood's leafy tranquillity and big-city energy converge.

NEIGHBORHOOD TOP 5

1. Have a drink or a meal at the **Signature Room** at the 95th.

2. Sunbathe with the beautiful people at **Oak Street Beach.**

3. Take one of the Chicago Architecture Foundation's amazing **boat tours** along the river.

4. Catch a glimpse of the **Tribune Tower** and find the pieces of the Taj Mahal, Parthenon, and other famous structures embedded in the base.

5. Experience the visual wit and acrobatics that characterize a **Lookingglass Theatre** performance.

QUICK BITES

For an inexpensive, hearty lunch, try **L'Appetito** (✉ *875 N. Michigan Ave.* ☎ *312/337–0691*), a deli and grocery off the Hancock Center's lower-level plaza that has some of the best Italian sandwiches in Chicago.

Behind and one level down from the Wrigley Building is the (in)famous **Billy Goat Tavern** (✉ *430 N. Michigan Ave.* ☎ *312/222–1525*), the inspiration for *Saturday Night Live's* classic "cheezborger, cheezborger" skit and a longtime haunt of local journalists, most notably the late columnist Mike Royko. Grab a greasy burger (and chips, of course) at this no-frills grill, or just have a beer and absorb the comic undertones.

Make a meal out of appetizers at **Bistro 110** (✉ *110 E. Pearson St.* ☎ *312/266–3110*). The artichoke hearts are heavenly, and the gooey French onion soup is not to be missed. There are ample choices of wine by the glass. The front bar-café area is perfect for casual dining.

Garrett Popcorn Shop (✉ *670 N. Michigan Ave.* ☎ *312/943–8464*) is a Chicago institution that has been selling popcorn on the Mag Mile for more than 50 years. Tourists and locals alike line up outside—even in the frigid months—to buy tasty warm popcorn mixed with things like macadamia nuts and caramel.

2

RIVER NORTH

Sightseeing
★★☆☆☆

Dining
★★★★☆

Lodging
★★★★☆

Shopping
★★★★☆

Nightlife
★★★★☆

Technically a part of Near North, River North is a neighborhood that commands a strong presence all its own. Bounded on the south and west by branches of the Chicago River, River North has eastern and northern boundaries that can be hard to define.

As in many other Chicago neighborhoods, the limits of River North have expanded as the area has grown more attractive; today they extend roughly to Oak Street on the north and Rush Street on the east.

Richly served by waterways and railroad tracks that ran along its western edge, the neighborhood was settled by Irish immigrants in the mid-19th century. As the 20th century approached, the area developed into a busy commercial, industrial, and warehouse district.

But as economic conditions changed and factories moved away, the neighborhood deteriorated, and River North became just another down-on-its-luck urban area.

In the 1970s, artists attracted by low rents and spacious abandoned storage areas and shop floors began to move into the neighborhood, and it eventually became the go-to spot for art lovers to gallery-hop.

Then developers caught the scent and began buying up properties with an eye to renovation. Today struggling artists might find it hard to afford a cup of coffee in this high-rent district dotted with tourist-pleasing restaurants and upscale retail shops.

WHAT'S HERE

The huge **Merchandise Mart,** on the river between Orleans and Wells streets, is so commanding that it has its own zip code as well as its own stop on the El's Brown and Purple lines. Miles of corridors on its top floors are lined with trade-only furniture and home-design showrooms. LuxeHome, a collection of 30 or so upscale stores with an emphasis on home design and renovation, takes up the bottom two floors.

At Dearborn and Kinzie streets is the splendid ornamental brickwork of **33 West Kinzie Street,** the home of Harry Caray's restaurant. (The loud—and delicious—restaurant, filled with flags and giant drawings of the late Cubs broadcaster and his big glasses, is on "Harry Caray Drive," an honorary designation.)

Southeast of here, just shy of the bridge that crosses the Chicago River, you can see the distinctive twin corncobs of **Marina City,** a residential complex that also includes the Hotel Sax Chicago (formerly a House of Blues hotel), the House of Blues nightclub, and a bowling alley. Fans of the old *Bob Newhart Show* may recognize Marina City from the backdrop in the show's opening credits.

A few blocks north, at the intersection of State and Ohio streets, are the **Tree Studios** shops and galleries, and the adjacent Medinah Temple, on Wabash Avenue, which houses a **Bloomingdale's Home & Furniture Store.**

THE ROOTS

The original Tree Studios were intended as living spaces for artists who were in town for the World's Columbian Exposition at the turn of the 20th century. They were used as living and working spaces by generations of creative types and were considered an artistic oasis until 2001, when a development group bought the studio buildings and the Medinah Temple.

Head west on either Ohio or Ontario Street, and as you approach LaSalle, then Wells streets, see the neighborhood transform into something of a dining Disneyland, with enormous outposts of national chains like Rainforest Café, Hooters, and the Hard Rock Café. Tourists clog the streets, eager to mob them all.

Things get a little more civilized again north on Wells Street to Superior Street, where you run into the area known as the **River North Gallery District.** Dozens of art galleries show every kind of work imaginable in the area bounded by Wells, Orleans, Chicago, and Erie streets—in fact, virtually every building on Superior Street between Wells and Orleans streets houses at least one gallery. Galleries welcome visitors, so feel free to stop into any that catch your eye. On periodic Fridays throughout the year the galleries coordinate their exhibitions and open their doors to the public for a special night to showcase new works.

Art lovers take note: though River North is still a good bet for great art, a growing number of artists have ditched the high-rent district for the cheaper, more industrial West Loop and Pilsen neighborhoods.

GETTING ORIENTED

GETTING HERE

The Merchandise Mart has its own stop on the El's Brown and Purple lines.

Traveling by car, there is a parking lot nearby at 350 N. Orleans Street. Or, if you are heading to the northern tip of the neighborhood, take Wells Street to Chicago Avenue.

You can also walk west from the Mag Mile a few blocks to get to the area.

MAKING THE MOST OF YOUR TIME

You can see all there is to see in about two hours, but add another hour or more if you want to wander leisurely in and out of the shops at Tree Studios or the galleries on Superior Street and the surrounding area. Step across the State Street Bridge for a great bird's-eye view of Chicago. You'll see the Tribune Tower and Trump Tower to the east and Marina City at your back.

For a reminder of the Chicago River's ongoing importance as a working river, wait for the bridge to rise to let boats pass underneath—kids especially love seeing the bridge in action. Duck into the Bloomingdale Home store in the former Medinah Temple and admire the ornate architecture and Moorish details while shopping for bath towels. Be sure to take in a meal while you're in the area. But be forewarned: Dining without reservations at one of the touristy restaurants can entail a wait on weekends and on nice days. Most galleries are closed Sunday and Monday.

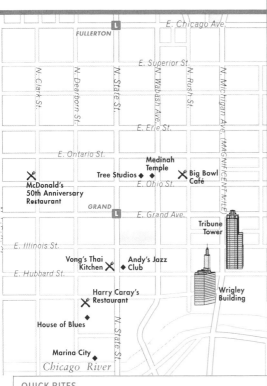

NEIGHBORHOOD TOP 7

1. Treat yourself to music during a Friday lunch at the infamous Andy's Jazz Club's **Jazz at Noon** series.

2. Spend an afternoon browsing the **art galleries.**

3. Pick up some ideas for your next home improvement project at **LuxeHome** in the Merchandise Mart.

4. Cheer on the Chicago Cubs from the comfort of a cozy barstool at **Harry Caray's Restaurant** at 33 W. Kinzie Street.

5. Admire the views north and south from the **Dearborn** or **State Street bridges** over the Chicago River.

6. Take the kids to **Ed Debevic's** for a burger with a side of sass.

7. Catch a performance at the **House of Blues** and then head across the street to **Bin 36** for wine flights and cheese plates.

QUICK BITES

For quality over kitsch, try **Big Bowl** (⊠ 60 E. Ohio St.), or fill up on both while devouring yummy Chicago deep-dish pizza at the graffiti-covered, tourist-happy **Gino's East** (⊠ 633 N. Wells St.).

Nestled under the El tracks at Superior and Franklin streets is **Brett's Kitchen** (⊠ 233 W. Superior St., River North ☎ 312/664–6354), an excellent spot for a sandwich or an omelet Monday through Saturday.

Want some fries to go with that shake, honey? The purposefully sassy waitstaff at **Ed Debevic's** (⊠ 640 N. Wells St.), a '50s-style diner, keeps the crowds entertained.

The great John-Georges Vongerichten gets casual at **Vong's Thai Kitchen** (⊠ 6 W. Hubbard St., River North ☎ 312/664–8664), where sharing satays, noodle dishes, and curries is encouraged.

LINCOLN PARK AND OLD TOWN

Sightseeing
★★★★☆

Dining
★★★★☆

Lodging
★★☆☆☆

Shopping
★★☆☆☆

Nightlife
★★★★☆

Old Town began in the 1850s as a modest neighborhood of working-class German families. Now you'll find a diverse population and some of the oldest—and most expensive—real estate in Chicago.

Old Town is bordered by Division Street to the south, Armitage Avenue to the north, Clark Street on the east, and Larrabee Street on the west, but its heart lies at the intersection of North Avenue and Wells Street. Besides its notable architecture, Old Town is home to the famous comedy clubs Zanies and the Second City.

Lincoln Park—the *park*—extends from North Avenue to Hollywood Avenue. It became the city's first public playground in 1864, named after the then recently assassinated president. The neighborhood adjacent to the original park, bordered by Armitage Avenue on the south, Diversey Parkway on the north, the lake on the east, and the Chicago River on the west, also became known as Lincoln Park.

WHAT'S HERE

There's a lot going on in Old Town and Lincoln Park. The yuck-it-up comedy clubs on Wells Street and raucous nightlife along North Lincoln Avenue and Halsted Street are a sharp contrast to the tranquillity at the lagoon in Lincoln Park at Fullerton Parkway.

You can hear the laughs emanating from Wells Street in Old Town most any night of the week. **Zanies** has been hosting stand-up shows by some of the country's most famous comics, from Jay Leno to Dave Chappelle, for 30 years. Just up the street is **The Second City,** the legendary improv company that's served as a training ground for generations of would-be superstars.

The **Chicago History Museum** (✉1601 N. Clark St., Lincoln Park ☎312/642–4600) (formerly the Chicago Historical Society), at North Avenue and Clark Street, is housed in a Georgian structure built in 1932. The beautiful people strut their stuff just to the east along the lake at **North**

Avenue Beach, while the beasts roar nearby on Stockton Drive at **Lincoln Park Zoo,** which is free to the public. A few blocks ahead there's a rather inconspicuous patch of grass where a garage once stood bearing the address **2122 N. Clark Street.** There's no marker, but it's the site of the infamous St. Valentine's Day Massacre, when seven men were killed on the orders of Al Capone on February 14, 1929.

DID YOU KNOW?

Another infamous Lincoln Park locale is the Biograph Theater (⊠ 2433 *N. Lincoln Ave., Lincoln Park* ☎ 773/871–3000), now home to the Victory Gardens Theater company, where notorious bank robber John Dillinger was shot and killed by the FBI in 1934.

One of the largest Catholic universities in the country, **DePaul University** has a 28-acre campus in Lincoln Park, bounded roughly by Webster Avenue on the south, Fullerton Avenue on the north, Halsted Street on the east, and Racine Avenue on the west. It serves more than 17,000 students, and has four other campuses in the Loop and suburbs. You might have a celebrity sighting or two on Halsted Street if you time a visit right to **Steppenwolf Theatre Company,** where ensemble members including Joan Allen, John Mahoney, Gary Sinese, and John Malkovich often perform or direct. The **Peggy Notebaert Nature Museum,** back in the park at Fullerton Parkway, is geared to kids, but outdoorsy adults will dig it, too.

On Wednesday and Saturday mornings from May to September the **Green City Market** takes over a large swath of grass at the south end of Lincoln Park. In addition to farmstands showcasing locally grown produce and sustainably produced meat, there are food booths and cooking demonstrations by local celebrity chefs, such as Rick Bayless of Frontera Grill.

OUR TIP

All ages get especially wide-eyed in the Notebaert's Judy Istock Butterfly Haven, where you get to commingle with 75 species of free-flying, brightly colored beauties—roughly 1,000 at any time.

Film buffs shouldn't leave Lincoln Park without a visit to **Facets Cinematheque,** which presents an eclectic selection of artistically significant films from around the world on its two screens. It also has a well-stocked video store (Facets Videotheque) that has more than 60,000 foreign, classic, and cult films.

Film fans—and younger visitors—also will relish a trip to **Oz Park,** between Webster and Dickens avenues and Burlington and Larrabee streets, for a chance to get up close with Dorothy and Toto. All the beloved movie characters are there in sculpture form. The Wizard's author, L. Frank Baum, lived in Chicago at the turn of the 20th century. The park also has a playlot for pint-size visitors.

GETTING ORIENTED

GETTING HERE	MAKING THE MOST OF YOUR TIME
Take the Howard (Red Line) train or the Ravenswood (Brown Line) train to either Armitage or Fullerton avenues. Sheffield Avenue will be the nearest north–south street in both cases. Buses 11, 22, 36, and 151 take you through the area, too. If you're driving, take Lake Shore Drive to Fullerton Avenue and drive west on Fullerton Avenue to Sheffield Avenue. Parking is scarce, especially evenings and weekends, so public transit or a cab is recommended.	You could take an hour or a whole day for Lincoln Park, depending on how you prefer to spend your time. Set aside at least a couple of hours if you plan on a leisurely shopping experience along Armitage, Halsted, and Webster avenues. Tack on a couple more hours for the Peggy Notebaert Nature Museum, especially with kids. And if it's a beautiful summer day, ditch whatever else you had planned and surrender yourself to hours of frolicking in the park and on the beach. If you have kids in tow, or simply love visiting urban beasts, set aside some time for the Lincoln Park Zoo. Come nightfall, make a beeline for The Second City or the Steppenwolf Theatre Company; do a little research ahead of time to decide what kind of performance you want to see—and how much you want to spend. Then you can plan to make a day out of enjoying Lincoln Park and Old Town. It's quintessential Chicago!

2

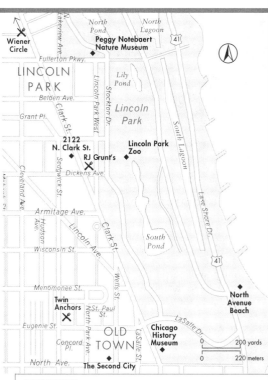

NEIGHBORHOOD TOP 7

1. Take a walk or a run, or a bike ride—along the **lakefront path** heading south from North Avenue beach, and take in the breathtaking views of the city along Lake Michigan.

2. Catch the free improv after the show every night except Friday at **Second City.**

3. See some of Hollywood's greats return to their roots to perform in a play at the **Steppenwolf Theatre Company.**

4. Browse the boutiques along **Armitage Avenue.**

5. Take refuge in the lush greenery of the **Lincoln Park Conservatory.**

6. Satisfy your late-night cravings after a stint at the bars with a stop at the **Wiener Circle** (at N. Clark St. and Wrightwood Ave.; walk north on Clark from Fullerton Pkwy.), where the surly service is part of the fun.

7. For a very different dining experience, splurge on a degustation at **Charlie Trotter's.**

QUICK BITES

Cafe Luigi (✉ 2548 N. Clark St., Lincoln Park ☎ 773/404–0200) is a blink-and-you'll-miss-it storefront that sells New York–style pizza slices, calzones, and sausage rolls to grateful East Coast expats.

Nookies, too (✉ 2114 N. Halsted St., Lincoln Park ☎ 773/327–1400) is open 24 hours on Friday and Saturday and serves heaping breakfasts anytime, making it a favorite of the neighborhood's late-night partying crowd. Cash only.

Just outside the park, **R. J. Grunt's** (✉ 2056 N. Lincoln Park West, Lincoln Park ☎ 773/929–5363) has been serving killer milk shakes and burgers and stocking a salad bar for healthy types since 1971.

Twin Anchors (✉ 1655 N. Sedgwick St., Lincoln Park ☎ 312/266–1616 ⊙ No lunch weekdays), a popular Old Town restaurant and tavern for more than 60 years, is famous for its barbecued ribs.

WICKER PARK AND BUCKTOWN

Sightseeing
★★☆☆☆

Dining
★★★★☆

Lodging
★☆☆☆☆

Shopping
★★★★☆

Nightlife
★★★★☆

Creative types still cluster in Bucktown and Wicker Park, a hip, somewhat grungy enclave of neighborhoods centered on Milwaukee, Damen, and North avenues. But they no longer lay exclusive claim to this funky part of town.

These days you'll find young families, thirtysomething professionals, and university students thrown into the mix along with the immigrant communities who have lived here for generations. There are also cutting-edge galleries, coffeehouses, and nightclubs. A sign of the changing times: chains like American Apparel and Urban Outfitters have opened outposts in this neighborhood, once considered a haven from corporate retail. In 2008 Marc Jacobs opened its first Chicago boutique, Marc by Marc Jacobs, in the area. Still, this area's eclectic shopping is a far cry from a suburban strip mall—or, for that matter, the Mag Mile.

Bucktown—which is said to have taken its name from the goats kept by the area's original Polish and German immigrants—encompasses the neighborhood surrounding Milwaukee Avenue north of North Avenue. The area south of North Avenue to Division Street is Wicker Park. Farther south still is Ukrainian Village, where the artsy types are now encroaching, but which still has a number of sights that are a testimony to the ethnic roots that remain strong in this neighborhood.

WHAT'S HERE

The anchor of the North-Milwaukee-Damen intersection is the striking triangular Art Deco–style **Northwest Tower Building**, a 12-story office building on North Avenue that's used as a reference point from miles around. Built in 1929 and nicknamed the Coyote Building for some unknown reason, it long served as the locus of the annual Around the Coyote Arts Festival, until its relocation to the West Loop in 2008. Opposite the Northwest Tower across the busy intersection is the distinctive three-story, terra-cotta **Flatiron Arts Building**. Its upper floors have long served as a sort of informal arts colony, providing studio and gallery space for a number of visual artists. The beautiful facade of the

North Avenue Baths Building (✉ *2039 W. North Ave., Bucktown*), just west of the intersection of Milwaukee and Damen avenues, is a clue to its past life, when it was a storied meeting spot for politicians who cut deals in the hot steam rooms, where it was difficult to plant wiretaps. Across the street is **Subterranean** (✉ *2011 W. North Ave., Bucktown* ☎ *773/278–6600*), a bar and dance club resting atop Prohibition era escape tunnels. Also near this intersection is the **Double Door,** a late-night music venue where homegrown acts like Veruca Salt and Liz Phair and legends like the Rolling Stones have played. **Earwax Café** is a vegan- and vegetarian-friendly hangout with a video-rentals department.

For a reality-television fix, check out the building at the corner of Winchester and North avenues, a former *Real World* house. Back on Damen, head north for some shopping—window or otherwise—at a collection of shops selling wares you won't likely find elsewhere. Hip fashionistas from around the city head to **p.45** for the latest finds from up-and-coming designers. Homebodies *oooh* and *ahhh* over the luxurious tabletop finds at **Stitch,** and antiques hunters like **Pavilion** and **Pagoda Red.**

At the southern border of Wicker Park, Division Street has become a shopping and dining destination in its own right. Bars, boutiques, and trendy restaurants line the once-gritty thoroughfare, which lent its name to journalist Studs Terkel's famous 1967 book about urban life. Heading west on the stretch of Division between Wolcott and Western avenues you'll pass by **Public I,** a popular boutique featuring clothing by independent designers; **Renegade Handmade,** an eclectic shop selling a wide variety of goods by local crafters; **Coco Rouge,** an upscale chocolatier hawking inventive spice-infused truffles; hip sushi spot **Mirai Sushi;** and **Crust,** the city's first certified organic restaurant, specializing in wood oven–fired flatbreads.

South of the North-Damen-Milwaukee intersection is the triangular **Wicker Park,** which was donated to the city in 1870 by politician Charles Wicker. Along Hoyne and Pierce streets nearby you'll find some of the biggest and best examples of Chicago's Victorian-era architecture. So many brewery owners built homes in this area that it was once dubbed "Beer Baron Row."

DID YOU KNOW?

Novelist Nelson Algren, whose book *Chicago: City on the Make* still wins praise for capturing the essence of the city, lived in the three-story home at **1958 West Evergreen Street.**

For a glimpse of how the working class lived at the turn of the 20th century, head a little farther south to the **Ukrainian Village Landmark District** (on Haddon Avenue and Thomas and Cortez streets between Damen and Leavitt avenues), a well-preserved group of workers' cottages and flats. Another place to glimpse the old immigrant populations' squat leaded-glass brick homes is on Homer Street between Leavitt and Oakley streets. Nearby on Chicago Avenue is the **Ukrainian Institute of Modern Art** (✉ *2320 W. Chicago Ave.* ☎ *773/227–5522*), which has three galleries that focus on sculpture, mixed media, and paintings.

GETTING ORIENTED

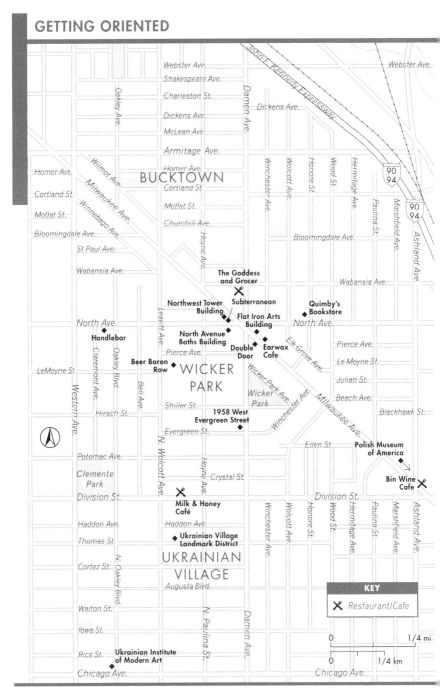

GETTING HERE

If you're driving, take the Kennedy to North Avenue, then go west on North Avenue until you reach the triangular inter-section where North meets Milwaukee and Damen avenues. Metered street parking is available but can be hard to come by, especially in the evening and on the weekend when the neighborhood is bustling. Be aware that many side streets restrict parking to residents with permits only. Most restau-rants in the area offer valet service—a good alternative to driving around for an hour looking for a spot. By El train, take the Blue Line to the Damen–North Avenue stop.

QUICK BITES

bin wine cafe (⌧ *1559 N. Milwaukee Ave., Wicker Park* ☎ *773/486–2233*) is a cozy little storefront where you can pair top-notch wines by the glass with global menu options.

To us, former caterer to the stars Debby Sharpe is both **The Goddess and Grocer** (⌧ *1646 N. Damen Ave., Buck-town* ☎ *773/342–3200*), serving up to-die-for sandwiches and salads that please vegans and carnivores alike at her gourmet takeout shop. You can eat at the small dining room next door.

Bike messengers and other folks with a hankering for healthy comfort food flock to the **Handlebar** (⌧ *2311 W. North Ave., Bucktown* ☎ *773/384–9546*) for mostly vegetarian fare. Don't pass up the smoked gouda mac and cheese side.

A sunny spot with a fireplace for cold winter days, **Milk & Honey Café** (⌧ *1920 W. Division St., Wicker Park* ☎ *773/395–9434*) packs in neighborhood types who crave the French toast at breakfast and inventive lunchtime sand-wiches served with housemade potato chips.

NEIGHBORHOOD TOP 5

2

1. Order a cup of coffee or a glass of wine and perch your-self at the window seat in a café—or at an outdoor table in warm weather—and get ready for some of the best **people-watching** in the city.

2. Catch some cutting-edge music at the **Double Door.**

3. **Shop for funky finds** at the shops along Division Street, Milwaukee Avenue, and Damen Avenue.

4. Explore the rich visual arts scene at the Flatiron Art Build-ing's **First Fridays** gallery openings on the first Friday of the month.

5. Browse the books and 'zines or catch a reading at eclectic **Quimby's Bookstore.**

MAKING THE MOST OF YOUR TIME

The best times for people-watch-ing are in the evening when the clubs and bars draw crowds, or during Sunday brunch when the restaurants do steady business. May through October you can take your place at an outdoor patio to savor the view of hip-sters and young families stroll-ing by, soaking up the sun.

The liveliest times to visit are late August, when Bucktown hosts its annual Arts Fest, and September, during the indie favorite Renegade Craft Fair.

LAKEVIEW INCLUDING WRIGLEYVILLE

Sightseeing
★★☆☆☆

Dining
★★★★☆

Lodging
★☆☆☆☆

Shopping
★★★★☆

Nightlife
★★★★☆

Lakeview is a massive North Side neighborhood made up of smaller enclaves that have their own distinct personalities. It's a mix that means that a few blocks' walk in one direction or another will surely lead to some interesting finds.

There's the beer-swilling, Cubby-blue-'til-we-die sports-bar fanaticism of Wrigleyville, home of the esteemed Wrigley Field; the out-and-proud colors of the gay bars, shops, and clubs along Halsted Street in Boystown; and an air of urban chic along Southport Avenue, where young families stroll amid the trendy boutiques and ice-cream shops.

Lakeview's first white settler was Conrad Sulzer, a grim-looking Swiss native and the son of a Protestant minister. Sulzer arrived in 1837, but the community was really established in the 1850s by James E. Rees and E. E. Hundley. Rees and Hundley built the Hotel Lake View—from which the neighborhood got its name—and then its first main road, which is now Broadway. By 1889 Chicago took the town for its own.

WHAT'S HERE

The venerable **Wrigley Field,** the ivy-covered home of the Chicago Cubs and the nation's second-oldest major league ballpark, is on the corner of Addison and Clark streets. Check out the **Harry Caray statue** commemorating the late Cubs announcer and sing "Take Me Out to the Ballgame" in his honor. Diagonally across the street is the **Cubby Bear Lounge** (⊠*1059 W. Addison St.* ☎*773/327–1662*), a Chicago institution since 1953. If you look up along Sheffield Avenue on the eastern side of the ballpark, you can see the rooftop patios where baseball fans pay high prices to root for the home team. Ticketless fans sit in lawn chairs on Sheffield during the games, waiting for foul balls to fly their way.

A long fly ball north of Wrigley is **Metro** (⊠*3730 N. Clark St.*), a former theater that's been converted to one of the city's best live-music venues. The Smashing Pumpkins got their start here. East on Grace Street is the

3800 north block of **Alta Vista Terrace,** a lovely residential street where 40 town houses completed as part of a single development in 1904 mirror one another diagonally across the block for a striking, harmonious effect. North again on Clark Street is **Graceland Cemetery,** which has crypts that are almost as strikingly designed as the city skyline.

2

DID YOU KNOW?

The names on the grave sites at Graceland read like a who's who from a Chicago history book: Marshall Field, George Pullman, Louis Sullivan, and Daniel Burnham are a few of the notables buried here. You can buy a walking-tour map at the entrance Monday through Saturday to explore on your own.

Right on Halsted Street is "Boystown," as locals often call it. Distinctive rainbow pylons line the street between Belmont and Addison avenues, marking the gay district. In June, Halsted is a sea of people, when Chicago's gay pride parade floats down the block.

On the side streets heading east and west of Boystown you'll find plenty of two- and three-story graystones and other vintage buildings on quiet tree-lined streets. Wandering Lakeview's residential streets, you might even feel transported back in time to 1920s or '30s Chicago. At least, that's what director Michael Mann must have thought. In spring 2008 a stretch of Newport Avenue between Clark and Halsted was temporarily transformed into a cobblestone thoroughfare while Mann was filming the John Dillinger flick *Public Enemies* (starring Johnny Depp). Belmont Avenue is a strip with a different character entirely. There are tattoo parlors and vintage-clothing stores, and just past the El tracks at Sheffield is the **Vic Theatre,** originally a luxurious vaudeville theater. Today it's a live-music venue that's most popular on Brew & View nights, when second- or third-run movies are screened, three bars are open, and the mood is festive.

A few blocks farther west you hit Southport Avenue, where the shopping seems to get more interesting all the time. There's not a Gap or Pottery Barn in sight—rather, the streets that travel north to Irving Park Road are lined with independent shops, many of which cater to well-dressed young women with money to burn. **Red Head Boutique** and neighboring **Krista K** are big favorites. Hipsters of both sexes, meanwhile, drool over the goods at **Jake.** Southport's main claim to fame, though, is the **Music Box Theatre,** a 1929 movie house where you can still see twinkling stars and clouds on the ceiling and hear live organ music before the independent and classic films are shown on its two screens.

Lakeview is also home to a high concentration of off-Loop theaters, many of which can be found within the small area bounded by Clark, Halsted, Belmont, and Broadway. Inside that rough square you'll find the risk-taking, experimental theater of **Red Tape Theatre Company**, the comedy-focused **Lakeshore Theater,** the historical plays of **Timeline Theater,** and **Briar Street Theatre,** the longtime Chicago performance spot for the Blue Man Group. Wander just a few blocks north on Clark Street to find **Live Bait Theater,** a veteran independent theater company that produces fresh, visually engaging works.

GETTING ORIENTED

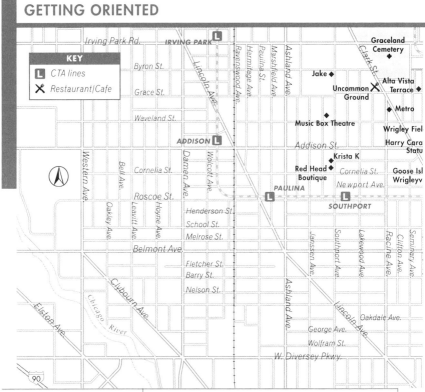

KEY

L CTA lines

X Restaurant/Cafe

GETTING HERE

If you're driving, take Lake Shore Drive north from the Loop to Belmont, but keep in mind that parking can be scarce. When the Cubs play, it's all but impossible—take public transit or give in and pay the exorbitant rates charged by enterprising residents with parking spots to spare.

Buses 22 and 36 will bring you here from points downtown, as will the Brown and Purple lines to Belmont or the Red Line to Addison. To get to the Southport Avenue shops, take the Brown Line to Southport.

MAKING THE MOST OF YOUR TIME

A quick walk through Wrigleyville and Lakeview will take about an hour and a half. Add another half-hour if you're wading through the post-Cubs-game crowds.

If you want to get a feel for the rest of the neighborhood, head to Graceland Cemetery—allow about an hour or two for a visit—or hit the boutiques along Southport Avenue.

You'll need a few hours more for watching an afternoon game at Wrigley Field, a pastime we consider one of the best ways to experience the *real* Chicago. To maximize the authenticity, choose a seat in the bleachers. Then follow the crowd after the game to a nearby Cubs-centric bar—such as the Cubby Bear or Murphy's Bleachers—to toast the recent win or drown your sorrows over a loss. Either method involves pitchers of beer. When night falls, catch a folk or rock show at Schubas Tavern or take in some live reggae at the Wild Hare.

NEIGHBORHOOD TOP 7

1. If you can score a ticket, sit in the bleachers with the locals at **Wrigley Field**—and be ready to throw the ball back onto the field if the opposing team nearly hits a homer into the stands.

2. If you can't score a ticket, hang out with the fans on **Sheffield Avenue,** who wait there to catch one of the long fly balls out of the park.

3. Catch an indie flick at the vintage **Music Box Theatre.**

4. Indulge in a scoop of Daley (as in Mayor Richard J. Daley's) Addiction at the homegrown **Bobtail Soda Fountain.**

5. Thumb through the extensive selection of vintage vinyl and new tracks at **Reckless Records.**

6. Meet Marshall Field, George Pullman, and the other famous "residents" of **Graceland Cemetery.**

7. Experience gay Chicago in **Boystown.**

QUICK BITES

The original Swedish **Ann Sather** (✉ 909 W. Belmont Ave., Lakeview ☎ 773/348–2378) has legendary breakfasts: lingonberry pancakes or giant cinnamon buns.

Bobtail Soda Fountain (✉ 2951 N. Broadway, Lakeview ☎ 773/880–7372) serves ice cream based on an old family recipe, with specialty flavors like Lakeview Bourbon Barhopper and Daley Fudge Addiction.

The **Chicago Diner** (✉ 3411 N. Halsted St., Lakeview ☎ 773/935–6696) is known for its yummy vegetarian food.

Goose Island Wrigleyville (✉ 3535 N. Clark St., Wrigleyville ☎ 773/832–9040) has a variety of its own beers and root beers on tap, plus good burgers.

Uncommon Ground (✉ 3800 N. Clark St., Wrigleyville ☎ 773/929–3680) might look like a typical neighborhood coffeehouse, until you try the Jamaican jerk pork chops and Guinness French onion soup.

FAR NORTH AND FAR NORTHWEST SIDES

Sightseeing
★★☆☆☆

Dining
★★★★☆

Lodging
★☆☆☆☆

Shopping
★★★★☆

Nightlife
★★★☆☆

The far north and northwest sides of Chicago are home to several of the city's most colorful, eclectic neighborhoods. History-rich Uptown was once a thriving entertainment district; there you can take in the beautiful architecture and striking old marquees.

Though it's been a bit gritty for decades, new condo developments and chains like Borders and Starbucks are arriving in the area. The area centered around Broadway and Argyle Street is known alternately as Little Saigon, Little Chinatown, and North Chinatown.

WHAT'S HERE

Uptown is filled with an interesting mix of entertainment venues that attract, well, a pretty interesting mix of people to the area on any given night. Just outside the Lawrence train station is the **Aragon Ballroom** (⊠ *1106 W. Lawrence Ave.* ☎ *773/561–9500*), its large sign heralding upcoming bands—who play everything from metal to mariachi—in its dreamy, piazzalike setting. South is the marquee of the **Riviera Theatre** (⊠ *4746 N. Racine Ave.* ☎ *773/275–6800*), which draws a mosh-pit-diving crowd to see grungy bands.

Nearby, Little Saigon (also known as Little Chinatown and North Chinatown) is a part of the **Argyle Strip,** which is anchored by the El's Argyle Street stop with its red pagoda. The Strip is teeming with storefront noodle shops and pan-Asian grocery stores. Roasted ducks hang in shop windows and fish peer out from large tanks.

Andersonville, just north of Uptown, still shows many signs of the Swedish settlers who founded the neighborhood. The **Swedish American Museum Center** has an interesting mix of exhibits, a separate museum complete with a Viking ship for kids, and a gift shop packed with Scandinavian items. An anchor of the area is the **Women & Children**

First bookstore, which stocks an extensive selection of feminist and children's books.

Farther north, **Devon Avenue** is where Chicagoans go when they crave Indian food, or, as the avenue moves west, a good Jewish challah. The Indian restaurants and shops start popping up just east of Western Avenue. At Talman Avenue the multicultural wares transform to Jewish specialties. There are butchers and bakers and windows decorated with Russian newspapers and handmade *matrioshkas* (nesting dolls). At **Three Sisters Delicatessen** (⊠*2854 W. Devon Ave.* ☎*773/973–1919*) you can pick up an imported teapot or a doll with your Russian rye. Pick up menorahs, mezuzahs, and even stuffed matzo-ball dog toys at **Rosenblum's World of Judaica** (⊠*2906 W. Devon Ave.* ☎*773/262–1700*).

Bordered by Foster Avenue to the north, Montrose Avenue to the south, Damen Avenue to the east, and the Chicago River to the west, Lincoln Square has long been known for its Teutonic heritage. As proof, it's home to not one but two annual German fests—**Mayfest** in late May (held around the neighborhood's iconic 30-foot-tall maypole) and **German-American Fest** in September. Both involve plenty of beer, brats, and German-style pretzels, as well as folks dressed in lederhosen. In the past 10 years, however, this quiet far Northwest Side neighborhood, named for the Abraham Lincoln statue near the Lawrence-and-Western intersection, has seen its currency rise, and a spate of trendy restaurants and boutiques have moved into the area.

Many credit Lincoln Square's renaissance to the relocation of the **Old Town School of Folk Music** in 1998 from its original home in Old Town to a long-vacant Art Deco building on North Lincoln Avenue. Today the area has a number of popular bars and restaurants—including **Tank Sushi, Bistro Campagne, La Bocca della Verita,** and the **Grafton**—all centered on a stretch of Lincoln Avenue between Montrose and Lawrence.

Visitors longing for a taste of Lincoln Square's ethnic roots shouldn't despair. There are still a handful of German restaurants and bars lining Lincoln Avenue—most notably, the **Chicago Brauhaus**, with its perennial Oktoberfest vibe and schnitzel dishes on the menu, and the divey German-owned **Huettenbar**. The Old World **Merz Apothecary** first opened in 1875 to cater to the area's German immigrants. On the third Friday of each month, visit the **DANK Haus** German Cultural Center just off Lincoln on Western Avenue; the sixth-floor Skyline Lounge has German beer on tap and a patio with a fabulous view of downtown to the southeast.

Another can't-miss site is the recently rehabbed **Krause Music Store** building. Formerly the Museum of Decorative Arts and now a private office space, the 1922 landmark was the last work commissioned by architect Louis Sullivan. Passersby often stop to admire the building's ornate green terra-cotta façade, with its elaborate wreathed medallion projecting above the roofline.

After shopping and dining your way through the Square, pause for a rest in **Giddings Plaza** with a view of the bronze, tiered **Giddings Square Fountain**. From May to October the plaza comes alive with frequent outdoor concerts. It's also adjacent to the tempting bakery–restaurant **Café Selmarie**, whose tarts and chocolate croissants are impossible to resist.

GETTING ORIENTED

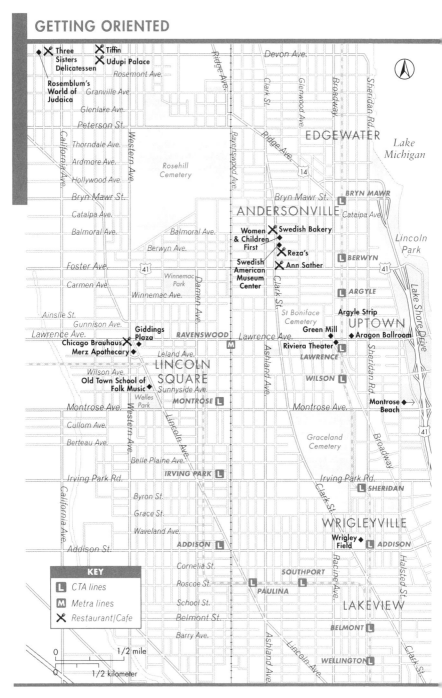

Three Sisters Delicatessen

Tiffin

Udupi Palace

Rosemont Ave.

Rosemblum's World of Judaica

Granville Ave.

Glenlake Ave.

Peterson St.

Thorndale Ave.

Ardmore Ave.

Hollywood Ave.

Rosehill Cemetery

EDGEWATER

Lake Michigan

Bryn Mawr St.

BRYN MAWR

Catalpa Ave.

Balmoral Ave.

Berwyn Ave.

Foster Ave.

Carmen Ave.

Winnemac Ave.

Winnemac Park

Balmoral Ave.

Bryn Mawr St.

ANDERSONVILLE Catalpa Ave

Women & Children First

Swedish Bakery

Reza's

Ann Sather

Swedish American Museum Center

Lincoln Park

BERWYN

ARGYLE

Ainslie St.

Gunnison Ave.

Lawrence Ave.

Chicago Brauhaus

Merz Apothecary

Giddings Plaza

RAVENSWOOD

Leland Ave.

Wilson Ave.

Old Town School of Folk Music

Sunnyside Ave.

Welles Park

LINCOLN SQUARE

MONTROSE

Montrose Ave.

Cullom Ave.

Berteau Ave.

Belle Plaine Ave.

Irving Park Rd.

IRVING PARK

Byron St.

Grace St.

Waveland Ave.

Addison St.

ADDISON

St Boniface Cemetery

Lawrence Ave.

Argyle Strip

Green Mill

Riviera Theater

LAWRENCE

WILSON

UPTOWN

Aragon Ballroom

Sheridan Rd.

Montrose Beach

Graceland Cemetery

Montrose Ave.

Irving Park Rd.

SHERIDAN

WRIGLEYVILLE

Wrigley Field

ADDISON

Cornelia St.

Roscoe St.

SOUTHPORT

PAULINA

School St.

Belmont St.

Barry Ave.

LAKEVIEW

BELMONT

WELLINGTON

KEY

L CTA lines

M Metra lines

✕ Restaurant/Cafe

0   1/2 mile

0   1/2 kilometer

GETTING HERE

Take the El's Red Line north from the Loop (toward Howard) and get off at the Lawrence stop for Uptown. In a car, take Lake Shore Drive north to Lawrence Avenue for Uptown or Foster Avenue for Andersonville. Devon Avenue is reachable via the El's Red Line (exit at the Morse Avenue station), then the 155 (Devon Avenue) bus. By car, head north up Western Avenue. For Lincoln Square, take the Brown Line El north from the Loop (toward Kimball) and exit at Western. By car, head north on Western Avenue; most of Lincoln Square's action takes place between Montrose and Lawrence.

MAKING THE MOST OF YOUR TIME

If you're planning on hitting all four neighborhoods, allow most of a day. Uptown will take about an hour; allow a couple of hours for Andersonville if you pop into the shops, and another hour to see the Swedish Museum. Devon Avenue takes about two hours—the street is crowded, especially evenings and on weekends, so walking is slow going there. Then end the day in Lincoln Square with a last peek at the boutiques followed by dinner at one of Lincoln Avenue's many restaurants.

LOCAL LIFE

Andersonville is one of the best places in Chicago to stock up on Swedish and other European foods and treats. If you have a sweet tooth, try the **Swedish Bakery** (⊠ *5348 N. Clark St., Far North Side* ☎ *773/561–8919*).

SAFETY

Be cautious in all of Uptown, especially at night. The neighborhood is slowly undergoing a resurgence, but there's still quite a bit of gang activity. Nevertheless, daytime walking, in pairs or groups, is just fine if you stick to the main drags of Broadway and Argyle.

QUICK BITES

Ann Sather (⊠ *5207 N. Clark St., Far North Side* ☎ *773/271–6677*) carries what may be the world's most addictive cinnamon rolls and lingonberry pancakes.

At **Reza's** (⊠ *5255 N. Clark St., Far North Side* ☎ *773/561–1898*) you can dine on such outstanding Persian cuisine as kebabs, *dolmeh* (stuffed green peppers), and charbroiled ground beef with Persian rice.

Another favorite down the street is **Tiffin** (⊠ *2536 W. Devon, Far North Side* ☎ *773/338–2143*), where the crowds are a testament to the quality of the curry.

The decor is reminiscent of a hotel lobby, but the South Indian vegetarian cuisine is scrumptious at **Udupi Palace** (⊠ *2543 W. Devon, Far North Side* ☎ *773/338–2152*).

NEIGHBORHOOD TOP 5

1. Gorge yourself on cinnamon rolls at **Ann Sather.**

2. Haggle over the prices of electronics, fabric, and jewelry on **Devon Avenue.**

3. Catch a Sunday-night poetry slam at the **Green Mill,** where it all began.

4. Browse the eclectic shops along **North Lincoln Avenue.**

5. Grab a pastry to go from **Café Selmarie** and take a seat facing the fountain in **Giddings Plaza.**

PILSEN, LITTLE ITALY AND UNIVERSITY VILLAGE

Sightseeing
★★☆☆☆

Dining
★★★★☆

Lodging
★☆☆☆☆

Shopping
★★☆☆☆

Nightlife
★☆☆☆☆

Stretching from the South Branch of the Chicago River to the Eisenhower Expressway (Interstate 290) this area west of the Loop on the south side of the city is a jumble of ethnic neighborhoods.

Formerly a neighborhood of immigrants from Bohemia, Czechoslovakia, the enclave of Pilsen is now home to the largest Mexican community in the Midwest—making up roughly 85% of the neighborhood's population. Pilsen is known for its dramatic, colorful murals that show scenes from Mexican history, culture, and religion. It's also home to a thriving arts community—if you're a gallery-hopping art collector, you must visit this neighborhood. Pilsen is bordered by Halsted Street on the east and Western Avenue on the west, and extends from 16th Street to the south branch of the Chicago River.

Chicago's Little Italy is to the north of Pilsen. This traditional ethnic neighborhood has been encroached upon by the expansion of the nearby university in recent years, but there are still plenty of yummy Italian restaurants, bakeries, groceries, and sandwich shops to explore. Stretching to Ashland Avenue on the west and Roosevelt on the south, Little Italy blends into University Village in its northeast corner.

The University of Illinois at Chicago anchors University Village. This booming residential area lies west of Roosevelt Road, primarily made up of a massive new mixed-use development that centers around Halsted Street and spans south to 14th Street.

WHAT'S HERE

The **National Museum of Mexican Art** (formerly the Mexican Fine Arts Center Museum), the nation's largest Latino museum, houses traditional and contemporary creations by international and local artists. In 2001 the museum tripled in size to accommodate state-of-the-art storage vaults for its 5,500-object permanent collection that spans pre-Cuauhtemoc artifacts, textiles, paintings, prints and drawings, and folk art.

SWEET TOOTH

If you like sweets or have kids in tow, keep an eye out for BomBon Bakery (✉ *1508 W. 18th St.* ☎ *312/733–7788*), which stocks a mind-boggling array of treats.

2

Halsted near 18th Street is home to an ever-growing cluster of art galleries and studios that have put Pilsen on the map as a go-to art destination. A large number of artists live and work in the mixed-use artists' community known as the Chicago Arts District (formerly Pilsen East), centered on Halsted Street and stretching from 16th Street to Cermak Road.

Be aware that most of the area's dozen or more galleries and studio spaces are open by appointment only; a few have limited weekend hours. Notable exceptions include the combined gallery–home furnishings boutique **Grid Gallery,** the eclectic **4Art Inc.,** and the contemporary ceramics–focused **Dubhe Carreño,** all of which are open Tuesday through Saturday (but call first to confirm). In addition, on the second Friday evening of each month many area artists open their studio doors to the public for the 2nd Fridays gallery walk.

In Little Italy the main thoroughfare is **Taylor Street,** which is best known for its Italian restaurants, though Thai food, tacos, and other ethnic food options are starting to fill the street as well.

The **National Italian American Sports Hall of Fame** (✉ *1431 W. Taylor St., Little Italy* ☎ *312/226–5566*) pays tribute to athletes like Rocky Marciano, Yogi Berra, and Phil Rizzuto.

On Polk Street is **St. Basil Greek Orthodox Church** (✉ *733 S. Ashland Ave., Little Italy* ☎ *312/243–3738*), a gorgeous Greek Revival building originally used as a Jewish synagogue. The bronze statue of Italian explorer Christopher Columbus that anchors **Arrigo Park** on Loomis Street was cast in Rome and brought to Chicago for the 1893 World's Columbian Exposition.

In University Village new luxury town homes and loft conversions mix with row houses and two-flats on a stretch of the city that not long ago was considered a wasteland. Retailers, including **Barbara's Bookstore** (✉ *1218 S. Halsted St., University Village* ☎ *312/413–2665*), a small local chain, have been lured to the area along with the new residents. The **Jane Addams Hull-House Museum** on the UIC campus (✉ *800 S. Halsted St., University Village* ☎ *312/413–5353*) is a city landmark as well as a memorial to Jane Addams, who launched innovative settlement-house programs. Nearby, you find the new home of the legendary **Maxwell Street Market,** which was not-so-gently nudged to the east at Canal Street and Roosevelt Road to make way for the new development.

GETTING ORIENTED

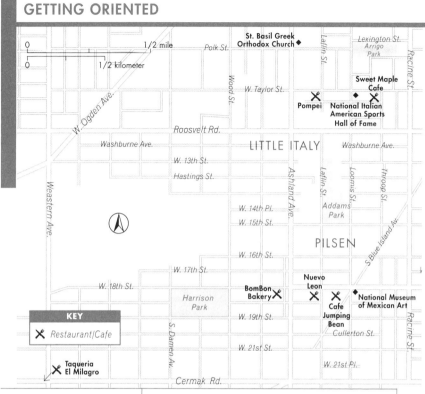

MAKING THE MOST OF YOUR TIME

Pilsen is busiest on weekends and on the first weekend of August during the Fiesta del Sol festival, as well as on Second Fridays (the second Friday of every month), when the neighborhood's art galleries stay open late for an art crawl. Little Italy is busier at night, when the restaurants and bars draw crowds. A visit to the University Village area is most rewarding on weekdays, when there's plenty of student activity on campus, or on Sunday, when you can check out the nearby Maxwell Street Market.

GETTING HERE

Take Interstate 290 west to the Damen Street exit. Go south on Damen to 19th Street. There's parking at the National Museum of Mexican Art. There's also metered parking on 18th Street and Ashland Avenue. You can also take the El's Blue Line from downtown to the 18th Street station. It's a station covered with colorful murals, and when you reach street level, take a look at the mosaic mural depicting Mexican women from pre-Columbian times to now.

To get to University Village, take the Blue Line to UIC/Halsted. The 9 Ashland bus will take you to UIC and Little Italy. If you're driving to Little Italy and University Village, take the Kennedy Expressway from either direction to the Taylor Street exit, then head west.

NEIGHBORHOOD TOP 4

1. Try the Italian lemonade—really a slushy Italian ice that comes in a rainbow of flavors—at **Mario's Lemonade Stand** on Taylor Street.

2. Gallery hop on **Second Fridays** in Pilsen, the monthly event when the art galleries stay open late.

3. Haggle over everything from TVs to tube socks at the legendary **Maxwell Street Market** on Sunday.

4. Three words: tres leches cake. Sample it at **BomBon Bakery** in Pilsen. Yum.

SAFETY

The area between Pilsen and Little Italy is railway tracks and vacant lots, and it isn't safe to walk between the two neighborhoods. If at all possible, try to drive to this area, park your car as you explore each individual neighborhood, and drive between the two. Or take the Blue Line to either UIC–Halsted or Racine to explore University Village and Little Italy, then hop back on and take it two more stops to 18th Street for Pilsen.

QUICK BITES

Cafe Jumping Bean (⊠ *1439 W. 18th St., Pilsen* ☎ *312/455–0019*), a cozy neighborhood coffee shop, displays original art by local artists on its walls. This eclectic gathering place has hot chocolate with Mexican spices, panini pizzas, and fresh sandwiches.

Pompei (⊠ *1531 W. Taylor St., Little Italy* ☎ *312/421–5179*) started as a bakery selling thick, bready squares of pizza back in 1909. Today it's a part of a growing local empire of restaurants that serve salads, house-made pasta, and that same delicious pizza.

Sweet Maple Cafe (⊠ *1339 W. Taylor St., Little Italy* ☎ *312/243–8908*) has a loyal following for their Southern-inspired breakfast. If you can stand the crowds on the weekend, it's worth the wait for grits, salmon cakes, and sweet-milk biscuits.

Taqueria El Milagro (⊠ *3050 W. 26th St., Pilsen*) is a reliably tasty taco joint adjacent to a tortilla factory.

PRAIRIE AVENUE AND CHINATOWN

Sightseeing
★★★☆☆

Dining
★★★★☆

Lodging
★☆☆☆☆

Shopping
★★☆☆☆

Nightlife
★☆☆☆☆

Geography is the main link between the Prairie Avenue Historic District and Chinatown. Prairie Avenue (two blocks east of Michigan Avenue, between 18th and 22nd streets) was Chicago's first Gold Coast.

Many prominent merchants and manufacturers, including George Pullman and Marshall Field, built their homes here in the 1870s through the 1890s, but now only a handful of buildings recall this vanished era. New condominium construction has helped give the area more of its old vim, but it's nothing compared to the compact commotion to the west in Chinatown, a neighborhood packed with restaurants and shops. Tour the historic commercial district along Wentworth and Archer avenues and you might just forget you're in the Midwest

WHAT'S HERE

In the 19th century many of the city's most prominent residents lived in what is now referred to as the **Prairie Avenue Historic District**. After the Chicago Fire of 1871, notable Chicagoans such as the Pullmans, the Fields, and the meatpacking family the Armours all built mansions in this neighborhood on the city's South Side.

Most of the 19th-century mansions are long gone, but you can still visit the National Historic Landmark **Glessner House Museum**(✉ *1800 S. Prairie Ave., Pilsen* ☎*312/326–1480*), a home designed by Henry Hobson Richardson, the architect of Boston's Trinity Church. Completed in 1887, the L-shaped mansion is characteristic of "Richardson Romanesque" style, with its stone construction and short towers.

Nearby, the **Clarke House** (✉*1855 S. Indiana St., Pilsen* ☎*312/326–1480*), built in 1836, has the distinction of being the city's oldest surviving building. The Greek Revival–style home was built for Henry B. Clarke, a wealthy local hardware dealer. Today the home also functions as a museum, revealing what life was like for a middle-class family in the early part of the 19th century.

WIDE
LOAD

Clarke House has been moved three times from its original location on Michigan Avenue between 16th and 17th streets. The last time, in 1977, it had to be hoisted above the nearby elevated train tracks.

While you're in the area, don't miss the **National Vietnam Veterans Art Museum**, on the corner of 18th Street and Indiana Avenue. The museum presents a rare perspective on war through works of visual art created by combat veterans. At the intersection of Calumet and Cullerton avenues is the **Wheeler Mansion** (⊠*2020 S. Calumet Ave., Prairie Avenue* ☎*312/945–2020*), another of the area's great mansions that was nearly replaced by a parking lot before it was saved and painstakingly restored in the late 1990s. Today it's a contemporary boutique hotel and a fun alternative to more traditional chain lodging options nearby.

Three blocks farther west, on Michigan Avenue, is the handsome Gothic Revival **Second Presbyterian Church** (⊠*1936 S. Michigan Ave., Prairie Avenue* ☎*312/225–4951*). Be sure to go inside this National Historic Landmark and take a look at the Tiffany stained-glass windows—one of the largest collections anywhere.

Next, walk south another block on Michigan Avenue for a tour of **Willie Dixon's Blues Heaven Foundation,** housed in the former Chess Records office and studios (⊠*2120 S. Michigan Ave.* ☎*312/808–1286*), where a cadre of music legends, from Etta James and Bo Diddley to Aretha Franklin and John Lee Hooker, have recorded.

DID YOU
KNOW?

The Rolling Stones immortalized the Willie Dixon address in a blues track they recorded here in 1964 titled—you guessed it—"2120 S. Michigan Avenue."

South of the Prairie Avenue district, where Wentworth Avenue and Cermak Road/22nd Street meet, is the entrance to Chinatown. Our favorite parts are the plethora of gift shops in **Chinatown Square** (on bustling Archer Avenue) and the mouthwatering smells from the area's many restaurants and bakeries.

The 11-block neighborhood is anchored by the Chinatown Gate and the enormous green-and-red pagoda towers of the Pui Tak Center, a church-based community center in the former On Leong Tong Building. Be sure to see the **Nine Dragon Wall** on Cermak Road, next to the El's Red Line Cermak-Chinatown stop, one of only four replicas worldwide of the Beijing original, and **Ping Tom Memorial Park** (⊠*300 W. 19th St., Chinatown*), a multi-acre site dedicated to a neighborhood civic leader, that has views of the Chicago River.

GETTING ORIENTED

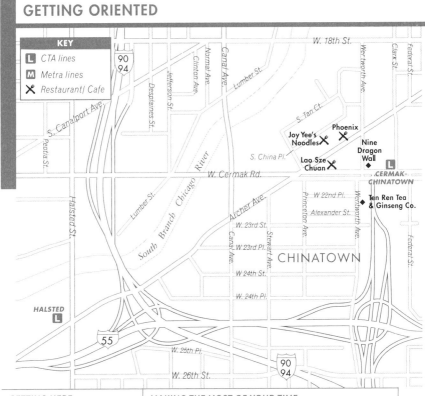

KEY

L CTA lines
M Metra lines
✕ Restaurant/ Cafe

GETTING HERE	MAKING THE MOST OF YOUR TIME

GETTING HERE

To get to Chinatown by car, drive south on Michigan Avenue and take a left at 18th Street, and travel four blocks to Cermak Road/East 22nd Street. There's an inexpensive outdoor parking lot adjacent to the Chinatown Gate on Wentworth Avenue. If you dine in the area, ask the restaurant to validate your parking receipt. For the Prairie Avenue Historic District, take Michigan Avenue to East 21st Street, then travel west to Prairie Avenue. Buses 1, 3, and 4 cover both of these areas, or you can take the El's Red Line south from the Loop to the Cermak–Chinatown stop.

MAKING THE MOST OF YOUR TIME

You can easily spend a few hours browsing the shops and sampling the goodies along Wentworth Avenue or at Chinatown Square. Add an hour or two more if you're going to tour one or more of the Prairie Avenue homes. Chinatown is particularly busy on weekends throughout the year, but the big draws are Chinese New Year in January or February and the summer fair in July. Later in July a dragon boat race draws thousands of spectators to view the ornately decorated boats on the south branch of the Chicago River.

SAFETY

Both of these areas are a little removed from the heart of the city and bordered by slowly gentrifying neighborhoods, so be cautious and aware if you are walking around the neighborhood at night. Better yet, limit your visit to well-lit and well-populated main streets after dark.

2

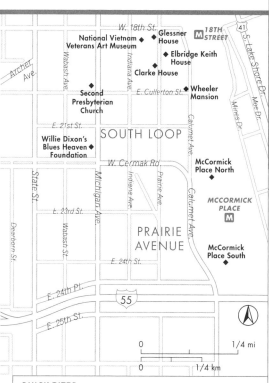

NEIGHBORHOOD TOP 3

1. Forgo traditional weekend brunch for dim sum with the locals at **Phoenix**.

2. Check out the digs where Chicago greats like Marshall Field and George Pullman lived in the **Prairie Avenue Historic District**.

3. Shop for tea and learn about ancient traditions at Chinatown shops like **Ten Ren Tea & Ginseng Co.** (✉ *2247 S. Wentworth Ave.60616* ☎ *312/842–1171*).

QUICK BITES

Joy Yee's Noodles (✉ *2159 S. China Pl., in Chinatown Square Mall, Chinatown* ☎ *312/328–0001*) has a mile-long menu of Pan-Asian dishes that arrive in a flash; they claim to have introduced bubble teas to Chicagoland. Who are we to argue while we sip away?

Lao Sze Chuan (✉ *2172 S. Archer Ave., Chinatown* ☎ *312/326–5040*) is the go-to spot for the best Szechuan in town. Try the twice-cooked pork and dry chili string beans. They're served super fast.

Phoenix (✉ *2131 S. Archer Ave., Chinatown* ☎ *312/328–0848*), a widely popular choice, is busiest during weekend dim sum, when cart after cart of tempting dumplings and other dishes are rolled before eager diners. The food's all about comfort, but we'll warn you that the service isn't.

TOURS

Package guided tours of both the Clarke House and the Glessner House Museum are available Wednesday through Sunday, and are free on Wednesday (☎ *312/326–1480*). Wednesday tours are walk-in only and tend to fill up, so arrive early to guarantee a spot.

The Chinatown Chamber of Commerce (☎ *312/326–5320*) conducts one-hour walking tours in English and can help you arrange lunch at a neighborhood restaurant. Tours must be arranged two weeks in advance.

HYDE PARK

Sightseeing
★★★★☆
Dining
★★☆☆☆
Lodging
★☆☆☆☆
Shopping
★☆☆☆☆
Nightlife
★★☆☆☆

Hyde Park is something of a trek from downtown Chicago, but it's worth the extra effort. Today the neighborhood is considered a vibrant, eclectic part of the city.

Best known as the home of the University of Chicago, the neighborhood only began to see significant growth in the late 19th century, when the university opened in 1892 and the World's Columbian Exposition attracted an international influx a year later.

The exposition spawned the Midway Plaisance and numerous Classical Revival buildings, including the behemoth Museum of Science and Industry. The Midway Plaisance still runs along the southern edge of the University of Chicago's original campus. Sprawling homes were soon erected for school faculty in neighboring Kenwood, and the area began to attract well-to-do types who commissioned famous architects to build them spectacular homes.

A number of architecturally riveting buildings are here, including two by Frank Lloyd Wright, the **Robie House** and **Heller House.** There's also a thriving theater scene and several art and history museums. Most impressive, though, is the diverse population with a strong sense of community pride and fondness for the neighborhood's pretty tree-lined streets, proximity to the lake, and slightly off-the-beaten-path vibe.

WHAT'S HERE

To get a good overview of the neighborhood, stop by the **Hyde Park Historical Society** (✉ *5529 S. Lake Park Ave., Hyde Park* ☎ *773/493–1893* ☉ *Weekends 2–4*), which sponsors lectures and tours.

One of Hyde Park's gems is **Jackson Park** (✉ *Bounded by E. 56th and 67th Sts., S. Stony Island Ave., and the lakefront*), which was designed by Frederick Law Olmsted (who also designed Central Park in New York City) for the World's Columbian Exposition of 1893. It has lagoons, a Japanese garden with authentic Japanese statuary, and the Wooded Island, a nature retreat with wildlife and 300 species of birds.

MR. OBAMA'S NEIGHBORHOOD

Hyde Park's most famous family spends most of its time in Washington, D.C., these days, and the Secret Service prevents visitors from getting close to their Chicago home. Still, you can experience many of the First Family's favorite neighborhood haunts. Start at **University of Chicago**, where Barack Obama taught law from 1992 to 2004. Make sure to look up: you'll see the university's iconic gargoyles on some buildings. From there, poke around at **57th Street Books** (*57th and Kimbark 773/684-1300*), recommended by Michelle Obama for its extensive collection of fiction and nonfiction and its youth-oriented programs. The store bills itself as "the first stop for serious readers."

With mind fed, it's time for some fresh air. Head east to Lake Shore Drive and walk to **Promontory Point** (*5491 S. Lake Shore Drive*) for a great view of Lake Michigan. If you walk to the lake along E. Hayes Drive, you'll pass by the basketball courts where President Obama likes to shoot hoops with his brother-in-law, Craig Robinson. If you need something extra sweet before heading to your next destination, get a scoop at the **Baskin Robbins** on 53rd and Dorchester; it's where President and Mrs. Obama shared their first kiss.

THE BIRDS

Harold Washington Park and Jackson Park have a notable parakeet population. Rumor has it they escaped from a cage at O'Hare Airport and settled in area parks. Somehow these tropics natives were able to survive the harsh Chicago winter and have become neighborhood fixtures.

The **University of Chicago** (✉*S. Ellis Ave.* ☎*773/702–1234*) dominates the physical and cultural landscape of Hyde Park and South Kenwood. Much of the original campus was designed by Henry Ives Cobb. Especially of note are the International House and the Rockefeller Memorial Chapel, which has a carillon with 72 bells; a university carillonneur gives regular performances. Stately Gothic-style quadrangles look like something straight out of Cambridge and Oxford. The university-run Court Theatre stages new and classic works.

DID YOU KNOW?

"The toasters," designed by I. M. Pei, are two U of C apartment buildings that sit on an island in the middle of the street, so named because, fittingly enough, the buildings look like two pieces of toast.

Frank Lloyd Wright's **Robie House** is a Prairie Style masterpiece and one of the most remarkable designs in modern American architecture. (It's also a place of interest for many young readers of the children's book *The Wright 3*, a fictional mystery that takes place at Robie House, which now conducts weekly tours geared to the book's fans.) **Heller House,** nearby on Harper Avenue between 52nd and 53rd streets, was designed in 1897 by Wright, 12 years prior to Robie House. Though not open to the public, the house's exterior shows his progression toward the Prairie Style he achieved with Robie. Other architecturally significant buildings here are the **Windermere House** and **Promontory Apartments.**

GETTING ORIENTED

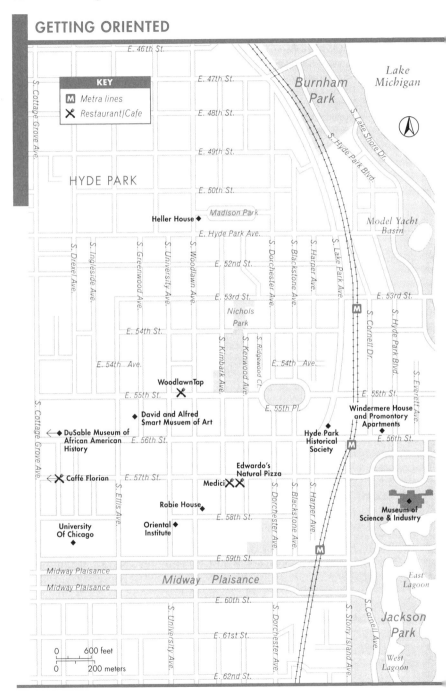

GETTING HERE

By car, take Lake Shore Drive south to the 57th Street exit and turn left into the parking lot of the Museum of Science and Industry. You can also take the Metra Railroad train from Randolph Street and Michigan Avenue; get off at the 55th Street stop and walk east through the underpass two blocks, then south two blocks.

MAKING THE MOST OF YOUR TIME

If you're visiting the Museum of Science and Industry, you'll probably be spending most of your day there. Try to go during the week to avoid crowds. You could wind down the day meandering through Jackson Park or the University of Chicago campus. Then wander the Midway Plaisance, an expanse of green separating the Hyde Park neighborhood from Woodlawn to the south. The Midway was the center of activity at the World's Columbian Exposition in 1893.

QUICK BITES

Caffé Florian (⊠ *1450 E. 57th St., Hyde Park* ☎ *773/752–4100*) serves pizza and Italian entrées as well as hearty sandwiches, homemade soups and salads, decadent desserts, and lots of java.

The deep-dish pies at **Edwardo's Natural Pizza** (⊠ *1321 E. 57th St., Hyde Park* ☎ *773/241-7960*) are considered by some to be the best in the city.

You'll find several spots on 57th Street where you can get a quick bite and relax. **The Medici** (⊠ *1327 E. 57th St., Hyde Park* ☎ *773/667-7394*) has served up its specialty pizzas, burgers, and sandwiches to generations of University of Chicago students who've carved their names into the tables.

Woodlawn Tap (⊠ *1172 E. 55th St., Hyde Park* ☎ *773/643-5516* ⏱ *Daily 11 AM–2 AM*) is a favored spot where locals and university students gather for a spoken-word reading or jazz concert along with pub grub.

SAFETY

Hyde Park is bordered to the west, south, and north by some less prosperous, and at times dangerous, areas. Use caution, especially in the evening, if you're uncertain about where you're heading.

TOURS

Tours of Frank Lloyd Wright's Robie House are conducted on Saturdays only, or take a free audio tour of the exterior (☎ *708/848-1976* ⊠ *adults $15, children 11–18 $12; 4 to 10 $5; 3 and under free).*

A self-guided tour of University of Chicago architecture, **A Walking Guide to the Campus,** is available for purchase in the University of Chicago Bookstore (⊠ *Visitor Center: Reynolds Club, 5706 S. University* ☎ *773/702-9739* ⊕ *www.uchicago.edu* ⏱ *Weekdays 9–5*).

NEIGHBORHOOD TOP 5

1. Get lost in the massive wonder of the **Museum of Science and Industry.**

2. Do some exotic-bird-watching in **Jackson Park,** where a tropical-parrot population roosts.

3. Tour Frank Lloyd Wright's fantastic **Robie House.**

4. Pack a picnic and enjoy the views from the beautiful **Promontory Point.**

5. Get in a heated debate with a U of C Nobel Laureate over a pint at the **Woodlawn Tap.**

Museums

WORD OF MOUTH

"Absolutely LOVE the Art Institute. When the kids were little, we lived in suburbs of Chicago and went almost every Saturday for their incredible children's programs. Very worthwhile membership if you live in the area. They really reach out to the community and there are many free opportunities. Don't visit Chicago without stopping here!"

—aliska

MUSEUMS PLANNER

Free Days

Always free:
Jane Addams Hull-House Museum
McCormick Tribune Freedom Museum
Museum of Contemporary Photography
National Museum of Mexican Art
Oriental Institute
Smart Museum
Ukrainian Institute of Modern Art

Sunday:
DuSable Museum of African American History

Monday:
Adler Planetarium & Astronomy Museum (selected months only)
Chicago Children's Museum (for kids 15 and younger first Mon. each month)

Tuesday:
Adler Planetarium & Astronomy Museum (selected months only)
Museum of Contemporary Art
Swedish American Museum Center (second Tues. each month)

Thursday:
Art Institute of Chicago (after 5 only)
Chicago Children's Museum (5–8 PM only)
Peggy Notebaert Nature Museum

Save Money

All the major museums are expensive; consider purchasing a Chicago CityPass instead of buying a single ticket. For about the price of admission to two museums, the pass lets you bypass the long lines and visit all of the big five—the Art Institute, Field Museum, Museum of Science and Industry, Adler Planetarium, and the Shedd Aquarium—plus the Hancock Observatory, anytime within nine days. For more information, see ⊕www.citypass.com.

Late Hours

Adler Planetarium & Astronomy Museum, first Friday of the month to 10 PM
Art Institute of Chicago, Thursday to 8 PM
Chicago Children's Museum, Thursday & Saturday to 8 PM
Museum of Contemporary Art, Tuesday to 8 PM
Museum of Contemporary Photography, Thursday to 8 PM
Oriental Institute, Wednesday to 8:30 PM
John G. Shedd Aquarium, Thursday to 10 PM (summer only)
Smart Museum, Thursday to 8 PM

Special Events

Tuesdays on the Terrace is a weekly summer event for mingling and live local jazz at the Museum of Contemporary Art. Cash bar. June–Sept., Tues. 5:30–8 PM.
DJs and local bands get things going at the Museum of Contemporary Art's First Fridays, a monthly preview of new work by Chicago artists. First Friday of every month, 6–10 PM. $15.
Feel like dinner, drinks, live jazz, and a view of the lake and the skyline? Get thee to Shedd Aquarium's Jazzin at the Shedd on the museum's terrace. June–Sept., Thurs. 5–10 PM. $10.

How Much Time?

Less than an hour:
Balzekas Museum of Lithuanian Culture
Jane Addams Hull-House Museum
Museum of Contemporary Photography
Museum of Holography
National Vietnam Veterans Art Museum
Polish Museum of America

1–2 hours:
DuSable Museum of African American History
Oriental Institute
Smart Museum of Art

2–3 hours:
Adler Planetarium & Astronomy Museum
Chicago Children's Museum
Chicago History Museum
National Museum of Mexican Art
Peggy Notebaert Nature Museum

Half day:
Museum of Contemporary Art
John G. Shedd Aquarium

Full day:
Art Institute of Chicago
Field Museum
Museum of Science and Industry

Best Gift Shops

Art Institute of Chicago. Find silk scarves, fine jewelry, glass paperweights, and other reproductions of artworks in the museum.

Field Museum. Everything dinosaur is sold in Field gift shops, but our guilty pleasure is the Mold-A-Rama vending machines on the lower level. These 1960s relics take heated colorful plastic and inject it into dinosaur molds.

Museum of Science and Industry. The Big Idea gift shop, on the entrance level, is packed with objects to tickle your mind, including chemistry sets, radio-controlled blimps, robot kits, and a kinetic solar-system model.

Museum of Contemporary Art. Pick up a Calder mobile or electronic chirping bird—you know, the stuff you never knew you always wanted.

Best Quirky Exhibits

Judy Istock Butterfly Haven, Peggy Notebaert Nature Museum. More than 20 local and international species of butterfly flutter through the butterfly atrium. Even more interesting are the cocoons in various stages of development. You might even catch a butterfly struggling out of its chrysalis.

Colleen Moore's Fairy Castle, Museum of Science and Industry. The MSI is full of quirky exhibits that make us wonder if we're still in a technology museum—there are live baby chicks and a moving exhibit of circus wagon miniatures—but one of the most beloved is the Fairy Castle. Built between 1928 and 1935, the final cost for this 8-foot-high palace with its 2,000 miniatures was $500,000.

Mesopotamian Gallery, Oriental Institute. The OI's largest gallery covers the entire sweep of Mesopotamian history, and includes a caveman's axe with the first trace of human blood and tablets that trace the history of writing.

Thorne Miniature Rooms, Art Institute. The 68 dollhouse-like rooms were designed by a Chicago socialite to display the miniatures she collected through her travels in Europe and America.

Updated by
Kelly Aiglon

Chicago's museums are the cultural heart of the city—so vital that the mayor rerouted Lake Shore Drive to create a verdant Museum Campus for the Adler Planetarium, Shedd Aquarium, and Field Museum. Treasures in Chicago's museums include Grant Wood's iconic painting *American Gothic,* at the Art Institute; "Sue," the largest T. rex ever discovered, at the Field Museum; and the only German U-boat captured during World War II, at the Museum of Science and Industry.

JUST THE HIGHLIGHTS, PLEASE

Head to the Art Institute for a quick art fix. For a tour of superlatives, see *Sky Above Clouds IV,* Georgia O'Keeffe's largest painting; the largest holding of Monet's *Grainstacks* anywhere; and *A Sunday on La Grande Jatte—1884,* Georges Seurat's greatest painting.

CULTURE VULTURE

Tour the world without leaving the city. First stop? Europe. Hit the **Balzekas Museum of Lithuanian Culture,** the **Swedish American Museum Center,** the **Polish Museum of America,** and the **Ukrainian Institute of Modern Art.** Swing by the **Oriental Institute** for relics of the Near East, or brush up on Latino history at the **National Museum of Mexican Art.**

IF YOU HAVE KIDS

Besides the Chicago Children's Museum, these are our favorite kids' exhibits, sure to capture the imagination of your young ones. Don't miss the **Fairy Castle** at the Museum of Science and Industry, **"Sue,"** the T. rex, at the Field Museum, and the **dolphin show** at the Shedd Aquarium's Oceanarium. For an extra-colorful experience, **chase butterflies** at the Peggy Notebaert Nature Museum.

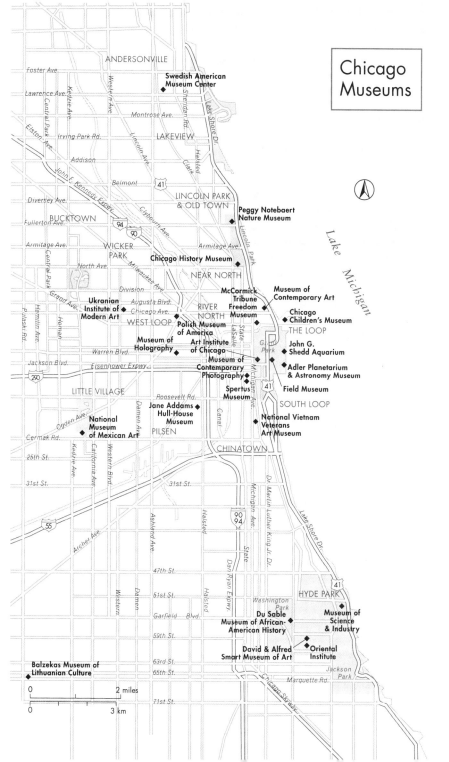

Chicago
Museums

ANDERSONVILLE

Swedish American
Museum Center

Foster Ave.

Lawrence Ave.

Montrose Ave.

LAKEVIEW

Elston Ave.

Irving Park Rd.

Addison

Central Park Ave.

Kedzie Ave.

Western Ave.

Sheridan Rd.

Lincoln Ave.

Halsted

Clark

Lake Shore Dr.

41

Belmont

Diversey Ave.

LINCOLN PARK
& OLD TOWN

John F. Kennedy Expwy.

Fullerton Ave.

BUCKTOWN

94

90

Peggy Notebaert
Nature Museum

Clybourn Ave.

Lincoln Park

Lake
Michigan

Armitage Ave.

WICKER
PARK

North Ave.

Central Park

Hamlin

Pulaski Rd.

Homan

Grand Ave.

Milwaukee Ave.

Armitage Ave.

Chicago History Museum

NEAR NORTH

Division

WEST LOOP

Augusta Blvd.

Chicago Ave.

Ukranian
Institute of
Modern Art

Museum of
Holography

Polish Museum
of America

Art Institute
of Chicago

RIVER
NORTH

McCormick
Tribune
Freedom
Museum

State

LaSalle

Museum of
Contemporary Art

Chicago
Children's Museum

THE LOOP

Grant
Park

John G.
Shedd Aquarium

Adler Planetarium
& Astronomy Museum

Warren Blvd.

Jackson Blvd.

290

Eisenhower Expwy.

LITTLE VILLAGE

Museum of
Contemporary
Photography

Spertus
Museum

Michigan Ave.

41

Field Museum

SOUTH LOOP

Roosevelt Rd.

Ogden Ave.

Cermak Rd.

Damen Ave.

National
Museum
of Mexican Art

Jane Addams
Hull-House
Museum

PILSEN

Canal

National Vietnam
Veterans
Art Museum

25th St.

CHINATOWN

31st St.

Kedzie Ave.

California Ave.

Western Blvd.

31st St.

Ashland Ave.

Halsted

90
94

Michigan Ave.

Dr. Martin Luther King Jr. Dr.

Lake Shore Dr.

55

Archer Ave.

47th St.

Damen

51st St.

Dan Ryan Expwy.

State

Garfield Blvd.

Washington
Park

HYDE PARK

41

59th St.

Du Sable
Museum of African-
American History

Museum of
Science
& Industry

Western

63rd St.

David & Alfred
Smart Museum of Art

Oriental
Institute

Balzekas Museum of
Lithuanian Culture

65th St.

Jackson
Park

Chicago Skyway

Marquette Rd.

0   2 miles

0   3 km

71st St.

A GUIDE TO THE ART INSTITUTE

The Art Institute of Chicago, nestled between the contemporary public art showplace of Millennium Park and the Paris-inspired walkways of Grant Park, is both intimate and grand, a place where the rooms are human-scale and the art is transcendent.

Come for the sterling collection of Impressionists and Old Masters (an entire room is dedicated to Monet), linger over the extraordinary and comprehensive photography collection, take in a number of fine American works, and discover paintings, drawings, sculpture, design, and photography spanning the ages.

The Art Institute is more than just a museum; in fact, it was originally founded by a small group of artists in 1866 as a school with an adjoining exhibition space. Famous alumni include political cartoonist Herblock and artists Grant Wood and Ed Paschke. Walt Disney and Georgia O'Keeffe both took classes, but didn't graduate. The School of the Art Institute of Chicago, one of the finest art schools in the country, is across the street from the museum; occasionally there are lectures and discussions that are open to the public.

ORIENTATION TO THE MUSEUM

- ✉ 111 S. Michigan Ave., South Loop
- ☎ 312/443–3600
- ⊕ www.artic.edu/aic/
- 🎟 Suggested $12, Students and Seniors $7, Free Thursday 5–8
- 🕐 Mon.–Wed. and Fri. 10:30–5, Thu. 10:30–8, Sat.–Sun. 10–5

Take in the museum's grandeur.

The Art Institute is a complicated jumble of four difficult-to-navigate buildings—you can only change buildings on the first level of the museum, and the map the museum gives out isn't very helpful. Here are some tips to help you find your way around:

- On the lower level are textiles, decorative arts, the Thorne Miniature Room, and the Kraft Education Center. The first level includes the non-European galleries, and American art to 1890. The second level holds American art from 1900 to 1950, European art from all periods, and Impressionism.

Photo op: Pose with one of the two bronze lions.

- Pinpoint the five or six works you'd really like to see or pick two or three galleries and wander around after getting yourself there.

- Guards expect visitors to ask for directions, so don't be shy.

- Buy the audio tour ($6) by the coatroom as you enter—it provides descriptions for every gallery and work in the museum. All you do is key in the gallery number and the voices of curators will guide you around the room.

- Don't miss the free rotating sculpture installations in the Bluhm Family Terrace, a 3,400-square-foot outdoor space on the West Pavilion's third floor, adjacent to the seasonally focused restaurant Terzo Piano (reservations recommended).

- Before your visit, download and listen to free podcasts from the Art Institute web site (www.artic.edu/aic)

FOR THE KIDS
Kids love the Kraft Education Center, which has rotating exhibits of child-friendly art (like paintings from picture books) and a permanent, interactive exhibit called *Faces, Places & Inner Spaces* that helps teach children how to look at different kinds of art. There's also a small stage with Kabuki costumes, actual paintings hung at kid-friendly levels, and computer-enhanced games. Nearby is the Touch Gallery, which was originally designed for the blind. You can run your fingers over several bronze works.

BEST PAINTINGS

AMERICAN GOTHIC (1930). **GALLERY 263**
Grant Wood won $300 for his iconic painting of a solemn farmer and his wife (really his sister and his dentist). Wood saw the work as a celebration of solid, work-based Midwestern values, a statement that rural America would survive the Depression and the massive migration to cities.

American Gothic (1930).

NIGHTHAWKS (1942). **GALLERY 262**
Edward Hopper's painting of four figures in a diner on the corner of a deserted New York street is a noir portrait of isolated lives and is one of the most recognized images of 20th-century art. The red-haired woman is the artist's wife, Jo.

THE CHILD'S BATH (1893). **GALLERY 273**
Mary Cassatt was the only American to become an established Impressionist and her work focused on the daily lives of women and children. In this, her most famous work, a woman gently bathes a child who is tucked up on her lap. The Bath was unconventional when it was painted because the bold patterns and cropped forms it used were more often seen in Japanese prints at the time.

Nighthawks (1942).

SKY ABOVE CLOUDS IV (1965). **GALLERY 249**
(not pictured) Georgia O'Keeffe's massive painting, the largest canvas of her career, is of clouds seen from an airplane. The rows of white rectangles stretching toward the horizon look both solid and ethereal, as if they are stepping stones for angels.

THE OLD GUITARIST (1903/04). **MODERN WING**
(not pictured) One of the most important works of Pablo Picasso's Blue Period, this monochromatic painting is a study of the crooked figure of a blind and destitute street guitarist, singing sorrowfully. When he painted it, Picasso was feeling particularly empathetic toward the downtrodden—perhaps because of a friend's suicide—and the image of the guitarist is one of dignity amid poverty.

The Child's Bath (1893).

GRAINSTACK (1890/91). **GALLERY 243**
The Art Institute has the largest collection of Monet's Grainstacks in the world. The stacks rose 15 to 20 feet tall outside Monet's farmhouse in Giverny and were a symbol to the artist of sustenance and survival.

Grainstack (1890/91)

THE MODERN WING

In May 2009 the Art Institute unveiled its highly anticipated Modern Wing. Designed by Pritzker Prize–winning architect Renzo Piano, designer of Paris's Pompidou Center, the 264,000-square-foot addition is almost a separate museum unto itself, providing 65,000 square feet of display space for the museum's extensive collection of modern and contemporary art. With the addition, the Art Institute became the country's second largest art museum.

A view of new wing

THE DESIGN
The rectangle of glass, steel, and limestone cost just under $300 million and took nearly four years to build. The airy, ultra-modern structure provides abundant natural light and dramatic views of Millennium Park through floor-to-ceiling windows. Green building features include a "flying carpet" canopy that filters sunlight through skylights in the third-floor galleries and a sophisticated lighting system that self-adjusts based on available light and temperature.

North Façade

THE COLLECTION
View works from major art movements of the 20th and 21st centuries, ranging from painting and sculpture to video and installation art. Notable artists represented in the collection include Eva Hesse, David Hockney, Jasper Johns, Kerry James Marshall, Joan Mitchell, Jackson Pollock, Gerhard Richter, and Andy Warhol.

GRIFFIN COURT
The light-filled central corridor provides a dramatic passageway to the three-story pavilions flanking it on both sides and to the street-level Pritzker Garden. Griffin Court also houses a ticket area, gift shop, coat check, education center, garden café, and balcony café.

Griffin Court

NICHOLS BRIDGEWAY
A 625-foot pedestrian bridge soars over Monroe Street and the Lurie Gardens, connecting the third floor of the Modern Wing's West Pavilion to the southwest corner of Millennium Park—and providing stunning views of the park, skyline, and lake.

BLUHM FAMILY TERRACE
Rotating sculpture installations occupy the free, 3,400-square-foot outdoor space on the West Pavilion's third floor, adjacent to the seasonally focused restaurant Terzo Piano (reservations recommended).

A painting from Gerhard Richter

ADLER PLANETARIUM AND ASTRONOMY MUSEUM

✉ 1300 S. Lake Shore Dr., South Loop

☎ 312/922–7827

🌐 www.adlerplanetarium.org

🎟 $19 museum admission and 1 show, $25 museum admission and 2 shows. Free days and discount weeks fall throughout the year

🕐 Mon.–Fri. 10 AM–4 PM (except 1st Fri. of month, when open until 10 PM); Sat. and Sun. 10 AM–4:30 PM; summer hours 9:30 AM–6 PM (except 1st Fri. of month when open until 10 PM).

Navigate your way through the solar system with interactive and state-of-the-art exhibits that appeal to planetarium traditionalists as well as technology-savvy kids and adults. The museum uses computer games, videos, short films, and hands-on devices to teach physics and astronomy basics like the Doppler effect. Two different planetariums and a 3-D theater unlock the mysteries of the stars.

TIPS

■ Additional charges apply for the Sky Theater planetarium shows and the StarRider interactive shows *(see admission prices, above)*, but don't skip them—they're the reason to go.

■ Take a quick (free) ride in the Atwood Sphere, a large metal globe with punched-out stars. It provided the nation's very first planetarium experience.

■ No need to purchase the museum's audio tour. The signs in the museum are comprehensive, and the narrative doesn't add much to the experience.

■ 2–3 PM on weekdays, the museum's Space Visualization Lab (a working laboratory where scientists, technicians, and artists drum up new ways to explore the universe) is open to the public.

HIGHLIGHTS

The Adler's traditional in-the-round Zeiss planetarium (called the Sky Theater) shows constellations and planets in the night sky. It's been around since the Adler opened in 1930 as the first public planetarium in the Western Hemisphere.

Peer through Chicago's largest public telescope at the Duane Observatory, located outside of and behind the main museum building. It gathers 5,000 times more light than the human eye, so filters are used to reduce the brilliant glare of the Moon.

See the restored Gemini 12, the spacecraft flown by Captain Jim Lovell and Buzz Aldrin in 1966, in the permanent exhibit "Shoot for the Moon." A collection of space artifacts once owned by Lovell is also on exhibit.

Take a digital journey into space on the interactive StarRider Theater, inside the high-tech Sky Pavilion. For some shows you use control buttons on your armrest to vote for what you see on screen. (Part of the technology is based on aircraft flight simulators.) Other shows wrap you in a 3-D universe of stars.

CHICAGO CHILDREN'S MUSEUM

✉ Navy Pier, 700 E. Grand Ave., Near North

☎ 312/527-1000

⊕ www.chichildrensmuseum.org

💳 $10, free Thurs. 5–8 PM and 1st Mon. of the month for children 15 and younger

🕐 Fri.–Wed. 10 AM–5 PM, Thurs. 10 AM–8 PM.

"Hands-on" is the operative concept for this brightly colored Navy Pier anchor. Kids play educational video games, climb through multilevel tunnels, run their own TV stations, and, if their parents allow it, get soaking wet.

TIPS

■ The museum issues readmission bracelets that let you leave the museum and come back on the same day—great idea for weary families that want to take a break to get a bite to eat or simply explore other parts of Navy Pier before coming back to the museum.

■ Grab a bite at the nearby space-themed McDonald's (☎ 312/832-1640) or bring a picnic and grab a sunny seat outside (in warm weather) or gather in the Crystal Ballroom (amid tropical plants and fountains).

■ Most families spend an average of three hours visiting the museum.

■ Hour-long art workshops at Artabounds are free.

■ The museum is designed for children 2 to 12 years.

■ Adults may not enter the museum without a child.

HIGHLIGHTS

Kids can don raincoats before they start splashing around in the WaterWays exhibit, which has oversize water tubs with waterwheels, pumps, brightly colored pipes, and splashing fountains. If everyone pumps hard enough, water squirts 50 feet into the air.

In the Big Backyard exhibit, children "shrink" to the size of bugs amid giant giggling flowers. Butterflies seem to flutter around their bodies and water appears to splash down on their heads, all through the magic of a tall video screen.

Parents, get ready for a workout. You and your children can scurry up a three-story-high rigging complete with crow's nest and gangplank on the Kovler Family Climbing Schooner. It's reminiscent of the boats that once sailed Lake Michigan. If you make it to the rope tunnels at the top, you can take in bird's-eye views of the museum, then slide back down to the lower level, where there are tanks of fish.

Crouch beside your child to search for fossils in Dinosaur Expedition. Brush away dirt to discover the bones of a Suchomimus, a kind of fish-eating dinosaur that's on display nearby. The exhibit re-creates a trip to the Sahara led by University of Chicago paleontologist Paul Sereno.

Collaboration is the watchword at Kraft Artabounds Studio, where kids participate in rotating group art projects that include activities like creating a castle out of clay.

FIELD MUSEUM

✉ 1400 S. Lake Shore Dr., South Loop

☎ 312/922–9410

⊕ www.fieldmuseum.org

🎫 $15

⊙ Daily 9 AM–5 PM; last admission at 4 PM.

★ More than 6 *acres* of exhibits fill this gigantic world-class museum, which explores cultures and environments from around the world. Interactive exhibits examine such topics as the secrets of Egyptian mummies, the people of Africa and the Pacific Northwest, and the living creatures in the soil. Originally funded by Chicago retailer Marshall Field, the museum was founded in 1893 to hold material gathered for the World's Columbian Exposition; its current neoclassical home opened in 1921.

TIPS

■ Don't hesitate to take toddlers to the Field; the new Crown Family PlayLab, designed for kids 2–6 years old, is where they play house in a faux pueblo, sort objects by shape and color, and compare their footprints to a dinosaur's.

■ It's impossible to see the entire museum in one visit. Try to get tickets to the special exhibit of the season (go to the Web site if you'd like to order in advance) and then choose a couple of subjects you'd like to explore, like North American birds or Chinese jade.

■ The Sue Store sells a mind-boggling assortment of dinosaur-related merchandise.

■ Bring young ones to 20-minute story times, when staff and volunteers read a dinosaur-themed book and direct an art project (weekends year-round and daily July and August).

■ The lobby of the museum includes the Corner Bakery. The dining room tucked in the back has sparkling views of the lake and the Museum Campus.

HIGHLIGHTS

Shrink to the size of a bug to burrow beneath the surface of the soil in the Underground Adventure exhibit ($8 extra). You'll come face-to-face with a giant, animatronic wolf spider twice your size, listen to the sounds of gnawing insects, and have other encounters with the life that teems under our feet.

Spend a couple of hours taking in contemporary and ancient Africa. Dioramas let you feel like you're stepping inside the homes and lives of Africans from Senegal, Cameroon, and the Sahara, while the remarkable Inside Ancient Egypt complex includes a working canal, a living marsh where papyrus is grown, a shrine to the cat goddess Bastet, burial-ceremony artifacts, and 23 mummies.

The Field's dinosaur collection is one of the world's best. You can't miss 65-million-year-old "Sue," the largest and most complete *Tyrannosaurus rex* fossil ever found—it's on permanent exhibit in the lobby. Also visit the McDonald's Fossil Preparation Laboratory, where you can watch paleontologists cleaning up bones. Another favorite is the Evolving Planet, which uses video technology to explain the dawn of single-cell organisms and the advent of dinosaurs.

MUSEUM OF CONTEMPORARY ART

✉ 220 E. Chicago Ave., Near North

☎ 312/280–2660

⊕ www.mcachicago.org

🎟 $12, free Tues.

🕓 Tues. 10 AM–8 PM, Wed.– Sun. 10 AM–5 PM.

TIPS

■ The back of the MCA is one of the best spots to have lunch in the city. Run by Wolfgang Puck, Puck's Café at the MCA has a tasty menu.

■ Try to catch one of the cutting-edge music and theater performances; one year, for example, the entire front of the museum was turned into a puppet theater. Check the Web site for more information.

■ In summer come for Tuesdays on the Terrace and be serenaded by local jazz bands. There's a cash bar from 5:30 to 8 PM and a full menu at the café.

■ On the first Friday of every month the museum hosts a party ($15) with live music and hors d'oeuvres from 6 PM to 10 PM.

■ A farmers' market sets up shop on Tuesday from mid-June through October. Pick up fresh snacks and enjoy a picnic in the museum's backyard (free-admission) sculpture garden.

★ **Fodor's Choice** A group of art patrons who felt the great Art Institute was unresponsive to modern work founded the MCA in 1967, and it's remained a renegade art museum ever since. It doesn't have any permanent exhibits; even the works from its collection are constantly rotating. This gives it a feeling of freshness, but it also makes it impossible to predict what will be on display at any time. Special exhibits are devoted mostly to original shows you can't see anywhere else.

HIGHLIGHTS

The MCA's dramatic quarters were designed by Berlin architect Josef Paul Kleihues. From the outside, the building looks like a home for modern art—it's made of square metal plates, with round bolts in each corner.

The MCA's growing 7,000-piece collection, which includes work by René Magritte, Alexander Calder, Bruce Nauman, Sol LeWitt, Franz Kline, and June Leaf, makes up about half the museum (pieces on view continually rotate). The other half is dedicated to temporary exhibitions.

The museum showcases work in all mediums, including paintings, sculpture, works on paper, photography, video, film, and installations.

Guided "Exhibition Focus" tours dedicated to short-run exhibits happen daily; "Highlights Tours," which provide a balanced sweep of the entire museum, are offered on weekends.

The MCA Store is the place to go for well-designed jewelry and quirky items for the home, from a porcelain eggshell from which a flower sprouts to goggles to be worn while chopping onions.

MUSEUM OF SCIENCE AND INDUSTRY

✉ 5700 S. Lake Shore Dr.,
Hyde Park

☎ 773/684–1414

⊕ www.msichicago.org

💲 $13; museum and Omni-
max admission $20; park-
ing $16

🕐 Memorial Day–Labor Day,
Mon.–Sat. 9:30–5:30, Sun.
11–5:30; Labor Day–Memo-
rial Day, Mon.–Sat. 9:30–4,
Sun. 11–4.

TIPS

■ Use the museum map
to plan out your visit. Your
best bet is to hit a couple of
highlights (the U-boat tour
alone will take at least an
hour) and then see a couple
of quirky exhibits.

■ If the kids get grouchy,
bring them to the Idea Factory, a giant playroom where
they can play with water can-
nons, blocks, and cranks. Limited to ages 10 and younger.

■ Relax with some ice cream
in the old-fashioned ice-cream
parlor, tucked away in a gen-
teel re-creation of an Illinois
main street.

■ On nice days, hordes of
sunbathers and kite-flyers
camp out on the giant lawn
out front—it's almost as
entertaining as the museum
itself. Lake Michigan is across
the street.

■ The museum has free-
admission days, but the
schedule changes often.
Check the Web site for details.

★ **Fodor's Choice** The beloved MSI is one of the most-visited sites in Chicago, and for good reason. The sprawling open space has 2,000 exhibits on three floors, with new exhibits being added constantly. The museum's high-tech interior is hidden by the Classical Revival exterior; it was designed in 1892 by D. H. Burnham & Company as a temporary structure to house the Palace of Fine Arts for the World's Columbian Exposition. It's the fair's only surviving building. On a nice day, take a walk behind the museum to the beautifully landscaped Jackson Park and its peaceful Osaka Garden, a Japanese-style garden with a waterfall.

HIGHLIGHTS

Descend into the depths of a simulated coal mine on a "miner"-led tour that explores the technology behind digging energy out of the ground.

The opulent and detailed-as-a-film-set Fairy Castle (really a giant dollhouse) has tiny chandeliers that flash with real diamonds and floors that are laid with intricate stone patterns. It's enough to make us daydream about what the world's fairy-tale characters might have lived in.

Tour the cramped quarters of the only U-505 German submarine captured during World War II (there's an additional fee). Don't feel like waiting in line? Explore just the free interactive exhibits surrounding the sub, which give stunning insight into the strategy behind the war at sea.

Learn how scientists can make frogs' eyes glow or watch baby chicks tap themselves out of their shells at the "Genetics–Decoding Life" exhibit.

The Omnimax Theater shows science- and space-related films on a giant screen.

JOHN G. SHEDD AQUARIUM

⊠ 1200 S. Lake Shore Dr., South Loop

☎ 312/939–2438

⊕ www.sheddaquarium.org

🎫 $27.50 all-access pass

🕐 Memorial Day–Labor Day, daily 9–6, Thurs. until 10; Labor Day–Memorial Day, weekdays 9–5, weekends 9–6.

TIPS

■ Catch live jazz on the Shedd's north terrace on Thursday evenings from 5 to 10 PM June through August. A gorgeous view of the lake and skyline can make for a magical night. Food and a bar are available.

■ Lines for the Shedd often extend all the way down the neoclassical steps. Buy a ticket in advance to avoid the interminable wait, or spring for a CityPass.

■ Soundings restaurant is an elegant stop for lunch. The menu is pricey, but the quiet tables look over Lake Michigan—and there are very few Chicago eateries that can say that.

■ Discount admission days are offered throughout the year. Check the Web site for updates.

★ Fodor's Choice Take a plunge into an underwater world at the world's largest indoor aquarium. Built in 1930, the Shedd is one of the most popular aquariums in the country, housing more than 8,000 aquatic animals in realistic waterscapes.

HIGHLIGHTS

"Amazon Rising" gives you an up-close look at the animals of the Amazon River, including piranhas, snakes, and stingrays. The 8,600-square-foot exhibit, designed to resemble a flooded forest, re-creates the rise and fall of floodwaters so visitors can see how animals respond.

Sharks swim by in their 400,000-gallon tank as part of the permanent exhibit "Wild Reef," which explores the marine biodiversity and coral reefs in the Indo-Pacific. Wild Reef also has colorful corals, stingrays that slide by under your feet, and other surprising creatures, all from the waters around the Philippines.

Stare down one of the knobby-headed beluga whales (they love to people-watch), observe Pacific white-sided dolphins at play, and explore the simulated Pacific Northwest nature trail in the spectacular Oceanarium, which has pools that seem to blend into Lake Michigan. We like the daily educational dolphin presentation. Be sure to get an underwater glimpse of the dolphins and whales through the viewing windows on the lower level, where you can also find a bunch of information-packed, hands-on activities.

In the 90,000-gallon Caribbean Reef exhibit in the main building, sharks, stingrays, a sea turtle, and other denizens of the deep dart around. It's most fun to observe when divers swim within, feeding the animals and talking to the crowd gathered outside.

OTHER MUSEUMS

Sometimes the best museums are ones that you can see in an hour or less. We like Chicago's smaller museums for the unexpected, interesting, and simply fun things you can find. Some of them highlight the diverse origins that built the city; others dedicate their space to history, archaeology, or specific types of art.

FOR HIDDEN GEMS

Balzekas Museum of Lithuanian Culture. Though many of the people who come here do so for research (the museum is a large repository for genealogical information), the Balzekas has a stunning collection of Lithuanian amber. Other exhibits—armor, rare maps, stamps, and coins—chronicle Lithuanian history. ✉ *6500 S. Pulaski Rd., Englewood* ☎ *773/582–6500* ⊕ *www.lithaz.org* ✂ *$5, free Mon.* ⊙ *Daily 10–4.*

WINDY CITY HISTORY

★

Chicago History Museum. The museum went through a major rehaul in late 2006 when it changed its name from the Chicago Historical Society in honor of its 150th birthday. The new permanent sights include a Costume and Textile Gallery and the exhibit entitled "Chicago: Crossroads of America," which demystifies historic tragedies like the Great Chicago Fire and Haymarket Affair. ✉ *1601 N. Clark St., Lincoln Park* ☎ *312/642–4600* ⊕ *www.chicagohistory.org* ✂ *$14, Mon. free* ⊙ *Mon.–Wed., Fri., and Sat. 9:30–4:30, Thurs. 9:30–8, Sun. noon–5.*

David and Alfred Smart Museum of Art. If you want to see art masterpieces but don't want to spend a long day wandering one of the major art museums, the Smart may be just your speed. The diverse, 10,000-piece permanent collection includes works by old masters; photographs by Walker Evans; furniture by Frank Lloyd Wright; and sculptures by Degas, Matisse, Rodin, and Henry Moore. Temporary exhibits are a great way to see startlingly good art in a smaller, intimate space. ✉ *5550 S. Greenwood Ave., Hyde Park* ☎ *773/702–0200* ⊕ *www.smartmuseum. uchicago.edu* ✂ *Free* ⊙ *Tues., Wed., and Fri. 10–4, Thurs. 10–8, weekends 11–5.*

DuSable Museum of African-American History. The DuSable is a colorful—and haunting—exploration of the African-American experience, set alongside the lagoons of Washington Park. There are handwritten lyric sheets from Motown greats, letters and memorabilia of scholar W. E. B. DuBois and poet Langston Hughes, and a significant African-American art collection. The most moving exhibit is one on slavery; the poignant, disturbing artifacts include rusted shackles used on slave ships. ✉ *740 E. 56th Pl., Hyde Park* ☎ *773/947–0600* ⊕ *www.dusablemuseum.org* ✂ *$3, free Sun.* ⊙ *Mon.–Sat. 10–5, Sun. noon–5.*

Jane Addams Hull-House Museum. The redbrick Victorian Hull House was the birthplace of social work. Social welfare pioneers and peace advocates Jane Addams and Ellen Gates Starr started the American settlement house movement in this house in 1889, and wrought near miracles in their surrounding community, which was then a slum for new immigrants. Pictures and letters add context to the two museum buildings, which re-create the homey setting the residents experienced. ✉ *800 S. Halsted St., University Village* ☎ *312/413–5353* ⊕ *www.uic. edu/jaddams/hull* ✂ *Free* ⊙ *Tues.–Fri. 10–4, Sun. noon–4.*

QUIET SPACES

North Terrace, Shedd Aquarium. The entire aquarium is mesmerizing; you might find yourself staring at placidly swimming fish for hours without getting bored. But for a truly peaceful experience during mild weather, push through the doors of the North Terrace and sit at a table overlooking Lake Michigan and the city skyline. The terrace is usually deserted even on the busiest summer days.

Mammal dioramas, Field Museum. Few visitors linger amid the long, darkened hallways of the North American mammal dioramas. Take a seat on a curved wooden bench and you won't be disturbed—unless the sight of stuffed and mounted bears and buffalo makes you queasy.

Main Street theater and Jackson Park, Museum of Science and Industry. Olde Chicago is re-created in a corner of the MSI, complete with cobblestones and iron lamps. At the end of the street is a small theater showing silent shorts of Buster Keaton. If you'd rather be in the sunshine, take a walk around Jackson Park's lagoons and bridges behind the museum, one of the most peaceful—and overlooked—spots in all of Chicago.

IF YOU ONLY HAVE TIME FOR ONE ★ **National Museum of Mexican Art.** Formerly the Mexican Fine Arts Museum Center, this sparkling site, the largest Latino museum in the country, is half art museum, half cultural exploration. After the big downtown museums, this is the one you shouldn't miss. Galleries house impressive collections of contemporary, traditional, and meso-American art from both sides of the border, as well as vivid exhibits that trace immigration woes and political fights. Every fall the giant Day of the Dead exhibit stuns Chicagoans with its altars from artists across the country. ⊠*1852 W. 19th St., Pilsen* ☎*312/738–1503* ⊕*www.nationalmuseumofmexicanart. org* ⊠*Free* ☉*Tues.–Sun. 10–5.*

McCormick Tribune Freedom Museum. This bi-level museum dedicated to the First Amendment and the rights it describes is located, fittingly, next door to Tribune Tower, office of the *Chicago Tribune* (the museum is a non-profit entity of the daily paper). Inside you'll find plasma touchscreens that allow you to zoom in on electronic versions of important documents, such as the Constitution and Bill of Rights, and decipher their passages. Use headsets at the "Voices of Freedom" exhibit to hear discourses by big-time politicos like Thomas Jefferson and John Adams. The whole concept feels middle-school field trip–like, but the high-tech, interactive experiences keep things interesting. ⊠*435 N. Michigan Ave., Downtown* ☎*312/222–4860* ⊕*www.freedommuseum. us* ⊠*Free* ☉*Wed.–Mon. 10–6.*

Museum of Contemporary Photography. "Contemporary" is defined here as anything after 1936. More than 7,000 works from American-born and American-resident photographers make this an impressive collection. Among the don't-miss works are photos by Dorothea Lange, Ansel Adams, and Nicholas Nixon. Curators constantly seek out new talent and under-appreciated established photographers, which means that there are artists here you probably won't see elsewhere. Rotating

The Local Art Scene

You don't need to be an art expert to explore the city's web of local neighborhood galleries. Just do as locals do and ready yourself with a free copy of *The Chicago Reader,* which has gallery and exhibition listings (available in many street dispensers, coffee shops, and record stores), or grab the *Chicago Gallery News* (or check it out on the Web at ⊕ *www.chicagogallery news.com*)—it's the best source for maps, gallery information, and exhibition listings. Most galleries provide complimentary copies.

Here's the skinny: Chicago is divided into gallery "districts," or communities. They each have their own feel and flavor. Stop by anytime during gallery hours—no need to make an appointment—even if you're just browsing. Gallery directors and staff are always available to answer questions or provide further information on their artists.

RIVER NORTH DISTRICT
The city's first organized art neighborhood remains a vibrant community and the hub of the gallery scene.

Zolla/Lieberman (*contemporary multimedia* ⊠ *325 W. Huron St.* ☎ *312/944–1990*).

Roy Boyd (*contemporary painting and sculpture* ⊠ *739 N. Wells St.* ☎ *312/642–1606*).

Carl Hammer (*American folk and outsider art* ⊠ *740 N. Wells St.* ☎ *312/266–8512*).

Ann Nathan Gallery (*contemporary painting and sculpture* ⊠ *212 W. Superior St.* ☎ *312/664–6622*).

Stephen Daiter Gallery (*vintage black-and-white photography* ⊠ *311 W. Superior St.* ☎ *312/787–3350*).

WEST LOOP DISTRICT
Lots of galleries have opened in multilevel warehouses on Randolph Street and throughout the rest of the neighborhood.

Packer Schopf Gallery (*emerging and mid-career artists* ⊠ *942 W. Lake St.* ☎ *312/226–8984*).

Rhona Hoffman (*established and emerging contemporary artists* ⊠ *118 N. Peoria St.* ☎ *312/455–1990*).

Donald Young Gallery (*local and international contemporary art* ⊠ *224 S. Michigan Ave.* ☎ *312/455–0100*).

EAST PILSEN DISTRICT
Most artists live in their galleries in this district south and west of the Loop, and the line between reality and fantasy is often outrageously blurred.

4ArtInc. (*contemporary, artist-run* ⊠ *1932 S. Halsted St.* ☎ *312/850–1816*)

WICKER PARK/BUCKTOWN
The area is home to a respectable chunk of the city's artists, but most show their work privately or in independent group shows. You can still see artists' studios if you wander around the **Flat Iron Building** (⊠ *1714 N. Damen Ave.*). Check out **Pagoda Red** (*Chinese and Tibetan art objects* ⊠ *1714 N. Damen Ave.* ☎ *773/235–1188*).

exhibits have included photojournalism and scientific photography. ✉*600 S. Michigan Ave., South Loop* ☎*312/663–5554* ⊕*www.mocp.org* ✉*Free* ⊙*Mon.–Wed., Fri., and Sat. 10–5, Thurs. 10–8, Sun. noon–5.*

Museum of Holography. Holography seems almost quaint in our age of 3-D digital renderings. Still, it's fun to spend an hour walking

from side to side in front of these glowing, three-dimensional, laser-etched portraits and pictures. ✉*1134 W. Washington Blvd., West Loop* ☎*312/226–1007* ✉*$5* ⊙*Wed.–Sun. 12:30–4:30.*

National Vietnam Veterans Art Museum. The chimelike sounds of more than 58,000 imprinted dog tags hanging from the ceiling entranceway are a melancholy memorial to the soldiers who lost their lives in the unpopular war. Take in the visual journal of the experiences of more than 122 artists who served in Vietnam through the 1,000-plus pieces of art on display here. ✉*1801 S. Indiana Ave., South Loop* ☎*312/326–0270* ⊕*www.nvvam.org* ✉*$10, free to service members* ⊙*Wed. and Fri. 11–5, Sat. 10–5.*

★ **Oriental Institute.** This gem began with artifacts collected by University of Chicago archaeologists in the 1930s (one is rumored to have been the model for Indiana Jones) and has expanded into an interesting, informative museum with a jaw-dropping collection from the ancient Near East, including the largest U.S. collection of Iraqi antiquities. There are amulets, mummies, limestone reliefs, gold jewelry, ivories, pottery, and bronzes from the 4th millennium BC through the 13th century AD. You won't be able to miss the 17-foot-tall statue of King Tut, excavated from the ruins of a temple in western Thebes in 1930. ✉*1155 E. 58th St., Hyde Park* ☎*773/702–9520* ⊕*www.oi.uchicago.edu* ✉*Free* ⊙*Tues. and Thurs.–Sat. 10–6, Wed. 10–8:30, Sun. noon–6.*

★ **Peggy Notebaert Nature Museum.** Walk among hundreds of Midwest species of butterflies and learn about the impact of rivers and lakes on daily life at this modern museum washed in natural light. Like Chicago's other science museums, it's geared to kids, with educational computer games to play and water turbines to control. But even jaded adults will be excited when bright yellow butterflies land on their shoulders. The idea is to study nature inside without forgetting graceful Lincoln Park outside. ✉*2430 N. Cannon Dr., Lincoln Park* ☎*773/755–5100* ⊕*www.naturemuseum.org* ✉*$9, free Thurs.* ⊙*Weekdays 9–4:30, weekends 10–5.*

Polish Museum of America. Chicago has the largest Polish population of any city outside Warsaw, and this museum in Ukrainian Village, just south of Wicker Park, celebrates that fact. Take a trip to the old country by strolling through exhibits of folk costumes, memorabilia from Pope John Paul II, Hussar armor, American Revolutionary War heroes Tadeusz Kosciuszko and Casimir Pulaski, pianist and composer Ignacy

Paderewski, and an 8-foot-long sleigh in the shape of a dolphin that's carved from a single log. It's also a good place to catch up on your reading; the library has 60,000 volumes. ⊠*984 N. Milwaukee Ave., Wicker Park* ☎*773/384–3352* ⊕*www.polishmuseumofamerica.org* ⊠*$5* ⊘*Fri.–Wed. 11–4.*

Spertus Museum. This museum addresses an intellectual puzzle: what does it mean to be Jewish in the modern world? Contemporary and traditional art and ritual objects illustrate daily life; a sobering Holocaust memorial with many photos and a tattered concentration camp uniform remind us to remember. The museum recently reopened in a stunning new location on the same block and added an expansive Children's Center. ⊠*610 S. Michigan Ave., South Loop* ☎*312/322–1747* ⊕*www. spertus.edu* ⊠ *$7* ⊘*Sun. and Wed. 10–5, Thurs. 10–6.*

★ **Swedish American Museum Center.** Though this tiny and welcoming museum does have changing exhibits that focus on the art and culture of Sweden, you don't have to be Swedish to find it interesting—much of the museum focuses on the immigrant experience. On permanent display, for example, are trunks immigrants brought with them to Chicago, and a map showing where in the city different immigrant groups settled. On the third floor, in the only children's museum in the country dedicated to immigration, kids can climb aboard a colorful Viking ship or "milk" a wooden cow, pulling rubber udders to collect streams of water in a bucket. ⊠*5211 N. Clark St., Far North Side* ☎*773/728–8111* ⊕*www.samac.org* ⊠*$4, free 2nd Tues. of month* ⊘*Tues.–Fri. 10–4, weekends 11–4.*

Ukrainian Institute of Modern Art. Modern and contemporary art fans head out to this small museum at the far western edge of the Ukrainian Village, near Wicker Park. Three permanent galleries feature mixed media, sculpture, painting, and even some digital art. Some of the most interesting works are abstract or playful versions of Old World themes, like Evan Prokopov's 1998 abstract bronze of a mother cradling her child. ⊠*2320 W. Chicago Ave., Wicker Park* ☎*773/227–5522* ⊕*www.uima-art.org* ⊠*Free* ⊘*Wed.–Sun. noon–4.*

Architecture

WORD OF MOUTH

"Add me to those who recommend the [Chicago Architecture Foundation's] architecture boat trip . . . very interesting, relaxing, and informative."

—musicfan

ARCHITECTURE PLANNER

In a Chicago Mood

Chicago has long been known as America's Second City, but as a visit here makes clear, this is no burg. A metropolis if there ever was one, Chicago hums with activity while its lakeside location lends a relaxed, breezy ambience. A great way to take advantage of this intermingling is to sit for a spell in Millennium Park or Grant Park and enjoy the march of buildings up Michigan Avenue. Known to some as the "Michigan Avenue Cliff," this stretch just west of the parks comprises a slew of noteworthy structures.

Good Reads

Architecture geeks won't need much introduction to the city's architectural history, but if you don't count yourself among that special breed, you might pick up *Chicago Architecture and Design*, a beautifully illustrated book with a good perspective by George A. Larson and Jay Pridmore. For a more in-depth yet highly readable study of some of the big names who worked here, check out Peter Blake's *The Master Builders*. And if you don't mind a bit of murder with your history lesson, there's Erik Larson's magnificent *The Devil in the White City*.

Walking Tours

The Chicago Architecture Foundation gives expertly guided tours. Chicago Greeter and InstaGreeter are free city services that match savvy Chicagoans with visitors for neighborhood tours. Friends of the Chicago River leads Saturday-morning tours during the warmer months.

Contacts Chicago Architecture Foundation (✉ Santa Fe Bldg., 224 S. Michigan Ave. ☎ 312/922–3432 ⊕ www. architecture.org). **Chicago Greeter/InstaGreeter** (✉ Visitor Information Center at Chicago Cultural Center, 77 E. Randolph St. ☎ 312/744–8000 ⊕ www.chicagogreeter.com). **Friends of the Chicago River** (✉ 40728 E. Jackson, Suite 1800 ☎ 312/939–0490 ⊕ www.chicagoriver.org).

Bus and Trolley Tours

A bus or trolley tour is a fun way to enjoy Chicago's architecture. Tours cost roughly $25 and last two hours or more.

Contacts Gray Line Tours (☎ 800/621–4153 ⊕ www. grayline.com). **Chicago Architecture Foundation** (*See Walking Tours*). **Chicago Trolley and Double Decker Co.** (☎ 773/648–5000 ⊕ www.chicagotrolley.com).

Boat Tours

The Chicago Architecture Foundation river tour is the most authoritative ($28 weekdays; $32 on weekends and holidays). You can purchase tickets at the Chicago ArchiCenter, 224 South Michigan Avenue, or through Ticketmaster at 312/902–1500 or www.ticketmaster.com. The boat-tour season runs from the end of April to mid-November — always call ahead. Other options include:

Mercury Chicago Skyline Cruiseline (☎ 312/332–1353 ⊕ www.mercuryskylinecruiseline.com). **Shoreline Sightseeing** (☎ 312/222–9328 ⊕ www.shorelinesightseeing. com). **Wendella Sightseeing Boats** (✉ 400 N. Michigan Ave. ☎ 312/337–1446 ⊕ www.wendellaboats.com). **Windy of Chicago Ltd** (☎ 312/595–5555 ⊕ www. tallshipwindy.com).

Updated
by Roberta
Sotonoff

4

Every great city has great buildings, but Chicago *is* its great buildings. Art, culture, food, and diversion are all part of the picture here, but everything Chicagoans do is framed by some of the most remarkable architecture to be found anywhere. From the sky-scraping of its tall towers to the horizontal sweep of the Prairie School, Chicago's built environment is second to none.

DECISIONS, DECISIONS, DECISIONS

Even if you're pressed for time, you can't leave town without seeing a few of the city's important buildings. The lovely **Reliance Building** on State Street (home to trendy Hotel Burnham) is steps away from the **Harold Washington Library** and just blocks from the Art Institute and Millennium Park. Mies van der Rohe's **860–880 North Lake Shore Drive** buildings are right on the lake and not too far from high-end shopping on the Magnificent Mile.

With so many significant skyscrapers packed into the Loop, it's tough to elevate any one above the rest. When it comes to early buildings, the **Rookery** is hard to beat. Looking like an impenetrable terra-cotta mass from the street, its heart is a graceful, covered court done up by Frank Lloyd Wright. And no matter how much you may dislike modern architecture, the **Inland Steel Building** is a beauty. Also worth a visit is the dizzying atrium of the squat **James R. Thompson Center,** a bold interpretation of a public building. Finally, for a swanky Art Deco number, stop by the **Carbide and Carbon Building,** home to the Hard Rock Hotel Chicago.

A TALL ORDER

If you came looking for tall buildings, Chicago certainly won't let you down. Among the tallest are the famous **Willis (Sears) Tower,** with its 103rd-floor observatory (on clear days you can see four states); the instantly recognizable **John Hancock Center,** with its crisscross braces and two huge antennae (not to mention a showy bar and restaurant on the 95th floor); and the formidable **Aon Center,** which towers over Millennium Park. And no building proclaims its sky-scraping ambition quite like **311 South Wacker Drive,** whose Gothic crown is ablaze with light at night.

IT'S WORTH THE TRIP

Nearby **Oak Park** is Frank Lloyd Wright's old stomping ground. The leafy community is chock-full of his work, from early examples of Prairie Style to a fascinating Unitarian church. A visit to **Glessner House**—H. H. Richardson's 1887 masterpiece in the Prairie Avenue Historic District—offers the voyeuristic appeal of poking through a great home. It's enough to motivate even those who don't know an I-beam from a flying buttress.

> **FINDING FACTS**
>
> For more information about the city's architectural treasures, contact the Chicago Architecture Foundation at 312/922–8687 or 312/922–3432 (online at ⊕*www. architecture.org*) or the Chicago Convention and Tourism Bureau at 312/567–8500 (online at ⊕*www.choosechicago.com/ architecture.html*).

THE LOOP

Defined by the El (the elevated train that makes a circuit around the area), the Loop is Chicago at its big-city best. A hub of retail, cultural, financial, and governmental activity, it's also home to the city's most notable skyscrapers. Ambitious walkers can cover a good part of the Loop and the surrounding areas in a day, but even a relatively short stroll will pass some top sites.

HISTORIC BUILDINGS

★ **Auditorium Building.** Hunkered down across from Grant Park, this 110,000-ton granite-and-limestone behemoth was an instant star when it debuted in 1889, boasting a 400-room hotel, offices, and a 4,300-seat theater. It didn't hurt the careers of its designers, Dankmar Adler and Louis H. Sullivan, either. The state-of-the-art theater included electric lighting and an air-conditioning system that used 15 tons of ice per day. Adler managed the engineering—the theater's acoustics are renowned—while Sullivan ornamented the space using mosaics, cast iron, art glass, wood, and plaster. During World War II the building was conscripted for use as a Servicemen's Center. Then Roosevelt University moved in. Thanks to Herculean restoration efforts, the theater—rechristened as the Auditorium Theatre of Roosevelt University—is once again one of the city's premiere performance venues. If you can't book a performance, call for tour details (Mon. 10:30 and noon; Thurs. 10:30). ⊠*50 E. Congress Pkwy., Loop* ☎*312/431–2389* ⊕*www.auditoriumtheatre. org* ⛟*Tour $10.*

Carson Pirie Scott & Co. (now the Sullivan Center). Built in 1899, the old-fashioned department store's flagship location closed its doors in 2007, and the building now goes by the Sullivan Center. While shopping—window or otherwise—is no longer an option, it's worth checking out the building's facade. The work of one of Chicago's most renowned architects, it combines Louis H. Sullivan's visionary expression of modern design with intricate cast-iron ornamentation. The eye-catching rotunda and the 11 stories above it are actually an addition Sullivan made to his original building. In later years D. H. Burnham & Co. and Holabird & Root extended Sullivan's smooth, horizontal scheme farther down State Street. ✉ *1 S. State St., Loop.*

WORLD'S **Chicago Cultural Center.** Built in1897
LARGEST as the city's original public library,
TIFFANY DOME this huge building houses the **Chi-**
★ **cago Office of Tourism Visitor Information Center,** as well as a gift shop, galleries, and a concert hall. Designed by the Boston firm Shepley, Rutan & Coolidge—the team behind the Art Institute of Chicago—it's a palatial affair of Carrara marble, mosaics, gold leaf, and the world's largest Tiffany glass dome. Building tours are offered Wednesday, Friday, and Saturday at 1:15 PM. There's live music on weekdays at 12:15 PM in the café. ✉ *78 E. Washington St., Loop* ☎ *312/346–3278 or 312/744–6630* ⊕ *www. cityofchicago.org/Tourism/CulturalCenter* ⊙ *Mon.–Thurs. 8–7, Fri. 8–6, Sat. 9–6, Sun. 10–6.*

> ### FOR SULLIVAN FANS
>
> Bear north to Lincoln Park to see the **Louis Sullivan row houses.** The love of geometric ornamentation that Sullivan eventually brought to such projects as the Carson Pirie Scott building is already visible in these row houses built in 1885. The terra-cotta cornices and decorative window tops are especially noteworthy. ✉ *1826–1834 N. Lincoln Park W, Lincoln Park* ⊕ *www.artic. edu/aic/libraries/rbarchives/ sullivan/extant.html*

Fine Arts Building. This creaky building was constructed in 1895 to house the showrooms of the Studebaker Company, then makers of carriages. Publishers and artists have used its spaces; today the principal tenants are professional musicians. Take a look at the handsome exterior, then step inside the marble-and-woodwork lobby. The motto engraved in the marble as you enter says, ALL PASSES—ART ALONE ENDURES. The building has an interior courtyard, across which strains of piano music and soprano voices compete with tenors as they run through exercises. Open Studios tours (4:30–9:30 on the second Friday of each month) include live music, galleries, and a peak at the studios. ✉ *410 S. Michigan Ave., Loop* ☎ *312/566-9800* ⊕ *www.fineartsbuilding.tv.*

CHECK OUT **Marquette Building.** Like a slipcover over a sofa, the clean, geometric
THE CHICAGO facade of the Marquette Building expresses what lies beneath: in this
WINDOWS case, a structural steel frame. Sure, the base is marked with roughly cut
★ stone and a fancy cornice crowns the top, but the bulk of the building mirrors the cage around which it is built. Inside is another story. The intimate lobby of this 1895 Holabird & Roche building is a jewel box of a space, where a single Doric column stands surrounded by a Tiffany glass mosaic depicting the exploits of French Jesuit missionary Jacques Marquette, an early explorer of Illinois. The building is a clear example of the Chicago style, from the steel skeleton to the Chicago Windows to the terra-cotta ornamentation. ✉ *140 S. Dearborn St., Loop.*

Monadnock Building. Built in two segments a few years apart, the Monadnock captures the turning point in high-rise construction. Its northern

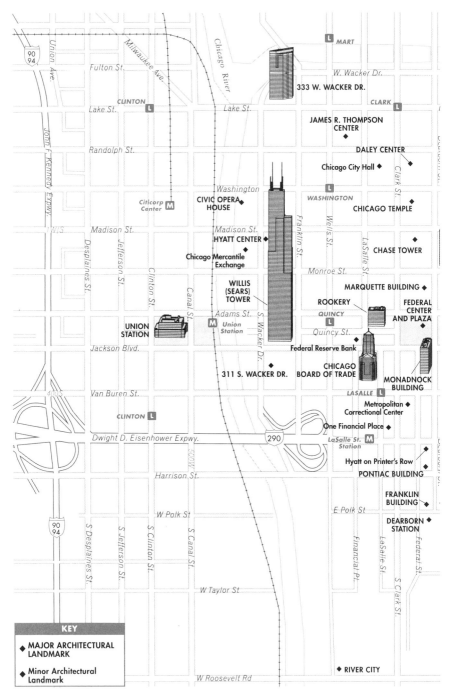

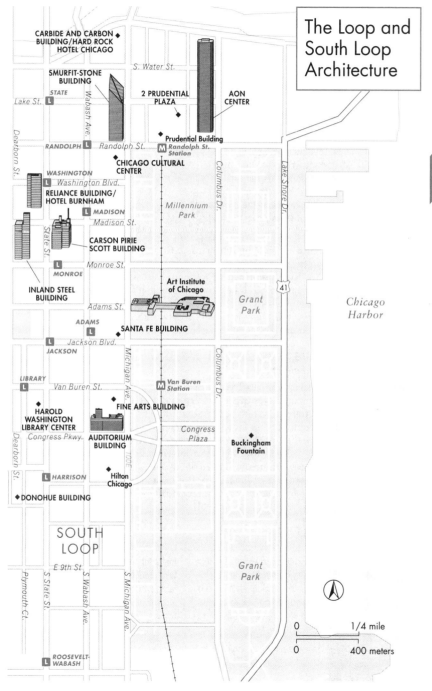

The Loop and South Loop Architecture

CARBIDE AND CARBON BUILDING/HARD ROCK HOTEL CHICAGO

SMURFIT-STONE BUILDING

STATE

Lake St.

Wabash Ave.

Dearborn St.

S. Water St.

2 PRUDENTIAL PLAZA

AON CENTER

RANDOLPH ▸ Randolph St.

Prudential Building

M Randolph St. Station

CHICAGO CULTURAL CENTER

WASHINGTON

Washington Blvd.

RELIANCE BUILDING/ HOTEL BURNHAM

MADISON

Madison St.

Millennium Park

Columbus Dr.

Lake Shore Dr.

4

CARSON PIRIE SCOTT BUILDING

State St.

Monroe St.

MONROE

INLAND STEEL BUILDING

Art Institute of Chicago

Adams St.

ADAMS

SANTA FE BUILDING

Grant Park

41

Chicago Harbor

JACKSON ▸ Jackson Blvd.

LIBRARY

Van Buren St.

Michigan Ave.

M Van Buren Station

Columbus Dr.

HAROLD WASHINGTON LIBRARY CENTER

Congress Pkwy.

FINE ARTS BUILDING

AUDITORIUM BUILDING

Congress Plaza

Buckingham Fountain

Dearborn St.

HARRISON

Hilton Chicago

◆ DONOHUE BUILDING

100E

SOUTH LOOP

E 9th St

Plymouth Ct.

S. State Ave.

S. Wabash Ave.

S. Michigan Ave.

Grant Park

ROOSEVELT-WABASH

0   1/4 mile

0   400 meters

WORLD'S COLUMBIAN EXPOSITION

In 1893 the city of Chicago hosted the **World's Columbian Exposition.** The fair's mix of green spaces and Beaux Arts buildings offered the vision of a more pleasantly habitable metropolis than the crammed industrial center that rose from the ashes of the Great Fire. However, a ruffled Louis Sullivan prophesied that "the damage wrought to this country by the Chicago World's Fair will last half a century." He wasn't entirely wrong in his prediction—the neoclassical style vied sharply over the next decades with the native creations of the Chicago and Prairie schools, all the while incorporating their technical advances. One of Hyde Park's most popular destinations—the Museum of Science and Industry—was erected as the fair's Palace of Fine Arts. It's the exposition's only building still standing.

half, designed in 1891 by Burnham & Root, was erected with traditional load-bearing masonry walls (6 feet deep at the base). In 1893 Holabird & Roche designed its southern half, which rose around the soon-to-be-common steel skeleton. The building's stone and brick exterior, shockingly unornamented for its time, led one critic to liken it to a chimney. The lobby is equally spartan: lined on either side with windowed shops, it's essentially a corridor, but one well worth traveling. Walk it from end to end and you'll feel like you're stepping back in time. ⊠ *53 W. Jackson Blvd. at S. Dearborn St., Loop* ⊕*www. monadnockbuilding.com.*

A CHICAGO LANDMARK
Fodor'sChoice
★

Reliance Building. The clearly expressed, gleaming verticality that characterizes the modern skyscraper was first and most eloquently articulated in this steel-frame tower in the heart of the Loop. Completed in 1895 and now home to the stylish **Hotel Burnham,** the building was a crumbling eyesore until the late 1990s, when the city initiated a major restoration. In the early and mid-1900s it was a mixed-use office building, and Al Capone's dentist reportedly worked out of what's now Room 809. Don't be misled when you go looking for this masterpiece—a block away, at State and Randolph streets, a dormitory for the School of the Art Institute

WHAT ARE YOU LOOKIN' AT?

Terra-cotta, a baked clay that can be produced as tiles or shaped ornamentally, was commonly used by Chicago architects after the Great Fire of 1871.

Heat resistant and malleable, the material proved an effective and attractive fireproofing agent for the metal-frame buildings that otherwise would melt and collapse. The facade of the Marquette Building at 140 S. Dearborn Street is a particularly fine example.

of Chicago shamelessly mimics this trailblazing original by Burnham, Root, and Charles Atwood. Once you've found the real thing, don't miss the mosaic floor and ironwork in the reconstructed elevator lobby. The building boasts early examples of the Chicago Window, which define the entire building's facade by adding a shimmer and glimmer to the surrounding white terra-cotta. ⊠*1 W. Washington St., Loop* ☎*312/782–1111* ⊕*www.burnhamhotel.com.*

GREAT CORNERS TO LOOK UP!
■ North Michigan Avenue and East Wacker Drive
■ West Adams and South LaSalle streets
■ North Michigan Avenue and East Chestnut Street

4

Fodor's Choice ★ **Rookery.** This 11-story structure, with its eclectically ornamented facade, got its name from the pigeons and politicians who roosted at the city hall that once stood on this site. Designed in 1885 by Burnham & Root, who used both masonry and the more modern steel-frame construction, the Rookery was one of the first buildings in the country to feature a central court that brought sunlight into interior office spaces. Frank Lloyd Wright, who kept an office here for a short time, renovated the two-story lobby and light court, eliminating some of the ironwork and terra-cotta and adding marble scored with geometric patterns detailed in gold leaf. The interior endured some less tasteful alterations after that, but it has since been restored to the way it looked when Wright completed his work in 1907. ⊠*209 S. LaSalle St., Loop* .

Santa Fe Building. Also known as the Railway Exchange Building, this structure was designed in 1904 by Daniel Burnham, who later moved his office here. The SANTA FE sign on its roof was put up early in the 20th century by the Santa Fe Railroad, one of several railroads that had offices here when Chicago was the rail center of the country. The fantastic **ArchiCenter of the Chicago Architecture Foundation** (☎*312/922–3432* ⊕*www.architecture.org* ⊙*Daily 9:30–6:30*) occupies this historic space. ⊠*224 S. Michigan Ave., Loop* .

Symphony Center. Orchestra Hall, home to the acclaimed Chicago Symphony Orchestra (CSO), lies at the heart of this music center. The hall was built in 1904 under the supervision of Daniel Burnham. The Georgian building has a symmetrical facade of pink brick with limestone quoins, lintels, and other decorative elements. Backstage tours are available by appointment for groups of 10 or more. ⊠*220 S. Michigan Ave., Loop* ☎*312/294–3000.*

FINDING THE ART DECO

FROM BUBBLY INSPIRATION ★ **Carbide and Carbon Building.** Designed in 1929 by Daniel and Hubert Burnham, sons of the renowned architect Daniel Burnham, this is arguably the jazziest skyscraper in town. A deep-green terra-cotta tower rising from a black-granite base, its upper reaches are embellished with gold leaf. The original public spaces are a luxurious composition in marble and bronze. The story goes that the brothers Burnham got their design inspiration from a gold-foiled bottle of champagne. So perhaps it's fitting that the building now houses the **Hard Rock Hotel Chicago,** party central for those who wouldn't be caught dead at the Four Seasons. ✉*230 N. Michigan Ave. Loop* ⊕*www.hardrockhotelchicago.com.*

★ **Chicago Board of Trade.** Rising dramatically at the end of LaSalle Street— heart of the city's financial district—Holabird & Root's building is a streamlined giant from the days when Art Deco was all the rage. The artfully lit marble lobby soars three stories; atop the roof stands Ceres, the Roman goddess of agriculture. Erected in 1930, this 45-story structure reigned as the city's tallest skyscraper until 1955, when the Prudential Center grabbed that title. ✉*141 W. Jackson Blvd., Loop* ☎*312/435–3590.*

Civic Opera House. The handsome home of the Lyric Opera of Chicago is grand indeed, with pink-and-gray Tennessee marble floors, pillars with carved capitals, crystal chandeliers, and a sweeping staircase to the second floor. Designed by Graham, Anderson, Probst & White, it combines lavish Art Deco details with classical touches. And the show goes on, with the Lyric Opera performing regularly on the great stage within. ✉*20 N. Wacker Dr., Loop* ☎*312/419–0033 Civic Opera House, 312/332–2244 Lyric Opera* ⊕*www.civicoperahouse.com.*

1950S AND BEYOND: MEET MODERNISM

Daley Center. Named for the late mayor Richard J. Daley, this boldly plain high-rise is the headquarters of the Cook County court system, but it's best known as the site of a sculpture by Picasso. Known simply as the *Picasso,* this monumental piece provoked an outcry when it was installed in 1967; baffled Chicagoans tried to determine whether it represented a woman or an Afghan hound. In the end, they gave up guessing and simply embraced it as a unique symbol of the city. The building was constructed in 1965 of Cor-Ten steel, which weathers naturally to an attractive bronze. In summer the building's plaza is the site of concerts, political rallies, and a weekly farmers' market (Thursday); during the holidays, the city's official Christmas tree is erected here, and Christkindl Market, a traditional German market selling food and gifts, takes over the area. ✉*Bounded by Washington Blvd., Randolph, Dearborn, and Clark Sts., Loop.*

MIES MEETS **Federal Center and Plaza.** Designed in 1959, but not completed until
CALDER 1974, this severe constellation of buildings around a sweeping plaza
★ was Mies van der Rohe's first mixed-use urban project. Fans of the International Style will groove on this pocket of pure modernism, while others can take comfort in the presence of the Marquette Building, which marks the north side of the site. In contrast to this dark ensemble are the great red arches of Alexander Calder's *Flamingo.* The piece was dedicated on the same day in 1974 that the artist's *The Universe* was unveiled at Willis (Sears) Tower. Calder went from one event to the other, riding through the streets in a brightly colored circus wagon accompanied by calliopes. The area is bound by Dearborn, Clark, and Adams streets and Jackson Boulevard. ✉*Dirksen: 219 S. Dearborn St., Loop* ✉*Kluczynski: 230 S. Dearborn St., Loop .*

★ **Inland Steel Building.** A runt compared to today's tall buildings, this crisp, sparkling structure from Skidmore, Owings & Merrill was a trailblazer back in the late 1950s. It was the first skyscraper built with external supports (allowing for wide-open, unobstructed floors within); the first to employ steel pilings (driven 85 feet down to bedrock); the city's first fully air-conditioned building; and the first to feature underground parking. As for looks, well, you might say it combines the friendly scale of the Reliance Building with the cool rigor of a high-rise by Mies. ⊠ *30 W. Monroe St., Loop* .

LATE MODERNISM GIVES WAY TO POSTMODERNISM

ENJOY THE
17-STORY
ATRIUM
★

James R. Thompson Center. People either hate or love the center: former governor James Thompson, who selected the Helmut Jahn design for this state government building, hailed it in his dedication speech in 1985 as "the first building of the 21st century." For others, it's a case of postmodernism run amok. A bowl-like form topped by a truncated cylinder, the building's sky-blue and salmon color scheme screams 1980s. But the 17-story atrium, where exposed elevators zip up and down and sunlight casts dizzying patterns through the metal-and-glass skin, is one of the most animated interiors to be found anywhere in the city. The sculpture in the plaza is Jean Dubuffet's *Monument with Standing Beast.* It's nearly as controversial as the building itself. The curved shapes, in white with black traceries, have been compared to a pile of melting Chicago snow. The **Illinois Artisans Shop** (☎ *312/814–5321*), on the second level of the Center, sells crafts, jewelry, and folk art by Illinois artists. ⊠ *100 W. Randolph St., Loop* .

Smurfit-Stone Building. Some wags have said this building, with its diamond-shape top, looks like a giant pencil sharpener. The slanted top carves through 10 floors of this 1984 building. The painted, folded-aluminum sculpture in the plaza is Yaacov Agam's *Communication X9.* You'll see different patterns in the sculpture depending on your vantage point. ⊠ *150 N. Michigan Ave., Loop* .

333 West Wacker Drive. This green-glazed beauty doesn't follow the rules. Its riverside facade echoes the curve of the Chicago River just in front of it, while the other side of the building is all business, conforming neatly to the straight lines of the street grid. This 1983 Kohn Pedersen Fox design is roughly contemporary to the James R. Thompson Center—but it has enjoyed a much more positive public reception. ⊠ *333 W. Wacker Dr., between W. Lake Street and N. Orleans St., Loop* .

CHECK OUT
THE ROOF
OWLS
★
☾

Harold Washington Library Center. Gargantuan and almost goofy (the huge, gargoyle-like sculptures atop the building look like something out of Harry Potter), this granite-and-brick edifice is a uniquely postmodern homage to Chicago's great architectural past. The heavy, rusticated ground level recalls the Rookery; the stepped-back, arched windows are a reference to the great arches in the Auditorium Theatre of Roosevelt University; the swirling terra-cotta design is pinched from the Marquette Building; and the glass curtain wall on the west side is a nod to 1950s modernism. The library was named for the first African-

Continued on page 124

tHE skY's THE LImIt

Talk about baptism by fire. Although Chicago was incorporated in 1837, it wasn't until after the Great Fire of 1871 that the city really started to take shape. With four square miles gone up in flames, the town was a clean slate. The opportunity to make a mark on this metropolis drew a slew of architects, from Adler & Sullivan to H. H. Richardson and Daniel H. Burnham—names renowned in the annals of American architecture. A Windy City tradition was born: the city's continuously morphing skyline is graced with tall wonders designed by architecture's heavy hitters, including Mies van der Rohe; Skidmore, Owings & Merrill; and, most recently, Santiago Calatrava. In the next four pages, you'll find an eye-popping sampling of Chicago's great buildings and how they've pushed—and continue to push—the definition of even such a lofty term as "skyscraper."

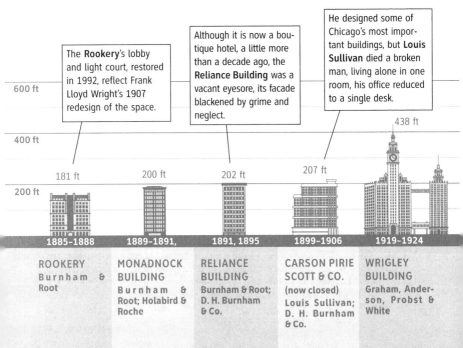

The **Rookery**'s lobby and light court, restored in 1992, reflect Frank Lloyd Wright's 1907 redesign of the space.

Although it is now a boutique hotel, a little more than a decade ago, the **Reliance Building** was a vacant eyesore, its facade blackened by grime and neglect.

He designed some of Chicago's most important buildings, but **Louis Sullivan** died a broken man, living alone in one room, his office reduced to a single desk.

600 ft
400 ft
200 ft

438 ft
181 ft
200 ft
202 ft
207 ft

1885–1888
1889–1891,
1891, 1895
1899–1906
1919–1924

ROOKERY
Burnham & Root

MONADNOCK BUILDING
Burnham & Root; Holabird & Roche

RELIANCE BUILDING
Burnham & Root; D. H. Burnham & Co.

CARSON PIRIE SCOTT & CO.
(now closed)
Louis Sullivan; D. H. Burnham & Co.

WRIGLEY BUILDING
Graham, Anderson, Probst & White

THE BIRTH OF THE SKYSCRAPER

Houses, churches, and commercial buildings of all sorts rose from the ashes after the blaze of 1871, but what truly put Chicago on the architectural map was the tall building. The earliest of these barely scrape the sky—especially when compared to what towers over us today—but in the late 19th century, structures such as William Le Baron Jenney's ten-story Home Insurance Building (1884) represented a bold push upward. Until then, the sheer weight of stone and cast-iron construction had limited how high a building could soar. But by using a lighter yet stronger steel frame and simply sheathing his building in a thin skin of masonry, Jenney blazed the way for ever taller buildings. And with only so much land available in the central business district, up was the way to go.

Although the Home Insurance Building was razed in 1931, Chicago's Loop remains a rich trove of early skyscraper design. Some of these survivors stand severe and solid as fortresses, while others manifest an almost ethereal quality. They—and their descendants along Wacker Drive, North Michigan Avenue, and Lake Shore Drive—reflect the technological, economic, and aesthetic forces that have made this city on the prairie one of the most dramatically vertical communities in the country.

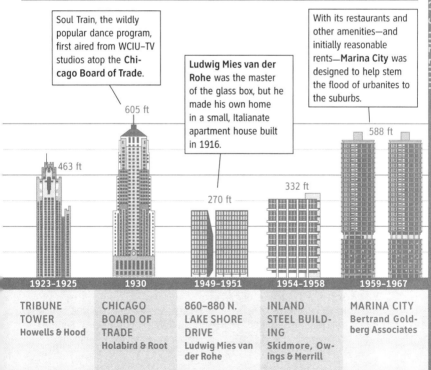

Soul Train, the wildly popular dance program, first aired from WCIU-TV studios atop the **Chicago Board of Trade**.

Ludwig Mies van der Rohe was the master of the glass box, but he made his own home in a small, Italianate apartment house built in 1916.

With its restaurants and other amenities—and initially reasonable rents—**Marina City** was designed to help stem the flood of urbanites to the suburbs.

463 ft

605 ft

270 ft

332 ft

588 ft

1923–1925	1930	1949–1951	1954–1958	1959–1967
TRIBUNE TOWER	CHICAGO BOARD OF TRADE	860–880 N. LAKE SHORE DRIVE	INLAND STEEL BUILDING	MARINA CITY
Howells & Hood	Holabird & Root	Ludwig Mies van der Rohe	Skidmore, Owings & Merrill	Bertrand Goldberg Associates

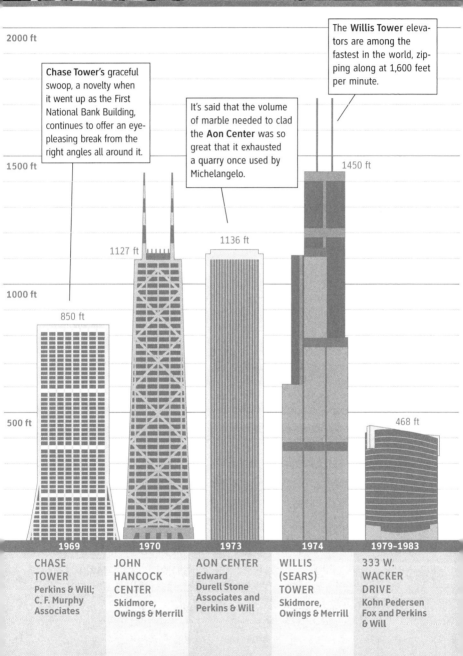

2000 ft

Chase Tower's graceful swoop, a novelty when it went up as the First National Bank Building, continues to offer an eye-pleasing break from the right angles all around it.

It's said that the volume of marble needed to clad the **Aon Center** was so great that it exhausted a quarry once used by Michelangelo.

The **Willis Tower** elevators are among the fastest in the world, zipping along at 1,600 feet per minute.

1500 ft

1450 ft

1127 ft

1136 ft

1000 ft

850 ft

500 ft

468 ft

1969	1970	1973	1974	1979–1983
CHASE TOWER	JOHN HANCOCK CENTER	AON CENTER	WILLIS (SEARS) TOWER	333 W. WACKER DRIVE
Perkins & Will; C. F. Murphy Associates	Skidmore, Owings & Merrill	Edward Durell Stone Associates and Perkins & Will	Skidmore, Owings & Merrill	Kohn Pedersen Fox and Perkins & Will

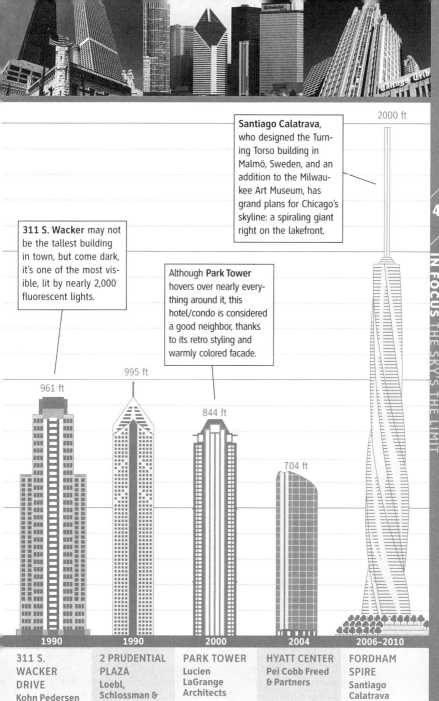

2000 ft

Santiago Calatrava, who designed the Turning Torso building in Malmö, Sweden, and an addition to the Milwaukee Art Museum, has grand plans for Chicago's skyline: a spiraling giant right on the lakefront.

311 S. Wacker may not be the tallest building in town, but come dark, it's one of the most visible, lit by nearly 2,000 fluorescent lights.

Although **Park Tower** hovers over nearly everything around it, this hotel/condo is considered a good neighbor, thanks to its retro styling and warmly colored facade.

995 ft

961 ft

844 ft

704 ft

1990	1990	2000	2004	2006–2010
311 S. WACKER DRIVE	2 PRUDENTIAL PLAZA	PARK TOWER	HYATT CENTER	FORDHAM SPIRE
Kohn Pedersen Fox	Loebl, Schlossman & Hackl	Lucien LaGrange Architects	Pei Cobb Freed & Partners	Santiago Calatrava

American mayor of Chicago, and the primary architect was Thomas Beeby, of the Chicago firm Hammond, Beeby & Babka.

The excellent **Children's Library** on the second floor, an 18,000-square-foot haven, has vibrant wall-mounted figures by Chicago imagist Karl Wirsum. Works by noted Chicago artists are displayed along a second-floor walkway above the main lobby. There's also an impressive Winter Garden with skylights on the ninth floor. Free programs and performances are offered regularly at the center. ☒ *400 S. State St., Loop* ☏ *312/747–4300* ⊕ *www.chipublib.org* ☯ *Mon.–Thurs. 9–9, Fri. and Sat. 9–5, Sun. 1–5.*

SKY-HIGH SANCTUARY

Chicago Temple. The Gothic-inspired headquarters of the First United Methodist Church of Chicago were built in 1923 by Holabird & Roche, complete with a first-floor sanctuary, 21 floors of office space, a sky-high chapel, and an eight-story spire (best viewed from the bridge across the Chicago River at Dearborn Street). Outside, along the building's east wall at ground level, stained-glass windows relate the history of Methodism in Chicago. Joan Miró's sculpture *Chicago* (1981) is in the small plaza just east of the church. ☒ *77 W. Washington St., Loop* ☏ *312/236-4548* ⊕ *www.chicagotemple.org.*

UP, UP, UP: THE SKYSCRAPERS

Aon Center. With the open space of Millennium Park at its doorstep, the Aon Center really stands out—even if its appearance isn't much to write home about. Originally built as the Standard Oil Building, the structure has changed names and appearances twice. Not long after it went up, its marble cladding came crashing down and the whole building was resheathed in granite. The massive building sits on a handsome (if rather sterile) plaza, where Harry Bertoia's wind-chime sculpture in the reflecting pool makes interesting sounds when a breeze blows. ☒ *200 E. Randolph Dr., Loop* .

PLAZA
BLISS: VISIT
THE MARC
CHAGALL
MOSAIC

Chase Tower. This building's graceful swoop—a novelty when it went up—continues to offer an eye-pleasing respite from all the right angles surrounding it. And its spacious plaza, with a mosaic by Marc Chagall called *The Four Seasons*, is one of the most enjoyable public spaces in the neighborhood. Designed by Perkins & Will and C. F. Murphy Associates in 1969, the building has been home to a succession of financial institutions (its most recent name was Bank One Plaza); names aside, it remains one of the more distinctive buildings around, not to mention one of the highest buildings in the Loop's true heart. ☒ *Bounded by Dearborn, Madison, Clark, and Monroe Sts., Loop* .

Hyatt Center. At 48 stories, the headquarters of this hospitality group is no giant, but it more than makes its mark on South Wacker Drive with a bold elliptical shape, a glass-faced street-level lobby rising 36 feet, and a pedestrian-friendly plaza. One of the city's newer towers, it displays a noticeable tweaking of the unrelieved curtain wall that makes many city streets forbidding canyons. Designed by Pei Cobb Freed & Partners, the building was completed in 2004. ✉ *71 S. Wacker Dr., Loop* .

CHECK OUT
THE 103RD
FLOOR
Fodor'sChoice
★
☾

Willis Tower. In Chicago, size matters. This soaring 110-story skyscraper, designed by Skidmore, Owings & Merrill in 1974, and previously named **Sears Tower** (the name was just changed by the new tenant, insurance broker Willis Group Holdings), was the world's tallest building until 1996 when the Petronas Towers in Kuala Lumpur, Malaysia, claimed the title (but Petronas counts its spire as part of the building). In 2004 Taipei 101 beat out the latter. Those bragging rights aside, the **Skydeck** is really something to boast about. Enter on Jackson Boulevard to take the ear-popping ride to the 103rd-floor observatory. Video monitors turn the 70-second elevator ride into a fun-filled, thrilling trip. On a clear day a whopping four states are visible: Illinois, Michigan, Wisconsin, and Indiana. (Check the visibility ratings at the security desk before you decide to ride up and take in the view.) At the top, interactive exhibits tell about Chicago's dreamers, schemers, architects, musicians, and sports stars. Computer kiosks in six languages help international travelers key into Chicago hot spots. Knee-High Chicago, a 4-foot-high exhibit with cutouts of Chicago sports and history at a child's eye-level, will entertain the kids. The Willis Tower also has spruced up the lower level with a food court, new exhibits, and a short movie about the city. Security is very tight, so figure in a little extra time for your visit to the Skydeck. Before you leave, don't miss the spiraling Calder mobile sculpture *The Universe* in the ground-floor lobby on the Wacker Drive side. ✉ *233 S. Wacker Dr.; for Skydeck, enter on Jackson Blvd. between Wacker Dr. and Franklin St., Loop* ☎ *312/875–9696* ⊕ *www.the-skydeck.com* ✉ *$12.95* ☽ *Apr.–Sept., daily 10–10; Oct.–Mar., daily 10–8.*

NIGHT LIGHTS
SUPREME
★

311 South Wacker Drive. The first of three towers intended for the site, this pale pink building is the work of Kohn Pedersen Fox, who also designed 333 West Wacker Drive, a few blocks away. The 1990 building's most distinctive feature is its Gothic crown, blindingly lighted at night. During migration season so many birds crashed into the illuminated tower that the building management was forced to tone down the lighting. The building has an inviting atrium, with palm trees and a splashy, romantic fountain. ✉ *311 S. Wacker Dr., at W. Jackson Blvd., Loop* ⊕ *www.311southwacker.com.*

WHAT ARE YOU LOOKIN' AT?

The Chicago Window, a popular window design used in buildings all over America (until air-conditioning made it obsolete), consists of a large fixed central pane with smaller moveable windows on each side. The picture window offered light, while the double-hung windows let in the Lake Michigan breeze. Developed in Chicago by engineer and architect William Le Baron Jenney, who pioneered the use of metal-frame construction in the 1880s, the Chicago Window helps to define buildings across the city.

Two Prudential Plaza. Nicknamed "Two Pru," this glass-and-granite giant is the older sibling of the 1955 tower at its feet (looking very 1950s indeed). Together with their neighbors they form a block-long business-oriented minicity. Two Prudential is the tallest reinforced concrete building in the city, and its blue detailing and beveled roof are instantly recognizable from afar. ⊠*180 N. Stetson Ave., Loop* ⊕*www.pruplazachicago.com.*

CURVES ON THE MARINA

River City. These concrete curves may look familiar; it was built in 1986 by Bertrand Goldberg, who also built the "corncobs" of Marina City. The complex features a 10-story atrium, commercial space, and 62-slip marina. It has great views of the water from the lobby. ⊠*800 S. Wells St., South Loop* .

SOUTH LOOP

Heading south from the heart of the Loop, you'll find Printers Row, where lofts that once clattered with linotype machines are now luxury real-estate morsels, as well as Dearborn Park, a residential enclave reclaimed from old rail yards.

HISTORIC BUILDINGS

Dearborn Station. Chicago's oldest standing passenger train station, a South Loop landmark, now serves as a galleria. Designed in Romanesque Revival style in 1885 by the New York architect Cyrus L. W. Eidlitz, it has a wonderful clock tower and a red-sandstone and redbrick facade ornamented with terra-cotta. Striking features inside are the marble floor, wraparound brass walkway, and arching wood-frame doorways. ⊠*47 W. Polk St., South Loop* ☎*312/554–8100* ⊘*Daily 8* AM–*5* PM.

Donohue Building. The first major printing facility in Printers Row, this 1883 building's main entrance is flanked by marble columns topped by ornately carved capitals, with tile work over the entrance set into a splendid granite arch. Note the beautiful ironwork and woodwork ornamenting the first-floor retail establishments. ⊠*711 S. Dearborn St., South Loop* .

Franklin Building. Built in 1888 and initially the home of the Franklin Company, a printing concern, this building has intricate decoration. The tile work on the facade leads up to *The First Impression*—a medieval scene illustrating the first application of the printer's craft. Above the entryway is a motto: THE EXCELLENCE OF EVERY ART MUST CONSIST IN THE COMPLETE ACCOMPLISHMENT OF ITS PURPOSE. ⊠*720 S. Dearborn St., South Loop* .

OLD SCHOOL HOLABIRD & ROCHE **Pontiac Building.** An early Chicago School skyscraper—note its classic rectangular shape and flat roof—the simple, redbrick, 14-story Pontiac was designed by Holabird & Roche in 1891 and is their oldest existing building in Chicago. ⊠*542 S. Dearborn St., South Loop* .

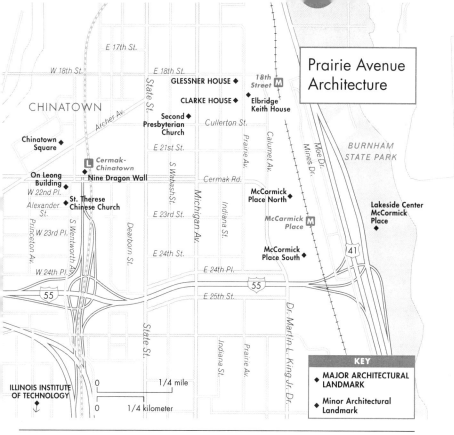

E 17th St.

W. 18th St.

E 18th St.

CHINATOWN

GLESSNER HOUSE ◆

CLARKE HOUSE ◆

18th
Street Ⓜ

Elbridge
Keith House

State St.

Archer Av.

Second ◆
Presbyterian
Church

Cullerton St.

Chinatown
Square

E 21st St.

Prairie Av.

Calumet Av.

Moe Dr.

Mines Dr.

BURNHAM
STATE PARK

Cermak-
Chinatown Ⓛ
Nine Dragon Wall

On Leong
Building

W 22nd Pl.

S Wabash St.

Cermak Rd.

Alexander
St.

St. Therese
Chinese Church

Michigan Av.

McCormick
Place North ◆

Lakeside Center
McCormick
Place ◆

E 23rd St.

Indiana St.

McCarmick
Place Ⓜ

Princeton Av.

S Wentworth Av.

Dearborn St.

E 24th St.

McCormick
Place South ◆

41

W 23rd Pl.

W 24th Pl.

55

E 24th Pl.

E 25th St.

55

State St.

Indiana St.

Prairie Av.

Dr. Martin L. King Jr. Dr.

ILLINOIS INSTITUTE
OF TECHNOLOGY

0   1/4 mile

0   1/4 kilometer

KEY
◆ MAJOR ARCHITECTURAL LANDMARK
◆ Minor Architectural Landmark

PRAIRIE AVENUE AND BEYOND

Heading even farther south parallel to the lakeshore, you'll find the Prairie Avenue Historic District; this was the neighborhood of choice for the city's movers and shakers in the mid-19th century. If you're a die-hard Mies van der Rohe fan, continue your journey south to check out his buildings on the campus of the Illinois Institute of Technology.

HISTORIC BUILDINGS

Clarke House. This Greek Revival dates from 1836, making it Chicago's oldest surviving building. It's a clapboard house in a masonry city, built for Henry and Caroline Palmer Clarke to remind them of the East Coast they left behind. The Doric columns and pilasters were an attempt to civilize Chicago's frontier image. The everyday objects and furnishings inside evoke a typical 1830s–60s middle-class home. ⊠*1827 S. Indiana Ave., Prairie Avenue District* ☎*312/745–0040* ☐*$10. Free Wed.; see Glessner House listing for combo-ticket information* ☉*Tours: Wed.– Sun. at noon and 2 PM.*

Fodor'sChoice   **Glessner House.** This fortresslike, Romanesque Revival 1886 residence is
★   the only surviving building in Chicago by architect H. H. Richardson,

MIES VAN DER ROHE, KOOLHAAS AND JAHN

Illinois Institute of Technology. "Less is more" claimed Mies van der Rohe, but for fans of the master's work, more is more at IIT. The campus holds an array of the kind of glass-and-steel structures for which he is most famous. Crown Hall is the jewel of the collection and has been designated a National Historic Landmark, but don't overlook the Robert F. Carr Memorial Chapel of St. Savior.

Additions to the campus include the McCormick Tribune Campus Center, designed by Dutch architect Rem Koolhaas, and new student housing by Helmut Jahn. The campus is about 1 mi west of Lake Shore Drive on 31st Street. Or take the El train's Green or Red Line to the 35th Street stop, and walk east two blocks to campus. ⊠ *S. State St. between 31st and 35th Sts., Douglas, south of Chinatown* ☏ *312/567–3000* ⊕ *www. iit.edu.*

who also designed Boston's Trinity Church. It's also one of the few great mansions left on Prairie Avenue, once home to such heavy hitters as retailer Marshall Field and meat-packing magnate Philip Armour. The area has lately seen the arrival of new, high-end construction, but nothing beats a tour of Glessner House, a remarkable relic of the days when merchant princes really lived like royalty. Enjoy the lavish interiors and the many artifacts, from silver pieces and art glass to antique ceramics and Isaac Scott carvings and furnishings. ⊠ *1800 S. Prairie Ave., Prairie Avenue* ☏ *312/326–1480* ⊕ *www.glessnerhouse.org* ✆ *$10. Combined admission to Glessner and nearby Clarke House $15. Free Wed.* ☉ *Tours Wed.–Sun. at 1 and 3* PM.

NEAR NORTH AND RIVER NORTH

Just a hop, skip, and a jump from the Loop's northern reaches and across the Chicago River are the Near North and River North neighborhoods. The magnet for most folks is North Michigan Avenue—aka the Magnificent Mile—a glittering stretch studded with shops and hotels. Saunter up this thoroughfare from the Michigan Avenue Bridge (or head south from Oak Street) and you'll see such sights as the Wrigley Building, the Tribune Tower, the Historic Water Tower, and the John Hancock Center.

HISTORIC BUILDINGS

Tribune Tower. In 1922 *Chicago Tribune* publisher Colonel Robert McCormick chose a Gothic design for the building that would house his paper, after rejecting a slew of functional modern designs by such notables as Walter Gropius, Eliel Saarinen, and Adolf Loos. Embedded in the exterior walls of the tower are chunks of material taken from famous sites around the world. Look for bits from the Parthenon, Westminster Abbey, the Alamo, St. Peter's Basilica, the Taj Mahal, and the Great Wall of China. On the ground floor are the studios of WGN

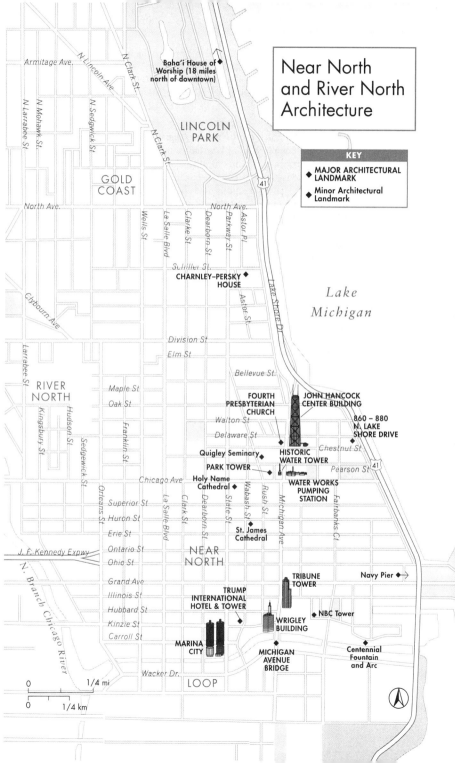

Near North and River North Architecture

KEY
◆ MAJOR ARCHITECTURAL LANDMARK
◆ Minor Architectural Landmark

Armitage Ave.

N Lincoln Ave.

N. Clark St.

Baha'i House of Worship (18 miles north of downtown) ◆

LINCOLN PARK

N. Clark St.

N Mohawk St.

N. Larrabee St.

N. Sedgwick St.

GOLD COAST

41

North Ave.

North Ave.

Wells St.

La Salle Blvd

Clarke St.

Dearborn St.

Parkway St.

Astor Pl.

Lake Shore Dr.

Lake Michigan

Clybourn Ave.

Schiller St.

CHARNLEY–PERSKY HOUSE ◆

Astor St.

Division St

Elm St

Bellevue St.

Larrabee St.

RIVER NORTH

Maple St

Oak St

FOURTH PRESBYTERIAN CHURCH ◆

JOHN HANCOCK CENTER BUILDING

860 – 880 N. LAKE SHORE DRIVE

Kingsbury St.

Hudson St.

Sedgwick St.

Franklin St.

Walton St.

Delaware St

Chestnut St.

Quigley Seminary ◆

HISTORIC WATER TOWER

PARK TOWER ◆

Pearson St.

41

Chicago Ave.

Holy Name Cathedral ◆

WATER WORKS PUMPING STATION

Orleans St.

La Salle Blvd

Clark St.

Dearborn St.

State St.

Wabash St.

Rush St.

Michigan Ave.

Fairbanks Ct.

Superior St

Huron St

Erie St

St. James Cathedral ◆

Ontario St

Ohio St

NEAR NORTH

J. F. Kennedy Expwy

Grand Ave

TRIBUNE TOWER ◆

Navy Pier ◆ →

N. Branch Chicago River

Illinois St

TRUMP INTERNATIONAL HOTEL & TOWER

Hubbard St

NBC Tower ◆

Kinzie St

WRIGLEY BUILDING

Carroll St

MARINA CITY

MICHIGAN AVENUE BRIDGE

Centennial Fountain and Arc

Wacker Dr.

LOOP

0   1/4 mi

0   1/4 km

radio, part of the *Chicago Tribune* empire, which also includes WGN-TV, cable-television stations, and the Chicago Cubs. (Modesty was not one of Colonel McCormick's prime traits: WGN stands for the *Tribune*'s self-bestowed nickname, World's Greatest Newspaper). ⊠*435 N. Michigan Ave., Near North* ☎312/222–3232 ⊕*www.chicago tribune.com.*

OFF THE BEATEN PATH ★ About 18 miles north of downtown Chicago (in Wilmette), rising near the lake, the **Baha'i House of Worship** is an intriguing, nine-sided building that incorporates architectural styles and symbols from many of the world's religions. With its delicate lacelike details and massive dome, the Louis Bourgeois design emphasizes the 19th-century Persian origins of the Baha'i religion. As symmetrical and harmonious as the building are the formal gardens that surround it. The temple is the U.S. center of the Baha'i faith, which advocates spiritual unity, world peace, race unity, and equality of the sexes. The visitor center has exhibits explaining the Baha'i faith; here you can also ask for a guide to show you around. ⊠*100 Linden Ave.* ☎847/853–2300 ⊕*www.us.bahai.org* ⊠*Free* ⊗*May–Sept., daily 10–8; Oct.–Apr., daily 10–5.*

Historic Water Tower. This famous Michigan Avenue structure, completed in 1867, was originally built to house a 137-foot standpipe that equalized the pressure of the water pumped by the similar pumping station across the street. Oscar Wilde uncharitably called it "a castellated monstrosity" studded with pepper shakers. Nonetheless, it remains a Chicago landmark and a symbol of the city's spirit of survival following the Great Chicago Fire of 1871. The small gallery inside has rotating art exhibitions of local interest. ⊠*806 N. Michigan Ave., at Pearson St., Near North* ⊠*Free* ⊗*Mon.–Sat. 10–6:30, Sun. 10–5.*

Water Works Pumping Station. Water is still pumped to some of the city residents at a rate of about 250 million gallons per day from this Gothic-style structure, which, along with the Water Tower across the street, survived the Great Chicago Fire of 1871. The acclaimed **Looking-glass Theatre** calls this place home. The station also houses a **Chicago Water Works Visitor Center** (☎877/244–2246 ⊕*www.877chicago. com* ⊗*Daily 7:30 AM–7 PM*), which has a sandwich shop. ⊠*163 E. Pearson St., at Michigan Ave., Near North .*

A NOD TO SEVILLE ★ **Wrigley Building.** Two structures built several years apart and later connected, the gleaming white Wrigley Building sports a clock tower inspired by the bell tower of the grand cathedral in Seville, Spain. The landmark headquarters of the chewing-gum company—designed by Graham, Anderson, Probst & White—was instrumental in transforming Michigan Avenue from an area of warehouses to one of the most desirable spots in the city. Be sure to check it out at night, when lamps bounce light off the building's gleaming terra-cotta facade. ⊠*400 and 410 N. Michigan Ave., Near North* ⊕*www.wrigley.com/wrigley/about/about_story_building.asp.*

TWO INTERPRETATIONS OF "TWINS"

Fodor's Choice
★
860–880 N. Lake Shore Drive. These twin apartment towers overlooking Lake Michigan were an early and eloquent realization of Mies van der Rohe's "less is more" credo, expressed in the high-rise. I-beams running up the facade underscore the building's verticality, while, inside, mechanical systems are housed in the center so as to leave the rest of each floor free and open to the spectacular views. Completed in 1951, the buildings were built in the famed International Style, which played a key role in transforming the look of American cities. ⊠*860–880 N. Lake Shore Dr., at E. Chestnut St., River North* .

SOME
CALL THEM
CORNCOBS
Marina City. Likened to everything from corncobs to the towers of Antonio Gaudí's Sagrada Familia in Barcelona, Goldberg's twin towers were a bold departure from the severity of the International Style, which began to dominate high-rise architecture beginning in the 1950s. Completed in 1967, the towers house condominium apartments (all pie-shape, with curving balconies). In addition to the apartments and marina, the complex now has four restaurants, the House of Blues nightclub, the Hotel Sax Chicago, and a huge bowling alley. ⊠*329 N. Dearborn St., River North* ☎*312/923–2000.*

BRIDGE OF BRIDGES

★
Michigan Avenue Bridge. Chicago is a city of bridges, and this is one of its most graceful. Completed in 1920, it features impressive sculptures on its four pylons representing major Chicago events: its exploration by Marquette and Joliet, its settlement by trader Jean Baptiste Point du Sable, the Fort Dearborn Massacre of 1812, and the rebuilding of the city after the Great Chicago Fire of 1871. The site of the fort, at the southeast end of the bridge, is marked by a commemorative plaque. As you stroll Michigan Avenue, be prepared for a possible delay; the bridge rises regularly to allow boat traffic to pass underneath. ⊠*Michigan Ave. at Wacker Dr., Near North* .

SKYSCRAPERS DELUXE

SKY-HIGH
"BIG JOHN"
Fodor's Choice
★
John Hancock Center. Designed by the same team that designed the Sears Tower (Skidmore, Owings & Merrill), this multi-use skyscraper is distinguished by its tapering shape and the enormous X braces, which help stabilize its 100 stories. Soon after it went up in 1970, it earned the nickname "Big John." No wonder: at 1,127 feet (1,502 feet counting the antennae at the top), 2.8 million square feet, and 46,000 tons of steel, there's nothing little about it. Packed with retail, parking, offices, a restaurant, and residences, it has been likened to a city within a city. Impressive from any angle, it offers mind-boggling views from a 94th floor observatory (as with Willis Tower, you can see to four states on clear days). For anyone afflicted with vertigo, a sensible option is a seat in the bar of the 95th floor Signature Room. The tab will be steep, but you'll be steady on your feet—*maybe.* ⊠*875 N. Michigan Ave., Near North* ☎*312/751–3681* ⊕*www.hancock-observatory.com and www.john*

hancockcenterchicago.com ✉*Observatory $15* ⊗*Daily 9* AM*–11* PM*; last ticket sold at 10:45* PM*.*

Trump International Hotel & Tower. The Chicago Sun-Times Building was torn down to make way for the real estate mogul's 92-story tower designed by Skidmore, Owings & Merrill. A spire elevates its height to a whopping 1,362 feet, and a concrete-reinforced structure (Willis Tower and the John Hancock Tower are reinforced by steel) adds stability. Still, the biggest thing the glassy, tiered monolith has going for it is an idyllic location along the Chicago River. While there's no viewing deck, the public can get picturesque views of downtown through the floor-to-ceiling windows of its 16th-floor restaurant, Sixteen, and bar, Rebar. ✉*401 N. Wabash Ave., Near North 60611* ⊕*www.trumpchicago hotel.com.*

Park Tower. A relative newcomer to the neighborhood (2000), this high-end hotel–condo combines retro touches (note the pitched roof) and quirky contemporary flourishes (check out the protruding bank of windows on the seventh floor). Designed by Lucien LaGrange Architects, the 67-story tower seems even taller than it really is (almost 900 feet), thanks to its unobstructed location across from the small park where the Historic Water Tower stands. ✉*800 N. Michigan Ave., at Chicago Ave., Near North* ⊕*www.parkhyatt.com.*

CHICAGO'S ANSWER TO A GOTHIC-REVIVAL CHURCH

REST YOUR FEET IN THE GRASSY COURTYARD **Fourth Presbyterian Church.** A welcome visual and physical oasis amid the high-rise hubbub of North Michigan Avenue, this Gothic Revival house of worship was designed by Ralph Adams Cram. Local architect Charles van Doren Shaw devised the cloister and companion buildings. The first big building erected on the avenue after the Chicago Fire, it counted among its congregants the city's elite. Noontime concerts are given every Friday in the sanctuary. ✉*126 E. Chestnut St., Near North* ☎*312/787–4570* ⊕*www.fourthchurch.org.*

WHAT ARE YOU LOOKIN' AT?

"**Curtain Wall**" is the term for the largely glass exterior surface of many modern buildings.

Unlike masonry construction, in which stone or brick support the weight of the building, a curtain wall is not a load-bearing system; rather, it is hung on the steel or concrete frame that holds the building up.

The Reliance Building (an early example), Willis Tower, and 333 W. Wacker Drive are all curtain-wall buildings.

FRANK LLOYD WRIGHT

1867–1959

The most famous American architect of the 20th century led a life that was as zany and scandalous as his architectural legacy was great. Behind the photo-op appearance and lordly pronouncements was a rebel visionary who left an unforgettable imprint on the world's notion of architecture. Nowhere else in the country can you experience Frank Lloyd Wright's genius as you can in Chicago and its surroundings.

Born two years after the Civil War ended, Wright did not live to see the completion of his late masterpiece, the Guggenheim Museum. His father preached and played (the Gospel and music) and dragged the family from the Midwest to New England and back before he up and left for good. Wright's Welsh-born mother, Anna Lloyd Jones, grew up in Wisconsin, and her son's roots would run deep there, too. Although his career began in Chicago and his work took him as far away as Japan, the home Wright built in Spring Green, Wisconsin—Taliesin—was his true center.

Despite all his dramas and financial instability (Wright was notoriously bad with money), the architect certainly produced. He was always ready to try something new—as long as it fit his notion of architecture as an expression of the human spirit and of human relationship with nature. By the time he died in 1959, Wright had designed over 1,000 projects, more than half of which were constructed.

Robie House, Chicago

WELCOME TO OAK PARK!

Oak Park is a leafy, quiet community just 10 miles west of downtown Chicago. When you arrive, head to the **Oak Park Visitors Center** (⊠ 158 N. Forest Ave. ☎ 708/848–1500 ⊕ www.visitoakpark.com ☉ Daily 10–5, until 4 in winter) and get oriented with a free map.

Next wander to the **Frank Lloyd Wright Home and Studio** (⊠ 951 Chicago Ave. ☎ 708/848–1606 🖨 708/848–1248 ⊕ www.wrightplus.org 🔟 $15; walking tour $15; combined $25 ☉ Tour times vary depending on the season. Tickets can be purchased in advance via the Web site). From the outside, the shingle-clad structure may not appear all that innovative, but it's here that Wright developed the

architectural language that still has the world talking.

Financed with a $5,000 loan from his mentor, Louis Sullivan, Wright designed the home when he was only 22. The residence manifests some of the spatial and stylistic characteristics that became hallmarks of Wright's work: there's a central fireplace from which other spaces seem to radiate and an enticing flow to the rooms. In 1974, the local Frank Lloyd Wright Home and Studio Foundation, together with the National Trust for Historic Preservation, embarked on a 13-year restoration that returned the building to its 1909 appearance.

Strolling Oak Park

GETTING HERE

To get to the heart of Oak Park by car, take the Eisenhower Expressway (I-290) west to Harlem Avenue. Head north on Harlem and take a right on Lake Street to get to the Oak Park Visitors Center at Forest Avenue and Lake Street (158 N. Forest Avenue), where there's ample free parking. You can also take the Green Line of the El to the last stop, the Harlem Avenue exit, or Metra's Union Pacific West Line from the Ogilvie Transportation Center in Citicorp Center downtown (500 W. Madison) to the Oak Park stop at Marion Street.

WOMEN, FIRE, SCANDAL . . . AND OVER 1,000 DESIGNS

The southeast entrance to the Frank Lloyd Wright Home & Studio in Oak Park.

1885 Wright briefly studies engineering at the University of Wisconsin.

1887 Wright strikes out for Chicago. He starts his career learning the basics with J. L. Silsbee, a residential architect. Later he joins the office of Adler & Sullivan as a drafter, just as the firm begins work on the massive Auditorium building.

1889 Wright marries Catherine Tobin; he builds her a home in suburban Oak Park, and they have six children together.

> "WHILE NEW YORK HAS REPRODUCED MUCH AND PRODUCED NOTHING, CHICAGO'S ACHIEVEMENTS IN ARCHITECTURE HAVE GAINED WORLD-WIDE RECOGNITION AS A DISTINCTIVELY AMERICAN ARCHITECTURE."

A leisurely stroll around the neighborhood will introduce you to plenty of **Frank Lloyd Wright houses.** All are privately owned, so you'll have to be content with what you can see from the outside. Check out 1019, 1027, and 1031 Chicago Avenue. These are typical Victorians that Wright designed on the sly while working for Sullivan.

For a look at the "real" Wright, don't miss the **Moore–Dugal Home** (1895) at 333 N. Forest Avenue, which reflects Wright's evolving architectural philosophy with its huge chimney and overhanging second story. Peek also at numbers 318, 313, 238, and 210, where you can follow his emerging modernism. Around the corner at 6 Elizabeth Court is the **Laura Gale House,** a 1909 project whose cantilevered profile foreshadows the thrusting planes Wright would create at Fallingwater decades later.

Between 1889 and 1913, Wright erected over two dozen buildings in Oak Park, so unless you're making an extended visit, don't expect to see everything. But don't leave town without a visit to

A landmark profile: the eastern facade of the architect's home and studio, Oak Park.

his 1908 **Unity Temple** (✉ 875 W. Lake St. ☎ 708/383–8873), a National Historic Landmark. Take a moment to appreciate Wright's fresh take on a place of worship; his bold strokes in creating a flowing interior; his unfailing attention to what was outside (note the skylights); and his dramatic use of concrete, which helps to protect the space from traffic noise.

4

IN FOCUS FRANK LLOYD WRIGHT

Interior, Unity Temple, Oak Park

1893 Wright launches his own practice in downtown Chicago.

1898 As his practice grows, Wright adds a studio to his Oak Park residence.

1905 Wright begins designing the reinforced concrete Unity Temple.

1908 Construction begins on the Robie House in Chicago's Hyde Park neighborhood.

Guided Tours

A great way to get to know Oak Park is to take advantage of the guided tours. Well-informed local guides take small groups on tours throughout the day, discussing various architectural details, pointing out artifacts from the family's life, and often telling amusing stories of the rambunctious Wright clan. Reservations are required for groups of 10 or more for the home and studio tours. Note that you need to arrive as early as possible to be assured a spot. Tours begin at the **Ginkgo Tree Bookshop,** which is part of the home and studio. The shop carries architecture-related books and gifts. You can pick up a map ($3.95) to find other examples of Wright's work that are within easy walking or driving distance, or you can join a guided tour of the neighborhood led by volunteers.

The Hemingway Connection

Frank Lloyd Wright wasn't the only creative giant to call Oak Park home. Ten years after Wright arrived, Ernest Hemingway was born here in 1899 in a proper Queen Anne, complete with turret. Wright was gone by the time Hemingway began to sow his literary oats. Good thing, too. It's doubtful the quiet village could have handled two such egos. *See* Get Out of Town: Brushing up your Ernest Hemingway pg. 26.

Frank Lloyd Wright's distinctive take on a modern dining room.

TIPS

Tickets go on sale every March 1 for the eagerly awaited annual **Wright Plus Benefit Housewalk,** your chance to see the interiors of some of Oak Park's most architecturally notable homes. Check out ⊕ www.wrightplus.org for more details.

Interior, Rookery, Chicago

1909 Wright leaves for Europe with Mamah Cheney, the wife of a former client; this puts an abrupt end to his family life, but Mrs. Wright does not consent to a divorce.

1911 Wright and Cheney settle at Taliesin, in Spring Green, Wisconsin.

1914 Mrs. Cheney, her two children, and several other people are killed by a deranged employee, who also sets fire to Taliesin. Wright rebuilds, as he does when the house burns again in 1922.

1915 With new mistress Miriam Noel in tow, the architect heads for Japan to oversee the building of the Imperial Hotel.

PRAIRIE STYLE PRIMER

Primarily a residential mode, Wright's Prairie style is characterized by ground-hugging masses; low-pitched roofs with deep eaves; and ribbon windows. Generally, Prairie houses are two-story affairs, with single story wings and terraces that project into the landscape. Brick and stone, earth tones, and unpainted wood underscore the perception of a house as an extension of the natural world. Wright designed free-flowing living spaces defined by alternating ceiling heights, natural light, and architectural screens. Although a number of other Chicago architects pursued this emerging aesthetic, Wright became its

> "ALL FINE ARCHITECTURAL VALUES ARE HUMAN VALUES, ELSE NOT VALUABLE."

acknowledged master. Though Wright designed dozens of Prairie style homes, the most well-known is Robie House, in Chicago's Hyde Park neighborhood. A dynamic composition of overlapping planes, it seems both beautifully anchored to the ground and ready to sail off with the arrival of a sharp breeze.

4

IN FOCUS FRANK LLOYD WRIGHT

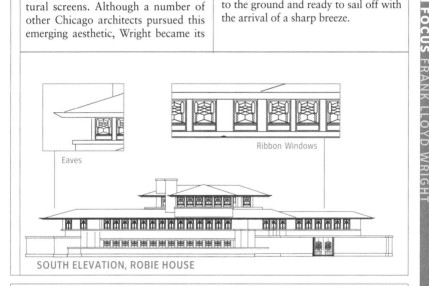

Ribbon Windows

Eaves

SOUTH ELEVATION, ROBIE HOUSE

The architect discusses a project with his assistants in Oak Park, 1958.

1922 Wright and his wife Catherine divorce.

1924 Wright marries Miriam Noel, but Noel is emotionally unsteady and the marriage implodes three years later.

1928 Wright marries Olga (Olgivanna) Lazovich Milanoff, who remains a compelling helpmate for the remainder of his life. They have one daughter together.

1930 The Taliesin Fellowship is launched; eager apprentices arrive at Spring Green to learn from the master.

WRIGHT BACK IN THE CITY

If you can't make it to Oak Park, there are a handful of notable—and memorable—Frank Lloyd Wright experiences to be had in the city.

★ Fodor's Choice Long and low, **Robie House** (1908–1910) grabs the ground and sends the eye zipping westward. Massive overhangs shoot out from the low-pitched roof and windows run along the facade in a glittering stretch. Inside, Wright's "open plan" echoes the great outdoors, as one space flows into another, while sunlight streaming through decorative leaded windows bathes the rooms in patterns. Robie House is nearing completion of a 10-year renovation but remains open to visitors. ⊠ 5757 S. Woodlawn Ave., Hyde Park ☎ 773/834–1847 💲 $15 ☾ Tour weekdays, hours vary; weekends every hour.

When he designed the **Isidore Heller House** in 1897, Frank Lloyd Wright was still moving toward the mature Prairie style achieved in the Robie House. As was common with Wright—and very uncommon then and now—the entrance to the Heller House is on the side of the structure. The house is not open to the public. ⊠ 5132 S. Woodlawn Ave., Hyde Park.

Frank Lloyd Wright designed the **Charnley–Persky House** with his mentor Louis Sullivan. This almost-austere residence represents one of Wright's first significant forays into residential design. Historians still squabble about who designed what here, but it's easy to imagine that the young go-getter had a hand in the cleanly rendered interior. Note how the geometric exterior looks unmistakably modern next to its fussy neighbors. ⊠ 1365 N. Astor St., Near North ☎ 312/915–0105 💲 Free Wed., $10 for Sat. tour that includes Madlener House (45 min). ☾ Apr.–Nov., tours Wed. at noon, Sat. at 10 AM and 1 PM; Dec.–Mar., 10 AM only. For larger groups, make reservations well in advance.

Stand outside the **Rookery** with its dizzyingly detailed facade and you'll think you've taken a wrong turn in your search for Wright. This early high-rise was designed by Burnham & Root. In 1905, Wright was hired to spruce up the building's interior court, which he lightened up by replacing terra-cotta with gilded white marble; adding pendant light fixtures; and gracing the stairway with urns, one of his favorite motifs. ⊠ 209 S. LaSalle St., Loop.

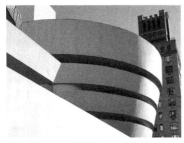

A New York icon: Wright's Guggenheim Museum.

1935 Fallingwater, the country home of Pittsburgh retailer Edgar J. Kaufmann, is completed at Bear Run, Pennsylvania.

1937 Wright begins construction of his winter getaway, Taliesin West, in Scottsdale, Arizona.

1956 Wright designs the Guggenheim Museum in New York. It is completed in 1959.

1957 Wright joins preservationists in saving Robie House from demolition.

1959 Wright dies at the age of 91.

Where to Eat

WORD OF MOUTH

"I went to Boka on North Halsted for my birthday dinner with a bunch of my girlfriends and had the best time. Absolutely wonderful food—extraordinary flavors and beautiful presentation without being pretentious and fussy. Then after dinner, if you skip dessert at Boka, you could stroll up to Armitage to window-peek and get Italian ice or ice cream."

—ChgoGal

Updated by
Kate Leahy

Chicago is a city sans snobbery when it comes to food. The collective appetite champions both haute and street cuisine. Mediocrity, at any price level, just doesn't fly here, which makes Chicago a reliably tasty town to tour.

Down low, Chicago is famed for hot dogs, deep-dish pizza, and Italian beef sandwiches. On the high end, the city launched celebrity chef Charlie Trotter, cutting-edge molecular gastronomist Grant Achatz of Alinea, and Rick Bayless, who introduced the nation to authentic regional Mexican cuisine at Frontera Grill.

The city is home to more than 7,000 restaurants, the most prominent of which cluster close to downtown expense accounts. But many of the most exciting restaurants that have opened in the past several years have been in residential neighborhoods, from Alinea in Lincoln Park to Spacca Napoli and Sola on the Far North Side to Takashi in Bucktown.

Local establishments, such as barbecue-centric Smoque and hot-dog spot Hot Doug's, both on the Far North Side, find that drawing crowds from all over the city is a matter of focusing on simple food and doing it well. At the same time, downtown development hasn't slowed down, attracting big name investors (Donald Trump) and spurring local restaurant groups to open new restaurants (Bin 36's new Italian concept, A Mano, is located underneath its River North location). Meanwhile, Chicago's steakhouse tradition continues to wield influence on the restaurant scene, though big-name chefs, including David Burke, have expanded expectations, taking the experience beyond men's-club exclusive.

In coming years expect to see more star Chicago chefs open casual eateries (Michael Kornick of mk has a burger concept on the way), eager to feed a populace that knows good food and isn't willing to accept anything less than the best.

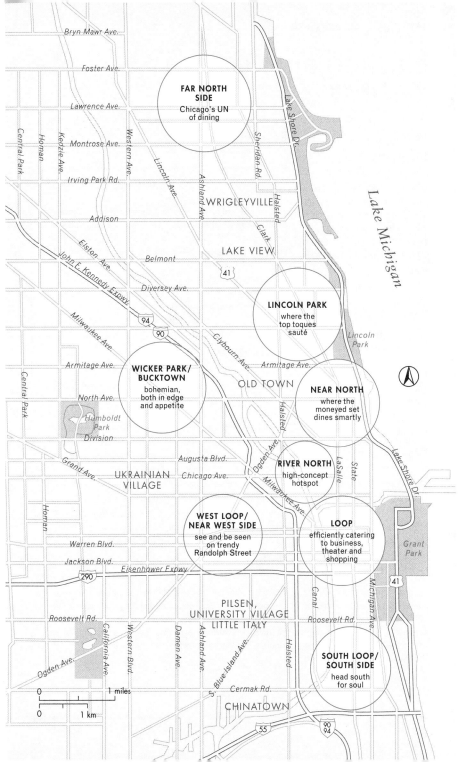

CHICAGO DINING PLANNER

Eating Out Strategy

Where should we eat? With thousands of Chicago eateries competing for your attention, it may seem like a daunting question. But fret not—our expert writers and editors have done most of the legwork.

The selections here represent the best this city has to offer— from hot dogs to haute cuisine.

Search "Best Bets" for top recommendations by price, cuisine, and experience. Sample local flavor in the neighborhood features. Or find a review quickly in the alphabetical listings. Delve in, and enjoy!

Smoking

Smoking is prohibited in all enclosed public spaces in Chicago, including restaurants and bars.

Tipping and Taxes

In most restaurants, tip the waiter 18%–20%. (To figure the amount quickly, just take 10% of the bill and double it.) Bills for parties of six or more sometimes include the tip already.

Reservations

Plan ahead if you're determined to snag a sought-after reservation. Some renowned restaurants are booked weeks or months in advance.

But you can get lucky at the last minute if you're flexible— and friendly. Most restaurants keep a few tables open for walk-ins and VIPs. Show up for dinner early (5:30 PM) or late (after 9 PM) and politely inquire about any last-minute vacancies or cancellations.

If you're calling a few days ahead of time, ask if you can be put on a waiting list. Occasionally, an eatery may ask you to call the day before your scheduled meal to reconfirm: don't forget or you could lose out.

What to Wear

In general, Chicagoans are neat but casual dressers; only at the top-notch dining rooms do you see a more formal style.

But the way you look can influence how you're treated— and where you're seated. Generally speaking, jeans will suffice at most table-service restaurants in the $ to $$ range. Moving up from there, many pricier restaurants require jackets, and a few insist on ties.

In reviews, we mention dress only when men are required to wear a jacket or a jacket and tie.

Note that shorts, sweatpants, and sports jerseys are rarely appropriate. When in doubt, call the restaurant and ask.

Children

Though it's unusual to see children in the dining rooms of Chicago's elite restaurants, dining with youngsters in the city does not have to mean culinary exile. Many of the restaurants reviewed in this chapter are excellent choices for families. They are marked with a ☺ symbol.

Wine

Although some of the city's top restaurants still include historic French vintages, most sommeliers are now focusing on small-production, lesser-known wineries. Some are even keeping their wine lists purposefully small, so that they can change them frequently to match the season and the menu. Half bottles are becoming more prevalent, and good wines by the glass are everywhere. Don't hesitate to ask for recommendations. Even restaurants without a sommelier on staff will appoint knowledgeable servers to lend a hand with wine selections.

Prices

If you're watching your budget, be sure to ask the price of daily specials recited by the waiter or captain. The charge for specials at some restaurants is noticeably out of line with the other prices on the menu. Beware of the $10 bottle of water; ask for tap water instead. And always review your bill.

If you eat early or late you may be able to take advantage of a prix-fixe deal not offered at peak hours. Most upscale restaurants offer great lunch deals, with special menus at cut-rate prices designed to give customers a true taste of the place.

Credit cards are widely accepted, but many restaurants (particularly smaller ones downtown) accept only cash. If you plan to use a credit card it's a good idea to double-check its acceptability when making reservations or before sitting down to eat.

WHAT IT COSTS

	¢	$	$$	$$$	$$$$
FOR ONE PERSON	under $10	$10–$18	$19–$27	$28–$36	over $36

Prices are per person for a typical main course or equivalent combination of smaller dishes. Note: if a restaurant offers only prix-fixe (set-price) meals, it has been given the price category that reflects the full prix-fixe price.

In This Chapter

Spotlight On

5

Orientation

Throughout the chapter, you'll see mapping symbols and coordinates (⊕) after property reviews. To locate the property on a map, turn to the Chicago Dining & Lodging Atlas at the end of this chapter. The first number after the (⊕) symbol indicates the map number. Following that is the property's coordinate on the map grid.

BEST BETS FOR CHICAGO DINING

With thousands of restaurants to choose from, how will you decide where to eat? Fodor's writers and editors have selected their favorite restaurants by price, cuisine, and experience in the Best Bets lists below. In the first column, Fodor's Choice properties represent the "best of the best" in every price category. You can also search by neighborhood for excellent eats—just peruse the following pages. Or find specific details about a restaurant in the full reviews, listed alphabetically later in the chapter.

Fodor's Choice ★

Alinea, p. 166
Avec, p. 195
Bin 36, p. 181
Blackbird, p. 195
Boka, p. 171
Hopleaf Bar, p. 162
Hot Doug's, p. 163
North Pond, p. 172
Urban Belly, p. 164

¢

Billy Goat Tavern, p. 176
Hot Doug's, p. 163
Milk & Honey Café, p. 201
Mr. Beef, p. 185
Smoque BBQ, p. 163

$

The Bristol, p. 201
Hopleaf Bar, p. 162
Mado, p. 200

MANA Food Bar, p. 201
Urban Belly, p. 164

$$

Avec, p. 195
Bin 36, p. 181
Frontera Grill, p. 183
Hot Chocolate, p. 200
Mercat a la Planxa, p. 193
Sola, p. 163

$$$

Blackbird, p. 195
Boka, p. 171
Graham Elliot, p. 184
Green Zebra, p. 196
North Pond, p. 172
Takashi, p. 200

$$$$

Alinea, p. 166
Charlie Trotter's, p. 171

L20, p. 171
Sixteen, p. 191
Spiaggia, p. 180

Best by Cuisine

AMERICAN

Billy Goat Tavern, p. 176
Epic Burger, p. 192
Hot Doug's, p. 163
Lou Mitchell's, p. 197

ASIAN

Red Light, p. 198
Urban Belly, p. 164

CHINESE

Lao Sze Chuan, p. 194
Phoenix, p. 195

FRENCH

Brasserie Jo, p. 181
Everest, p. 173
L20, p. 171
Le Bouchon, p. 200
Les Nomades, p. 177
Marché, p. 197

ITALIAN

A Mano, p. 181
Osteria via Stato, p. 185
Spacca Napoli, p. 163
Spiaggia, p. 180
Terragusto, p. 164

JAPANESE

Japonais, p. 184
Kamehachi, p. 177
Takashi, p. 200

LATIN AMERICAN

Coobah, p. 165
Nacional 27, p. 185

MEXICAN

De Cero Taqueria, p. 196
Frontera Grill, p. 183
Salpicón, p. 179
Topolobampo, p. 191

PIZZA

Piece, p. 201
Pizzeria Uno, p. 186
Spacca Napoli, p. 163

SPANISH

Café Ba-Ba-Reeba, p. 171

Café Iberico, p. 182

Mercat a la Planxa, p. 193

Custom House, p. 192

David Burke's Prime-house, p. 182

Gibsons Steakhouse, p. 176

Keefer's, p. 184

THAI

Arun's, p. 162

Thai Classic, p. 166

Vong's Thai Kitchen, p. 191

VEGETARIAN

Green Zebra, p. 196

Lula Café, p. 163

MANA Food Bar, p. 201

Best by Experience

BAR FOOD

Hopleaf Bar, p. 162

Juicy Wine Company, p. 196

Rockit Bar & Grill, p. 186

Twin Anchors Restaurant & Tavern, p. 180

BUSINESS DINING

NoMI, p. 178

Seasons Restaurant, p. 179

Sepia, p. 199

Spiaggia, p. 180

Tavern at the Park, p. 175

CAFÉ EATS

Bin 36, p. 181

Café Selmarie, p. 162

Julius Meinl Café, p. 165

Milk & Honey, p. 201

Pierrot Gourmet, p. 178

CHICAGO CLASSICS

Billy Goat Tavern, p. 176

Gene & Georgetti, p. 183

Mr. Beef, p. 185

Twin Anchors Restaurant & Tavern, p. 180

Pizzeria Uno, p. 186

CHILD-FRIENDLY

Ann Sather, p. 164

Café Selmarie, p. 162

Ed Debevic's, p. 183

Eleven City Diner, p. 192

Piece, p. 201

Scoozi!, p. 186

Smoque BBQ, p. 163

GOOD FOR GROUPS

Fogo de Chão, p. 183

Park Grill, p. 174

The Parthenon, p. 198

HOT SPOTS

Avec, p. 195

Blackbird, p. 195

The Bristol, p. 201

Green Zebra, p. 196

L20, p. 171

Sepia, p 199

BEST HOTEL DINING

Avenues, p. 176

Custom House, p. 192

Mercat a la Planxa, p. 193

Seasons Restaurant, p. 179

Sixteen, p. 191

MOST INNOVATIVE

Alinea, p. 166

Avenues, p. 176

Charlie Trotter's, p. 171

Graham Elliot, p. 184

Moto, p. 197

LATE-NIGHT DINING

Avec, p. 195

Hopleaf Bar, p. 162

Nacional 27, p. 185

Red Light, p. 198

Vivo, p. 199

PRETHEATER MEAL

Atwood Café, p. 173

Boka, p. 171

Rhapsody, p. 175

Riva, p. 178

Sola, p. 163

QUIET MEAL

Arun's, p. 162

Avenues, p. 176

Charlie Trotter's, p. 171

Les Nomades, p. 177

North Pond, p. 172

SPECIAL OCCASION

Charlie Trotter's, p. 171

Everest, p. 173

L20, p. 171

North Pond, p. 172

TRU, p. 180

BEST VIEWS

NoMI, p. 178

North Pond, p. 172

Park Grill, p. 174

Sixteen, p. 191

Spiaggia, p. 180

5

FAR NORTH SIDE

Some of Chicago's best ethnic food is found on the Far North Side, a vast catchall district north of Irving Park Road running all the way to suburban Evanston.

Within its borders lie several food-happy neighborhoods, none more lively than Devon Avenue, traditional home to Chicago's Indian community and lined with Indian restaurants, Bollywood video stores, and sari shops as well as Russian bakeries and Israeli eateries.

Two classic Chicago neighborhoods, the Swede-settled Andersonville and the German enclave Lincoln Square, have lured a critical mass of retailers, delis, bars, and restaurants that warrant an afternoon or evening out. Both are pedestrian-friendly; Lincoln Square lies on the Brown Line El, though Andersonville is better reached via cab. To reach the other dining destinations in this area, such as **Arun's** (⊠ *4156 N. Kedzie Ave.* ☎ *773/539–1909*), **Hot Doug's** (⊠ *3325 N. California Ave.* ☎ *773/751–1500*), and **Smoque BBQ** (⊠ *3800 N. Pulaski Rd.* ☎ *773/545–7427*), you may want to consider renting a car, or expect a longish cab ride from downtown.

GASTROPUBBING

Hopleaf Bar (⊠ *5148 N. Clark St.* ☎ *773/334–9851*) owner Michael Roper pairs food and beer, with sometimes surprising results. Here's what Roper recommends: Belgian-style mussels paired with Belgian blond ales like Leffe or Triple Karmeliet. Why: "Steamed with herbs and shallots, the mussels go great with blonds." For a snack, try a sandwich of ham, Gruyère cheese, and apple-tarragon slaw with a hoppy Lagunitas. Why: "Bigger, hoppier beers stand up to cured ham and bold cheese." On a cold night, dig into: Flemish beef stew with a pint of St. Bernardus Apt 12. Why: "Rich, malty St. Bernardus matches the caramelized beef."

NOSHING UP NORTH

German (Lincoln Square) vs. Swede (Andersonville). Germans settled Lincoln Square, and the Swedes populated Andersonville, two north-side neighborhoods not far apart. Do one, or make it a double header.

	LINCOLN SQUARE	ANDERSONVILLE
Shop	Since 1875, Chicagoans have been shopping at **Merz Apothecary** (⊠4716 N. Lincoln Ave., south of Lawrence Ave. ☎773/989–0900) for homeopathic remedies, health-promoting tonics and teas, and hard-to-find European lozenges and fennel digestive drops.	Stop into **City Olive** (⊠5408 N. Clark St., north of Foster Ave. ☎773/878–5408) for a carefully selected range of olive oils and non-edibles, including olive serving dishes and olive oil–based lotions.
Sip	Try a stein of Spaten or a shot of the Goldwasser, a spiced citrus liqueur with flakes of 22k gold, at the Bavarian-themed **Huettenbar** (⊠4721 N. Lincoln Ave., south of Lawrence Ave. ☎773/561–2507).	Drink free coffee at the stand-up bar while noshing on pastries at **Swedish Bakery** (⊠5348 N. Clark St. ☎773/561–8919). Our favorites are the buttery spritz cookies and cinnamon streusel coffee cake.
Sup	The old-school **Chicago Brauhaus** (⊠4732 N. Lincoln Ave. ☎773/784–4444) serves up mugs of suds, platters of brats, and jovial tunes by a live oompah band nightly.	Herring salad, Swedish meatballs, and smorgasar (open-faced sandwiches) are on the menu at **Svea** (⊠5236 N. Clark St. ☎773/275–7738).

CHICAGO HOT DOGS

Two far-flung spots on the North Side warrant the trek for a dog. At **Superdawg Drive-In,** carhops deliver your chow (⊠*6363 N. Milwaukee Ave., at Devon Ave.* ☎*773/763–0660*). Serving haut dogs, **Hot Doug's** does the classic Chicago all-beef as well as a rotating range of exotic "encased meats," including kangaroo and rabbit (⊠*3324 N. California Ave., at Henderson St.* ☎*773/279–9550*).

Belgian
Hopleaf Bar, $

Bistro
Bistro Campagne, $$

Café
Café Selmarie, $

German
Chicago Brauhaus, $

Hot Dogs
Hot Doug's, ¢

Italian
Spacca Napoli, $
Terragusto, $

New American
Sola, $$

Scandinavian
Svea, ¢

Southern
Smoque BBQ, ¢

Thai
Arun's, $$$$

5

LINCOLN PARK AND LAKEVIEW

Of Chicago's 77 official neighborhoods, the North Side's popular Lincoln Park is definitely worth exploring. From a food perspective, this neighborhood is host to several of Chicago's best restaurants, including Charlie Trotter's and Alinea.

Named for the lakefront park it borders, Lincoln Park is often a first stop for recent Chicago transplants moving to the city as well as the permanent residence of families inhabiting pricey brownstones. On commercial thoroughfares such as Clark, Halsted, and Armitage, you can spend an afternoon bouncing back and forth from great restaurants and cafés to hip shops.

For more casual fare, head north of Lincoln Park to Lakeview, which includes the sub-districts of Wrigleyville, which buffers Wrigley Field and hosts many bars serving beer and brats, and Boy's Town, which refers to the gay district along Halsted between Belmont and Diversey. Here the bars are equally raucous but the food is more refined.

URBAN GARDEN

Chef Bruce Sherman has an idyllic spot in **North Pond** (✉ *2610 N. Cannon Dr.* ☎ *773/477–5845*), a restaurant lodged in a former skater's warming hut on the edge of a duck pond in the heart of Lincoln Park. To this greensward he has added a kitchen garden, growing almost all his own herbs and many of his own vegetables in the height of summer, resulting in urban-farm-to-table salads and sorbets. The only challenge is keeping the neighbors out of the garden. "Have people helped themselves? Of course, we're in a public park," Sherman says.

LINCOLN PARK—A TOP CHEF HUB

From the corner of Armitage Avenue and Halsted Street, head a half block west and you'll arrive at Charlie Trotter's, kitchen of the eponymous chef. The other way, two blocks south, is Alinea with its chef Grant Achatz, in many ways the next-generation Trotter.

Restaurant name	CHARLIE TROTTER'S (⊠816 W. Armitage Ave. ☎773/248–6228)	ALINEA (⊠1723 N. Halsted St. ☎312/867–0110)
What the name means	Eponymous (Don't you know who I am?)	A typographical symbol signifying the start of a new thought
Culinary Style	Modern American; meticulous presentation; dedication to organic and free-range products	Cutting-edge American; daring presentation; flavor is as important as form
Menu	8-course degustation menus (grand and vegetable) change daily	12-course tasting menu or 24-course "tour;" menu changes often
Wow Factor	Restrained. Sources luxury ingredients (Iranian pistachios, Spanish percebes) from around the world	Unleashed. Custom service pieces reinvent fork and knife into spindles, tabletop pedestals.
Theater Analogy	Shakespearean drama	Performance art

EATING AROUND WRIGLEY FIELD

Hungry fans can find good eats in any direction, though most options run north and south of the ballpark. Go south on Sheffield Street three blocks to **Sheffield's** (⊠3258 N. Sheffield St., at School St. ☎773/281–4989) for pulled-pork barbecue best consumed in the beer garden. Go south on Clark two blocks to **Tryst** (⊠3485 N. Clark St., at Cornelia Ave. ☎773/755–3980) for small plates such as chicken satay and beef sliders paired with strong martinis. Go north on Sheffield three blocks to **Pizza Rustica** (⊠3913 N. Sheridan Rd., at Byron St. ☎773/404–8955, BYOB) for pizza and pastas from an Italian owner.

American
Kitsch'n on Roscoe, $
North Pond, $$$
Orange, ¢–$

Asian Fusion
Yoshi's Cafe, $$

Bistro
Mon Ami Gabi, $$

Café
Julius Meinl Cafe, ¢

Cutting-Edge
Alinea, $$$$

French
Geja's Cafe, $$$$

Italian
Mia Francesca, $

Latin American
Coobah, $

New American
Boka, $$$
Charlie Trotter's, $$$$
Erwin Cafe, $$

Scandinavian
Ann Sather, $

Seafood
L2O, $$$$

Spanish
Café Ba-Ba-Reeba!, $

Thai
Thai Classic, ¢

Turkish
Turquoise Restaurant and Cafe, $$

5

THE LOOP

Business, theater, and shopping converge in the Loop, the downtown district south of the Chicago River distinguished by the elevated train that circles it.

Long the city's financial center, the Loop is commuter central for inbound office workers. It is also Chicago's historic home of retail, where the flagship Marshall Field's (now Macy's) and Carson Pirie Scott (now defunct) made State Street a great shopping street. Newcomers like Old Navy and TJ Maxx update the mix, appealing to tourists as well as locals.

As a theater district, the Loop hosts the Tony-awarded Goodman Theater, which mounts its own productions, as well as the Oriental, Palace, and Bank of America theaters, which generally run Broadway tours.

In feeding these diverse audiences, Loop restaurants run the gamut from quick-service to high-volume and special-occasion. Beware noontime and pre-curtain surges (you'll need a reservation for the latter).

NEW BAGEL?

Hannah's Bretzel
(✉ *180 W. Washington Ave., at Wells St.* ☎ *312/621–1111*) aims to replace the New World–popularized bagel with the Old World–ubiquitous soft pretzel. A bretzel, that is, made of organic wheat and cooked in imported German ovens by Stuttgart native and former ad exec Florian Pfahler, who quit the corporate world to train in the art of baking bretzels. Get them spread with organic butter, stuffed with Gruyère and cucumbers, or slathered in Nutella. The results are lighter and tastier than a bagel sandwich, closer to a baguette with serious holes.

TOP PICKS FOR DINING IN THE LOOP

Whether you're looking for pretheater eats, a quick bite on the go, or an intimate dining room, restaurants in the Loop deliver some of the city's best dining experiences.

☞ *For pre-theater dining, try*: Italian pastas and chops at **Petterino's** (✉*150 N. Dearborn St., at Randolph St.* ☎*312/422–0150*), adjacent to the Goodman Theater; **312 Chicago** (✉*136 N. LaSalle St., at Randolph St.* ☎*312/696–2420*) for seasonal Italian adjacent to the Palace Theater; or **Rhapsody** (✉*65 E. Adams St., at Michigan Ave.* ☎*312/786–9911*) for contemporary American.

☞ *For a break while shopping, stop into*: **Atwood Café** (✉*1 W. Washington Ave., at State St.* ☎*312/368–1900*) for seasonal American comfort food and picture-window views of the bustle; **Seven on State** (✉*111 N. State St., 7th fl., at Randolph St.* ☎*312/781–1000*), within Macy's, for upscale food-court fare; or **Patty Burger** (✉*72 E. Adams St., at Wabash Ave.* ☎*312/987–0900*) for burgers in a retro diner setting.

☞**Everest** (✉*440 S. LaSalle St., 40th fl., at Van Buren St.* ☎*312/663–8920*) serves chef Jean Joho's refined French food and city views. Try **Park Grill** (✉*11 N. Michigan Ave., at Randolph St.* ☎*312/521–7275*) in thronged Millennium Park for contemporary fare.

FAST FOOD WITH A PEDIGREE

One of Chicago's most acclaimed chefs, Rick Bayless of Frontera Grill, has opened a fast-food outlet in the Loop. Bayless call his efforts "authentic Mexican street food" at **Frontera Fresco** in the Seven on State (✉*111 N. State St., 7th fl., at Randolph St.* ☎*312/781–1000*) food court in Macy's serving *tortas* (Mexican sandwiches), tamales, and quesadillas with Bayless's authentic regional flair.

American
Atwood Café, $$
Park Grill, $$
Tavern at the Park, $$

French
Everest, $$$$

International
Aria, $$$
Shikago, $$

Italian
312 Chicago, $$
Petterino's, $$
Trattoria No. 10, $$

New American
Rhapsody, $$

Russian
Russian Tea Time, $$

Seafood
Catch 35, $$
Nick's Fishmarket, $$$

Southern
Heaven on Seven, $

Steakhouse
The Grillroom Chophouse & Winebar, $$
Morton's, The Steakhouse, $$$$

5

NEAR NORTH

Chicago's tony Near North district, home to shopping's Magnificent Mile and the residential Gold Coast, specializes in upscale restaurants that suit the clientele like a bespoke suit.

It's the land of posh hotels (Peninsula, Ritz-Carlton, Four Seasons, Park Hyatt) and their posh dining rooms (Avenues, The Café, Seasons Restaurant, and NoMI, respectively), as well as stand-alone stars like Tru, Spiaggia, and Les Nomades. Even the Mag Mile's toniest retailers such as Polo/Ralph Lauren with the see-and-be-seen RL restaurant are in on the feed. If you're planning on dining on Michigan Avenue while you shop it, expect to spend like a platinum cardholder.

Just to the west of the Gold Coast lies the equally moneyed but more liberal Old Town district, home to Second City improv theater and a spate of restaurants that the actors can afford, at least once in a paycheck cycle.

EXPER-CHEESE

Contemporary Italian restaurant **Spiaggia** (✉ *980 N. Michigan Ave.* ☎ *312/280–2750*) works hard to get things right, down to installing a *cava di stagionatura,* or cheese cave. Why? It ages the cheese properly, says chef Tony Montuano, by controlling the temperature and humidity of between 15 and 40 cheeses the restaurant serves before or after dinner. Stocking those is Remy Ayesh, Spiaggia's *formaggiaio*—or cheese guy. Don't expect an atmospheric, bat-dwelling cave; this one's a 7-by-3-foot cooler visible from the dining room. Occasionally Ayesh will give a tour of the "cave" to help cheese aficionados choose their cheese.

CHICAGO'S CHICEST TABLES

If you want to rub elbows with Chicago's glitterati—real-estate scions, ladies who lunch, and local media figures—head to:

✕ **RL** (✉*115 E. Chicago Ave.* ☎*312/475–1100*), especially at lunch when shoppers at Ralph Lauren/Polo rest their Amex cards and order the lobster club.

✕ **NoMI** (✉*800 N. Michigan Ave.* ☎*312/239–4030*), on the 7th floor of the Park Hyatt Chicago. Be sure to specify that you want a table overlooking the landmark Water Tower under the Dale Chihuly chandeliers.

✕ **Gibsons Steakhouse** (✉*1028 N. Rush St..* ☎*312/266–8999*), a classic Chicago meat market popular with moneyed men, particularly those who play on and manage sports teams.

✕ **Bar at the Peninsula Chicago** (✉*108 E. Superior St., at Michigan Ave.* ☎*312/573–6766*), where local society types start their evenings with Champagne and end with privately blended bourbon in the leather-walled, art-filled barroom.

✕ **TRU** (✉*676 N. St. Clair St.* ☎*312/202–0001*), where there's an Andy Warhol silkscreen on the wall, a caviar course served on a table-top crystal staircase, and a multicourse dessert tasting for the truly indulgent.

BEST REFUELING STOPS FOR SHOPPERS

Around the corner from Tiffany & Co., **Pierrot Gourmet** (✉*108 E. Superior St.* ☎*312/573–6749*), run by the Peninsula Chicago hotel, serves savory soups and "tartines," open-face sandwiches. Three blocks from designer-lined Oak Street, **Big Bowl** (✉*6 E. Cedar St.* ☎*312/640–8888*) does a savory and speedy job with Asian stir-fry and noodles (and tiki-inspired tropical drinks). At Nordstrom, look no farther than the **Nordstrom Café** (✉*55 E. Grand Ave., at Michigan Ave.* ☎*312/464–1515*) on the 4th floor for paninis and salads.

American
Mike Ditka's, $$$
Pump Room, $$
RL, $$
Signature Room at the 95th, $$$
Twin Anchors Restaurant, $$
Viand, $$

Bistro
Bistro 110, $$
Bistrot Margot, $$

Burger
Billy Goat Tavern, ¢

Café
Fox & Obel Market, ¢
Pierrot Gourmet, $

Chinese
Shanghai Terrace, $$

Cutting-Edge
Avenues, $$$$

French
Les Nomades, $$$$

Italian
Spiaggia, $$$$

Japanese
Kamehachi, $

Mexican
Salpicón, $$

New American
NoMI, $$$$
Seasons Restaurant, $$$$
TRU, $$$$

Seafood
McCormick/Schmick's, $$$
Riva, $$$

Southern
Table Fifty-Two $$$

Steakhouse
Gibsons Steakhouse, $$$$

5

RIVER NORTH

The Chicago River bends around this 19th-century-factory district, which was refurbished and reclaimed in the 1980s by art galleries, urban-living pioneers, and chef-owned eateries to become a crown jewel in the city's dining scene.

Today the art and design trades—the mammoth Chicago Merchandise Mart anchors River North—patronize the area's trendy eateries, including Japonais, Sushi Samba Rio, and Nacional 27, as well its refined restaurants, such as mk, Naha, and Topolobampo. But while these notable restaurants have flourished, other independent eateries in the area have been forced out by soaring real-estate values and new high-rise developments. In the place of casual indie concepts, chains like Rainforest Café and ESPN Zone have taken root and gained market share.

In spite of all the change, down-home Chicago fare still thrives here, including the classic Italian beef sandwich and the famed deep-dish pizza, making River North the go-to district whether your tastes run high or low.

FOODIE DRINKS

Come cocktail hour grab a stool at the creative bar run by innovative mixologist Adam Seger at **Nacional 27** (✉ *325 W. Huron St.* ☎ *312/664–2727*). "I get most of my ideas from chefs and from food," says Seger, a regular farmers' market shopper who was inspired by an arugula, warm goat cheese, and mango herb-dressed salad to create his signature mango-ginger-habañero daiquiri. On Thursday evenings he pours mini drinks ($3.95 each) so you can try several. The in-demand Seger also works as beverage director at **Osteria via Stato** (✉ *620 N. State St.* ☎ *312/642–8450*), where he creates seasonal "gastro-tails" as specials. *Salut!*

A STEAKHOUSE FOR ANY OCCASION

Steakhouses are a dime a dozen in River North, with its ample warehouse-sized buildings and proximity to the city center. With a meat market this robust, you can afford to be a little picky. Here are our top picks for various dining situations:

☞ A festive atmosphere that's great for groups: **Fogo de Chão** (✉ *661 N. LaSalle St.* ☎ *312/932–9330*) is an all-you-can-eat Brazilian churrascaria. The restaurant's name, which means "fire on the ground," refers to a traditional gathering around the fire with good food, family, and friends. The celebratory mood is reproduced here with interactive elements: using a two-sided red and green chip, guests indicate when they're ready to have costumed gaucho cowboys come to their table to carve the skewered and grilled meats (you can stop and start as many times as you'd like). Guests can also watch their meat being roasted in dramatic fire pit while traveling back and forth to the lavish salad bar.

☞ A Chicago classic with Italian-American flavor: **Gene & Georgetti** (✉ *500 N. Franklin St.* ☎ *312/527–3718*). Founded in 1941, this is Chicago's oldest steakhouse, and a current favorite of local politicians. On the walls you'll find autographed photos from Frank Sinatra and Lucille Ball, and on the menu you'll encounter Italian-American favorites like spaghetti and meatballs, along with classic favorites like creamed spinach. Don't miss the famed "garbage salad"—a kitchen-sink creation of greens with vegetables and meats.

☞ A stylish setting that ladies will love: **Keefer's** (✉ *20 W. Kinzie St.* ☎ *312/467–9525*) boasts a sleek, modern bistro feel, and has a broader menu than most steakhouses, with seafood, entrée salads, and roasted chicken and chops. But don't mistake this award-winning venue for steakhouse lite: its 22-ounce T-bone and 17-ounce corn-fed New York strip steak can compete with the manliest offerings in town. On the wine list you'll find more than 110 labels, with plenty of big reds.

American
Bin 36, $$
Ed Debevick's, ¢
Rockit Bar & Grill, $$
Weber Grill Restaurant, $$
Wildfire, $$

Asian
SushiSamba Rio, $$

Bistro
Cyrano's Bistrot Wine Bar, $$

Brasserie
Brasserie Jo, $$

Brazilian
Fogo de Chão, $$$$

Chinese
Ben Pao, $

International
Vermilion, $$

Italian
A Mano, $$
Coco Pazzo, $$
Pizzeria Uno, $
Scoozi!, $$

Japanese
Japonais, $$$

Latin American
Nacional 27, $$

Mexican
Frontera Grill, $$
Topolobampo, $$$

New American
Aigre Doux, $$$
Graham Elliot, $$$
mk, $$$
Naha, $$$

Seafood
Joe's Seafood, $$–$$$
Shaw's Crab House, $$$

Steakhouse
David Burke's Primehouse, $$$$
Gene and Georgetti, $$$$
Harry Caray's Italian Steakhouse, $$
Keefer's, $$$$

Thai
Vong's Thai Kitchen, $$

5

SOUTH LOOP AND SOUTH SIDE

The South Side of Chicago is a vast district of largely undistinguished culinary reputation that makes its foodie islands—Chinatown and South Loop—shine all the brighter.

If you're planning on exploring the South Side, especially Chicago's soul foodie Army & Lou's and other stand-alone classics, plan to drive, as distances are great and public transportation isn't, even to hubs such as the University of Chicago.

That said, you can actually spend time on foot in two rewarding South Side districts not far from the Loop. Begin at the South Loop adjacent to downtown which can easily feed Museum Campus visitors. The newly gentrifying district is home to a host of new condos and lofts, which have drawn a range of interesting diners, restaurants, and bars, primarily on Wabash Avenue. Farther south and easily accessed via the Red Line El, Chinatown is Chicago's colorful Chinese neighborhood, where traditional dim-sum specialists neighbor trendy bubble tea shops. Recently a new generation of Asian-Americans from Chicago and the suburbs have rediscovered Chinatown, energizing the scene.

CLASSIC SPOTS

Go out of your way to **Army & Lou's** (✉ 422 E. 75th St. ☎ 773/483–3100), a soul food favorite since 1945, for catfish, chitterlings, and smothered chicken served by bow-tied waiters on way-south 75th Street. Have the corned-beef sandwich with a side of sass from the countermen at **Manny's Coffee Shop & Deli** (✉ 1141 S. Jefferson St. ☎ 312/939–2855) near the Maxwell Street Market, the city's best deli. It's truly a no-frills place, but Hyde Parkers embrace the vintage cafeteria **Valois** (✉ 1518 E. 53rd St., at S. Harper Ave. ☎ 773/667–0647) for breakfast (pancakes), lunch (mac-'n-cheese), or dinner (barbecued ribs).

AFTERNOON IN CHINATOWN

Herbal-medicine shops, trinket sellers, candy specialists, dim-sum servers, bakeries, and noodle shops make Chinatown an entertaining day away within the city. Top stops include:

☞ Herb shop: **Yin Wall City** (✉ *2347 S. Wentworth Ave. at 23rd Pl.* ☎ *312/808–1122*) for ginseng and Japanese mushrooms.

☞ Bakery: **Tasty Place** (✉ *2306 S. Wentworth Ave. at 23rd St.* ☎ *312/842–8802*) for coconut buns and chestnut cakes.

☞ Dim Sum: **Phoenix** (✉ *2131 S. Archer Ave.* ☎ *312/328–0848*) for barbecued pork buns and shrimp dumplings plucked from carts that wheel around the room on the weekend.

☞ Hot Pot: **Lao Sze Chuan** (✉ *2172 S. Archer Ave.* ☎ *312/326–5040*) for the all-you-can-eat Chinese fondue, where diners cook their own veggies, noodles, and meat in boiling broth at the table.

☞ Noodles: **Joy Yee's Noodle** (✉ *2159 S. China Pl., at Cermak Rd.* ☎ *312/328–0001*) for standout sugarcane-shrimp-pork vermicelli.

BEST MUSEUM EATS

For visitors to the adjacent Museum Campus there's a South Loop dish for every interest:

☞ For visitors to the Ancient Americas exhibit at the Field Museum, the chicken in mole sauce at **Zapatista** (✉ *1307 S. Wabash Ave., at 13th St.* ☎ *312/435–1307*).

☞ For Shedd Aquarium goers, the albacore tuna sandwich and lox at **Eleven City Diner** (✉ *1112 S. Wabash Ave., at 11th St.* ☎ *312/212–1112*).

☞ For show-goers in the Adler Planetarium's StarRider Theater, the very theatrical **Opera** (✉ *1301 S. Wabash Ave.* ☎ *312/461–0161*), with its renowned golden shrimp appetizer.

American
Eleven City Diner, $
Epic Burger, ¢
Manny's Coffee Shop and Deli, ¢

Bistro
Chez Joël Bistro Français, $$

Chinese
Emperor's Choice, $
Lao Sze Chuan, ¢
Opera, $$
Phoenix, $

Italian
Gioco, $$
Pompei, ¢

Southern
Army and Lou's, ¢
Soul Queen, ¢

Spanish
Mercat a la Planxa, $$

Steakhouse
Custom House, $$$

5

WEST LOOP AND NEAR WEST SIDE

Near enough to downtown to draw a critical mass of diners, but far enough away to keep the rents somewhat down, the West Loop—and particularly Randolph Street within it—has emerged as Chicago's restaurant row, lined with upscale eateries of every ethnic persuasion.

Most restaurants here warrant a full meal, but if you haven't the time or the attention span, it's easy enough to stroll the street and feast on small bites.

The West Loop runs essentially from the south branch of the Chicago River to Ashland Avenue on the east and west, Fulton Street and Grand Avenue on the north and south, respectively. Beyond it to the north lies the unbounded but up-and-coming Near West Side. Its culinary contributions, including West Town Tavern, Juicy Wine Company, and Green Zebra, are easy to reach by cab or the El's Blue Line train.

VA-VA-VEG

Chef Shawn McClain earned raves nationwide for giving veggies the gourmet treatment at **Green Zebra** (✉ *1460 W. Chicago Ave., at Greenwood Ave.* ☎ *312/243–7100*). But don't call it vegetarian, McClain says. It's "flexitarian," mostly veggie but not strictly. "The restaurant is vegetable-focused," he says, "but we frequently have one fish and one chicken dish on the menu for guests who want some protein." The menu changes often, but may include dishes like a blue-cheese agnolotti with brussels sprouts, vanilla-port-swirled "ice cream," and chanterelle mushroom popovers.

EAT YOUR WAY DOWN RANDOLPH STREET

Foodies from around the city and beyond flock to Randolph Street, aka Chicago's Restaurant Row, for excellent eats. From pizza and pasta to curry and sushi, the flavors here are sure to satisfy any culinary craving. Here are our top recommendations, dish by dish, restaurant by restaurant. Choose your own food tour from the selections below. Bon appétit!

SOUTH SIDE OF RANDOLPH STREET (the numbers refer to street addresses):

No. 615 : Marinated olives and truffle-scented focaccia at **Avec** (☎ 312/377–2002).

No. 619 : Wood-grilled sturgeon at **Blackbird** (☎ 312/715–0708).

No. 833 : Rotisserie chicken and pommes frites at **Marché** (☎ 312/226–8399).

No. 945 : "Fire Breather" sausage-pepperoni-hot-pepper pizza at **Tomato Head Pizza** (✉ At Sangamon St. ☎ 312/226–1616).

No. 1235 : Cheddar and black beans, fried into a dish called "scrapple" at **Ina's** (☎ 312/226–8227).

No. 1415 : Seasonal flatbreads at the **Tasting Room** (✉ At Ogden Ave. ☎ 312/942–1313).

NORTH SIDE OF RANDOLPH STREET:

No. 814 : Chipotle chicken tacos at **De Cero Taqueria** (☎ 312/455–8114).

No. 820 : Emerald jumbo prawn curry at **Red Light** (☎ 312/733–8880).

No. 832 : Dragonfly martini at **Dragonfly Mandarin** (✉ At Green St. ☎ 312/787–7600).

No. 838 : Grilled calamari at **Vivo** (☎ 312/733–3379).

No. 842 : Dragon rolls (tempura shrimp, eel, and avocado) at **Sushi Wabi** (☎ 312/563–1224).

No. 1400 : Slow-cooked pork belly with jicama slaw at **one sixtyblue** (☎ 312/850–0303).

American
Ina's, $
Lou Mitchell's, ¢
West Town Tavern, $$

Asian
Red Light, $$

Bistro
La Sardine, $$

Brasserie
Marché, $$

Cutting-Edge
Moto, $$$$

Greek
Costa's, $–$$
The Parthenon, $

Italian
Vivo, $$

Japanese
Sushi Wabi, $

Mexican
De Cero Taqueria, $

New American
Avec, $$
Blackbird, $$$
Green Zebra, $$$
Juicy Wine Company, $
one sixtyblue, $$$
Otom, $$
Publican, $
Sepia, $$$

Steakhouse
Carmichael's Chicago Steakhouse, $$

5

WICKER PARK AND BUCKTOWN

Chicago's bohemian 'hoods — neighbors Wicker Park and Bucktown — are a venturesome El stop away from downtown's deep pockets.

Artists and musicians are responsible for its 1990s rise from blighted to trendy, and although real estate prices have increased significantly, residents prize the independent spirit here, from the local record labels and hole-in-the-wall bars to one-of-a-kind boutiques and funky eateries.

Though Starbucks is, as expected, already on the scene, the food landscape here is fittingly fun and diverse, and surprisingly good at any hour, whether you want breakfast (ok, brunch, since no one gets up that early), lunch, or dinner. A handful of Bucktown and Wicker Park restaurants qualify as destinations themselves, but the best way to approach the area is to come out in the afternoon to nosh and troll the shops, stop into a bar for a drink, then head to dinner, followed by a show at Double Door, a music club.

SWEET SPOTS

A trio of sweet spots puts the cherry on the Wicker Park/Bucktown sundae. For south of the border palates, order a banana split served with crispy plaintains, Mexican chocolate, strawberry ice cream, and *cajeta* (caramelized condensed milk) at **Adobo Grill** (✉ 2005 W. Division St. ☎ 773/252–9990). Old-school fans line up for ice-cream sundaes at the family-owned **Margie's Candies** (✉ 1960 N. Western Ave. ☎ 773/384–1035) dating from 1921. Progressive foodies rave about the salted caramel ice cream at **Hot Chocolate** (✉ 1747 N. Damen Ave. ☎ 773/489–1747), a restaurant owned by acclaimed pastry chef Mindy Segal.

WICKER PARK TWO WAYS

There are two equally satisfying ways to dine in Wicker Park and Bucktown: With money or without much.

	LOW PROFILE	HOT SPOT
Foodie haunts	**Milk & Honey Café** (⊠1920 W. Division St., at Damen Ave. ☏773/395–9434) distinguishes breakfast with house-made granola, and lunch with sandwiches such as crab cake with chipotle mayo.	Acclaimed chef Shawn McClain runs **Spring** (⊠2039 W. North Ave., at Damen Ave. ☏773/395–7100), serving gorgeous and savory Asian-inspired seafood in a former Russian bathhouse.
Music with your meal	**Smoke Daddy** (⊠1804 W. Division St., at Wood St. ☏773/772–6656) serves up finger-lickin' barbecue like pulled-pork sandwiches and rib platters along with live R&B nightly.	Mariachi music mingles with Dylan tunes at nightspot **Angels & Mariachis** (⊠1721 W. Division St. ☏773/227–7772), a self-proclaimed "rock cantina" serving up Tex-Mex fare.
Unexpected flavors	Aficionados line up down the block on weekends for brunch at **Bongo Room** (⊠1470 N. Milwaukee Ave., at Honore St. ☏773/489–0690), including stacks of apple-currant French toast.	Rare beverage finds at **Takashi** (⊠1952 N. Damen Ave., at Cortland Ave. ☏773/772-6170), such as a sweet wine made with yuzu (a Japanese citrus), complement a globally inspired menu.

American
Hot Chocolate, $$
Mado, $

Bistro
Le Bouchon, $$

Café
Milk & Honey Café, ¢

International
Feast, $

Japanese
Takashi, $$$

New American
Spring, $$$

Pizza
Crust, $
Piece, $

Southern
Smoke Daddy, $

5

WHERE ROCKERS DINE

Come for the New Haven–style free-formed pizza and house-made brews at **Piece** (⊠*1927 W. North Ave., at Damen Ave.* ☏*773/772-4422*). Stick around for the Saturday-night live-band karaoke. Co-owner Rick Nielsen is a member of Cheap Trick. Given his rep and the pies, rockers from near (Billy Corgan of Smashing Pumpkins fame, Al Jourgensen of Ministry, producer Steve Albini) and far (Todd Rundgren) frequently dine here.

FAR NORTH SIDE

$$$$ ╳**Arun's.** The finest Thai restaurant in Chicago—some say in the country—
THAI is also the most expensive, featuring only 12-course tasting menus for
a flat $85. That said, the kitchen readily adjusts its offerings to food
preferences and, of course, distastes. The kitchen artfully composes six
appetizers, four entrées, and two desserts using the freshest ingredients.
Results might include shrimp-filled golden pastry baskets, whole tama-
rind snapper, and veal medallions with ginger-lemongrass sauce. Arun's
out-of-the-way location in a residential neighborhood on the northwest
side doesn't discourage a strong following among locals and visiting
foodies. ⊠*4156 N. Kedzie Ave.* ☎*773/539–1909* ⌖*Reservations
essential* ▤*AE, D, DC, MC, V* ⊗*Closed Mon. No lunch.* ✛*2:A1*

$$ ╳**Bistro Campagne.** This is the place to dine on the North Side for rustic
BISTRO French fare: crispy roast chicken, steak piled with frites, goat-cheese
salads, and ale-steamed mussels. The lovely, wood-trimmed Arts and
Crafts interior provides instant attitude adjustment; in warmer weather,
aim to get a table in the torch-lit garden. Prices are reasonable, includ-
ing those for the French-centric wine list. ⊠*4518 N. Lincoln Ave.*
☎*773/271–6100* ▤*AE, MC, V* ⊗*No lunch.* ✛*2:B1*

$ ╳**Café Selmarie.** For a light meal in Lincoln Square, line up at this
CAFÉ bakery-turned-café, a longstanding favorite among locals. Breakfast
☺ gets you brioche French toast and corned-beef hash with eggs; lunch
ranges from goat-cheese salads to turkey and Brie sandwiches; and
dinner runs to panko-crusted tilapia and roast chicken. Don't miss
the sink-your-teeth-in pastries (you can also buy them to go at the
front counter). Pass summer waits pleasantly in the neighboring plaza;
during other seasons, you're out in the cold. ⊠*4729 N. Lincoln Ave.*
☎*773/989–5595* ▤*MC, V* ✛*2:B1*

$ ╳**Chicago Brauhaus.** The German immigrants who settled in Lincoln
GERMAN Square have mostly moved on, making room for a new generation of
urban hipsters. But they leave behind the Brauhaus, an Oktoberfest of a
restaurant featuring a live band playing nightly polkas and waltzes that
bring old-timers and new converts to the dance floor. Though the atmo-
sphere is the draw over the food, you can't go wrong with the bratwurst
and sauerkraut or the schnitzel. Large tables easily accommodate
groups. The spacious bar and a good selection of German beers draw
oompah-loving drinkers. ⊠*4732 N. Lincoln Ave.* ☎*773/784–4444*
▤*AE, D, MC, V* ⊗*Closed Tues.* ✛*2:B1*

$ ╳**Hopleaf Bar.** True beer aficionados know beer is food. So when hops
BELGIAN devotee Michael Roper added a dining room onto the back of his
Fodor's Choice beloved tavern, swillers thrilled to sop their suds with delectable spe-
★ cialties such as Belgian-style mussels steamed in white ale with herbs,
venison meat loaf with a root-vegetable gratin, and duck Reuben
sandwiches on marble rye. Arrive early to avoid waiting in the bar
for a table. But don't bring the kids; Roper insists that only those of
legal drinking age can eat here. ⊠*5148 N. Clark St.* ☎*773/334–9851*
▤*AE, D, DC, MC, V* ✛*2:D1*

¢ ✕**Hot Doug's.** Don't tell the zealots who have made Hot Doug's famous
HOT DOGS that these are *just* hot dogs—these "encased meats" go beyond your
Fodor'sChoice standard Vienna wiener. The gourmet purveyor wraps buns around
★ chipotle chicken sausage, smoked crawfish and pork sausage with
☺ spicy remoulade, rabbit sausage, and even rattlesnake sausage on occasion. Make the trek on a Friday or Saturday, when the artery-clogging
duck-fat fries are available. The clientele is a curious mix of hungry
hard-hats and serious foodies, neither of which care about the lack of
frills. ✉ *3324 N. California Ave.* ☎ *773/279–9550* ▭ *No credit cards*
☻ *Closed Sun. No dinner.* ✛ *3:A2*

$$ ✕**Lula Café.** For the kind of modern cooking made from locally sourced
AMERICAN ingredients that distinguishes downtown chefs—but at half the price
and with zero attitude—locals throng Lula Café, a quick walk from the
Logan Square El stop. This bohemian storefront of closely set wooden
tables and chairs serves stellar cuisine such as wild bass with blood
orange and olives, and maple-scented rabbit with rosemary sweet
potatoes. Menus are seasonal, change frequently, and champion farm
sources; in fact the restaurant holds prix-fixe farm dinners each Mon-
day. Open for breakfast and lunch too, Lula is a neighborhood hang-
out for arty neighbors during the day, drawing from far and wide for
dinner, when weekend waits are common. ✉ *2537 N. Kedzie Blvd.*
☎ *773/489–9554* ▭ *AE, MC, V* ☻ *Closed Tues.* ✛ *3:A2*

¢ ✕**Smoque BBQ.** The sweet smoky aroma wafting out of this casual barbe-
SOUTHERN cue spot always attracts a crowd. While the line to order at the counter
starts out the door on weekends, it moves quickly as chowhounds catch
up on neighborhood news. If you can't make up your mind between
brisket or shredded pork shoulder (both tender and cooked for more
than 12 hours), order the half-and-half—a sandwich with half of each.
Or try a slab of ribs. A side of vinegar-spiked slaw, rich baked beans,
and cornbread round out the meal, and kids love the creamy mac and
cheese. Smoque is BYOB, so pick up a beer or two before arriving if
desired. ✉ *3800 N. Pulaski Rd.* ☎ *773/545–7427* ✍ *Reservations not
accepted* ▭ *AE, D, MC, V* ☻ *Closed Mon.* ✛ *2:A3*

$$ ✕**Sola.** While you can dine very well in Chicago's neighborhoods,
NEW AMERICAN most local joints aren't as ambitious as Sola, which would be right at
home downtown and probably far more expensive there. Now North
Side visitors don't have to travel far for ginger-glazed salmon, bacon-
wrapped pork tenderloin, and wasabi-crusted mahimahi. Chef-owner-
surfer Carol Wallack's affinity for Hawaii shows in Pacific Rim fare like
seaweed salad and Kauai prawns. Proving its affection for the neighborhood, the restaurant is fronted by a wall of windows and warm within,
thanks to a gas fireplace. Go around the corner to Byron Street to find
the front door. ✉ *3868 N. Lincoln Ave.* ☎ *773/327–3868* ▭ *AE, D,
DC, MC, V* ☻ *No lunch Mon.–Wed.* ✛ *2:C2*

$ ✕**Spacca Napoli.** Despite Chicago's renown for deep-dish pizza, locals
ITALIAN are lately swept away by Neapolitan pies bested by this bright, 68-seat
Fodor'sChoice Ravenswood gem. Finely ground Italian flour, imported buffalo moz-
★ zarella, hand-stretched dough, and a brick, wood-fired oven built by
Italian craftsmen are credited for producing bubbling, chewy crusts that
edge savory, uncut, thin pies that diners eat with a fork. Antipasti and

5

desserts like tiramisu round out the short menu. The proprietors shun takeout and turn up the lights a little too high, but the food wins out, accounting for out-the-door waits, even on weekdays. In summer, angle for a table on the pleasant sidewalk patio, which seats more than 40. ⊠*1769 W. Sunnyside Ave.* ☎*773/878–2420* ▭*AE, MC, V* ⊗*Closed Mon. closed for lunch Tues.* ✛*2:D1*

WORD OF MOUTH

"If you feel like getting out of downtown and up to Roscoe Village, I can recommend Terragusto on Addison and Wolcott. Excellent rustic northern Italian; organic local ingredients, pasta is hand-rolled there every morning, etc."
—TwoFatFeet

¢ ✕**Svea.** The North Side's Andersonville neighborhood, once a haven

SCANDINAVIAN   for Swedes, plays host to the humble Svea, a Swedish version of an American diner. There are Swedish pancakes with lingonberries and Swedish rye *limpa* bread with eggs in the morning, and open-face Swedish meatball sandwiches at lunch. The digs are no-frill, but the service is friendly. ⊠*5236 N. Clark St.* ☎*773/275–7738* ▭*No credit cards* ⊗*No dinner.* ✛*2:D1*

$$ ✕**Terragusto.** Chicago storefront dining doesn't get any better than this

ITALIAN   Italian haunt in Roscoe Village. Bring your own wine and sit down in the exposed-brick dining room for dishes comprised mainly of organic and sustainable ingredients and pastas made that day by your chef-cum-waiter. The house specializes in family-style service, enabling diners to choose an antipasto, salad, a couple of pastas, and entrées to split, making it a nice choice for groups who like to graze. Though it occupies an unlikely corner of Addison Street in Roscoe Village, it's only about a mile from Wrigley Field and neighbors the Brown Line El stop. ⊠*1851 W. Addison St.* ☎*773/248–2777* ▭*AE, D, DC, MC, V* ⊗ *Closed Mon. and Tues. No lunch.* ✛*2:C3*

$ ✕**Urban Belly.** It's easy to strike up a conversation with local foodies

ASIAN   at this favorite casual BYOB Asian street-food spot. And there's a lot to discuss: should you go for a bowl of udon noodles swimming in a chile-lime broth or the pho-spiced duck dumplings and "phat rice" (fried rice with diced pork belly and short rib)? Either way, it's hard to go wrong with anything chef Bill Kim (formerly of Le Lan) creates in his tiny kitchen. But come early: despite the restaurant's out-of-the-way location in the residential Avondale neighborhood, seating at the four long communal tables is first-come, first-served, and spots fill up quickly. ⊠*3053 N. California Ave.* ☎*773/583–0500* ▭*AE, MC, V* ⊗*Closed Mon.* ✛*2:A5*

LAKEVIEW

$ ✕**Ann Sather.** This Scandinavian restaurant, opened since 1945, is a Chi-

SCANDINAVIAN   cago institution, with good reason: the aroma of fresh cinnamon rolls,

ⓒ   Swedish pancakes with lingonberries, and waffles put this place on the map, and it still draws a mob that lines up down the block for weekend breakfasts. Sure, you could try the usual eggs Benedict, but why not sample the potato pancakes with apple sauce instead? Lunches offer similar Scandinavian specialties as well as standard café sandwiches and salads. ⊠*909 W. Belmont Ave.* ☏*773/348–2378* ▤*AE, D, DC, MC, V* ⊘*No dinner* ⊹*2:F4*

$ ✕**Coobah.** Loud and lively Coobah loves a good party. Unlike lots of

LATIN AMERICAN lounge-restaurants, however, this one doesn't rely on the mojitos and sangria to distract you from so-so food. Indeed, dishes such as tamale-baked tilapia, mussels sautéed with chili paste, and spicy pork tamales distinguish the kitchen. Weekend brunches, held 10 AM to 3 PM, lend a Latin accent to eggs and sandwiches. ⊠*3423 N. Southport Ave.* ☏*773/528–2220* ▤*AE, D, DC, MC, V* ⊘*No lunch weekdays* ⊹*2:D3*

$$ ✕**Erwin Cafe.** Striking a pose between friendly and refined, this spot

NEW AMERICAN has comforting food, a cozy setting, and polished service. Chef Erwin Drechsler often patrols the dining room of his namesake restaurant, greeting regulars. The straightforward, seasonal menu may not look all that differentiated from other upscale American menus—skate sautéed with zucchini, cherry tomatoes, garlic, and fingerling potatoes, wood-grilled flank steak with buttermilk scallion mashed potatoes, and one of the city's best burgers—but the skillful cooking and vibrant flavors give you new respect for simplicity. The booths by the front windows are the best for views of neighborhood comings and goings. ⊠*2925 N. Halsted St.* ☏*773/528–7200* ▤*AE, D, DC, MC, V* ⊘*Closed Mon. No lunch weekdays* ⊹*2:F5*

¢ ✕**Julius Meinl Cafe.** Viennese coffee roaster Julius Meinl operates this

CAFÉ very European café in an unexpected location at the intersection of Addison and Southport, just a few blocks from Wrigley Field. Comfortable banquettes and a supply of international newspapers bid coffee sippers to stick around. Vegetable focaccia and pear and Brie sandwiches, hazelnut and blue-cheese salads, *Frittaten* (Austrian beef broth with crepe noodles), and loads of European pastries feed the peckish. We love the Austrian breakfast of poached egg, ham, and Emmentaler cheese—this is the only place in the city that serves it. Classical and jazz combos entertain Fridays and Saturdays. ⊠*3601 N. Southport Ave.* ☏*773/868–1857* ▤*AE, D, MC, V* ⊹*2:D3*

$ ✕**Kitsch'n on Roscoe.** If you love all things '70s, you'll love Kitsch'n as

AMERICAN much as the regulars. It's a diner in retro garb, with lava lamps and vintage toasters–turned–table lamps. Dine, with tongue firmly in cheek, on pesto-dyed "green eggs and ham" and Twinkies tiramisu. Or play it straight with hefty tuna and grilled-cheese sandwiches. Weekends are jammed; midweek is better for relaxing. ⊠*2005 W. Roscoe St.* ☏*773/248–7372* ▤*AE, MC, V* ⊘*No dinner Sun. and Mon.* ⊹*2:B4*

$ ✕**Mia Francesca.** Moderate prices and a smart, urbane style drive cease-

ITALIAN less crowds to this Lakeview storefront. Enlightened Italian dishes like classic bruschetta, *quattro formaggi* (four-cheese) pizza, sausage and wild-mushroom pasta, and roast chicken are made with fresh ingredients and avoid stereotypical heaviness. With the exception of one pricey veal dish, the limited meat options keep the prices low here. While you wait for one of the small, tightly spaced tables—and you *will* wait—you can have a drink at the bar. Or travel to other Francesca locations, such as Francesca's Forno in Wicker Park or Francesca's on Taylor in Little Italy. ⊠*3311 N. Clark St.* ☏*773/281–3310* ▤*AE, D, MC, V*

5

⊘ *No lunch weekdays.* ✉*1576 N. Milwaukee Ave.* ☎*773/770–0184* ✉*1400 W. Taylor St.* ☎*312/829–2828* ⊹*2:F4*

¢–$ ✗**Orange.** Follow Wrigleyville's weekend crowds to the cheerful break-
AMERICAN fast spot for inventive, and thronged, breakfasts. If you think breakfast has become too dull, try the Orange approach, which is to treat break-fast with the same innovation and focus on presentation that chefs tend to reserve for dinner. Examples include pan-seared oatmeal, fruit sushi, kebab-style skewered French toast, or jam-filled pancakes. Standard stuff is done right, too: the fruit is juiced on-site and the omelets are big enough to take you through lunch. Yet eating at this morning hot spot requires some planning. Arrive early or prepare to wait as long as an hour for tables, especially on game days, or try Orange's two other locations in Roscoe Village or in the South Loop. ✉*3231 N. Clark St.* ☎*773/549–4400* ▭*D, MC, V* ⊘*No dinner* ✉*2011 W. Roscoe St.* ☎*773/248–0999* ✉*75 W. Harrison St.* ☎*312/447–1000* ⊹*2:F4*

¢ ✗**Thai Classic.** With apologies to Chinatown, Chicago is really a Thai
THAI town when it comes to outstanding Asian food. The assets at Thai Clas-sic include a prime location a few blocks south of Wrigley Field, good service, and even better dishes. Not only are prices low, but there is no liquor license (pick up a six-pack of Singha beer from the liquor store down the street), saving you the mark-up. Bargain hunters should hit the $11.95 buffet, available Saturday afternoon and all day Sunday. Come on foot during Cubs games when parking is near impossible. ✉*3332 N. Clark St.60657* ☎*773/404–2000* ▭*AE, D, DC, MC, V* ⊹*2:F4*

$ ✗**Turquoise Restaurant and Café.** The bustling Turkish-owned café attempts
TURKISH to please every palate with a mixed menu of continental and Turkish foods, but it's the latter that star here. Can't-miss items include lamb begendi, *sogurme* (a smoked eggplant, yogurt, and walnut dip), and homemade noodles with feta and dill. Vested waiters, white tablecloths, and wood-trimmed surroundings outclass the neighborhood lot. ✉*2147 W. Roscoe St.* ☎*773/549–3523* ▭*AE, D, DC, MC, V* ⊹*2:B4*

$$ ✗**Yoshi's Café.** Decades ago Yoshi's launched as a pricey fine-dining res-
ASIAN FUSION taurant in the 'hood. We offer this history lesson to say that while the atmosphere went jeans-casual and the prices south, the cooking qual-ity remained, and remains, high. Yoshi Katsumura turns out informal French-Asian cuisine, like duck breast with baked quail egg in brioche or roasted Japanese pumpkin filled with tofu (it's good enough to con-vert a carnivore). Sunday brunch includes the expected eggs along with a Japanese-inspired breakfast (rice, tofu, and seaweed). ✉*3257 N. Halsted St.* ☎*773/248–6160* ▭*AE, DC, MC, V* ⊘*Closed Mon. and Sun. brunch.* ⊹*2:F4*

LINCOLN PARK

$$$$ ✗**Alinea.** Believe the hype and book well in advance. Chicago's most
CUTTING-EDGE exciting restaurant demands an adventurous spirit and a serious commit-
Fodor'sChoice ment of time and money. If you have four hours and $225 to spare, the
★ more than 20-course tasting menu is the best way to experience young whiz Grant Achatz's stunning cutting-edge food. The gastronomic roller coaster (there's also a less pricey 12-course version for $145) takes you on a journey through intriguing aromas, visuals, flavors, and textures.

Continued on page 171

CULINARY MAVERICKS STORM WINDY CITY

Step into the kitchen, but don't forget your protective goggles. Whether "negative searing" at minus 30 degrees Fahrenheit or serving you an edible menu (literally—it's printed on soybean-based paper), this trio of young chefs in Chicago is redefining haute cuisine.

Just a few years ago, three young chefs, each a veteran of local icon Charlie Trotter's kitchen, took a simultaneous gamble on the sophistication and daring of Chicago diners, unveiling cutting-edge menus the likes of which the Windy City had never seen before. Though a visit to their restaurants— Alinea, Moto, and Graham Elliot— demands an adventurous palate, all three places have instantly thrived.

The chefs leading these restaurants— Grant Achatz, Homaro Cantu, and Graham Elliot Bowles—have brought an American touch to techniques and ideas first explored and popularized in Europe, toying with devices and chemicals more suited to a lab than a kitchen. This marriage of science and cooking is known as molecular gastronomy. Though following in the footsteps of chefs like Heston Blumenthal in Britain and Ferran Adrià in Spain, the Chicago pack prided themselves on being trailblazers, not imitators. "For Picasso to do something that looked like a Dalí would've been a sham," says Cantu. "It's the same thing in these restaurants. There's a certain amount of pride in originality."

Before long the national press began to take notice. "One chef is unique," says Bowles. "Two could be a fluke, but three guys doing this stuff in the same city, maybe something is going on." Writers from *GQ, Gourmet, The New York Times,* and *Vogue* gushed over Chicago's new "sci-fi" cuisine. The city, they wrote, had become the capital of avant-garde food in America.

by Jay Cheshes

GRANT ACHATZ

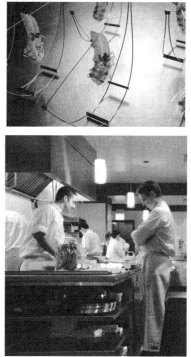

(previous page) From Alinea, a spiral of quince wrapped in prosciutto. (clockwise from top left) Grant Achatz; bacon with butterscotch, apple, and thyme; inside the Alinea kitchen; mango disc with sesame oil, soy, and bonito flakes.

Born into a restaurant family in Michigan, Achatz, who turned 30 a few years before his colleagues, is the triumvirate's senior statesman. After working at Charlie Trotter's and at Thomas Keller's French Laundry in Napa Valley, he began experimenting with molecular gastronomy at Trio in the Chicago suburbs. In 2005 he launched Alinea, his first solo project, just up the block from the Steppenwolf Theatre. The restaurant was named the best in the country by *Gourmet* barely a year after it opened.

Techniques & Trademarks

There are two dining options at Alinea—long (12 courses) and longer (24 courses). "When we first opened we were serving 28 courses," says the chef. "People were fatiguing. When you cross over four hours you're getting into dangerous territory." Tiny one- to four-bite courses flow one into the next, with sweet dishes not just ending the meal but also interrupting it midway.

"It breaks the monotony," Achatz says. Though ingredients are as likely to be flash-frozen on a stainless steel "anti-griddle" (at minus 30 degrees Fahrenheit) as seared on an old-fashioned Japanese charcoal barbecue, not much of this food (served on pedestals and prongs) will look familiar. In the kitchen you'll also find an immersion circulator (for cooking vacuum-sealed food "*sous-vide*" and containers of calcium lactate and sodium alginate (for encasing liquids in a yolk-like skin so they explode when you bite them).

HOMARO CANTU

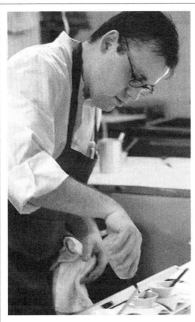

Cantu, the most wildly experimental and scientifically minded of the Chicago chefs, worked in kitchens up and down the West Coast before landing at Charlie Trotter's, where he eventually rose to the position of sous chef. Moto, opened in 2004 in a desolate stretch of the city's meatpacking district, is equal parts restaurant and mad-scientist workshop. The chef, who holds numerous food patents, sells innovations perfected in the restaurant's basement kitchen to corporate and government clients (including NASA).

(clockwise from top left) Homaro Cantu; steamed sea bass; deconstructed mac-and-cheese; edible menu made of soybeans with food-based inks.

Techniques & Trademarks

The kitchen at Moto resembles a James Bond villain's lair. When the industrial laser is turned on, protective-goggle-clad chefs work in near darkness on orders transmitted by a computer-generated voice. The daily changing prix-fixe menus (in 10- or 20-course options) are printed to order in soy-based ink on edible paper (one of the chef's many patents). Here, theatricality and trompe l'oeil presentations rule. "When you order a tasting menu it's like going out for a night at the opera," Cantu says. "You don't get to choose Act One, Scene Five; you get the entire production as the composer intended you to see it." You might encounter chemically treated lychee purée, mimicking pasta dough, molded into translucent rigatoni. Or a new wave "nitro" sushi roll made with liquid nitrogen—treated tofu skin that emits cool smoke through your mouth and nose when you bite into it.

GRAHAM ELLIOT BOWLES

(clockwise from top left) Graham Elliot Bowles; Aged Cheddar risotto, with PBR onions, green apple, Wisconsin bacon, and Cheez-Its.; Short rib stroganoff with cremini mushrooms, egg noodles, shallot marmalade, and crème fraîche.; Caesar salad, with romaine lettuce, white anchovies, Parmesan fluff, and brioche "twinkie".

After making his professional debut at the pastoral Jackson House Inn in rural Vermont, Bowles worked alongside Cantu at Charlie Trotter's. The chefs, who started two weeks apart, became good friends. Later Bowles returned to the Jackson House, where he first experimented with molecular gastronomy (and where *Food & Wine* named him one of America's best new chefs). Just as his colleagues were launching their own places, he landed the position of chef de cuisine at Avenues, the flagship restaurant of Chicago's Peninsula Hotel where he won numerous awards for his inventive cooking. After his four-year stint at Avenues, Chef Bowles decided to leave his highly-lauded post to open his own restaurant, Graham Elliot.

Techniques & Trademarks

Officially opening its doors in June 2008, Chef Bowles' eponymous restaurant is what he likes to call "bistronomic"— a juxtaposition of haute cuisine and a bistro-style approach. He believes his restaurant to be an extension of himself, and that too is seen in the food. An inventive take on buffalo wings is served with blue-cheese foam and Budweiser bubbles, and the cheddar risotto is served with green apple and Cheez-Its. Though his food is recognizable, it remains thought-provoking—and delicious. "It's more whimsical," says Bowles. "It's fine dining redefined."

The menu changes frequently, but you might find green beans perched on a pillow that emits nutmeg-scented air, sweetbreads served with burnt bread and toasted hay, and apple cider paired with walnut milk, cinnamon, and vegetable ash. Though some dishes—they range in size from one to four bites—may look like science projects, there's nothing gimmicky about the endless procession of bold and elegant tastes. The hours fly by in the windowless bi-level dining room, aided by the effortless service and muted decor. ⊠*1723 N. Halsted St.* ☎*312/867–0110* ⚑*Reservations essential* ▤*AE, D, DC, MC, V* ☉*Closed Mon. and Tues. No lunch.* ✛*3:E3*

$$$
NEW AMERICAN

✕**Boka.** If you're doing Steppenwolf pretheater dinner on North Halsted, this unpretentious, though upscale spot gets foodies' stamp of approval, particularly with Charlie Trotter alumnus Giuseppe Tentori in the kitchen. A seasonally driven menu includes standouts such as chamomile-dusted quail with caramelized fennel, and venison with brussels sprouts, wild rice, dates, juniper berries, and a chestnut cake. The slick lounge and outdoor patio both serve food, drawing a following independent of curtain time. ⊠*1729 N. Halsted St.* ☎*312/337–6070* ▤*AE, MC, V* ☉*No lunch* ✛*3:E3*

$
SPANISH

✕**Café Ba-Ba-Reeba!** It has a kitschy name and is jammed with partying Lincoln Parkers, so at first you wouldn't expect much food-wise here, but expat Spaniards swear it's the best in town. Colorful Mediterranean-style interiors encourage the fiesta feel. The large assortment of cold and warm tapas ranges from garlic potato salad to beef tenderloin with blue cheese. It's worth visiting the entrée menu for paella and skewered meats. In warm weather six different flavors of sangria flow freely on the outdoor patio. ⊠*2024 N. Halsted St.* ☎*773/935–5000* ▤*AE, D, DC, MC, V* ☉*No lunch weekdays* ✛*3:E2*

$$$$
NEW AMERICAN

✕**Charlie Trotter's.** Plan well in advance to dine at top toque Charlie Trotter's namesake (or call the day of and hope for a cancellation). One of the nation's most acclaimed chefs, Trotter prepares his menus daily from the best of what's available globally. The results are daring, multi-ingredient dishes that look like art on a dinner plate. Menus follow a multicourse, $155 degustation format ($130 for the vegetarian version). For a worthwhile splurge, order the wines-to-match option. This temple of haute cuisine occupies a stately Lincoln Park town house. ⊠*816 W. Armitage Ave.* ☎*773/248–6228* ⚑*Reservations essential. Jacket required* ▤*AE, DC, MC, V* ☉*Closed Sun. and most Mon. No lunch* ✛*3:E2*

$$$
FRENCH

✕**Geja's Cafe.** For every course there's a fondue at this Lincoln Park longtimer. Start with the cheese fondue, then progress to the sampler plate of shellfish, chicken, beef, and vegetables cooked in a fondue pot of hot oil (the tables are riveted to the floor to avoid disaster). Finish by dunking fruits and sweets in liquid chocolate, if you've got room. Candlelight, cozy dining nooks, walls filled with empty wine bottles, and strumming guitarists mean this place is packed on Valentine's Day. ⊠*340 W. Armitage Ave.* ☎*773/281–9101* ▤*AE, D, DC, MC, V* ☉*No lunch* ✛*3:G2*

$$$$
SEAFOOD

✕**L20.** Well before he opened this fine dining shrine to the sea, Chef Laurent Gras began tempting diners by logging menu ideas onto his blog. The results of his experiments can be found on L20's four-course prix-fixe menu and 12-course tasting menu, in which hard-to-find fish varieties—such as *shimaaji*, Japanese mackerel, or *kinmedai*, fatty tuna—are smoked, cured, seared, or foamed. Guests also have the opportunity to taste delicacies such as wagyu beef imported from Miyazaki, Japan, at an additional cost. Deciphering the menu may take some assistance, but the serene, earth-toned dining room and professional staff help soothe any worries. Tradition, in the form of delicate soufflés and macaroons, return at the end of the meal for a sweet sendoff. ⊠*2300 N. Lincoln Park W.* ☎*773/868–0002* ⊟*AE, D, DC, MC, V* ☉*Closed Tues.* ✛*3:G1*

$$ ✗**Mon Ami Gabi.** While this restaurant's corporate owner, Chicago-
BISTRO based Lettuce Entertain You, has opened up satellite restaurants in the suburbs and in Las Vegas, the original has not lost its charm. This little piece of Paris re-creates a classic bistro with views of Lincoln Park that could pass—with the help of a couple of glasses of *vin* from the rolling wine cart—for the Tuileries. Park-front windows let in ample natural light, warming the wood-trimmed interior. Best bites include several versions of steak frites, as well as bistro essentials such as steamed mussels and skate with crispy garlic chips. But chef Gabino Sotelino also serves a rotating list of specials, from cassoulet served on Sunday to Dover sole on Thursday. ⊠*2300 N. Lincoln Park W.* ☎*773/348–8886* ⊟*AE, D, DC, MC, V* ☉*No lunch* ✛*3:G1*

$$$ ✗**North Pond.** A former Arts and Crafts–style warming house for ice-
AMERICAN skaters at Lincoln Park's North Pond, this gem in the woods fittingly
Fodor'sChoice champions an uncluttered culinary style. Talented chef Bruce Sherman
★ emphasizes organic ingredients, wild-caught fish, and artisanal farm products. Menus change seasonally, but order the Midwestern favorite walleye pike if available. Like the food, the wine list seeks out small craft producers. The food remains top-notch at lunch but the scene, dense with strollers and high chairs, is far from serene. ⊠*2610 N. Cannon Dr.* ☎*773/477–5845* ⊟*AE, D, DC, MC, V* ☉*Closed Mon. No dinner Tues. Jan.–Apr. No lunch Oct.–May* ✛*2:H6*

NORTH LOOP

$$ ✗**312 Chicago.** Part handy hotel restaurant, part Loop power diner, and
ITALIAN all Italian down to its first-generation chef, 312 Chicago earns its popularity with well-executed dishes that range from rigatoni with sausage to veal medallions with porcini mushrooms. We're tempted to carbo-load on the house-baked bread alone. Tables in the bi-level eatery are quieter aloft, though you still may see the occasional hotel guest wander through, looking for the elevator. ⊠*Hotel Allegro, 136 N. LaSalle St.* ☎*312/696–2420* ⊟*AE, D, DC, MC, V* ☉*No lunch Sat.* ✛*1:C6*

$$$ ✗**Aria.** Can't decide between Moroccan, Asian, or Mediterranean?
INTERNATIONAL Take your globe-trotting taste buds to Aria, which roams the world larder with abandon: Asian-inspired sashimi tuna salad, free-range chicken breast seasoned with Moroccan spices, Argentine churrasco, Malaysian-inspired soy-glazed cod, Hong Kong barbecue duck and lobster chow mein, and the requisite American steaks. Among generous freebies, tandoori-baked naan bread with Indian-inspired dipping

sauces arrives before the meal, and a trio of exotically spiced potatoes comes with the entrées. In the convivial lounge, a small-plate menu and a full sushi bar cater to abbreviated but equally adventurous appetites. ✉*Fairmont Chicago, 200 N. Columbus Dr.* ☎*312/444–9494* 🖃*AE, D, DC, MC, V* ✛*1:F6*

$$
AMERICAN

✕**Atwood Café.** The Loop can be all business, even after hours, but we found an enclave of personality at this spot in the Hotel Burnham. Mahogany columns, cherrywood floors, gold café curtains, and curvy banquettes provide color, and floor-to-ceiling windows provide light. The mostly American menu includes reliables like pan-roasted chicken breast and thick pork chops, peppered by contemporary fare such as crispy red-lentil cakes and smoked paprika-grilled salmon fillet. ✉*Hotel Burnham, 1 W. Washington St.* ☎*312/368–1900* 🖃*AE, D, DC, MC, V* ✛*4:F1*

$$
SEAFOOD

✕**Catch 35.** Eavesdrop on advertising types who do the after-five mix-and-mingle at this spot in the lobby of the Leo Burnett Building. When it comes to the menu, have it your way: fish or shellfish comes grilled, seared, or baked. Classic seafood appetizers are delivered with a twist, such as coconut- and beer-battered shrimp, calamari rings with pepper oil and fried Thai basil, and seared scallops with chive pot stickers. The restaurant, with its marble, granite, and beautifully set woodwork, is an inviting space to relax, while the multilevel dining room provides plenty of eye candy, plus glimpses of the Chicago River beyond. Come in the evening from Tuesday through Saturday in order to catch the musical stylings of a local jazz trio. ✉*35 W. Wacker Dr.* ☎*312/346–3500* 🖃*AE, D, DC, MC, V* ⊘*No lunch weekends* ✛*1:D6*

$$$$
FRENCH

✕**Everest.** No one expects romance at the top of the Chicago Stock Exchange, but Everest does its best to throw you a curve wherever and whenever. Consider the trip: two separate elevators whisk you 40 stories up, where you have sweeping views of the city's sprawl westward. Then there's the food. It's French, but with an Alsatian bent—a nod to Chef Jean Joho's roots. He might just add Alsace Riesling to his risotto. And finally, there's the redesigned space, where modern sculpture melds with art nouveau. The whole experience, from the tuxedoed waiters to the massive wine list, screams "special occasion!" ✉*440 S. LaSalle St.* ☎*312/663–8920* ⌕*Reservations essential. Jacket required* 🖃*AE, D, DC, MC, V* ⊘*Closed Sun. and Mon. No lunch* ✛*4:F2*

$$
STEAKHOUSE

✕**The Grillroom Chophouse & Winebar.** If you're going to see a performance at the Bank of America Theatre across the street, you're close enough to dash over here for a drink at intermission (we love the lengthy by-the-glass wine selections). Pre- and post-curtain, the clubby confines fill with showgoers big on beef, though there are also ample raw bar, seafood, and pasta choices. For the most relaxing experience, come after Act I commences. ✉*33 W. Monroe St.* ☎*312/960–0000* 🖃*AE, D, DC, MC, V* ⊘*No lunch weekends* ✛*4:F2*

$
SOUTHERN

✕**Heaven on Seven.** Every day is Mardi Gras at Heaven on Seven, which pursues a good time all the time. The restaurant, with two locations in the city, has a menu centered around a daring collection of hot sauces, and the food, though it's well shy of ambrosia, is plentiful and filling. Some guests find the menu too spicy for their kids, but would go back for the well-priced Mardi Gras jambalaya, fried oyster po'boy, cheese grits, and chicory coffee. Cheddar-jalapeño biscuits and chocolate peanut-butter pie are great menu bookends. ☒ *111 N. Wabash Ave.* ☎*312/263–6443* ☒*600 N. Michigan Ave.* ☎*312/280–7774* ☐*AE, D, DC, MC, V* ☼*Closed Sun. Dinner served 3rd Fri. of month* ✛*1:E4, Wabash* ✛*1:E6.*

$$$$ ✕**Morton's, The Steakhouse.** Morton's in the Gold Coast neighborhood
STEAKHOUSE can be more fun, but this is Chicago's best steakhouse, a spin-off of the Gold Coast original. Excellent service and a good wine list add to the principal attraction: beautiful, hefty steaks cooked to perfection. A kitschy tradition mandates that everything you order, from gargantuan Idahos to massive slabs of beef, is brought to the table for your approval before the chef gets started. White tablecloths and chandeliers create a classy feel. It's no place for the budget conscious, but for steak lovers it's a 16-ounce (or more) taste of heaven. ☒*65 E. Wacker Pl.* ☎*312/201–0410* ☐*AE, D, DC, MC, V* ☼*No lunch weekends* ✛*1:D2*

$$$ ✕**Nick's Fishmarket.** While the original owners of this Chicago institution
SEAFOOD sold it years ago, and its current owners have opened satellite locations in the suburbs, locals continue to frequent Nick's for its great downtown location, fresh seafood, and prime steaks. The bold and pricey menu matches the well-paid power lunchers who get down to business over Pacific fish, California abalone, and Maine lobster paired with wines from California or Australia. If your purse strings are tight, angle for a spot at the Grill, where the lobster comes in bisque and windows frame the Marc Chagall mosaic on the plaza outdoors. ☒*51 S. Clark St.* ☎*312/621–0200* ☐*AE, D, DC, MC, V* ☼*Closed Sun. No lunch Sat.* ✛*4:F2*

$$ ✕**Park Grill.** Location trumps service at Park Grill, where a seat on the
AMERICAN patio in summer, in full view of Millennium Park, is among the best in the city. Sadly, the waitstaff lapses—grin and bear it with another drink from the outdoor bar. The menu is divided between small, medium, and large plates, offering a something-for-everyone selection. The burgers are first-rate, as is the more ambitious seasonal fare such as blood-orange and endive salad, lamb ribs spiked with garam masala, and pineapple-glazed salmon. A grab-and-go window supplies park picnics. In winter the scene moves indoors, as indulgent calorie consumers watch ice-skating athletes through picture windows. ☒*Millennium Park, 11 N. Michigan Ave.* ☎*312/521–7275* ☐*AE, D, DC, MC, V* ✛*4:G1*

$$ ✕**Petterino's.** Goodman, Palace, and Oriental theatergoers pack Pet-
ITALIAN terino's (next door to the Goodman lobby) nightly. Not that the Italian supper club with framed caricatures of celebs past and present couldn't stand on its own merits. The deep, red-leather booths make a cozy stage for old-school classics like steak Diane, shrimp *de jonghe* (covered in garlicky bread crumbs then baked), tomato bisque, Bookbinder soup, plus prime steaks, seafood, and the ever-present pasta. Although the show is usually next door, for live open-mike cabaret, seek out Petterino's Monday nights and order a drink from the large, well-stocked

bar. ✉*150 N. Dearborn St.* ☎*312/422–0150* ▭*AE, D, DC, MC, V*
✛*1:D6*

$$
NEW AMERICAN
✕**Rhapsody.** Attached to the Symphony Center, home of the Chicago
Symphony, Rhapsody is more than a handy spot for a preconcert din-
ner. This restaurant combines fine-dining ambitions with a pleasant
urban greenhouse setting graced with potted palms and picture win-
dows. Despite a few chef changes in recent years, the food is consistently
solid. Rhapsody's handsome bar, pouring an expansive wine-by-the-
glass selection, is a perfect post-performance hangout. ✉*65 E. Adams
St.* ☎*312/786–9911* ▭*AE, D, DC, MC, V* ⊗*Closed Sun. mid-June–
mid-Sept. No lunch weekends* ✛*4:G2*

$$
RUSSIAN
✕**Russian Tea Time.** Exotica is on the menu and in the air at this spot
that's favored by visitors to the nearby Art Institute and Symphony
Center. Mahogany trim, samovars, and balalaika music set the stage
for dishes from Russia and neighboring republics (the owners hail from
Uzbekistan), including Ukrainian borscht, *blinis* (small, savory pan-
cakes) with salmon caviar, Moldavian meatballs, and game sausages.
Chilled vodka flights (three shots) help the herring go down. ✉*77 E.
Adams St.* ☎*312/360–0000* ⌦*Reservations essential* ▭*AE, D, MC,
V* ✛*4:G2*

$
INTERNATIONAL
✕**Shikago.** With its ever-changing and reasonably-priced menu, Shikago
lets foodies sample Asian specialties without skipping a car payment
for the privilege. With its simple design, chunky wooden tables, and
soft ambient-techno music, the restaurant draws a mixed crowd; power
suits by day, and hip up-and-comers by night. The Vietnamese spring
rolls, a crispy blend of mango and Korean-style short ribs, and the
glazed rack of lamb are excellent. Enter on Adams Street or you might
miss it. ✉*190 S. LaSalle St.* ☎*312/781–7300* ▭ *AE, D, DC, MC, V.*
⊗*Closed Sun. No lunch Sat.* ✛*4:F2*

$$
AMERICAN
✕**Tavern at the Park.** Given its unique take on American classics and
its splendid view of Chicago's Millennium Park, it would be a mistake
to pass up this near-Michigan Avenue gem. Noise from the bar carries
up to the second floor, giving this spacious restaurant a lively feel. The
prime-rib sliders and sticky fried shrimp are perfect starters before mov-
ing on to the blackened sea scallops and fettuccine or the slow-roasted
prime rib. Though many favor the warm blueberry-apple bread pudding
for dessert, the fried banana split shouldn't be missed. Don't plan on
lunch without a reservation—local businesspeople have already made
this their new hangout. ✉*130 E. Randolph St.,* ☎*312/552–0070* ▭
AE, D, DC, MC, V ⊗ *Closed Sun.* ✛*1:F6*

$$
ITALIAN
✕**Trattoria No. 10.** It's hard to camouflage a basement location, but Trattoria No. 10 gives it a good go with terra-cotta colors, arched entryways,
and quarry-tile floors, all of which evoke Italy. Pretheater diners crowd
in for the house specialty ravioli filled with seasonal stuffings, classic
antipasti selections like caprese salad with vine-ripened tomatoes and
bufala mozzarella, and substantial *secondi piatti* like wagyu steak with
roasted corn and pancetta. Cheap chowsters, meanwhile, elbow into the
bar for the $12 nibbles buffet served from 5 to 7:30 PM weekdays with
a $6 drink minimum. ✉*10 N. Dearborn St.* ☎*312/984–1718* ▭*AE,
D, DC, MC, V* ⊗*Closed Sun. No lunch Sat.* ✛*4:F1*

5

NEAR NORTH

$$$$ ✕**Avenues.** The least ostentatious of the city's cutting-edge restaurants,
CUTTING-EDGE Avenues in the Peninsula Hotel lives a double life. The contemporary
black-lacquered decor aims to satisfy business travelers and other hotel
guests, but true culinary connoisseurs come here for something else altogether. Filling the not-insignificant shoes of former chef Graham Elliot
Bowles is Curtis Duffy, who has worked with some of Chicago's top
toques, including Grant Achatz of Alinea and Charlie Trotter of eponymous Charlie Trotter's. Expect creative cuisine that is at once familiar
and progressive as Duffy finds his stride. ⊠*Peninsula Hotel, 108 E.
Superior St.* ☎*312/573–6754* ▤*AE, D, DC, MC, V* ⩍*Reservations
essential. Jacket required.* ⊙*Closed Sun. and Mon. No lunch* ✛*1:E3*

¢ ✕**Billy Goat Tavern.** The late comedian John Belushi immortalized the
BURGER Goat's short-order cooks on *Saturday Night Live* for barking, "No
Pepsi! Coke!" and "No fries! Cheeps!" at customers. They still do the
shtick at this subterranean hole-in-the-wall favored by reporters posted
nearby at the *Tribune* and the *Sun-Times*. Griddle-fried "cheezborg-
ers" are the featured chow, and people-watching the favored sport.
⊠*430 N. Michigan Ave., lower level* ☎*312/222–1525* ▤*No credit
cards* ✛*1:E5*

$$ ✕**Bistro 110.** The knock against Bistro 110 is that it can be noisy and
BISTRO chaotic, but we consider that a testament to its popularity. Besides
the lively bar scene and Water Tower views, the real draw is the food
from the wood-burning oven. The kitchen consistently offers excel-
lent renditions of French classics like roast chicken, and vegetarians
praise the roasted-vegetable platter. The Sunday jazz brunch makes
things more crowded—and louder—than usual. ⊠*110 E. Pearson St.*
☎*312/266–3110* ▤*AE, D, DC, MC, V* ✛*1:E2.*

$$ ✕**Bistrot Margot.** We love this Old Town bistro for its faithfully executed
BISTRO menu, budget-friendly prices, and Parisian art nouveau interior, even
if we have to sit a little too close for comfort to our neighbors. Chef-
owner Joe Doppes whips up silky chicken-liver pâté, succulent *moules
marinières* (mussels in white wine), escargots simmered in rich garlic
butter, and soul-satisfying coq au vin. Head up to the second floor for
additional seating—it has more of an intimate French country-home
feel. Table spacing is tight and crowds are abundant, warranting your
best behavior. ⊠*1437 N. Wells St.* ☎*312/587–3660* ▤*AE, D, MC,
V* ✛*3:G3*

¢ ✕**Fox & Obel Market, Café & Catering.** Skip the tourist-trap funnel-
CAFÉ cake fare at Navy Pier. This riverside gourmet market a block away
is a toothsome escape. The prepared fine and organic foodstuffs are
treated with reverence, and although service is cafeteria-style, selections
are decidedly more sophisticated. We like the Cuban sandwich with
smoked Black Forest ham, breaded pork, and Swiss cheese, and the
pan-seared mahimahi topped with shrimp. But first, a word of warn-
ing: attractive chocolate bars, exotic charcuterie, and worldly cheeses
sold in the upscale grocery can be budget busters. ⊠*401 E. Illinois St.*
☎*312/410–7301* ▤*AE, D, MC, V* ✛*1:G4*

$$$$ ✕**Gibsons Steakhouse.** Chicago movers and shakers mingle with con-
STEAKHOUSE ventioneers at Gibsons, a lively, homegrown, Gold Coast steakhouse

renowned for overwhelming portions, good service, and celebrity spotting. Generous steaks and chops center the menu, but there are plenty of fish options, including planked whitefish and massive Australian lobster tails. One dessert will feed a table of four. Reservations aren't required but are near essential given the hoards of fans. ✉*1028 N. Rush St.* ☎*312/266–8999* ⌖*Reservations essential* ▤*AE, D, DC, MC, V* ✥*1:D1*

$ ✕**Kamehachi.** It seems like there's a sushi spot on practically every corner in Chicago, but when Kamehachi opened in Old Town in 1967 it was the first. Quality fish, updated decor, and eager-to-please hospitality keep fans returning. Behind the busy sushi bar, chefs manage both restaurant orders and the many take-out calls from neighbors. We find combinations, including maki rolls, nigiri sushi, and miso soup, are often a bargain, running from $13 to $30. Belly up to the sushi bar, or take a seat in the upstairs lounge or in the flowering garden (in season). The Streeterville spin-off offers semiprivate tatami rooms ideal for groups. ✉*1400 N. Wells St.* ☎*312/664–3663* ☾*No lunch Sun.* ✉*240 E. Ontario* ☎*312/587–0600* ✉*320 N. Dearborn St.* ☎*312/744–1900* ▤*AE, D, DC, MC, V* ☾*No lunch Sun.* ✥*1:F4; 3:G3*

JAPANESE

$$$$ ✕**Les Nomades.** Intimate and elegant don't make headlines, but Les Nomades holds a torch for tender refinements. Wood-burning fireplaces and original art warm the dining rooms of the Streeterville brownstone. A carefully composed menu of contemporary French food includes the usual suspects, such as duck consommé and warm asparagus with crispy poached egg, plus earthy indulgences like roasted squab breast with crispy sweetbreads. Compose your own prix-fixe dinner from the menu; four courses cost $115; five courses cost $130. ✉*222 E. Ontario St.* ☎*312/649–9010* ⌖*Reservations essential. Jacket required* ▤*AE, D, DC, MC, V* ☾*Closed Sun. and Mon. No lunch* ✥*1:F4*

FRENCH

$$$ ✕**McCormick & Schmick's.** If you're the indecisive type, don't even think about dining here. This link in the Oregon-based chain updates its massive menu twice daily to list the freshest fish available. Expect at least six varieties of oysters, specialties like blue lump crab cakes and several dozen fish, like Barcelona anchovies and Hawaiian marlin. Wood paneling, cozy booths, and high ceilings generate a clubby setting. We love the bar, not just for the cheap happy-hour nibbles, but because the bartenders squeeze all the juices that go into the fresh and zesty cocktails. ✉*41 E. Chestnut St.* ☎*312/397–9500* ▤*AE, D, DC, MC, V* ✥*1:D2*

SEAFOOD

$$$ ✕**Mike Ditka's.** NFL Hall-of-Famer Mike Ditka was one of only two coaches to take the Bears to the Super Bowl. Sure, it was in 1985, but Bears fans have long memories, and they still love "Da Coach" as well as his clubby, sports-themed restaurant where local performer John Vincent does dead-on impressions of Frank Sinatra Tuesdays through Saturdays. The dark-wood interior, upstairs cigar lounge, and sports memorabilia are predictable, but the menu clearly aims to please large and diverse audiences. Café staples (salads, fish) and bar food (burgers, meat loaf) join steakhouse fare (steaks, chops) and a few unexpected indulgences (crab and Parmesan-crusted lemon sole). ✉*Tremont Hotel, 100 E. Chestnut St.* ☎*312/587–8989* ▤*AE, D, MC, V* ✥*1:E2*

AMERICAN

5

$$$$
NEW AMERICAN
✕**NoMI.** The expensive linens, Jaune de Chrome china, and Isamu Noguchi sculpture make NoMI completely luxurious, but the vibe here is casual, as if all this elegance were everyday and not special-occasion (although jackets are recommended for men). This is the place to go if you're celebrating the latter or traveling on a generous expense account—you'll have one of the city's best tables, overlooking the historic Water Tower from a seven-story perch. The menu leans French, with strong Asian and Mediterranean accents. ⊠*Park Hyatt Hotel, 800 N. Michigan Ave.* ☎*312/239–4030* ▭*AE, D, DC, MC, V* ✣*1:E3*

$
CAFÉ
✕**Pierrot Gourmet.** Despite the legions of shoppers on Michigan Avenue, there are few casual cafés to quell their collective hunger, making this bakery-patisserie-café a welcome neighbor. Lunches center on upscale greens like herb salad with olives and Parmesan, along with open-face *tartine* sandwiches on crusty, house-made sourdough. Break midafternoon for a *tarte flambé,* an Alsatian flat bread with cheese and cream, accompanied by a glass of Riesling. Solos are accommodated at the magazine-strewn communal table. Meals are served all day long. The upscale Peninsula hotel runs Pierrot, accounting for both the high quality and the high cost. ⊠*Peninsula Hotel, 108 E. Superior St.* ☎*312/573–6749* ▭*AE, D, DC, MC, V* ✣*1:E3*

$$
AMERICAN
✕**Pump Room.** The Pump Room clings to its old-time Chicago fame, when celebrities passing through town via rail beat it to the restaurant to see and be seen. The likes of Frank Sinatra, Bette Davis, and Humphrey Bogart held court in the storied Booth One, and publicity photos taken there line the entrance to the restaurant. In keeping with tradition, the booth is off-limits to all but A-list celebs who, truthfully, don't show like they used to. Now the restaurant's main dining room is closed for renovations, but new management is working hard to lure the next generation with a more casual bistro menu served in the bar. ⊠*Ambassador East Hotel, 1301 N. State Pkwy.* ☎*312/266–0360* ▭*AE, D, DC, MC, V* ☾*No lunch* ✣*3:H4*

$$$
SEAFOOD
✕**Riva.** Riva's got the lock on upscale dining in the middle of junk-food–central Navy Pier. The restaurant relies a bit too much on the views—which, gazing southward over Lake Michigan, are admittedly fantastic—when it should concentrate on better cooking. Opt for simpler preparations, such as grilled salmon or various pastas, over the menu's more ambitious efforts. Grilled fish, shellfish, and steaks are pricey, though the hordes that crowd the place, especially in summer, don't seem to mind (good service helps). A casual grill downstairs, which spills onto the pier's promenade in summer, is kinder to your wallet. ⊠*700 E. Grand Ave.* ☎*312/644–7482* ▭*AE, D, DC, MC, V* ✣*1:H4*

$$
AMERICAN
✕**RL.** Power brokers, moneyed locals, and Michigan Avenue shoppers keep the revolving doors spinning at RL, the initials of designer Ralph

Lauren who lent his name and signature soigné style to the eatery that adjoins his Polo/Ralph Lauren store. The cozy confines cluster leather banquettes under hunt-club-style art hung on wood-paneled walls. The menu of American classics, including steak tartare, Dover sole in butter, and steak Diane flamed tableside, suits the country-club-in-the-city setting. ⊠*115 E. Chicago Ave.* ☎*312/475–1100* ▭*AE, DC, MC, V* ✛*1:E3*

$$ ✕ **Salpicón.** Anyone who does authentic Mexican in Chicago operates in
MEXICAN the shadow of Frontera Grill's Rick Bayless, which makes it easier for those in the know to snag a table at Salpicón. Chef Priscila Satkoff grew up in Mexico City, and her renditions of mole poblano and grilled fish with salsa fresca have unforced flair. Wash 'em down with a belt of one of 100 tequilas or choose from the extensive selection of vintage wines. Once you try the Mexican-style Sunday brunch, with dishes like skirt steak and eggs, you'll never go back to eggs Benedict. ⊠*1252 N. Wells St.* ☎*312/988–7811* ▭*AE, D, DC, MC, V* ⊗*No lunch* ✛*3:G4*

$$$$ ✕ **Seasons Restaurant.** How the Four Seasons's boîte manages to please
NEW AMERICAN business diners and traveling families is a mystery worthy of a hotel-school case study. Service is suave, the room elegant, and the seasonal food refined; altogether, it's an ideal spot for power-dining appointments. At the same time, the hotel makes a big deal about being family-friendly, which, if you read between the lines a bit, means there's a children's menu for better-behaved clans (it *is* still the Four Seasons). Fixing for a good deal and a quick lunch? There's an affordable three-course daily lunch menu that's served within an hour. Dinner menus include five- and eight-course tasting options. Reservations are essential for Chicago's best (and most expensive) Sunday brunch. ⊠*Four Seasons Hotel, 120 E. Delaware Pl.* ☎*312/649–2349* ▭*AE, D, DC, MC, V.* ⊗*No dinner Sun.–Tues.* ✛*1:E2*

$$ ✕ **Shanghai Terrace.** As precious as a jewel box, and often as pricey, this
CHINESE red, lacquer-trimmed 80-seater hidden away in the Peninsula Hotel reveals the hotelier's Asian roots. Come for upscale dim sum, stylishly presented, and luxury-laden dishes such as steamed fish, Kobe beef rolls, roasted quail with pickled pear, and wok-fried lobster. Meanwhile, a patio seating up to 70 during warmer months lets you revel in a relaxing meal four stories above the madding crowds of Michigan Avenue. Though fans admire the attentive, professional service, some warn that diners with larger appetites might leave feeling unsatisfied. ⊠*Peninsula Hotel, 108 E. Superior St.* ☎*312/573–6744* ▭*AE, D, DC, MC, V* ⊗*Closed Sun.* ✛*1:E3*

$$$ ✕ **Signature Room at the 95th.** When you've got the best view in town and
AMERICAN a lock on the prom business, do you need to be daring with the food? Signature Room isn't; making a formal affair of dishes such as rack of lamb and grilled salmon while couples ogle the skyline views from the John Hancock's 95th floor. Avoid the clichés by calling here at lunch: the $18 buffet gets you good and stuffed, and the daytime light lets you see Lake Michigan. The appeal of the lavish and pricey Sunday brunch? The abundance of food. Brunch reservations essential. ⊠*John Hancock Center, 875 N. Michigan Ave.* ☎*312/787–9596* ▭*AE, D, DC, MC, V* ✛*1:E2*

$$$$ ╳**Spiaggia.** Refined Italian cooking dished alongside three-story picture-
ITALIAN window views of Lake Michigan make Spiaggia one of the city's top
eateries. The tiered dining room guarantees good sight lines from each
table. Chef Tony Mantuano prepares elegant, seasonal dishes such as
veal-filled pasta with fennel pollen, roast guinea hen with truffle sauce,
or Mediterranean bass with saffron potato puree. Oenophiles consider
the wine list scholarly. For Spiaggia fare, minus the luxury ingredients, try lunch or dinner at the casual Cafe Spiaggia next door. ✉*980
N. Michigan Ave.* ☎*312/280–2750* ≜*Reservations essential. Jacket
required* ⊟*AE, D, DC, MC, V* ⊗*No lunch* ✥*1:E2*

$$$ ╳**Table Fifty-Two.** If it feels as if everyone is a regular at chef Art Smith's
SOUTHERN Gold Coast restaurant, they very well might be. Oprah's former per-
sonal chef is not short of friends and admirers. Yet newcomers lucky
enough to score a reservation feel just as welcome in its cozy, country-
home environs, particularly when the complimentary Parmesan cheese
biscuits arrive. While the menu strays to Asia and Europe, at its core is a
formidable Southern lineup of dishes such as Low Country shrimp with
stone-ground grits, a fried-green-tomato Napoleon, and fried chicken
(a Sunday-only special). Save room for Smith's hummingbird cake, a
homey banana and pineapple cake topped with cream-cheese frosting.
If you're in the neighborhood without a reservation, walk in and see if
the chef's counter is available: the restaurant keeps five seats open in
front of the pizza oven. ✉*52 W. Elm St.* ☎*312/573–4000* ≜*Reserva-
tions essential* ⊟*AE, MC, V* ⊗*Closed Mon.* ✥*3:G4*

$$$$ ╳**TRU.** Chefs Rick Tramonto and, on pastries, Gale Gand do fine din-
NEW AMERICAN ing with a sense of humor. The quite serious food is leavened by the
presentations: caviar atop a tabletop crystal staircase, between-course
sorbets in cones, or dishes served over a mini fishbowl occupied by a
live fighting fish. The dining room resembles a gallery, with white walls
and carefully chosen art, including an Andy Warhol. The menu starts
with a basic three-course prix-fixe, priced at $95, and escalates to nine
courses. Several of those are dessert, so save space. ✉*676 N. St. Clair
St.* ☎*312/202–0001* ≜*Reservations essential. Jacket required* ⊟*AE,
D, DC, MC, V* ⊗*Closed Sun. No lunch* ✥*1:F3*

$$ ╳**Twin Anchors Restaurant & Tavern.** For a taste of classic Chicago, stop
AMERICAN into Twin Anchors, which has been dishing baby back ribs since 1932.
The nautically-themed brick tavern was a favorite of Frank Sinatra,
who still croons nightly on the jukebox. If you're not in the mood for
a messy slab of mild or zesty ribs, the main draw on the menu, order
the battered codfish fry or the roasted chicken. In truth, dinner here is
really less about cuisine and more about the scene—local and touring
celebs often visit, and many locals are loyal regulars—but lovers of bar-
rooms with personality don't mind the typically long waits during prime
time. ✉*1655 N. Sedgwick St.* ☎*312/266–1616* ≜*Reservations not
accepted* ⊟*AE, D, DC, MC, V* ⊗*No lunch weekdays* ✥*3:G3*

$$ ╳**Viand.** Ebullient chef-owner Steve Chiappetti's personality is written
AMERICAN all over Viand, a lively restaurant and bar that's a breath of fresh air
after the seriously designer-centric Michigan Avenue, just a half block
away. "Dining should be fun," says the chef, and so it is here where
Oscar-style statuettes deliver chopsticks and the Junk Food Cart des-
sert option packs homemade Oreos, marshmallows, and brownies in a

mini shopping cart. Don't miss the braised lamb, the four-cheese ravioli with truffle sauce, and a chat with the friendly chef. Adjacent to a Courtyard by Marriott, the restaurant serves breakfast, lunch, and dinner and has a steady bar trade. ⊠*155 E. Ontario St.* ☎*312/255–8505* ▭*AE, MC, V* ✛*1:F4*

RIVER NORTH

$$$
NEW AMERICAN

✕**Aigre Doux.** Hidden in the shadows of its neighbor, the mammoth Merchandise Mart, this stylish spot in an unsung locale warrants searching out for the considerable talents of its husband-and-wife chef-owners. He does the savories, she the sweets. Aigre Doux (which means "sweet and sour") serves deftly accented dishes like heirloom squash risotto, braised rabbit pizza, and roasted lobster bucatini. Stay for desserts like sticky toffee pudding and caramelized apple bread pudding. Attentive service, a selective wine list, and modern decor including exposed light bulbs create a chameleon setting conducive, like the chefs' marriage, to both business and romance. ⊠*230 W. Kinzie St.* ☎*312/329–9400* ▭*AE, D, DC, MC, V* ⊙*Closed Sun. No lunch* ✛*1:C5*

$
ITALIAN

✕**A Mano.** The proven restaurant team behind Bin 36 turned the space beneath their popular wine-centric restaurant into this Italian spot. True to its name, A Mano prides itself on making almost everything—from the pastas to the fennel sausage—by hand. Start with a plate of salumi while you peruse the Italian wine list, or snack on thin-crust pizza baked in the brick oven. To avoid the din (the open kitchen is in the middle of the dining room and conversation can be difficult on busy nights), dine early or on the patio in warm weather. ⊠*335 N. Dearborn St.* ☎*312/629–3500* ▭ *AE, D, DC, MC, V* ✛*1:D5*

$
CHINESE

✕**Ben Pao.** Snagging our award for the most Zen Chinese restaurant in town is this spot with minimalist black-and-gray decor and soothing water walls. The food livens up the scene, with spicy dragon noodles and plenty of the tried-and-true sesame chicken and kung pao chicken. A dozen or so small-plate starters, generous main courses, and several sides encourage sharing, making this a good choice for the gang. ⊠*52 W. Illinois St.* ☎*312/222–1888* ▭*AE, D, DC, MC, V* ⊙*No lunch weekends* ✛*1:D4*

$$
AMERICAN
Fodor's Choice
★

✕**Bin 36.** This hip hybrid—fine-dining establishment, lively wine bar, and wineshop—serves wine any way you want it: by the bottle, glass, half glass, and as flights of multiple 2½ ounce tastings. The menu similarly encourages sampling, with lots of small-plate grazing choices. Contemporary entrées, such as braised lamb shank and peppercorn-crusted swordfish, are helpfully listed with wine recommendations. An all-glass west wall and 35-foot ceilings lend loft looks to the sprawling space, which can be noisy. Nonetheless, it's a good choice for group gatherings, and, since it's open all day, between-standard-mealtime nibbles. ⊠*339 N. Dearborn St.* ☎*312/755–9463* ▭*AE, D, DC, MC, V.* ✛*1:D5*

$$
BRASSERIE

✕**Brasserie Jo.** Come for the frites alone at Jean Joho's fun and more affordable brasserie (he of Everest fame). It's authentic down to its zinc-topped bar proffering complimentary hard-boiled eggs. Stay for the *choucroute Alsacienne* (smoked meats with Alsatian-style sauerkraut), sautéed skate wing, steamed mussels, fillet of trout, classic *coq* *au vin*, and steak tartare. It's most charming when it's bustling, though peak hours will force you to wait for a table. ⊠*59 W. Hubbard St.* ☎*312/595–0800* ▭*AE, D, DC, MC, V* ⊘*No lunch* ✛*1:D5*

$ ✕**Cafe Iberico.** A Spanish expat from Galicia runs this tapas place hailed
SPANISH by a range of fans from visiting Spaniards to family clans, dating couples, and cheap chowhounds. You can easily build a meal from the many $3.95–$8.50 small plates on offer like baked goat cheese, Spanish ham, grilled squid, and skewered beef. When busy, it's loud and boisterous, which is only annoying on weekends when the wait can stretch to hours. Only parties of six or more may make dinner reservations for Sunday through Thursday. ⊠*739 N. LaSalle St.* ☎*312/573–1510* ▭*AE, D, DC, MC, V* ✛*1:C3*

$$ ✕**Coco Pazzo.** The spread of antipasti that greets you upon entrance into
ITALIAN this Tuscan-inspired restaurant is a sign of things to come. This restaurant serves lusty, aggressively seasoned fare, such as homemade pasta with rabbit ragu, herb-crusted half lamb rack, and wood-grilled Florentine steaks. Stop in at lunch for pizzas fresh from the wood-fired oven. Swagged draperies and discreet but professional service work hard to soften the open loft setting of exposed brick walls and wood floors. Meanwhile, the well-rounded, exclusively Italian wine list is nothing to sniff at—*Wine Spectator* has lauded its selection ranging from popular to boutique producers. ⊠*300 W. Hubbard St.* ☎*312/836–0900* ▭*AE, DC, MC, V* ⊘*No lunch weekends* ✛*1:C5*

$$$ ✕**Crofton on Wells.** We like this place because it's really good and still
NEW AMERICAN manages to be rather low-key. Chef-owner Suzy Crofton breaks a few contemporary-dining rules: she doesn't pack tables too closely together in the small space, and she keeps the noise level down. Her food is similarly short on clichés but gratifyingly long on flavor. Dig into spicy herb- and chipotle-roasted Amish chicken with Yukon Gold mashed potatoes and smoky molasses au jus, or grilled venison with baby arugula and sweet-potato spaetzle. But the menu is not meat-centric: with at least three vegetarian entrées on the menu each night, consider this a place to bring vegetarian friends. ⊠*535 N. Wells St.* ☎*312/755–1790* ⌀*Reservations essential* ▭*AE, D, DC, MC, V* ⊘*Closed Sun. No lunch.* ✛*1:C4*

$$ ✕**Cyrano's Bistrot Wine Bar & Cabaret.** Cyrano's flies under the radar in
BISTRO restaurant-rich River North, which works to your advantage if you want a spontaneous meal. Chef and owner Didier Durand presents the food of his birthplace, Bergerac, in this cheerful restaurant. Traditional starters such as onion tart, lobster bisque, pâtés, and rillettes lead into mains of rotisserie duck, cassoulet, and rabbit fricassee. The wine list includes many vintages from lesser-known producers in southern France. The lower-level cabaret, Café Simone, is open on weekends and offers half-size entrées at half the price. ⊠*546 N. Wells St.* ☎*312/467–0546* ▭*AE, D, DC, MC, V* ⊘*Closed Sun. No lunch weekends* ✛*1:C4*

$$$$ ✕**David Burke's Primehouse.** New York celebrity chef David Burke runs
STEAKHOUSE Primehouse in the boutique James hotel, and though local reception was initially cautious—after all, what could a New Yorker teach a Chicagoan about steak?—the restaurant has been roundly embraced for its convivial setting and sense of playfulness, including identifying

207L, the steer responsible for producing the menu's prime beef. Don't miss Burke's innovative cuts, including a 28-day-dry-aged rib eye and the bone-in filet mignon. Interactive elements including tableside tossed Caesar salads and fill-your-own doughnuts for dessert feed the considerable energy in the generally packed room. The best seats are the red-leather booths along the walls. ⊠*616 N. Rush St.* ☎*312/660–6000* ▤*AE, D, MC, V* ✛*1:E4*

¢ ✕**Ed Debevic's.** Gum-snapping waiters in garish costumes trade quips
AMERICAN and snide remarks with customers at this tongue-in-cheek re-creation
☾ of a 1950s diner, but it's all good, clean fun (except perhaps when they dance on the counter without removing their shoes). The menu is deep and cheap with 10 different hamburgers, five chili preparations, four hot dogs, a large sandwich selection, and "deluxe plates" such as meat loaf, pot roast, and chicken-fried steak. The place is crawling with kids. Unlike a real 1950s diner, however, Ed's has a selection of cocktails and wines for their parents. ⊠*640 N. Wells St.* ☎*312/664–1707* ◿*Reservations not accepted* ▤*AE, D, DC, MC, V* ✛*1:C4*

$$$$ ✕**Fogo de Chão.** Gaucho-clad servers parade through the dining room
BRAZILIAN brandishing carved-to-order skewered and grilled meats in this all-you-can-eat Brazilian churrascaria. Diners warm up with a trip to the lavish salad bar. Then, using a plate-side chip, signal green for "go" to bring on lamb, pork loin, ribs, and several beef cuts, stopped only by flipping the chip to red. You can restart as often as you like. If that's not enough, there are starchy sides and desserts included in the $49.50 price as well; only drinks are extra. Compared to traditional steakhouses, this carnivorous all-inclusive feast is a bargain. Go on a busy night (Thursday, Friday, or Saturday) to ensure the meat's tender, and not dried out from reheating. ⊠*661 N. LaSalle St.* ☎*312/932–9330* ▤*AE, D, DC, MC, V* ☾*No lunch weekends* ✛*1:C3*

$$ ✕**Frontera Grill.** Devotees of chef-owner Rick Bayless queue up for his
MEXICAN distinct fare at this casual restaurant brightly trimmed in Mexican folk art. Bayless annually visits Mexico with the entire staff in tow. Servers, consequently, are encyclopedic on the food, typified by trout in yellow mole, red chili-marinated pork, and black-bean tamales filled with goat cheese. The reservation policy is tricky: a limited number are accepted for parties of all sizes. Otherwise, do as most do and endure the two-margarita wait. ⊠*445 N. Clark St.* ☎*312/661–1434* ▤*AE, D, DC, MC, V* ☾*Closed Sun. and Mon.* ✛*1:D5*

$$$$ ✕**Gene and Georgetti.** This old-school steakhouse, in business since
STEAKHOUSE 1941, is a Chicago institution. It thrives on the buddy network of high-powered regulars and celebrities who pop into the historic River North joint to carve up massive steaks, good chops, and the famed "garbage salad"—a kitchen-sink creation of greens with vegetables and meats. In addition, Italian-American classics such as eggplant parmigiana and veal Vesuvio are on offer along with simple seafood dishes like lobster tail, salmon, and whitefish. Service can be brusque if you're not connected, and prices can be steep, but the vibe is Chicago to the core. ⊠*500 N. Franklin St.* ☎*312/527–3718* ▤*AE, DC, MC, V* ☾*Closed Sun.* ✛*1:C4*

5

$$$

NEW AMERICAN

✗**Graham Elliot.** Guests groove to the tunes of Wilco and The Police while sampling Chef Graham Elliot Bowles's inventive fare, some of which foodies may recognize from the chef's stint orchestrating elaborate tasting menus at Avenues. Yet much of the menu, from "BLT-style" salmon (salmon served with pancetta vinaigrette) to pork prime rib will satisfy diners in far fewer courses than the old Avenues tasting menu did. Service can be unconventional: servers take dessert orders at the start of the meal, for example. Yet the boisterous space with exposed brick walls succeeds in combining a casual vibe with fine-dining flourish. Bowles calls it "bistronomic;" his fans simply call it good eating. ⊠ *217 W. Huron St.* ☎*312/624–9975* ⊟*AE, D, DC, MC, V* ⊘*Closed Sun.* ✛*3:G5*

$$

STEAKHOUSE

✗**Harry Caray's Italian Steakhouse.** Famed Cubs announcer Harry Caray died in 1998, but his legend lives on as fans continue to pour into the namesake restaurant where Harry frequently held court. Italian-American specialties including pastas and chicken Vesuvio share menu space with top-quality prime steaks and chops. The wine list has won a number of national awards. If you're looking for a classic Chicago spot to catch a game, the generally thronged bar serves items off of the restaurant menu. Holy cow! ⊠*33 W. Kinzie St.* ☎*312/828–0966* ⊟*AE, D, DC, MC, V* ✛*1:D5*

$$$

JAPANESE

✗**Japonais.** Style and substance come together at sleek and chic Japonais. Don't be intimidated by the lengthy menu. Trust servers to direct you to savories such as breaded oysters, sweet-vinegar-seaweed salad, and a raft of winning maki-roll combinations including octopus with spicy tuna. Traditional tables are supplemented by a couch-filled lounge also serving the entire menu. Downstairs an indoor-outdoor bar provides seasonal seating along the Chicago River—don't attempt it on weekends unless you have sharp elbows. ⊠*600 W. Chicago Ave.* ☎*312/822–9600* ⊟*AE, DC, MC, V* ⊘*No lunch weekends* ✛*1:A3*

$$–$$$

SEAFOOD

✗**Joe's Seafood, Prime Steaks & Stone Crab.** You might wonder what a South Floridian like Joe's is doing so far from the ocean. Apparently, raking it in. Unlike the original, Joe's Stone Crab in Miami Beach, this outlet doesn't close when the Florida crabs are out of season in summer, which explains the extra emphasis on other denizens of the deep and prime steaks. One thing this restaurant does share with the Miami original is its popularity—though the restaurant takes reservations, you can expect to wait when it's packed with hungry guests. ⊠*60 E. Grand Ave.* ☎*312/379–5637* ⊟*AE, D, DC, MC, V* ✛*1:E4*

$$$$

STEAKHOUSE

✗**Keefer's.** Few steakhouses advertise their broiler men, but the barrier-busting Keefer's hired acclaimed chef John Hogan to run the kitchen. Hogan's definition of a steakhouse menu breaks all conventions by including his signature bistro fare, inventive daily specials (pray for the seafood-rich bouillabaisse), and plenty of fish offerings as well as New York strips and hefty porterhouses. The circular room drops the he-man pose, too. All of which explains why Keefer's pulls the most diverse and gender-balanced crowd of the meat market. ⊠*20 W. Kinzie St.* ☎*312/467–9525* ⊟*AE, D, DC, MC, V* ⊘*Closed Sun. No lunch Sat.* ✛*1:D5*

$$$
NEW AMERICAN

✕ **mk.** Foodies and fashionistas favor owner-chef Michael Kornick's ultrahip spot for its sleek look and elegant menu. Occupying a renovated warehouse, mk weights brick walls and soaring ceilings with fine linens, expensive flatware, and designer wine stems. Menus change with the season and hew to two or three dominant flavors à la halibut with braised baby fennel and kalamata olives, and rack of pork with mustard greens. It's not cheap, but it is special. ⊠ *868 N. Franklin St.* ☎ *312/482–9179* ⊟ *AE, DC, MC, V* ⊘ *No lunch* ✛ *1:C2*

¢
AMERICAN

✕ **Mr. Beef.** A Chicago institution for two-fisted Italian beef sandwiches piled with green peppers or giardiniera and provolone cheese, Mr. Beef garners citywide fans from area hard-hats to restaurateurs and TV personalities. Service and setting—two indoor picnic tables and a dining rail—are fast-food no-nonsense. This workingman's favorite is, go figure, located near River North's art galleries. ⊠ *666 N. Orleans St.* ☎ *312/337–8500* ⊟ *No credit cards* ⊘ *Closed Sun. No dinner* ✛ *1:B3*

$$
LATIN AMERICAN

✕ **Nacional 27.** Here's a bit of trivia to spring on fellow diners: there are 27 nations south of the U.S. border, and it's the cuisine of those 27 that supposedly comprise the pan-Latin menu here. That may be an exaggeration, but the menu does offer variety. Try the tiny barbecued lamb tacos appetizer and follow with the slow-cooked pork Cubano with coconut rice, black beans, and plantains. The circular bar draws a following independent of the food. After 11 PM on weekend nights the floor in the middle of the dining room is cleared for salsa and merengue dancing. ⊠ *325 W. Huron St.* ☎ *312/664–2727* ⊟ *AE, D, DC, MC, V* ⊘ *Closed Sun. No lunch* ✛ *1:B3*

$$$
NEW AMERICAN

✕ **Naha.** Cousins Carrie and Michael Nahabedian lend their name (well, the first two syllables, anyway) and considerable culinary and hospitality skills to this upscale venture. In a clean space done in shades of cream and sage, Naha presents eye-catching dishes such as wood-grilled Spanish sausage, honey-lacquered duck breast, or wild bass in saffron broth. Wine is treated with reverence, from the well-chosen selection of vintages to the high-quality stemware. Solos and social-seekers can sit at the convivial bar and order from the main menu. ⊠ *500 N. Clark St.* ☎ *312/321–6242* ⊟ *AE, D, DC, MC, V* ⊘ *Closed Sun. No lunch Sat.* ✛ *1:D4*

$$$
ITALIAN

✕ **Osteria via Stato.** It's no-brainer Italian here, where the shtick is to feed you without asking too many questions. If you opt for the $39.95 prix-fixe, you pick an entrée from the $36 prix-fixe, and waiters do the rest, working the room with several communal platters of antipasti, then pasta, followed by your entrée, and dessert. There's even a "just bring me wine" program that delivers preselected Italian vino to your table throughout your meal. The results are savory enough, but Osteria shines brightest at making you feel comfortable. If conversation is important, make a reservation here. Or, for a faster meal, dine in the pizza bar. ⊠ *620 N. State St.* ☎ *312/642–8450* ⊟ *AE, D, DC, MC, V* ⊘ *No lunch Sun.* ✛ *1:D4*

5

$ ✗**Pizzeria Due.** Serving up one-inch-thick pizzas in a comfortable,
ITALIAN   though well-worn dining room, Pizzeria Due is where everyone goes
☺   when they've found out that Uno, the original home of Chicago's deep-
dish pizza up the street, has an hour-plus wait. The caveat is that Due
quickly builds its own waiting list, and it's not unusual to wait for more
than an hour here as well. The best strategy for dining out at either
spot is to arrive early or opt to come at lunch. Once here, go for the
signature dish, but feel free to customize. Due fans like the option of
ordering individual-sized pizzas rather than getting the table to agree
on fillings. ✉*619 N. Wabash Ave.* ☎*312/943–2400* ▭*AE, D, DC,
MC, V* ✛*1:E4*

$ ✗**Pizzeria Uno.** Chicago deep-dish pizza got its start here in 1943, and
ITALIAN   both local and out-of-town fans continue to pack in for filling pies.
Housed in a Victorian brownstone, Uno offers a slice of old Chicago
in dim paneled rooms with reproduction light fixtures. Spin-off Due
down the street handles the overflow. Plan on two thick, cheesy slices
or less as a full meal. This is no quick-to-your-table pie, so do order
salads and be prepared to entertain the kids during the inevitable wait.
✉*29 E. Ohio St.* ☎*312/321–1000* ✛*1:E4.*

$$ ✗**Rockit Bar & Grill.** A classic tavern for the club set, Rockit Bar &
AMERICAN   Grill serves upscale bar food, pours creative cocktails, and aims to
please everyone from celebrity visitors (given wide berth in the barroom
upstairs) to kids (served Lincoln Log-like stacks of peanut butter- and
jelly-brioche French toast for brunch). The extensive menu spans salads,
sandwiches, and burgers (try the Kobe version), as well as comfort-food
entrées like Thanksgiving turkey and pesto-cream pasta with salmon.
Oprah-famed-designer Nate Berkus did the rustic-chic interiors, includ-
ing tree-stump cocktail tables and antler chandeliers. After dinner, head
upstairs to shoot some pool and check out the singles scene. ✉*22 W.
Hubbard St.* ☎*312/645–6000* ▭*AE, MC, V* ✛*1:D5*

$$ ✗**Scoozi!** This ever-popular trattoria continues to attract a yuppie crowd
ITALIAN   after 5 PM and plenty of wandering suburbanites on the weekend. You'll
☺   recognize it by the gigantic tomato over the front door; inside, a sprawling, two-level dining room presents loft-chic looks of exposed-brick
walls, open-truss ceiling, and steel garage doors. This place is nothing if not chameleon; groups love the shareable antipasti and pizzas,
families with kids meld right into the cacophony, and couples find
the energy relieves the focus on a boring date. ✉*410 W. Huron St.*
☎*312/943–5900* ▭*AE, D, DC, MC, V* ⊗*No lunch* ✛*1:B3*

$$$ ✗**Shaw's Crab House.** Hands down, this is one of the city's best seafood
SEAFOOD   spots. Though it's held an exalted position for a long time, the restau-
rant doesn't rest on its laurels. The kitchen stays on track, turning out
famed classics like silky crab cakes and rich halibut while updating the
menu with sushi, maki, and fresh tartare selections. The seafood salad
served at lunch is loaded and big enough for two. (Lunch, by the way,
is a good bargain, with well-priced entrées and $1 desserts). The city's
chief specialist in bivalves nurtures a split personality, spanning a clubby
main dining room in nautically themed loft digs and a lively exposed-
brick bar where shell shuckers work harder than the barkeeps. ✉*21 E.
Hubbard St.* ☎*312/527–2722* ▭*AE, D, DC, MC, V* ✛*1:E5*

Continued on page 191

CHICAGO'S HOLY TRINITY:
Pizza, Hot Dogs & Italian Beef Sandwiches

Long before Chicago's dining scene got all gussied up with boldface-named chefs and swanky hot spots, the City of Big Shoulders perfected hearty, gut-busting food for the Average Joe. Until you've pigged out on deep-dish pizza at Lou Malnati's or Gino's East, sunk your teeth into a loaded hot dog at Superdawg Drive-in, and wiped the grease off your face after devouring an Italian beef sandwich at Al's Beef, you haven't done Chicago. So go on, leave your diet plans at home and get ready to sample the best of the big city.

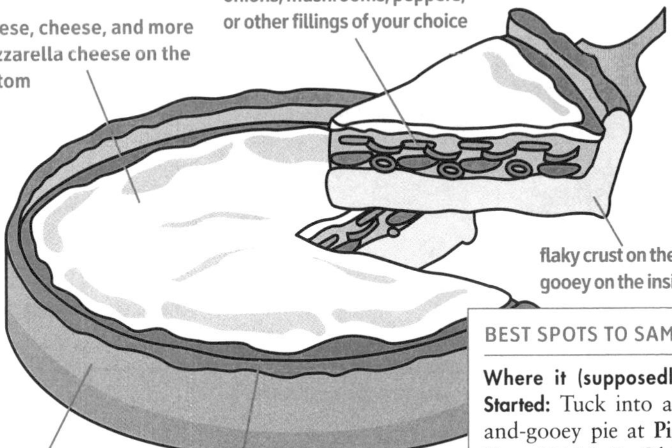

cheese, cheese, and more mozzarella cheese on the bottom

sausage, pepperoni, olives, onions, mushrooms, peppers, or other fillings of your choice

flaky crust on the outside, gooey on the inside

two-inch-high deep dish pan

spicy tomato sauce on top

TASTE 1 | DEEP-DISH PIZZA

A CALORIC HISTORY

Pizza—in one form or another—has been around since the sixth century B.C., but it only gained heft when it settled into this brash, entrepreneurial city. Pizzeria Uno founder Ike Sewell generally gets the credit for turning pizza inside out in 1943. His knife-and-fork creation started with a layer of cheese, followed by the toppings, and then the sauce, all tucked into a doughy crust that he yanked up the sides of a deep pan.

THE CRUST CONTROVERSY

The founders of Lou Malnati's pizzeria worked in Ike's kitchen at Pizzeria Uno and claim that *they* were the ones actually doing the cooking. They broke off and opened up Lou Malnati's in 1971, in Lincolnwood, a northern suburb of Chicago, and a classic Chicago rivalry was born. Today, there are more than 25 locations of Lou Malnati's in Chicago and its surrounding suburbs.

BEST SPOTS TO SAMPLE

Where it (supposedly) All Started: Tuck into a rich-and-gooey pie at **Pizzeria Uno** (⊠ 29 E. Ohio St. ☎ 312/321-1000 ⊕ www. unos.com), where you'll be sure to encounter a wait.

Most Authentic: Aficionados of **Lou Malnati's** (⊠ 439 N. Wells St. ☎ 312/828-9800 ⊕ www. loumalnatis.com) claim that their favorite pies have more flavor and like that there are fewer tourists to clog up the joint. If you're really feeling indulgent, order yours with a butter crust. Trust us.

Worth the Wait: Join the out-the-door line at **Gino's East** (⊠ 633 N. Wells St. ☎ 312/943-1124 ⊕ www. ginoseast.com) for caloric pies and a chance to add to the graffiti on the walls.

Easiest to Find: The ubiquitous **Giordano's** (⊠ 730 N. Rush St. ☎ 312/951-0747) has 12 locations throughout the city besides this one.

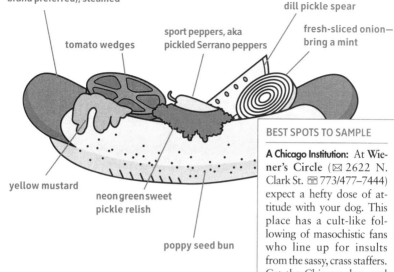

100% beef hot dog (Vienna Beef brand preferred), steamed

dill pickle spear

sport peppers, aka pickled Serrano peppers

fresh-sliced onion— bring a mint

tomato wedges

yellow mustard

neon green sweet pickle relish

poppy seed bun

TASTE 2 | **HOT DOGS**

A DOG IS BORN

The iconic Chicago-style hot dog got its start at the 1893 World's Fair's Columbian Exposition. Emil Reichel and Sam Ladany, Austro-Hungarian immigrants hawked a beef frankfurter sandwich in a steamed bun piled with mustard, relish, onion, tomato, dill pickle, hot peppers, and celery salt. When the Fair moved on, the cravings persisted, launching an on-going affair with the Chicago-style hot dog.

HOW MUCH GARDEN CAN ONE BUN HOLD?

If you've walked a square block of Chicago, chances are you've passed a hot dog. Dog dealers lodge under El stops, on street corners, and at sports arenas. The one thing they all have in common? Their dogs get "dragged through the garden," or loaded with the aforementioned veggies, unless otherwise specified. Make sure to never add ketchup to your Chicago-style hot dog: a major no-no among hot dog aficionados. Don't forget to grab a fistful of napkins—these dogs are messy.

BEST SPOTS TO SAMPLE

A Chicago Institution: At Wiener's Circle (✉ 2622 N. Clark St. ☎ 773/477–7444) expect a hefty dose of attitude with your dog. This place has a cult-like following of masochistic fans who line up for insults from the sassy, crass staffers. Get the Chicago dog, and don't ask for any substitutions. You've been warned.

Get 'em Retro Style: Look for the boy dog and girl dog on the roof of **Superdawg Drive-In** (✉ 6363 N. Milwaukee Ave. ☎ 773/763–0660 ⊕ www. superdawg.com), where carhops deliver your chow.

Poshest Pick: For a weiner on a higher plane, check out **Hot Doug's** (✉ 3324 N. California Ave. ☎ 773/ 279–9550 ⊕ www.hot dougs.com). In addition to the classic Chicago beef, encased meats include kangaroo or rabbit on a rotating menu.

Italian roll, split length-wise

thinly sliced, well-done
beef in its juices

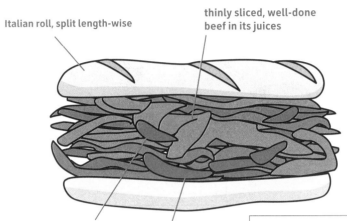

sautéed green bell peppers
(optional)

hot giardiniera peppers

TASTE 3 | **ITALIAN BEEF SANDWICHES**

IT'S ALL ABOUT THE BEEF

Italian immigrants in Chicago happily adapted to the locally abundant meat supply to produce the now-classic Italian beef sandwich. Hard hats and desk jockeys crowd beef stands at lunch, joined by the occasional visiting celebrity. Don't expect much in the way of atmosphere: Here it's Formica counters, fluorescent lights, and big shoulder–to–big shoulder intimacy.

GRAB YOUR NAPKINS

The two-fister, a popular lunchtime staple, stuffs an Italian roll, split length-wise, with thin slices of medium beef. Authentic Italian beef sandwiches use sirloin rump, top round, or bottom round that's wet-roasted and dripping in a broth that's spiked with garlic, oregano, and spices. The whole thing is topped with hot giardiniera, a spicy relish of peppers, diced carrots, cauliflower, celery, and olives in oil. If you've ordered it "wet," it comes with an extra ladle of juice and a stack of napkins; if you order a cheesy beef, they melt a slice or two of mozzarella over the whole mess.

BEST SPOTS TO SAMPLE

Roll up Your Sleeves: Plant your elbows at the window counter or a picnic table in the "elegant dining room" at **Mr. Beef** (✉ 666 N. Orleans St. ☎ 312/337–8500), where famous fans get their mugs on the wall.

Join the Masses: On Little Italy's Taylor Street, standing-room-only crowds of students and local business folk pack **Al's Beef** (✉ 1079 W. Taylor St., ☎ 312/226–4017, ⊕ www.alsbeef.com).

Soak Up Nostalgia: The cavernous space at **Portillo's** (✉100 W. Ontario St. ☎ 312/587–8910) is decked out with Capone-era gangster photos and an antique car that hangs from the ceiling. Fans rave about their Italian beef sandwich, and you can buy souvenirs to commemorate the occasion.

$$$$ ✗**Sixteen.** Uninterrupted views of the landmark Wrigley Building, Lake
NEW AMERICAN Michigan, and the Chicago River make it easy to overlook the food at
Sixteen—but you shouldn't. Located on the sixteenth floor (hence the
name) of the sleek Trump International Hotel & Tower, the restaurant
serves chef Frank Brunacci's unique fusion of European and Asian flavors. Dishes like Tasmanian trout or truffle lasagna are a treat for that
special occasion, while coconut-lemongrass soup and upscale lobster
rolls are perfect for a power lunch. The best deal might be at breakfast,
when house-made crumpets, breakfast quesadillas with fried eggs, and
freshly squeezed juices are an indulgent accompaniment to sunrise over
the lake. ✉*Trump International Hotel and Tower, 401 N. Wabash Ave.*
☎*312/588–8030* ⊟ *AE, D, DC, MC, V* ✛*3:H6*

$$ ✗**SushiSamba Rio.** *Sex and the City* made SushiSamba a star in New
ASIAN York, and look-alike hotties make the Chicago version a scene. The
trendy Brazilian–Japanese hot spot combines a nightclub vibe—dra-
matic multilevel design, freely flowing cocktails, the co-ed bathroom—
with an inventive menu. All the usual sushi suspects are here, as well
as offbeat sashimi choices, Brazilian-style marinated fish, and fusion
rolls that don't always work. For best results sample the menu with an
adventurous, party-hardy crowd on Wednesday, when there's a band
and samba dancers. An all-weather rooftop lounge, popular with the
late-night crowd, serves cocktails (try the sparkling sake) and the
full menu. ✉*504 N. Wells St.* ☎*312/595–2300* ⊟*AE, DC, MC, V*
✛*1:C4*

$$$ ✗**Topolobampo.** Chef-owner Rick Bayless wrote the book on regional
MEXICAN Mexican cuisine—several books, actually—and here he takes his faith-
fully regional food upscale. Next door to the more casual Frontera Grill,
Topolobampo is the higher-end room, with a more subdued mood and
luxury menu, though it shares Frontera's address, phone, and dedication to quality. The ever-changing offerings showcase game, seasonal
fruits and vegetables, and exotic preparations: adobo-marinated lamb
and rock hen in a sauce of almonds and tomatoes are two examples.
✉*445 N. Clark St.* ☎*312/661–1434* ⊟*AE, D, DC, MC, V* ☾*Closed
Sun. and Mon. No lunch Sat.* ✛*1:D5*

$$ ✗**Vermilion.** Vermilion touts itself as a Latin–Indian fusion restaurant,
INTERNATIONAL but its best dishes are strictly Eastern, such as tamarind-glazed ribs
(marinated in a special ingredient: Coca-Cola). Lots of small-plate
options—led by the lamb chops and scallops—encourage sampling.
Despite cool fashion photography on the walls and techno music in the
air, the welcome here is warm. Late-night dining hours draw a club-
going crowd. ✉*10 W. Hubbard St.60610* ☎*312/527–4060* ⊟*AE, D,
DC, MC, V* ☾*No lunch Sat.* ✛*1:D5*

$$ ✗**Vong's Thai Kitchen.** The casual spin-off of chef Jean-Georges Vonger-
THAI ichten's New York Thai–French fusion Vong, this eatery concentrates
solely on Thai fare with upmarket accents and pretty presentations.
Look for shrimp-and-crab pad Thai and a laundry list of curries ranging
from mild to extra hot. Candles and palms boost the romance quotient
by night, but this is also a strong candidate for a working lunch. ✉*6
W. Hubbard St.* ☎*312/644–8664* ⊟*AE, D, DC, MC, V* ☾*No lunch
Sun.* ✛*1:D5*

$$ ✕**Weber Grill Restaurant.** How cheesy is it to dine at a brand extension
AMERICAN of a popular backyard grill? Okay, a little, but get over yourself and
look for the red kettle cooker outside Weber Grill, where restaurant-
sized versions of the namesake appliance demonstrate their versatility.
Suburban Chicago–based Weber takes on the range of grill cookery at
its River North restaurant, offering burgers, ribs, steaks, chops, veg-
gie sides, and novelties like "beer-can chicken" on the extensive menu.
Adjacent to the Hilton Garden Inn, the restaurant also serves stan-
dard breakfast fare. Spacious booths line the State Street windows and
make for the best views of Chicago foot traffic. ⊠ *539 N. State St.*
☎ *312/467–9696* ⊟ *AE, D, DC, MC, V* ✛ *1:E4*

$$ ✕**Wildfire.** This is as close as you can get to the grill without staying
AMERICAN home and firing up the barbie. A triple hearth of roaring fires runs along
the back wall of the supper club–style joint that plays a soundtrack of
vintage jazz. No culinary innovations here, just exceptional chopped
salad, roasted prime rib, and salmon roasted on a cedar plank, along
with wood-fired pizzas and fried calamari. Top taste: the horseradish-
crusted filet mignon. ⊠ *159 W. Erie St.* ☎ *312/787–9000* ⊟ *AE, D,
DC, MC, V* ⊘ *No lunch* ✛ *1:C4*

SOUTH LOOP AND SOUTH SIDE

SOUTH LOOP

$$$ ✕**Custom House.** Chef Shawn McClain established his renown with
STEAKHOUSE Asian-influenced "steakhouse" seafood at Spring and vegetables at
Green Zebra before giving the standard Chicago steakhouse model a
much-needed update with Custom House. The Printers Row restaurant
features sandstone walls, cozy leather booths and picture windows, a
handsome but not overly masculine setting that mirrors the food. You
can get a New York strip or a flatiron steak, of course, but venturesome
carnivores should try the braised veal cheeks or roast quail. Outstand-
ing sides include gratin potatoes with sheep's-milk cheese, and desserts
have a comforting quality in dishes like malted-milk chocolate mousse.
⊠ *Hotel Blake, 500 S. Dearborn St.* ☎ *312/523–0200* ⊟ *AE, D, DC,
MC, V* ⊘ *No lunch weekends* ✛ *4:F2*

$ ✕**Eleven City Diner.** For all its great food, Chicago is not a big deli town,
AMERICAN which endears Eleven City Diner, an old-school deli and family res-
ⓒ taurant in the South Loop, to the locals. You can get breakfast all day
(bagel and lox, "hoppel poppel" scrambled eggs with salami, potatoes,
onions, and peppers), deli staples like matzoh-ball soup and pastrami
and corned-beef sandwiches, and diner options including burgers, and
soda-fountain floats and malts from the staff soda jerk. Breaking from
the deli tradition, Eleven City sells beer, wine, and cocktails. In keep-
ing with its theme there's an old-fashioned candy counter on your way
out. ⊠ *1112 S. Wabash Ave.,* ☎ *312/212–1112* ⊟ *AE, D, DC, MC,
V* ✛ *4:G3*

$ ✕**Epic Burger.** After walking through exhibits at the Art Institute, follow
AMERICAN the local college crowd to this order-at-the-counter eatery. While the
ambience is kitschy (think bright orange walls and televisions broad-
casting cartoons) the food is, as owner David Friedman describes it,

"more mindful." Friedman sources grass-fed, corn-finished beef for Epic's burgers, which are shaped by hand, cooked to order, and served atop fresh buns on biodegradable plates. In addition, burger add-ons include Wisconsin cheese, nitrate-free bacon, and an organic fried egg. While this might mean the meal costs more than other counter-service spots, it all goes back to Friedman's goal of building a greener burger joint. ✉ *517 S. State St.South Loop* ☎*312/913–1373* ▭ *AE, MC, V.*

$$ ✕**Gioco.** The name means "game" in Italian, and the restaurant fulfills
ITALIAN the promise not with venison, but in the spirit of playing a game. The decor is distressed-urban, with plaster-spattered brick walls and well-worn hardwood floors, but the menu is comfort-Italian, with rustic fare like homemade garganelli pasta with prosciutto, roasted pork chops, and sausage-stuffed quail. The Speakeasy Room, a private dining space with its own rear-alley entrance, is an homage to the building's notorious past under Prohibition. ✉ *1312 S. Wabash Ave.* ☎*312/939–3870* ▭*AE, DC, MC, V* ✛*4:G4*

¢ ✕**Manny's Coffee Shop and Deli.** Kibitzing counter cooks provide com-
AMERICAN mentary as they sling the chow—thick pastrami sandwiches, soul-nurturing matzoh-ball soup, and piping-hot potato pancakes—at this classic Near-South-Side cafeteria. Though they occasionally bark at dawdlers, it's all in good fun; looking for seating in two teeming, fluorescent-lit rooms is not. Don't try to pay the hash-slingers; settle up as you leave. ✉*1141 S. Jefferson St.* ☎*312/939–2855* ⚲*Reservations not accepted* ▭*AE, MC, V* ⊘*Closed Sun.* ✛*4:E4*

$$ ✕**Mercat a la Planxa.** Within the renovated Blackstone Hotel, this Cat-
SPANISH alan-inspired restaurant offers a stylish respite from Michigan Ave. Philadelphia-based chef Jose Garces returned to his native Chicago for the project, creating a menu of small and midsize plates of cured meats, seared fish and a variety of vegetable sides, all of which can be shared. Be sure to try the *cocas*, flatbreads topped with ingredients such as bean purée, shrimp, and chorizo. The mostly American Mercat burger with padrón peppers and onion jam (lunch only) also has several fans. Don't let the small, cramped bar at the entrance fool you: once you walk up the stairs, you'll encounter an airy dining room with a view of Grant Park. ✉ *638 S. Michigan Ave.* ☎*312/765–0524* ▭*AE, DC, MC, V*

$$ ✕**Opera.** Creative Chinese fare and theatrical design share the stage at
CHINESE Opera. Only top-flight ingredients and sparing sauces go into the cooking, distinguishing the five-spice duck egg roll, say, or lobster spring roll or roasted Scottish salmon from more familiar take-out fare. Former film-storage vaults—the building was once used by Paramount Studios—now hold a series of tables for two, providing intimacy for those who want it. Everyone else revels in the eye candy that includes Asian newspaper collages, oversize suspended lamps, and a multicolor-glass-wrapped wine cellar. ✉*1301 S. Wabash Ave.,* ☎*312/461–0161* ▭*AE, DC, MC, V* ⊘*No lunch weekends* ✛*4:G4*

SOUTH SIDE

$ ✕ **Army and Lou's.** First-rate home-cooked soul food banners this Far
SOUTHERN South Side institution. The fried chicken is arguably the city's best, but leave room for outstanding corn bread, chicken gumbo, mustard greens, and sweet-potato pie. The setting is surprisingly genteel for such down-

home fare: waiters in bow ties, tables with starched white cloths, and African and Haitian art on the walls. On Sunday, dress up and join the after-church crowds. ⊠ *422 E. 75th St.* ☎*773/483–3100* ⊟*DC, MC, V* ⊘*Closed Tues.* ✢*4:E6*

$$ ✕**Chez Joël Bistro Français.** Breaking Taylor Street's Italian allegiance,
BISTRO Chez Joel waves the flag for France. The sunny, cozy bistro, run by brothers Joël and Amed Kazouini, serves well-prepared classics like steak frites, coq au vin, escargots, and bouillabaisse. It's a good pasta-free date choice, and a favorite of locals thanks to its authentic bistro feel. Check out the full bar and the reasonably priced wine list favoring French and Californian selections. On a warm Chicago day, ask for a seat outside on the patio. ⊠*1119 W. Taylor St.* ☎*312/226–6479* ⊟*AE, D, DC, MC, V* ⊘*Closed Mon. No lunch weekends* ✢*4:C3.*

¢   ✕ **Pompei.** Cheap, cheerful, and fast—what's not to love about Pompei?
ITALIAN Little Italy's only casual café with a strong kitchen specializes in square slices of pizza, each under $4, with toppings ranging from shredded onions and sausage to bread crumbs and tomato. One to two easily makes a meal. Between University of Illinois Chicago students and Rush University Medical Center workers, Pompei is jammed at lunch. If you can tolerate the self-serve system at dinner, the evening hours are more relaxing. If pizza's not your thing, salad, generous sandwiches, and handmade pastas are also on the menu. ⊠*1531 W. Taylor St.* ☎*312/421–5179* ⊟*AE, D, DC, MC, V* ✢*4:B4*

¢   ✕**Soul Queen Restaurant.** Since 1971, family-owned and -operated Soul
SOUTHERN Queen has been sating everyone, from the famished music fans who frequent Stony Island's many jazz clubs to luminaries such as Mohhamad Ali, with one of the most generous buffets in town. For $7.75, help yourself to fried chicken, chicken and dumplings, ham hocks, turkey wings and legs, black-eyed peas, succotash, mac and cheese, peach cobbler, and more. The spread gets even more elaborate on Sunday, when the price goes up $3. ⊠*9031 S. Stony Island Ave.* ☎*773/731–3366* ⚱*Reservations not accepted* ⊟*MC, V* ✢*4:G6*

CHINATOWN

$ ✕**Emperor's Choice.** This sophisticate sets out to prove that Chinese spe-
CHINESE cialties can go well beyond deep-fried prawns and kung pao chicken. It succeeds with strong seafood offerings, such as baked clams, Peking-style lobster, or Dungeness crab, fried and served whole seasoned with salt. It also offers a separate menu including "delicacies" such as shark's-fin soup and pork belly. While the restaurant accommodates groups of 10 easily, seating is generally cramped and not for serenity-seekers, but the decent prices, good food, and friendly service make up for the surroundings. Discounted parking (with validation) is available in the Cermak/Wentworth lot. ⊠*2238 S. Wentworth Ave.* ☎*312/225–8800* ⊟*AE, D, MC, V* ✢*4:F6*

¢   ✕**Lao Sze Chuan.** If you're looking for spice, filling food, and great
CHINESE prices in Chinatown, check out this Szechuan kitchen. Chilies, garlic, and ginger seem to go into every dish, whether it's chicken, eggplant, or dumplings. The digs are nothing to write a postcard home about, but you'll feel smug for choosing it once the feast is finished. ⊠*2172 S. Archer Ave.* ☎*312/326–5040* ⊟*AE, D, DC, MC, V* ✢*4:F6*

$ ✗**Phoenix.** This bustling dim sum house can feel overwhelming with
CHINESE the hordes of diners who flock here on weekends, and service can be
brusque. Even so, it delivers. First Phoenix softens you up with second-
floor picture-window views that frame the Loop skyline. Then, just
when you're most vulnerable, it develops the food punch—and it's a
pretty good one, too. The dim sum, dispensed from rolling carts daily
from 8 AM to 3 PM on weekends is a big draw (servers often don't
speak English; just smile and point at what you want—and don't miss
the barbecue pork buns or the shrimp dumplings). Arrive before noon
on weekends or stew as you wait—and wait. ✉*2131 S. Archer Ave.*
☎*312/328–0848* ▱*AE, D, DC, MC, V* ✚*4:F6*

PILSEN

$ ✗**Nuevo León.** Fill up on the exotic (tripe soup) or the familiar (tacos)
MEXICAN at this bustling, family-run restaurant in the heart of Pilsen, Chicago's
Mexican neighborhood. Big tables accommodate big families, lending
a fiesta feel to the scene. Fans love the authentic food, including *chila-
quiles* (eggs scrambled with tortillas) for breakfast to dinners of shrimp
fajitas, chiles rellenos, and enchiladas. Brush up your Spanglish; not all
servers are fluent in English, though all are welcoming to newcomers.
To wash it all down, order a tall glass of *horchata*, a milky, cinnamon-
flecked rice beverage, or bring a couple of beers; Nuevo León is BYOB.
✉*1515 W. 18th St.* ☎*312/421–1517* ✍*Reservations not accepted*
▱*No credit cards* ✚*4:B5*

WEST LOOP AND NEAR WEST SIDE

$$ ✗**Avec.** Go to this Euro-style wine bar when you're feeling gregari-
MEDITERRANEAN ous; the rather stark space has seating for only 48 people, and it's
Fodor'sChoice all at communal tables. The results are loud and lively, though hap-
★ pily the shareable fare—a mix of small and large Mediterranean dishes
from a wood-burning oven—is reasonably priced. It's as popular as its
next-door neighbor Blackbird (and run by the same forces), and only
early birds are guaranteed tables. The doors open at—yikes!—3:30 PM.
✉*615 W. Randolph St.* ☎*312/377–2002* ✍*Reservations not accepted*
▱*AE, D, MC, V* ✎*No lunch* ✚*1:A6*

$$$ ✗**Blackbird.** Being cramped next to your neighbor has never been as fun
NEW AMERICAN as it is at this hot spot run by foodie chef Paul Kahan. Celebs pepper
Fodor'sChoice the sleek see-and-be-seen crowd who delve into creative dishes. While
★ the menu changes constantly, you'll always find choices that highlight
seasonal ingredients, such as rack of lamb with leeks and *spigarello*
(wild broccoli) in the spring, or grilled sturgeon with sauerkraut gnoc-
chi in the winter. It all plays out against a minimalist backdrop of white
walls, blue-gray banquettes, and aluminum chairs. Reservations aren't
required, but they might as well be; the dining room is typically booked
solid on Saturday night. ✉*619 W. Randolph St.* ☎*312/715–0708*
✍*Reservations essential* ▱*AE, D, MC, V* ✎*Closed Sun. No lunch*
Sat. ✚*1:A6*

$$ ✕**Carmichael's Chicago Steakhouse.** The look here is old-time Chicago—
STEAKHOUSE oak and brass, black-and-white photographs, and waiters dressed in
suspenders and shirtsleeve garters—though the true vintage is late
1990s. We forgive them the ruse for the well-priced (under $40) Angus
steaks, which make this one of the more reasonable top-tier steakhouses
in town. Orange-sesame glazed salmon is a good nonbeef option. Live
jazz lures prowling carnivores to the lush garden in summer. ⊠*1052
W. Monroe St.* ☎*312/433–0025* ⊟*AE, D, DC, MC, V* ⊘*No lunch
weekends* ✛*4:C2*

$–$$ ✕**Costa's.** Greektown is fairly labeled monotonous, cuisine-wise. But
GREEK Costa's, a favorite among University of Illinois Chicago students, bet-
ters its many neighbors in both looks and taste. The multilevel Hellenic
interior has terra-cotta tile work and rough-textured white walls and
archways. There's a generous assortment of *mezes* (tapaslike Greek
appetizers), traditional salt fish, a variety of kebabs, *dolmades* (stuffed
grape leaves), fish flown in fresh daily, and roast leg of lamb. Live piano
and the enthusiasm of diners tend to send the decibels soaring. ⊠*340
S. Halsted St.* ☎*312/263–9700* ⊟*AE, D, DC, MC, V* ✛*4:D2*

$ ✕**De Cero Taqueria.** Sometimes you want celebrity chef–made regional
MEXICAN Mexican, and sometimes you just want a really good taco. For the latter,
as well as zesty margaritas, a convivial setting, and lick-the-mortar-clean
guacamole, grab a table at De Cero, the Mexican standout on Randolph
Street's restaurant row. The highlight of the menu is the taco list. Each of
16 tacos is priced individually and made to order for a mix-and-match
meal. Top choices include chipotle chicken, braised duck with corn
salsa, and beef tenderloin tips braised with mushrooms. Though the
spot is wood-tables-and-benches casual and very loud, beat the crowds
by phoning ahead, especially on weekends. ⊠*814 W. Randolph St.*
☎*312/455–8114* ⊟*AE, MC, V* ⊘*Closed Sat. No lunch* ✛*4:D1*

$$$ ✕**Green Zebra.** Chef Shawn McClain of Spring fame took the vegetable
NEW AMERICAN side dish and ran it up the marquee. The result gives good-for-you veg-
gies the star treatment in a sleek shop suave enough to attract the likes
of Gwyneth Paltrow. All dishes are small and change seasonally. You
might see roast beets with horseradish foam or sunchoke ravioli with
melted goat cheese and hazelnuts. The occasional chicken or fish dish
makes do for carnivores. ⊠*1460 W. Chicago Ave.* ☎*312/243–7100*
⊟*AE, D, DC, MC, V* ✛*3:C5*

$ ✕ **Ina's.** It's so cozy you almost feel like you're at a diner—there's the
AMERICAN loving presence of owner Ina Pinkney, reliable chow, and a regular fol-
lowing. But dishes like vegetable hash and "scrapple"—polenta mixed
with cheddar and black beans, fried into a disk, and served with eggs
and chorizo—at breakfast and Southern fried chicken, pork tender-
loin, and several fish entrées at dinner, there's something for everyone.
Close to Oprah's studio and loft dwellers up and down Randolph,
Ina's regularly generates a queue, especially on weekends. ⊠*1235 W.
Randolph St.* ☎*312/226–8227* ⊟*AE, D, DC, MC, V* ⊘*No dinner
Sun. and Mon.* ✛*4:C1*

$ ✕**Juicy Wine Company.** Rodney Alex's smart wine bar is proof that a
NEW AMERICAN minimal kitchen (limited to what will fit behind the bar's counter) can
still thrill foodies. Simple preparations, such as duck rillette panini

seasoned with Hawaiian sea salt and aged goat cheese and slices of rare *jamón ibérico,* prized Spanish ham, serve to compliment the real draw: hand-picked wines from around the world poured in crystal glasses large enough to contain an entire bottle of wine. While the two-story, cork-lined space becomes a late-night hangout, head there on weekends for $5 drinks and a $5 brunch menu with offerings such as chicken and waffles. ☒ *694 N. Milwaukee Ave.* ☎*312/492–6620* ▭ *AE, D, DC, MC, V* ✛*3:E6*

$$ ✕**La Sardine.** We don't know if the sardine reference was meant to
BISTRO telegraph the seating arrangements, but, yes, it's snug here. Still, you'll find it easier to tolerate your neighbors with a solid menu of traditional bistro favorites including warm goat-cheese salad, bouillabaisse, and roasted chicken with potatoe purée. Since it's across the street from Harpo Studios (where Oprah tapes her talk show), audience members and producers alike converge at La Sardine. ☒*111 N. Carpenter St.* ☎*312/421–2800* ▭*AE, D, DC, MC, V* ☉*Closed Sun. No lunch Sat.* ✛*4:C1*

¢ ✕**Lou Mitchell's.** Shelve your calorie and cholesterol concerns; Lou
AMERICAN Mitchell's heeds no modern health warnings. The diner, a destination
☺ close to Union Station since 1923, specializes in high-fat breakfasts and comfort-food lunches. Start the day with eggs and homemade hash browns by the skillet (BYO Lipitor). Later break for meat loaf and mashed potatoes. Though you have to deal with out-the-door waits, staffers dole out doughnut holes and Milk Duds to pacify hunger pangs. ☒*565 W. Jackson Blvd.* ☎*312/939–3111* ▭*No credit cards* ☉*No dinner* ✛*4:E2*

$$ ✕**Marché.** If all the world's a stage, everyone from the waiters to the
BRASSERIE patrons are players at this theatrical West Loop brasserie. The set: a lively, loftlike room trimmed in paintings from local artists and wright-iron metal work. The program: classic French onion soup and house-made pâté, braised lamb, and an excellent steak tartare. The finale: classic American and French desserts, from bread pudding to profiteroles. Ovations at your discretion. ☒*833 W. Randolph St.* ☎*312/226–8399* ▭*AE, DC, MC, V* ✛*4:D1*

$$$$ ✕**Moto.** Mad-scientist chef Homaro Cantu has become a cult figure in
CUTTING-EDGE the Windy City. His restaurant-cum-laboratory is sequestered in the city's still working meatpacking district. Many of the techniques perfected in the basement kitchen are later put to use in the chef's work with NASA and corporate America. Inside the minimalist dining room patrons pay for the privilege of being literal guinea pigs. The daily changing multicourse menus—available in 10- and 20-course options— are printed on edible paper. Flavors are seared into wine glasses by

an industrial laser, rigatoni is fashioned from lychee puree, and frozen flapjacks are "cooked" tableside on a liquid-nitrogen-filled box. The spectacle is big but the portions are small. ⊠ *945 W. Fulton Market 60607* ☎ *312/491–0058* ⌕ *Reservations essential* ☰ *AE, MC, V* ✛*4:D1*

$$$
NEW AMERICAN

✕ **one sixtyblue.** Never mind that former Chicago Bulls superstar Michael Jordan owns a piece of this place, or that the private, cigar-friendly room has entertained its share of celebs. The real reason to travel to the tail end of West Randolph Street's restaurant row is chef Michael McDonald. His approachable food balances challenge-me tastes, like slow-cooked pork belly, with standbys like grilled hanger steak. Save room for dessert: pastry chef Stephanie Prida's desserts include brown-butter carrot cake. The leather-sofa lounge makes a sexy site for nibbles and drinks. ⊠ *1400 W. Randolph St.* ☎ *312/850–0303* ☰ *AE, D, DC, MC, V* ⊘ *Closed Sun. No lunch* ✛*4:B1*

$$
NEW AMERICAN

✕ **Otom.** With its bright colors and wide-open dining room, Otom is a fine addition to this industrial-chic part of town. The one-page menu offers a manageable selection of simple yet delicious appetizers and entrées that fit with the restaurant's warm atmosphere. The salmon ceviche is a must when available, and the short-rib is a delight. Meat lovers should try the lamb shank, but beware the colossal portion. To top it off, Otom offers eight cocktails. The chef's sweet-potato flan is a seasonal standout. ⊠ *951 W. Fulton Market* ☎ *312/491–5804* ☰ *AE, MC, V* ⊘ *Closed Sun. No lunch* ✛*4:D1*

$
GREEK

✕ **The Parthenon.** The claim to fame here is the *saganaki*, the Greek flaming-cheese dish, which the Parthenon says it invented in the late 1960s, thereby introducing "opa!" to the American vocabulary. So ordering flaming cheese here is a rite of passage for any first-time visitors, yet regulars return to this literal Greektown hot spot for lamb and chicken preparations, often skewered on sticks. In fact, the restaurant also takes credit for being the first to serve gyros stateside. True or not, indulge the legends and stick to these classics. When going, be sure to ask for pita bread and a side of *tzatziki*, a yogurt- and cucumber-based dipping sauce. The food is cheap and the atmosphere festive and family-friendly, generating happy campers. ⊠ *314 S. Halsted St.* ☎ *312/726–2407* ☰ *AE, D, DC, MC, V* ✛*4:D2*

$
AMERICAN

✕ **The Publican**. Don't call this beer-focused hot spot a gastropub. Chef Paul Kahan (of Blackbird fame) prefers "beer hall." Certainly the long communal tables, in which beer connoisseurs sample from a selection hovering around 100 brews, imparts the bustling space with the air of an Oktoberfest celebration. (Wine is also available.) Yet Chef de Cuisine Brian Huston's seafood- and pork-focused menu gives a decided nod to pub fare. Diners share shucked oysters and just-fried pork rinds before tucking into grilled, smoky country ribs, fried perch, and *potée* (braised pork belly, tenderloin, and sausage). Arrive early, as seating is first-come, first-served except for Sundays, when reservations are accepted for Huston's four-course, prix-fixe menu. ⊠ *837 W. Fulton Market* ☎ *312/733–9555* ☰ *AE, MC, V* ⊘ *No lunch* ✛*4:D1*

$$
ASIAN

✕ **Red Light**. Sultry, all-red decor and a club sound track stoke the high-energy vibe (read: loud) at Red Light. Chinese, Thai, Vietnamese, and Indonesian dishes commingle on the pan-Asian menu, which is heavily weighted with appetizers to encourage nibbling. Standout dishes include pork dumplings with hoisin-cognac sauce, jumbo prawn curry, a miso-lobster seafood stew, and the signature "chocolate bag" dessert filled with white-chocolate mousse. ✉ *820 W. Randolph St.* ☎ *312/733–8880* ▭ *AE, D, DC, MC, V* ◷ *No lunch weekends* ✛*4:D1*

$$$ **NEW AMERICAN** ✕ **Sepia.** While the name evokes nostalgia for the building's gritty past as a print shop, Sepia is thoroughly forward-thinking in both its design (think glassed-in chandeliers and leather-topped tables) and its simple, seasonal dishes created by Chef Andrew Zimmerman. Order flatbread for the table while you review the menu, which includes appetizers such as grilled octopus or pork rillettes and entrées such as skate served with a raisin-caper sauce. Meanwhile, a well-chosen, international wine list and thoughtfully prepared classic cocktails satisfy oenophiles and mixologists alike. Though reservations can be hard to come by for dinner, seats at the communal tables are first-come, first-served. ✉ *123 N. Jefferson St.* ☎ *312/441–1920* ▭ *AE, D, DC, MC, V* ✛*4:E1*

$$ **JAPANESE** ✕ **Sushi Wabi.** This funky West Loop sushi restaurant dances to an industrial-pop beat—on weekend evenings, at least, when the DJ turns up the beat (club attitude suffices on weekdays). The urban-chic brick-and-exposed-steel interior draws a young, martini-swilling crowd. Superior sushi and maki rolls along with straightforward entrées such as grilled peppercorn-crusted tuna with soy and lemon bring substance to the style haunt. ✉ *842 W. Randolph St.* ☎ *312/563–1224* ▭ *AE, D, DC, MC, V* ◷ *No lunch weekends* ✛*4:D1*

$$ **ITALIAN** ✕ **Vivo.** Vivo was trendy on this west-of-the-Loop stretch long before Randolph Street's restaurant row got hot, and it still manages to be a trendsetter. Slightly more about scene—brick walls, black ceiling, open wine racks, and lots of pretty people—than cuisine, Vivo manages reliable Italian fare. You can't go wrong with osso buco, house-made ravioli, and free-range lamb chops. ✉ *838 W. Randolph St.* ☎ *312/733–3379* ▭ *AE, DC, MC, V* ◷ *No lunch weekends* ✛*4:D1*

$$ **AMERICAN** ✕ **West Town Tavern.** While it's a little off the beaten path, trust your cabbie to get you here. The handsome wood bar and brick walls may be tavern staples, but the open kitchen and oversize dining-room mirror promise more than cheeseburgers. The menu delivers with a mix of upscale comfort foods (try the house-made potato chips with balsamic syrup and Parmesan cheese—and pizza-style flat breads) and gussied-up American classics like pepper-crusted beef tenderloin in a zinfandel sauce. The focused wine list globe-trots for value. ✉ *1329 W. Chicago Ave.* ☎ *312/666–6175* ▭ *AE, MC, V* ◷ *Closed Sun. No lunch* ✛*3:D5*

5

BUCKTOWN AND WICKER PARK

BUCKTOWN

$
INTERNATIONAL

✕**Feast.** The cozy fireplace and sofa-filled lounge create a fittingly social setting for the arty Bucktown locals who dine here regularly. If you can't find something to eat here, you're not hungry. World cuisines from Cuba to India mingle freely on an expansive, bold menu; try the maple-glazed chicken, barbecue salmon over corn buttermilk hot cakes, or chimichurri skirt steak. ⊠*1616 N. Damen Ave.* ☎*773/772–7100* ⊟*AE, DC, MC, V* ✛*3:B3*

$$
AMERICAN

✕**Hot Chocolate.** The city's most celebrated pastry chef, Mindy Segal, strikes out solo at Hot Chocolate, a hit with, as you might expect, a really great dessert selection ranging from a creative soufflé tart with salted caramel ice cream and homemade pretzels to a myriad milk shakes and hot-chocolate flavors with homemade marshmallows. How sweet, and how swamped, it is. The savory menu is well-crafted, with choices such as a Berkshire pork tenderloin with spaetzle and a tuna melt made with tuna poached in olive oil, wild capers, and Wisconsin cheese. ⊠*1747 N. Damen Ave.* ☎*773/489–1747* ⊟*AE, MC, V* ☾*Closed Mon.* ✛*3:B3*

$$
BISTRO

✕**Le Bouchon.** The French comfort food at this charming-but-cramped bistro in Bucktown is in a league of its own. The onion tart has been a signature dish of owner Jean-Claude Poilevey for years; he also does a succulent sautéed rabbit and a definitive *salade Lyonnaise* (mixed greens topped with a creamy vinaigrette and a poached egg). Save room for the fruit tarts. Don't attempt Le Bouchon on weekends without a reservation. ⊠*1958 N. Damen Ave.* ☎*773/862–6600* ⊟*AE, D, DC, MC, V* ☾*Closed Sun. No lunch* ✛*3:B2*

$
AMERICAN

✕**Mado.** Subtle, smoky aromas from a wood grill unleash appetites at this modest Bucktown restaurant where the chalkboard posting the daily-changing menu of chef-owners Rob and Alli Levitt doubles as the dining room's main design element. Dishes are similarly understated: radishes with creamy salted butter, wood-grilled mushrooms, and slow-cooked pork belly showcase locally grown or raised foodstuffs. Small portions encourage menu exploration, and the best bet is to start with a few antipasti—like ricotta-topped bruschetta with hazelnuts, and arugula—to share. Although desserts change constantly, seek out Alli Levitt's shortbread cookies when available. Mado is waiting for its liquor license and is temporarily BYOB; call ahead to see if status has changed. ⊠*1647 N. Milwaukee Ave.* ☎*773/342–2340* ⊟*AE, D, MC, V.* ☾*Closed Mon. No lunch* ✛*3:A3*

$$$
JAPANESE
Fodor'sChoice
★

✕**Takashi.** It's not often that a chef who has made a name for himself in Las Vegas retreats to a neighborhood restaurant. But that's exactly what Takashi Yagihashi did when he left his post as executive chef of Okada at Wynn Las Vegas. At his intimate, dinner-only restaurant, Yagihashi serves forth French- and American-inspired small and large plates with Japanese accents, such as duck fat–fried chicken with a ginger-flecked Napa cabbage slaw, and soy- and ginger-braised caramel pork belly with pickled daikon. While the upstairs is quiet and relaxed, request a seat downstairs to peek at the action in the glassed-in kitchen.

⊠ *1952 N. Damen Ave.* ☎*773/772–6170* ▤*AE, D, MC, V* ⊗*Closed Mon.* ✛*3:B2*

WICKER PARK

$ ✕**The Bristol.** While Bucktown isn't wanting for dining options, this
AMERICAN self-proclaimed "eatery and bar" sets itself apart by focusing intently on the food. Tru alumnus Chef Chris Pandel sources local produce and features meat from sustainably raised animals. As a consequence, it isn't rare to find braised goat on the daily-changing menu. He also offers playful takes on more familiar fare, turning out popular small plates such as pierogi (termed "lazy" because it lacks a filling), chicken wings stuffed with chorizo, and baked-to-order monkey bread. Arrive early; seating in the boisterous dining room is first come, first served. Or wait in the lounge upstairs for a spot to free up. ⊠*2152 N. Damen Ave.* ☎*773/583–0500* ▤*AE, DC, MC, V* ⊗*No lunch* ✛*3:B1*

$ ✕**Crust.** There are only a handful of restaurants around the country
PIZZA that are certified organic, and despite the bureaucracy required for the distinction (every ingredient used has to be approved by a third-party certifier), this casual hipster spot is one of them. Feast on globally inspired flatbread served on wooden pizza peels; from basilico, a simple mozzarella, tomato, and basil rendition; to *flamkuchen*, which boasts bacon, caramelized onion, béchamel, and caraway seeds. Complement the main event with sides of roasted vegetables, local beers, or organic sodas. While Crust doesn't take reservations, call ahead to have your name added to the list; the wait can be more than an hour on Friday and Saturday nights. ⊠*2056 W. Division St.* ☎*773/235–5511* ⚐*Reservations not accepted* ▤*AE, D, MC, V* ✛*3:A4*

$$ ✕**MANA Food Bar.** It's easy to miss this slim, stylish restaurant amid the
VEGETARIAN new clothing boutiques and bars along Division Street. But those in the know squeeze in for globally inspired vegetarian and vegan fare. Dishes are small; plan to order a few to share. The health-conscious among you will delight in Chef Jill Barron's dishes of red quinoa salad and curried cauliflower with brown rice. But carnivores won't miss their meat with mushroom sliders and hearty, sweet-potato pancakes served with apple-cranberry chutney. Apart from the food, the list of sake-based cocktails fills the seats along the long wooden bar: try the refreshing cucumber "sakerita" when it's available. ⊠*1742 W. Division St.* ☎*773/342–1742* ▤*AE, D, MC, V* ⊗*No lunch Mon.–Thurs.* ✛*3:C4*

¢ ✕**Milk & Honey Café.** Wicker Park's Division Street has long been a prowl
CAFÉ of night owls. But with the advent of spas and boutiques in the area, not to mention the many work-from-home locals, the boho neighborhood needed a good breakfast and lunch spot. Milk & Honey exceeds expectations with hearty (eggs) and healthful (granola) breakfasts, and creative sandwiches (avocado with smoked Gouda) at lunch. Choice seats change with the season: out on the sidewalk café in warm weather; in near the fireplace in cooler temperatures. ⊠*1920 W. Division St.* ☎*773/395–9434* ▤*AE, MC, V* ⊗*No dinner* ✛*3:B4*

$ ✕**Piece.** The antithesis of Chicago-style deep-dish pizza, Piece's flat
PIZZA pies mimic those made famous in New Haven, Connecticut. The some-
☾ what free-form, eat-off-the-baking-sheet pizzas come in plain (tomato

5

sauce, Parmesan, and garlic), white (olive oil, garlic, and mozzarella), or traditional red, with lots of topping options. Salads like the greens with Gorgonzola and pears are more stylish than expected, and house-brewed beers pair perfectly with the chow. It's good enough that multip-ierced Wicker Parkers are willing to risk dining alongside local families (with kids in tow) in this former garage space. ⊠*1927 W. North Ave.* ☎*773/772–4422* ▭*AE, D, DC, MC, V* ✛*3:B3*

$ ✕**Smoke Daddy.** A rib and blues emporium, in the gentrified though
SOUTHERN still funky Wicker Park, Smoke Daddy serves up tangy barbecued ribs with generously supplied napkins for swabbing stray sauce. Today fans pack bar stools and booths for the chow, which includes richly flavored smoked pulled pork and homemade fries, as well as for the no-cover R&B and jazz bands that play nightly after 9:30. A short walk from the Division Street El stop makes this barbecue spot an ideal point from which to explore the neighborhood's hipster scene. ⊠*1804 W. Division St.,* ☎*773/772–6656* ▭*AE, D, MC, V* ✛*3:B4*

$$$ ✕**Spring.** Leave pretense downtown. Chef Shawn McClain's artistic
NEW AMERICAN but unfussy fish preparations—from Kumomoto oysters with grated fresh wasabi root to Atlantic skate wing, white polenta, and roasted cauliflower—distinguish the sophisticated Spring from other seasonal restaurants. While warm orange tones have replaced the restaurant's original green-hued interior, original white glazed-tile walls hark back to the space's former life as a bathhouse. ⊠*2039 W. North Ave.* ☎*773/395–7100* ▭*AE, DC, MC, V* ☉*No lunch* ✛*3:B3*

Chicago Dining & Lodging Atlas

KEY	
□	*Hotels*
■	*Restaurants*
■	*Restaurant in Hotel*
Ⓜ	*Subway Station*

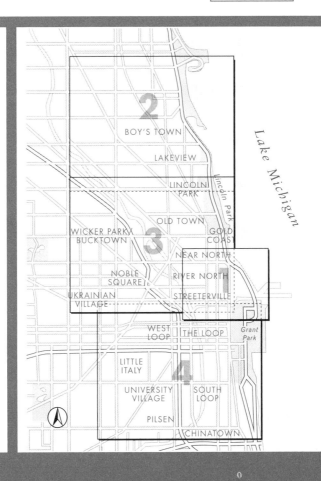

2

BOY'S TOWN

LAKEVIEW

LINCOLN PARK

Lake Michigan

Lincoln Park

OLD TOWN

3

WICKER PARK BUCKTOWN

GOLD COAST

NEAR NORTH

NOBLE SQUARE

RIVER NORTH

1

UKRAINIAN VILLAGE

STREETERVILLE

WEST LOOP

THE LOOP

Grant Park

LITTLE ITALY

4

UNIVERSITY VILLAGE

SOUTH LOOP

PILSEN

CHINATOWN

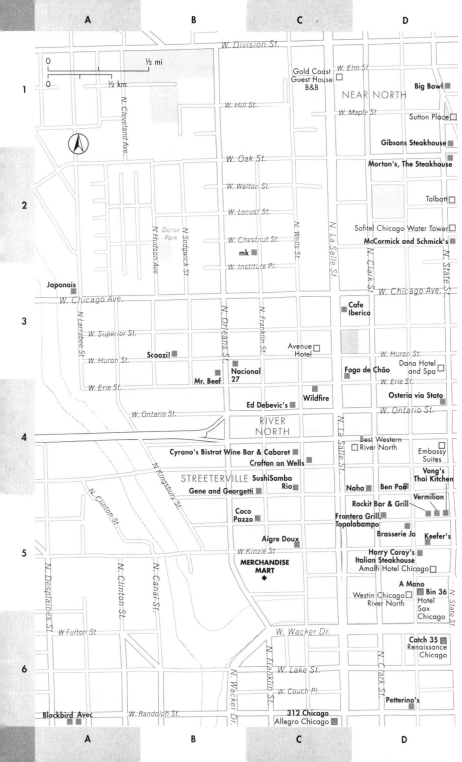

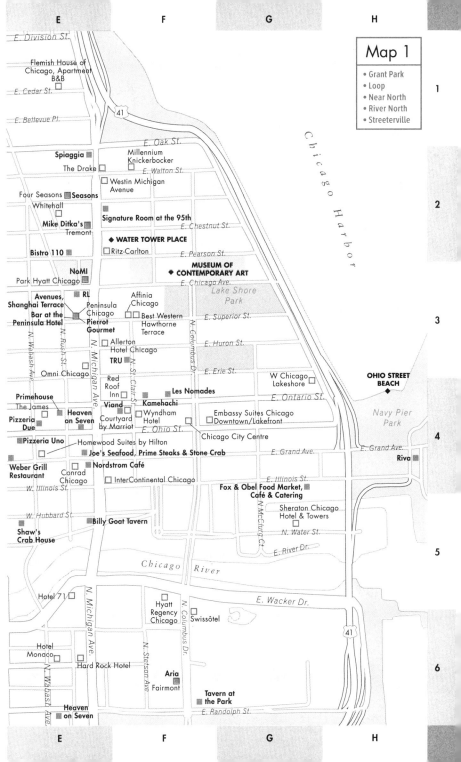

Map 1

- Grant Park
- Loop
- Near North
- River North
- Streeterville

E. Division St.

Flemish House of
Chicago, Apartment
B&B

E. Cedar St.

E. Bellevue Pl.

E. Oak St.

Spiaggia
The Drake

Millennium
Knickerbocker
E. Walton St.

Westin Michigan
Avenue

Four Seasons ■ Seasons
Whitehall

Mike Ditka's
Tremont

Bistro 110

Signature Room at the 95th

E. Chestnut St.

◆ WATER TOWER PLACE

NoMI
Park Hyatt Chicago

□ Ritz-Carlton

E. Pearson St.

◆ MUSEUM OF
CONTEMPORARY ART

E. Chicago Ave.

Lake Shore
Park

Avenues,
Shanghai Terrace
Bar at the
Peninsula Hotel

RL
Peninsula
Chicago
Pierrot
Gourmet

Affinia
Chicago

□ □ Best Western
Hawthorne
Terrace

E. Superior St.

Allerton
Hotel Chicago

TRU ■

E. Huron St.

Omni Chicago

E. Erie St.

Red
Roof
Inn

■ Les Nomades

W Chicago
Lakeshore

Primehouse
The James

Heaven
on Seven

Viand

Kamehachi

E. Ontario St.

OHIO STREET
BEACH

Navy Pier
Park

Pizzeria
Due

Courtyard
by Marriott

Wyndham
Hotel

E. Ohio St.

Embassy Suites Chicago
Downtown/Lakefront

Chicago City Centre

Pizzeria Uno

Homewood Suites by Hilton

E. Grand Ave.

E. Grand Ave.

Riva ■

Weber Grill
Restaurant

Conrad
Chicago

■ Joe's Seafood, Prime Steaks & Stone Crab

■ Nordstrom Café

□ InterContinental Chicago

W. Illinois St.

E. Illinois St.

Fox & Obel Food Market, ■
Café & Catering

W. Hubbard St.

■ Billy Goat Tavern

Sheraton Chicago
Hotel & Towers

N. Water St.

Shaw's
Crab House

Chicago River

E. River Dr.

Chicago River

E. Wacker Dr.

Hotel 71

Hyatt
Regency
Chicago

□ Swissôtel

Hotel
Monaco

Hard Rock Hotel

Aria
Fairmont

Tavern at
the Park

Heaven
on Seven

E. Randolph St.

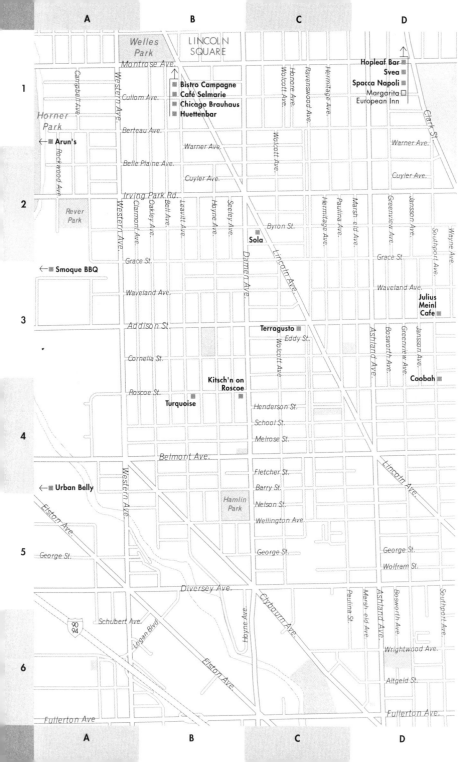

A

Welles Park

LINCOLN SQUARE

B

C

D

Montrose Ave.

Campbell Ave.

Western Ave.

Cullom Ave.

Honore Ave.
Wolcott Ave.
Ravenswood Ave.
Hermitage Ave.

Hopleaf Bar ■
Svea ■
Spacca Napoli ■
Margarita □
European Inn

Clark St.

1

Horner Park

Berteau Ave.

Rockwood Ave.

■← ■ Arun's

Warner Ave.

Wolcott Ave.

Warner Ave.

■ Bistro Campagne
■ Café Selmarie
■ Chicago Brauhaus
■ Huettenbar

Belle Plaine Ave.

Cuyler Ave.

Cuyler Ave.

Irving Park Rd.

Western Ave.

Clarmont Ave.
Oakley Ave.
Bell Ave.
Leavitt Ave.
Hoyne Ave.
Seeley Ave.

Damen Ave.

Byron St.

Lincoln Ave.

Hermitage Ave.
Paulina Ave.
Marsh. eld Ave.

Greenview Ave.
Janson Ave.
Wayne Ave.
Southport Ave.

2

Rever Park

Sola ■

Grace St.

Grace St.

Smoque BBQ ■←

Waveland Ave.

Waveland Ave.

Julius
Meinl
Cafe ■

3

Addison St.

Terragusto ■

Eddy St.

Wolcott Ave.

Ashland Ave.
Bosworth Ave.
Greenview Ave.
Janson Ave.

Cornelia St.

Coobah ■

Roscoe St.

Kitsch'n on
Roscoe ■

Turquoise ■

Henderson St.

School St.

Melrose St.

4

Belmont Ave.

Fletcher St.

Western Ave.

Barry St.

Lincoln Ave.

Urban Belly ■←

Hamlin
Park

Nelson St.

Wellington Ave.

Elston Ave.

George St.

5

George St.

George St.

Wolfram St.

Diversey Ave.

Hoyne Ave.
Clybourn Ave.

Paulina St.
Marsh. eld Ave.
Ashland Ave.
Bosworth Ave.
Southport Ave.

90
94

Schubert Ave.

Logan Blvd.

Wrightwood Ave.

6

Elston Ave.

Altgeld St.

Fullerton Ave

Fullerton Ave.

A

B

C

D

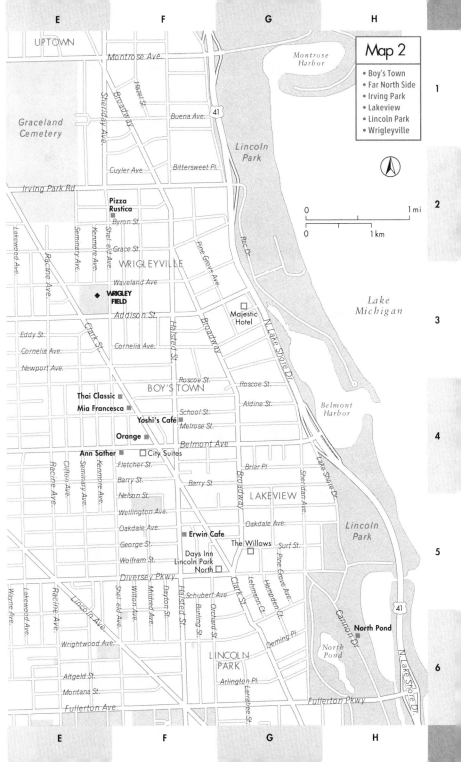

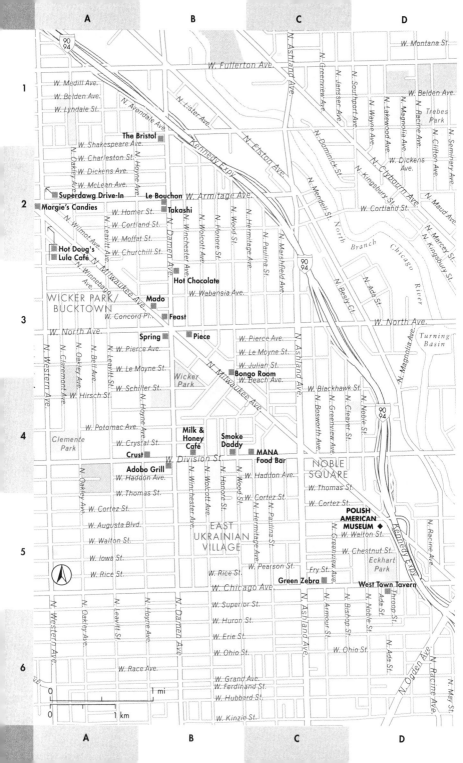

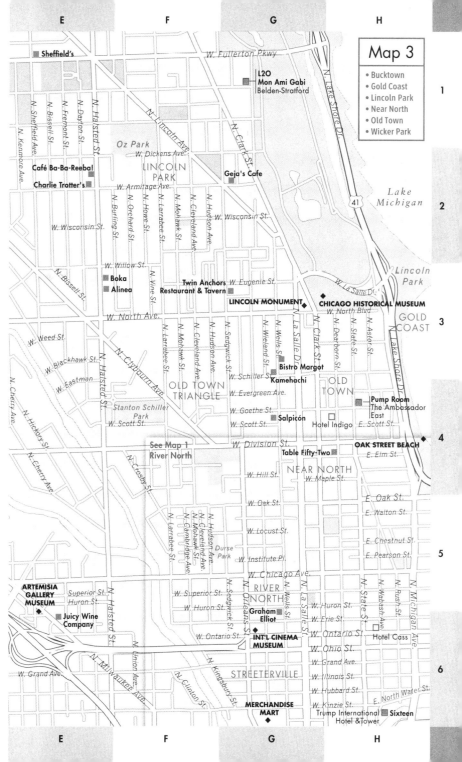

Map 3

- Bucktown
- Gold Coast
- Lincoln Park
- Near North
- Old Town
- Wicker Park

Sheffield's

W. Fullerton Pkwy.

L2O
Mon Ami Gabi
Belden-Stratford

N. Sheffield Ave.
N. Bissell St.
N. Fremont St.
N. Dayton St.
N. Halsted St.
N. Kenmore Ave.

N. Lincoln Ave.

N. Clark St.

Oz Park
W. Dickens Ave.
LINCOLN
PARK
W. Armitage Ave.

Geja's Cafe

Café Ba-Ba-Reeba!
Charlie Trotter's

Lake
Michigan

41

N. Burling St.
N. Orchard St.
N. Howe St.
N. Larrabee Ave.
N. Mohawk St.
N. Cleveland Ave.
N. Hudson Ave.

W. Wisconsin St.

W. Wisconsin St.

N. Bissell St.

W. Willow St.

Lincoln
Park

Boka
Alinea

N. Vine St.

Twin Anchors
Restaurant & Tavern

W. Eugenie St.

W. La Salle Dr.

LINCOLN MONUMENT

CHICAGO HISTORICAL MUSEUM
W. North Blvd.

GOLD
COAST

W. North Ave.

N. Clybourn Ave.

N. Larrabee St.
N. Mohawk St.
N. Cleveland Ave.
N. Hudson Ave.
N. Sedgwick St.
N. Wieland St.
N. Wells St.
N. La Salle St.
N. Clark St.
N. Dearborn St.
N. State St.
N. Astor St.

N. Halsted St.

W. Weed St.

W. Blackhawk St.

W. Eastman

OLD TOWN
TRIANGLE

Stanton Schiller
Park
W. Scott St.

Bistro Margot
W. Schiller St.
Kamehachi
W. Evergreen Ave.

OLD
TOWN

W. Goethe St.

Salpicón

W. Scott St.

Pump Room
The Ambassador
East

Hotel Indigo

E. Scott St.

N. Cherry Ave.
N. Hickory Ave.

See Map 1
River North

W. Division St.

OAK STREET BEACH

E. Elm St.

N. Cherry Ave.

N. Crosby St.

Table Fifty-Two

NEAR NORTH

W. Hill St.
W. Maple St.

W. Oak St.

E. Oak St.

E. Walton St.

N. Larrabee St.
N. Cleveland Ave.
N. Mohawk Ave.
N. Hudson Ave.
N. Cambridge Ave.

W. Locust St.

Durso
Park

W. Institute Pl.

E. Chestnut St.

E. Pearson St.

W. Chicago Ave.

ARTEMISIA
GALLERY
MUSEUM

Superior St.
Huron St.

Juicy Wine
Company

N. Halsted St.

N. Orleans St.

N. Sedgwick St.

RIVER
NORTH
W. Superior St.
W. Huron St.

W. Ontario St.

N. Cleveland Ave.

N. Wells St.

N. La Salle St.

Graham
Elliot

INT'L CINEMA
MUSEUM

N. State St.
N. Wabash Ave.
N. Rush St.
N. Michigan Ave.

W. Huron St.

W. Erie St.

W. Ontario St.

Hotel Cass

W. Ohio St.

N. Milwaukee Ave.

N. Union Ave.

W. Grand Ave.

N. Kingsbury St.

N. Clinton St.

STREETERVILLE

W. Grand Ave.

W. Illinois St.

W. Hubbard St.

W. Kinzie St.

E. North Water St.

MERCHANDISE
MART

Trump International
Hotel & Tower

Sixteen

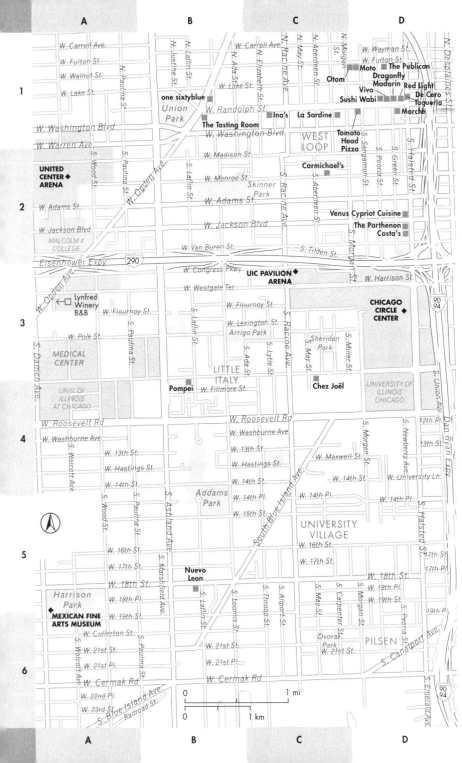

A

W. Carroll Ave.
W. Fulton St.
W. Walnut St.

1 W. Lake St.

N. Justine St.
N. Laflin St.

W. Washington Blvd

W. Warren Ave

UNITED CENTER ◆ ARENA

2 W. Adams St.

W. Jackson Blvd

MALCOLM X COLLEGE

Eisenhower Expy 290

W. Ogden Ave.

Lynfred Winery B&B

3 W. Flournoy St.

W. Polk St.

MEDICAL CENTER

UNIV OF ILLINOIS AT CHICAGO

W. Roosevelt Rd

4 W. Washburne Ave.

W. 13th St.

W. Hastings St.

W. 14th St.

S. Damen Ave.
S. Wolcott Ave.
S. Wood St.
S. Paulina St.

5

W. 16th St.
W. 17th St.
W. 18th St.

Harrison Park
◆ **MEXICAN FINE ARTS MUSEUM**

W. 18th Pl.
W. 19th St.

W. Cullerton St.

6 W. 21st St.
W. 21st Pl.

W. Cermak Rd

W. 22nd Pl.
W. 23rd St.

S. Blue Island Ave.
Railroad St.

B

N. Ada St.
N. Elizabeth St.

W. Carroll Ave.

W. Lake St.

one sixtyblue ■

Union Park

W. Randolph St.

The Tasting Room ■

W. Washington Blvd

W. Madison St.

W. Monroe St.

W. Adams St.

Skinner Park

W. Jackson Blvd

W. Van Buren St.

W. Congress Pkwy

W. Westgate Ter

W. Flournoy St.

W. Lexington St.
Arrigo Park

S. Laflin St.
S. Ada St.
S. Lytle St.

LITTLE ITALY

Pompei ■ W. Fillmore St.

W. Roosevelt Rd

W. Washburne Ave.

W. 13th St.

W. Hastings St.

W. 14th St.

Addams Park

W. 14th Pl.

W. 15th St.

Nuevo Leon ■

S. Ashland Ave.
S. Marshfield Ave.
S. Laflin St.

W. 18th St.

W. 19th St.

W. 21st St.
W. 21st Pl.

W. Cermak Rd

0   1 mi
0   1 km

C

N. Racine Ave.
N. May St.
N. Aberdeen St.
N. Morgan St.

W. Carroll Ave.

W. Lake St.

Ina's ■   **La Sardine** ■

WEST LOOP

Carmichael's ■

S. Racine Ave.
S. Aberdeen St.

W. Adams St.

W. Jackson Blvd

S. Tilden St.

UIC PAVILION ◆ ARENA

S. May St.
S. Miller St.
S. Morgan St.

Sheridan Park

Chez Joël ■

UNIVERSITY OF ILLINOIS CHICAGO

W. Roosevelt Rd

W. Washburne Ave.

W. Maxwell St.

W. 14th St.

W. 14th Pl.

UNIVERSITY VILLAGE

W. 16th St.

W. 17th St.

S. Loomis St.
S. Throop St.
S. Allport St.
S. May St.
S. Carpenter St.
S. Morgan St.

W. 18th St.
W. 18th Pl.
W. 19th St.

Dvorak Park

PILSEN

W. 21st St.

D

N. Morgan St.
W. Wayman St.
W. Fulton St.
W. Fulton St.

Moto ■ **The Publican** ■

Dragonfly

Otom **Madarin** ■ **Red Light**

Vivo **De Cero**

Sushi Wabi **Taqueria**

Marché ■

S. Sangamon St.
S. Peoria St.
S. Green St.
S. Halsted St.

Tomato Head Pizza ■

Venus Cypriot Cuisine ■

The Parthenon ■
Costa's ■

W. Harrison St.

CHICAGO CIRCLE CENTER ◆

90 94

S. Union Ave.
Dan Ryan Expy

12th Pl.
13th St.

S. Newberry Ave.

W. University Ln

S. Halsted St.

W. 14th Pl.

17th Pl.

19th Pl.

S. Peoria St.

S. Canalport Ave.

S. Emerald Ave.

90 94

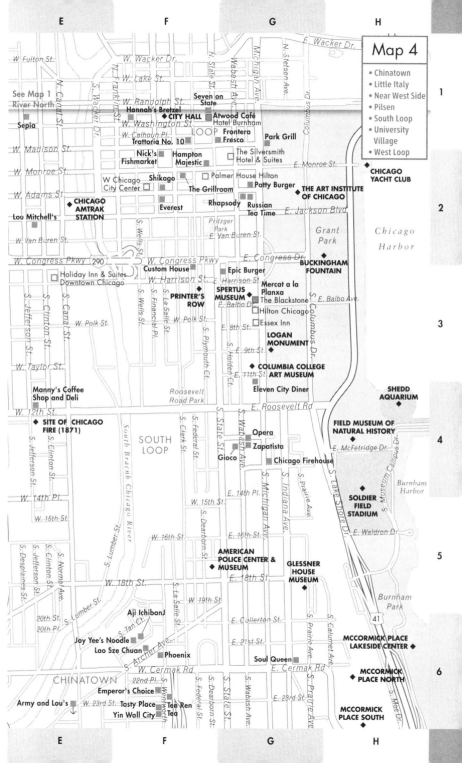

Where to Stay

WORD OF MOUTH

"We also had drinks at the Peninsula Hotel one night. What a swank place! We were very happy with the Park Hyatt, but we would also be interested in staying at the Peninsula for a future visit as the vibe is so cool!"

—mah1980

Updated by Jo Napolitano

Chicago hotel rates are as temperamental as the city's climate. And just as snow in April and 70-degree weather in November are not uncommon, it is widely accepted that a hotel's room rates may drop $50 to $100 overnight—and rise again the next day. It all depends on the season (summers are priciest, unsurprisingly) and what's happening in town (big conventions at McCormick Place, like February's annual Chicago Auto Show, throw a wrench in the system, kicking up rates citywide).

Even so, it's wise to shop around. Focus on a neighborhood of interest, such as the Michigan Avenue area, also called Near North, and you'll find budget chains like Embassy Suites, where prices start at $189, and luxury properties like the Four Seasons Hotel Chicago within a few blocks of each other.

On the lower end, expect well-maintained yet boxy and sparsely decorated rooms. The good news is that free Wi-Fi is now a feature of most budget-friendly hotels, like the Best Western and Holiday Inn chains, or local outfits like the Essex Inn.

Top-tier hotels have no problem filling their rooms: in some cases, this has little to do with amenities. Instead, their vibrant bar scenes are the draw, as is the case at the W Chicago Lakeshore, W Chicago City Center, and the James Hotel. Rooms at these hot spots usually don't go for under $300, but the "it" factor is huge, with attractive crowds queuing at the bar and lounging in the restaurants.

Looking forward, Ian Schrager, who co-founded Studio 54, announced his plans to partner with Marriott International Inc. to open a new boutique hotel called "Edition" just off the Magnificent Mile.

WHERE SHOULD I STAY?

	NEIGHBORHOOD VIBE	PROS	CONS
The Loop	Mostly historic hotels of architectural interest in an area trolled by business-people on weekdays and shoppers on weekends. The scene has become increasingly hip over the years.	Accessible public transportation and abundant cabs; packed with business types during the day; the area has recently blossomed into a worthy nighttime destination.	El train noise; construction common; streets can sometimes be bare in late evening. It draws an older, more established crowd.
South Loop and West Loop	Mixed residential and business neighborhoods that are gentrifying, although empty buildings and storefronts are common. This area has seen a lot of new life in the last couple of years.	Hotels are cheaper; streets are quieter; Museum Campus and McCormick Place are within easy reach; family-friendly; appealing to hipster set with many new lounges and restaurants.	Long walks to public transportation; minimal shopping; quiet at night with many darkened streets. If you're looking for entertainment, it might require a quick drive or a long walk.
Near North	The pulse of the city, on and around North Michigan Avenue, has ritzy high-rise hotels, plenty of shopping and restaurants. The farther north you go, streets become residential.	Many lodging options, including some of the city's most luxurious hotels. Lively streets abuzz until late night; safe. The shopping couldn't be better for those with deep pockets.	Some hotels on the pricey side; crowded sidewalks; popular tourist destination. And don't expect to find many bargains here.
River North	Lots of chains, from hotels to restaurants to shops, patronized mostly by travelers. Though this is a tourist haven, the area has become home to many art galleries and antiques stores.	Affordable lodging; easy access to public transportation; attractions nearby are family-friendly, especially during the day; high concentration of nightclubs.	Area might be too touristy for some. This is Chicago's home for chain restaurants; parking is a drag.
Lincoln Park	Small, boutique hotels tucked on quiet, tree-lined streets with many independent shops and restaurants. Pedestrian-friendly area; you don't need a car to find a restaurant, bar, or bank.	Low crime; great paths for walks; lots of parkland. From hot dogs to sushi, this place has it all; eclectic collection of shops and restaurants, ranging from super-affordable to the ultrapricey.	Limited hotel selection; long walks to El train. Parking is almost impossible in some spots, and garages don't come cheap; very young and trendy crowd.
Lakeview and North of the City	Especially lively around Wrigley Field, where both Chicagoans and travelers congregate in summertime; the area's lodging is mid-sized boutique hotels and B&Bs.	Low crime; moderately priced hotels; shopping and dining options at all price ranges, including many vintage-clothing boutiques; a plethora of sports-theme bars.	Congested traffic; panhandlers common, especially around El stations and Wrigley Field. Parking is nightmarish when the Cubs are playing in town.

6

CHICAGO LODGING PLANNER

Strategy

Where should we stay? With hundreds of Chicago hotels, it may seem like a daunting question. But fret not—our expert writers and editors have done most of the legwork. The selections here represent the best this city has to offer—from the best budget motels to the sleekest designer hotels. Scan "Best Bets" on the following pages for top recommendations by price and experience. Or find a review quickly in the listings. Search by neighborhood, then alphabetically. Happy hunting!

In This Chapter

Facilities

Unless otherwise noted in the individual descriptions, all the hotels listed have private baths, central heating, air-conditioning, and private phones. Almost all hotels have Internet and phones with voice mail, as well as valet service. Many now have wireless Internet (Wi-Fi) available, although it's not always free.

Need a Reservation?

Yes. Hotel reservations are an absolute necessity when planning your trip to Chicago—hotels often fill up with convention traffic, so book your room in advance.

Orientation

Throughout the chapter, you'll see mapping symbols and coordinates (⊕) after property reviews. To locate the property on a map, turn to the Chicago Dining & Lodging Atlas at the end of the Where to Eat chapter. The first number after the ⊕ symbol indicates the map number. Following that is the property's coordinate on the map grid.

Prices

The prices we've printed are based on standard double rooms at high season, excluding holidays. Although we list all the facilities that are available at a property, we don't specify what is included and what costs extra, as those policies are subject to change without notice.

WHAT IT COSTS

	¢	$	$$	$$$	$$$$
FOR TWO PEOPLE	under $150	$151–$219	$220–$319	$320–$419	over $420

Prices exclude service charges and Chicago's 15.4% room tax.

BEST BETS FOR CHICAGO LODGING

Fodor's offers a selective listing of quality lodging experiences at every price range, from the city's best budget motel to its most sophisticated luxury hotel. Here we've compiled our top recommendations by price and experience. The best properties—those that provide a remarkable experience in their price range—are designated in the listings with the Fodor's Choice logo. Check here for our top recommendations, then read the review in the listings, which are organized alphabetically within each neighborhood.

Fodor's Choice ★

The Blackstone, p. 238

Dana Hotel and Spa, p. 236

Essex Inn, p. 239

Flemish House of Chicago, p. 227

Four Seasons Hotel, p. 227

Hotel Burnham, p. 221

Hotel Sax Chicago, p. 237

The James Hotel, p. 239

Park Hyatt Chicago, p. 230

Peninsula Chicago, p. 230

Ritz-Carlton Chicago, p. 232

Sofitel Chicago Water Tower, p. 233

Trump International Hotel & Tower, p. 238

Best by Price

¢

Margarita European Inn, p. 218

City Suites Hotel, p. 218

$

Flemish House of Chicago, p. 227

Best Western Hawthorne Terrace, p. 218

Essex Inn, p. 239

Hampton Majestic, **p. 229**

Millennium Knickerbocker Hotel, p. 230

$$

Hard Rock Hotel, p. 221

Hyatt Regency Chicago, p. 222

Hotel Sax Chicago, p. 237

W Chicago Lakeshore, p. 234

$$$

The Blackstone, p. 238

Four Seasons Hotel, p. 227

Hilton Chicago, p. 239

Hotel Burnham, p. 221

Trump International Hotel & Tower, p. 238

$$$$

Park Hyatt Chicago, p. 230

Peninsula Chicago, p. 230

Ritz-Carlton Chicago, p. 232

Sofitel Chicago Water Tower, p. 233

Best by Experience

BEST SPA

Four Seasons Hotel, p. 227

The James Hotel, p. 229

Trump International Hotel & Tower, p. 238

W Chicago Lakeshore, p. 234

BEST CONCIERGE

Fairmont Chicago, p. 220

Hotel Monaco, p. 222

Renaissance Chicago Hotel, p. 222

Ritz-Carlton Chicago, p. 232

GREAT POOLS

Essex Inn, p. 239

Hilton Chicago, p. 239

Hotel InterContinental Chicago, p. 229

Peninsula Chicago, p. 230

Trump International Hotel & Tower, p. 238

MOST KID-FRIENDLY

Best Western River North, p. 236

Essex Inn, p. 239

Holiday Inn & Suites Downtown, p. 239

Homewood Suites, p. 228

Hotel Allegro Chicago, p. 221

6

EVANSTON

¢ 🖵**Margarita European Inn.** While the tiny rooms, shared bathrooms, and narrow corridors recall a college dormitory, you won't find a more charming place to stay in Chicago's near north suburbs. The Inn was formerly an all-girls residence club built in the late 1920s, and a lot of its original features, including the iron-girded elevator shaft and antiques-laden parlor, remain intact. The staff is small but helpful. The best feature is the "borrowing" library, where guests can swap their rare and used books for those of others. If you're in no rush to go downtown, eat at the lower-level Va Pensiero restaurant, a fancy Italian spot that serves more than 10 kinds of grappa and dishes like pancetta-wrapped pork tenderloin. **Pros:** a quaint, off-the-beaten path find; close to Northwestern University and a gorgeous downtown area. **Cons:** breakfast is merely adequate; spotty service. ⊠*1566 Oak Ave., Evanston* ☎*847/869–2273* 🖷*847/869–2353* ⊕*www.margaritainn. com* 🗷*42 rooms, 22 with bath* ₼*In-hotel: restaurant, Wi-Fi, parking (fee)* ☰*AE, D, DC, MC, V* ⦿|*CP* ⊹*2:D1*

LAKEVIEW

Seemingly light-years away from the downtown buzz, Lakeview hotels entice with their proximity to Wrigley Field and the summertime street festivals for which the neighborhood is known. As you venture farther north, accommodations tend to be quainter and spaces more intimate.

$ 🖵**Best Western Hawthorne Terrace.** This 59-room hotel is centrally located and offers all essential amenities at a reasonable price. There's little room to relax in the American colonial–style lobby, but rooms are inviting enough; deluxe rooms come with whirlpool tubs. A stay here includes free continental breakfast and use of business facilities and a fitness center. The hotel's front terrace becomes a place to see and be seen in the summer months, especially when street festivals roar into town. **Pros:** proximity to Wrigley Field; helpful staff; close to popular bars and restaurants. **Cons:** parking is not ideal; some guests have complained of billing problems. ⊠*3434 N. Broadway, Lakeview* ☎*773/244–3434 or 866/378–9792* 🖷*773/244–3435* ⊕*www.hawthorneterrace.com* 🗷*46 rooms, 13 suites* ₼*In-room: safe, microwave, refrigerator, DVD (some), Wi-Fi. In-hotel: gym, laundry service, parking (fee)* ☰*AE, D, DC, MC, V* ⦿|*CP* ⊹ *1:F3*

¢ 🖵**City Suites Hotel.** The neighborhood is eclectic, being the stomping grounds for the city's Goth and punk kids, but it's safe and pretty appealing if you want to escape the sometimes stiff downtown scene. European travelers love the hotel for its cozy, residential feel (it's a mostly suites property, and two-thirds of the rooms have separate sitting areas and pull-out couches). Its proximity to the El train is both a blessing and a curse; you'll have easy access to downtown and the North Side, but the rumbling noise into the wee hours might not make for the most restful night. Amenities include complimentary continental breakfast, afternoon cookies, free wireless Internet access, luxury robes, and access to a nearby health club. **Pros:** located near the Briar Street Theater's Blue Man Group; close to public transportation. **Cons:** rooms are on the small side; an underwhelming breakfast. ⊠*933 W. Belmont Ave. Lakeview* ☎*773/404–3400 or 800/248–9108* 🖷*773/404–3405* ⊕*www.cityinns. com* ⇌*16 rooms, 29 suites* &*In-room: refrigerator, Wi-Fi. In-hotel: concierge, parking (fee)* ⊟*AE, D, DC, MC, V* ¶⊙¶*CP* ⊹*2:F4*

$$ 🛈 **Majestic Hotel.** It's no wonder lovey-dovey couples are a big part of this hotel's clientele; everything here—from the roaring fireplace in the lobby to wood-laden, cozy rooms with Victorian-style furnishings— says romance. Rely on the friendly concierge for just about anything, including reservations at the many restaurants in the lively Boystown and Wrigleyville neighborhoods just outside the door. Transportation can be tricky; because the hotel is on a quiet side street, you'll have to walk a block to flag a cab, and the El train is at least five minutes away on foot. **Pros:** great ambience; friendly staff; quiet at night. **Cons:** furnishings are a bit dated; the small elevator can be a hassle for guests with lots of luggage. ⊠*528 W. Brompton Ave., Lakeview* ☎*773/404–3499 or 800/727–5108* 🖷*773/404–3495* ⊕*www.cityinns.com* ⇌*28 rooms, 23 suites* &*In-room: refrigerator (some), Wi-Fi. In-hotel: concierge, laundry service, parking (fee)* ⊟*AE, D, DC, MC, V* ¶⊙¶*CP* ⊹*2:G3*

$ 🛈 **The Willows.** The lobby of this 1920s boutique hotel, designed in 19th-century French Provincial style, opens onto a tree-lined street in Lakeview, a lively area three blocks from the lake and central to stores, restaurants, and movie theaters. Its prime location and proximity to the El make it a top choice for visitors to Chicago. The complimentary continental breakfast and afternoon cookies make it an inviting alternative to local bed-and-breakfasts. Workout buffs don't despair: although there is no on-site fitness center, guests have access to a local Bally's Total Fitness Club. **Pros:** just steps away from bars, restaurants, and public transit. **Cons:** modestly decorated rooms. ⊠*555 W. Surf St., Lakeview* ☎*773/528–8400 or 800/787–3108* 🖷*773/528–8483* ⊕*www.cityinns.com* ⇌*51 rooms, 4 suites* &*In-room: Wi-Fi. In-hotel: concierge, laundry facilities, laundry service, parking (fee)* ⊟*AE, D, DC, MC, V* ¶⊙¶*CP* ⊹*2:G5*

LINCOLN PARK

Three miles of lakefront parkland draw people to this neighborhood— and most hotels here are just blocks away. Room rates are decidedly lower than those downtown, the downside being that you'll invest more in transportation to hit top sites. Parking is easier, but never a snap; plan on using the valet.

$$ 🛈 **Belden-Stratford.** The 70 rooms—all with full kitchens or kitchenettes—are apartments for long-term rental, but on any given night there are plenty available for overnight stays at very reasonable rates. Don't be fooled; the feel is not that of a generic, extended-stay hotel. Its lobby, in fact, looks palatial, thanks to the polished gold chandelier, grand piano, and hand-woven tapestries. The lobby and hallways are praised for being quiet, so families should prepare to clam up their kids. The biggest treat is the on-site dining at French restaurant Mon Ami Gabi. Another highlight? The Lincoln Park Zoo is across the street and the lakefront is just a few blocks farther. **Pros:** extremely well maintained; excellent location. **Cons:** the quality of rooms is inconsistent. ⊠*2300*

N. Lincoln Park W., Lincoln Park ☎773/281–2900 *or* 800/800–8301 ☏773/880–2039 ⊕*www.beldenstratfordhotel.com* ☚*10 rooms, 60 suites* ♿*In-room: kitchen, Internet, Wi-Fi. In-hotel: Restaurant, gym, laundry facilities, laundry service, parking (fee)* ▭*AE, D, DC, MC, V* ⊹*3:G1*

$ 📺**Days Inn Chicago.** This award-winning Days Inn is one of the more
☾ luxurious in the sometimes so-so chain. This boutique hotel offers an affordable stay in a prime location. The updated look of its guest rooms is one of cheery mixed patterns and light-wood furniture, white linens, and duvets. Complimentary continental breakfast and free Wi-Fi are available to all guests, as well as free use of a nearby health club. **Pros:** great location; knowledgeable staff makes it a good value for the price. **Cons:** the location—bustling even very late at night—can make it a little noisy for some guests. ⊠*644 W. Diversey Pkwy., Lincoln Park* ☎773/525–7010 *or* 888/576–3297 ☏773/525–6998 ⊕*www. daysinchicago.net* ☚*129 rooms, 2 suites* ♿*In-room: safe, refrigerator (some), Wi-Fi. In-hotel: laundry facilities, laundry service, parking (fee), no-smoking rooms* ▭*AE, D, DC, MC, V* ⎥◎⎢*CP* ⊹*2:G5*

THE LOOP

Chicago's business district, laced with overhead train tracks, is a desirable—if slightly noisy—place to stay. Hotels here tend to be moderately priced; many are housed in historic buildings, giving them a charm you won't find along glitzier North Michigan Avenue. Easy access to the Art Institute and Millennium Park is a plus.

$$ 📺**Fairmont Chicago.** On a quiet block near the Loop, this 45-story pink-granite tower fluctuates between the understated and the opulent, with a huge, glistening chandelier in the foyer. Good thing that it caters to the chatty; there are three telephones per room (including one hanging conspicuously on the bathroom wall). Suites offer stunning views of Lake Michigan and feature dining rooms. Coveted whirlpools are only available in grand suites, which, housed on the top floor, also boast fireplaces, libraries, and kitchenettes. Aria, an upscale Asian/American restaurant within the Fairmont, attracts plenty of locals; a massive 2008 renovation updated the rooms with plush new carpets and dramatic artwork. **Pros:** spacious rooms; a short walk from the heart of the city. **Cons:** no pool; not good for children. ⊠*200 N. Columbus Dr., The Loop* ☎312/565–8000 *or* 800/526–2008 ☏312/856–1032 ⊕*www. fairmont.com* ☚*622 guest rooms, 65 suites* ♿*In-room: safe, refrigerator (upon request), Internet. In-hotel: restaurant, room service, bars, spa, concierge, laundry service, public Wi-Fi, parking (fee), no-smoking rooms, some pets allowed* ▭*AE, D, DC, MC, V* ⊹*1:F6*

$ 📺**Hampton Majestic, Chicago Theatre District.** The Hampton Majestic is located in one of the most high-traffic areas of town. It offers stunning and quiet guest rooms with rust-color walls, white sheets, and chocolate-brown furnishings. Online pictures, which can make the rooms look orange, don't do the place justice. The sheer curtains are a perfect touch. The downstairs lobby, nondescript and filled with luggage, is not at all a reflection of the rest of the space. The service is responsive and the common areas are large. Give this place a chance; it will truly surprise you. **Pros:** steps from the Art Institute; unique style; great complimentary breakfast. **Cons:** a hike to the Magnificent Mile; the lobby can seem too crowded with furniture. ✉ *22 W. Monroe, The Loop* ☎ *312/332–5052* ⊕ *www.hamptonmajestic.com* ↪ *135 rooms* ⚘ *In-room: Wi-Fi. In-hotel: room service, gym, laundry service, concierge, public Internet, parking* ▤ *AE, D, DC, MC, V* ⦿❘*CP* ✛ *4:F1*

$$ ⬚ **Hard Rock Hotel.** We're not huge fans of the ubiquitous restaurant chain, but the hotel—flashy, loud, and packed with plasma TVs—has our approval. Set within the 40-story Carbide and Carbon Building, it touts modern rooms adorned with rock-and-roll paraphernalia and a brilliant dining concept called China Grill. Ask for a tower room, offering striking views of Michigan Avenue, Millennium Park, and the Chicago River. Complimentary issues of *Time Out Chicago* keep guests in the know about what's happening in the city. **Pros:** well-appointed rooms with great views; good location; Aveda bath products. **Cons:** the dim lighting can be bothersome to some. ✉ *230 N. Michigan Ave., The Loop* ☎ *312/345–1000 or 866/966–5166* 📠 *312/345–1012* ⊕ *www. hardrockhotelchicago.com* ↪ *361 rooms, 20 suites* ⚘ *In-room: safe, DVD, Internet. In-hotel: restaurant, room service, bar, gym, concierge, public Wi-Fi, parking (fee), some pets allowed, no-smoking rooms* ▤ *AE, D, DC, MC, V* ✛ *1:E6*

$$$ ⬚ **Hotel Allegro Chicago.** Theater lovers will relish an opportunity to stay
🕑 at this recently renovated, Art Deco–theme hot spot. The new, eclectic decor—including pop art–inspired chairs and sofas—is a hit, and the lobby's black-and-gray wallpaper looks super sharp. The service is solid, and the rooms are a treat with their muted metallic walls and blue mohair headboards. The bathrooms are well crafted, with gleaming new gray marble and updated sinks and vanities. Rent a suite if space is your thing. The building, staying true to its original architecture, kept the rooms on the smaller side. **Pros:** Aveda products in the bathrooms; yoga equipment available upon request. **Cons:** small bathrooms and closets. ✉ *171 W. Randolph St., The Loop* ☎ *312/236–0123 or 800/643–1500* 📠 *312/236–0917* ⊕ *www.allegrochicago.com* ↪ *451 rooms, 32 suites* ⚘ *In-room: Wi-Fi, refrigerator. In-hotel: 2 restaurants, room service, 2 bars, gym, children's program, laundry service, concierge, public Internet, parking (fee), no-smoking rooms, some pets allowed* ▤ *AE, D, DC, MC, V* ✛ *1:C6*

$$$ ⬚ **Hotel Burnham.** Making creative use of a city landmark, this hotel is
Fodor's Choice housed in the famed 13-story Reliance Building, which D.H. Burnham
★ & Company built in 1895. The refurbished interior retains such original details as Carrara marble wainscoting and ceilings, terrazzo floors, and mahogany trim. Guest rooms, which were once the building's offices, are compact. But we'll overlook the lack of wiggle room thanks to perks like the "pillow library," which offers everything from firm to hypoallergenic pillows. On the ground floor, the intimate Atwood Cafe has a stylish mahogany bar and serves contemporary American fare, including its popular potpies. **Pros:** property has a storied past; beautifully restored building; good location. **Cons:** small guest rooms may make it difficult to sprawl out. ✉ *1 W. Washington St., The Loop* ☎ *312/782–1111 or 877/294–9712* 📠 *312/762–3554* ⊕ *www.burnhamhotel.com* ↪ *103*

rooms, 19 suites ☉In-room: safe, Wi-Fi, refrigerator. In-hotel: restaurant, room service, bar, gym, concierge, laundry service, public Wi-Fi, parking (fee), some pets allowed ☰AE, D, DC, MC, V ✥4:F1

$$$ ⊞**Hotel Monaco.** A registration desk fashioned after a classic steamer ⟳ trunk, and meeting rooms named for international destinations such as Tokyo and Paris inspire wanderlust here. We love each room's bay windows (the Monaco is the only hotel in the city that has 'em) and the pet goldfish in a bowl provided on request. It's clear that this hotel has humor: look to the honor bars stocked with plush goldfish for the kids. Complimentary Starbucks coffee is available from 6 to 9 AM, and all guests are offered free wine each night from 5 to 6 PM. **Pros:** free coffee and wine; comfortable beds. **Cons:** small gym for a hotel of this size and splendor. ✉225 N. Wabash Ave., The Loop ☎312/960–8500 or 866/610–0081 🖷312/960–1883 ⊕www.monaco-chicago.com ⇦172 rooms, 20 suites ☉In-room: safe, Wi-Fi, refrigerator. In-hotel: restaurant, room service, bar, gym, concierge, laundry service, parking (fee), some pets allowed ☰AE, D, DC, MC, V ✥1:E6

$$ ⊞**Hyatt Regency Chicago.** This 2,000-plus-room hotel is one of the largest in Chicago, with illuminated signs that guide you through the labyrinth of halls. Ficus trees, bamboo, and gushing fountains fill the two-story atrium lobby. In the comfortably sized guest rooms black-and-white photographs of Chicago landmarks give things an authentic spin. The in-house Stetson's Chop House is a convenient dining option for guests who don't want to travel far for a good meal. **Pros:** great winter rates; excellent location; just steps from numerous attractions. **Cons:** thin walls can make it easy to overhear neighbors; some guests say service didn't meet expectations for a hotel of this caliber. ✉151 E. Wacker Dr., The Loop ☎312/565–1234 or 800/233–1234 🖷312/239–4414 ⊕www.chicagohyatt.com ⇦2,019 rooms, 119 suites ☉In-room: safe, Internet. In-hotel: 5 restaurants, room service, gym, spa, concierge, laundry service, parking (fee), no-smoking rooms ☰AE, D, DC, MC, V ✥1:F5

$$$ ⊞**Palmer House Hilton.** The grand palais feel of this historic property is conveyed by the huge lobby ceiling mural, which was restored in 1996 by a Florentine gentleman who restores art in the Sistine Chapel. Rooms—reached via a winding maze of corridors—are adequately sized. With more than 1,600 rooms, the property can seem overwhelming; luckily, one executive level has its own lobby and concierge, providing a hotel-within-a-hotel feel. A 2008 renovation led to a state-of-the-art fitness center and spa, a new restaurant and bar, refurbished guest rooms, and a restored ballroom. **Pros:** recently renovated rooms with historic character left intact. **Cons:** rooms not always spotless; some rooms quite small. ✉17 E. Monroe St., TheLoop ☎312/726–7500 or 800/445–8667 🖷312/263–2556 ⊕www.hilton.com ⇦1,639 rooms, 88 suites ☉In-room: Wi-Fi, kitchenette (some). In-hotel: restaurant, room service, bar, pool, gym, concierge, laundry service, public Wi-Fi, parking (fee), no-smoking rooms, some pets allowed ☰AE, D, DC, MC, V ✥ 4:F2

$$ ⊞**Renaissance Chicago Hotel.** The cosmopolitan Renaissance Chicago, situated on the south bank of the Chicago River, puts a premium on

a good night's sleep: there's no missing the seven—yep, seven—fluffy white pillows on each bed. When you're not catching some Z's, you can enjoy views of the Chicago skyline right from your room. Stay on the hotel's slightly pricier "club levels" for a more exclusive feel and access to a private business center. **Pros:** excellent service, even when the hotel is packed to capacity; spacious rooms for a good value. **Cons:** guests complained about problems at check-in; can get pricey during high season. ✉ *1 W. Wacker Dr., The Loop* ☎ *312/372–7200 or 800/468–3571* 🖶 *312/372–0093* ⊕ *www.renaissancechicagodowntown.com* ➷ *513 rooms, 40 suites* ♿ *In-room: Wi-Fi. In-hotel: 2 restaurants, room service, bar, pool, gym, spa, concierge, laundry service, public Internet, public Wi-Fi, parking (fee), no-smoking rooms, some pets allowed* ▭ *AE, D, DC, MC, V* ✥ *1:D6*

$$$　🏨 **The Silversmith Hotel and Suites.** Don't be fooled by the tiny front entrance located under the El. The guest rooms—with their 12-foot ceilings—are unusually large, each with natural light. The lobby is enormous, one of the largest in the city and covered with oak. The guest-room colors—muted greens and beiges—are soft on the eyes. The furnishings are Frank Lloyd Wright–inspired, and the window seats are a treat. Steps from Millennium Park and the Art Institute, it's perfect for art and theater lovers. Popular with business folk; also great for families. **Pros:** conveniently located near public transportation. **Cons:** the entrance can be hard to find; some guests complain about outside noise. ✉ *10 S. Wabash Ave., The Loop* ☎ *312/795–6500* ⊕ *www.silversmithhotel.com* ➷ *143 rooms, 63 suites* ♿ *In-room: safe, refrigerator, Internet, Wi-Fi. In-hotel: restaurant, room service, bar, gym, laundry service, concierge, public Internet, public Wi-Fi, parking (fee), some pets allowed* ▭ *AE, D, DC, MC, V* ⧖EP ✥ *4:G2*

$$　🏨 **Swissôtel.** The Swissôtel's triangular Harry Weese design allows for panoramic vistas of the city, lake, or river. The comfortable, contemporary rooms have a condo feel, with two-line phones and marble bathrooms. A 42nd-floor fitness center, pool, and spa manage to draw even the most exercise-reticent, thanks to the bird's-eye views. Guests also enjoy the convenience of having The Palm restaurant located in the hotel; you don't have to travel far for a high-quality meal. **Pros:** guests love the view, the pool, and the location; modern rooms with great amenities; in-house destination restaurant. **Cons:** pricey parking fees. ✉ *323 E. Wacker Dr., The Loop* ☎ *312/565–0565 or 888/737–9477* 🖶 *312/565–0540* ⊕ *www.swissotelchicago.com* ➷ *621 rooms, 40 suites* ♿ *In-room: safe, Wi-Fi. In-hotel: 2 restaurants, room service, bars, pool, gym, spa, concierge, laundry service, parking (fee), no-smoking rooms* ▭ *AE, D, DC, MC, V* ✥ *1:F6*

$$$　🏨 **W Chicago City Center.** Bellhops in slick black pants and T-shirts, plus a welcome mat imprinted with "Well, Hello There," are early indicators that this hotel is hip. The couch-filled lobby (nicknamed the Living Room) is seemingly always dark (during our visit, candles were flickering at noon), and kaleidoscopic-looking film projections on walls complement ambient music. Rooms cater to the business traveler, with desks, WebTV, and cordless phones. **Pros:** with its sleek design and nightclub vibe, this hip and trendy hot spot is an ideal draw for a

A Beautiful Stay in the Neighborhood

Chicago is, famously, a city of neighborhoods. Chicagoans like to define themselves by where they hang their hat, with attendant pride, snobbery, or aspirations to street cred (of all kinds). For visitors, setting up a temporary base in one of the neighborhoods offers many advantages. This is especially true for leisure travelers. Without an expense account to ease downtown's hotel bills and menu shock, staying right in downtown can get very costly very quickly.

When choosing accommodations, it pays to look beyond the Loop and the Magnificent Mile.

A walk up Clark Street or Lincoln Avenue in Lincoln Park opens up miles of reasonably priced dining possibilities. Along one short stretch of the former you'll pass an excellent fusion restaurant, a take-out crepe place, a grocery store, and a couple of diners where the waitress might call you "hon." Remember that the next time you're called something else in the Loop.

There's also better and cheaper parking. Downtown you'll usually pay at least $30 a day. Rates at garages in outlying neighborhoods run less. There's even a chance, albeit rather remote, of finding street parking. Some days that's like saying there's a chance of a Republican mayor, but it happens.

The best reason to stay in a neighborhood is the chance to immerse yourself in the rhythms of the city. You get a chance to live as most Chicagoans live. In the neighborhoods you'll see the sky. You'll have countless independently owned restaurants and shops to browse in.

If you'd like to be somewhat near downtown, the happening Lincoln Park and Lakeview neighborhoods offer a handful of hotels. As a bonus, accommodations are relatively near the lakefront. Most also have relatively easy access to public transportation or routes well traveled by cabs. A determined walker can even get from Lincoln Park to the Magnificent Mile in a half hour.

Getting to downtown sights from farther afield may sound like too much trouble. But keep in mind that thousands upon thousands of Chicagoans make the trip every day. And, like them, you'll come home to something vital and intriguing at night. Much of the Loop, on the other hand, turns into a ghost town after rush hour. In places like Lakeview the starting gun goes off at 7 PM.

The neighborhood experience isn't for everyone. Those determined to "see it all" may find the journey in from such outposts takes too much time. Also, small hotels and B&Bs cannot offer the same pampering and facilities that are typical at the luxury digs downtown.

It's a search for small moments, for random encounters, for something indefinable—the vibe, you might say—that most appeals to visitors who stay in outer neighborhoods. Each district's rhythm is different. And it's easier to hear the city's songs away from the hustle and bustle, and tall buildings.

youngish visitor. **Cons:** some have complained of brusque staff. ✉*172 W. Adams St., The Loop* ☎*312/332–1200 or 800/621–2360* 🖷*312/917–5771* ⊕*www.whotels. com* ➯*358 rooms, 12 suites* ♿*In-room: safe, DVD, Internet, Wi-Fi. In-hotel: restaurant, room service, bar, gym, spa, concierge, laundry service, public Wi-Fi, parking (fee), no-smoking rooms, some pets allowed* ▤*AE, D, DC, MC, V* ✛*4:F2*

NEAR NORTH

With a cluster of accommodations around North Michigan Avenue (the "Magnificent Mile"), this area is where new hotels are springing up or reinventing themselves, thanks to multimillion-dollar renovations. Prices hover at the high end, but there are a few deals to be found if you're willing to forgo a pool or concierge service. Consider the area's proximity to great shopping part of the bargain.

$$$ 🏨**Allerton Hotel Chicago.** Named a National Historic Landmark in 1999, this limestone building was a residential "club hotel" for men when it opened in 1924. A 1999 renovation restored the limestone facade and overhauled the interior. A 2008 renovation left it with a more contemporary, residential feel. The bed linens are white with navy piping, and the rooms are a mix of muted blues and grays. If you want to stay in a place in the middle of it all, this may be your hotel of choice. **Pros:** newly renovated rooms; delightful concierge and doormen. **Cons:** guest rooms and bathrooms are on the small side. ✉*701 N. Michigan Ave., Near North* ☎*312/440–1500* 🖷*312/440–1819* ⊕*www.theallerton hotel.com* ➯*359 rooms, 84 suites* ♿*In-room: safe, Internet. In-hotel: restaurant, room service, bar, gym, concierge, laundry service, parking (fee), no-smoking rooms* ▤*AE, D, DC, MC, V* ✛*1:E3*

$$ 🏨**The Ambassador East.** One of the few hotels in the residential Gold Coast neighborhood, this small 1920s property is a 10- to 15-minute cab ride from the Loop. The secluded setting makes it popular with celebs and literary figures, and the world-famous Pump Room still attracts a loyal following (Humphrey Bogart and Lauren Bacall celebrated their wedding in Booth One). Rooms have a certain amount of glitz, with jewel tones and cherry-wood furniture. Bookworms, take heed: the "author" suite has held book signings by the likes of John Grisham and Maya Angelou. **Pros:** the hotel is just a few minutes away from great restaurants and bars; courteous staff. **Cons:** hotel is overdue for a renovation ✉*1301 N. State Pkwy., Near North* ☎*312/787–7200* 🖷*312/787–4760* ⊕*www.theambassadoreasthotel.com* ➯*230 rooms, 55 suites* ♿*In-room: refrigerator, kitchen (some), Wi-Fi. In-hotel: restaurant, room service, bar, gym, public Internet, concierge, laundry service, parking (fee), no-smoking rooms, some pets allowed* ▤*AE, D, DC, MC, V* ✛*3:H4*

6

$$ 🖥 **The Avenue Hotel Chicago.** Just yards away from Michigan Avenue, this high-tech, environmentally friendly property has recently completed a $35 million renovation that includes pull-out leather couches and zebra-striped chairs in every room. Ask for a room on the tech floor; they're a little more expensive, but come with iMacs and color printers. Young children will adore the kids rooms with their colorful bedding, Wii gaming systems, Baby Einstein toys, and rubber duckies for the tub. Kids rooms are very popular and go fast, so book in advance. **Pros:** the rooms are generously sized considering the location; the staff is accommodating; great concierge. **Cons:** elevators and pool are small; you might hear the din of sirens as the hotel is next to a hospital. ✉*160 East Huron* ☎ *312/787-2900* ⊕*www.avenuehotelchicago.com* ⇘*200 rooms, 150 suites* ⚴*In-room: refrigerator (some), Internet, Wi-Fi. In-hotel: 2 restaurants, room service, 2 bars, 1 pool, gym, laundry service, Internet terminal, Wi-Fi, parking (fee), some pets allowed* ⊟*AE, D, DC, MC, V*

$$$$ 🖥 **Conrad Chicago.** This hotel's Art Deco–inspired lobby has a contemporary feel, with clean-lined furniture and creative floral arrangements. Rooms—featuring European duvets, oversize pillows, plush bathrobes, and slippers—aim to pamper. Don't leave without checking out the building's limestone facade, cut from the same quarries as the Empire State Building and Tribune Tower, and depicting figures from ancient mythology and the zodiac. **Pros:** large TVs; beautifully appointed lobby. **Cons:** antiquated heating and cooling systems; it takes two elevators to reach some rooms. ✉*521 N. Rush St., Near North* ☎*312/645-1500* 🖷*312/645-1550* ⊕*www.conradchicago.com* ⇘*278 rooms, 33 suites* ⚴*In-room: safe, Internet, Wi-Fi. In-hotel: 2 restaurants, room service, bar, gym, concierge, laundry service, public Wi-Fi, parking (fee), no-smoking rooms, some pets allowed* ⊟*AE, D, DC, MC, V* ✛*1:E4*

$$$$ 🖥 **Drake Hotel.** Built in 1920, the grande dame of Chicago hotels presides over the northernmost end of Michigan Avenue. The lobby, inspired by an Italian Renaissance palace, is all cream-colored walls and chandeliers dating from the 1920s. The sounds of a fountain and harpist beckon at the Palm Court, a traditional setting for afternoon tea. There's live jazz in the Coq d'Or on Thursday, Friday, and Saturday nights, and the Cape Cod Room serves to-die-for crab cakes. The downsides? No swimming pool (a bummer for the price you're paying), and some rooms are tiny. **Pros:** hotel has retained its character; beautiful lobby. **Cons:** rooms are in need of an update. ✉*140 E. Walton Pl., Near North* ☎*312/787-2200 or 800/553-7253* 🖷*312/787-1431* ⊕*www.thedrakehotel.com* ⇘*535 rooms, 74 suites* ⚴*In-room: safe, Wi-Fi, refrigerator. In-hotel: 4 restaurants, room service, bar, gym, concierge, laundry service, public Wi-Fi, parking (fee), no-smoking rooms* ⊟*AE, D, DC, MC, V* ✛*1:E2*

$ 🖥 **Embassy Suites Chicago Downtown/Lakefront.** Every guest in this all-suites hotel has a view of either Lake Michigan or the Chicago skyscrapers. In addition, they also have room to roam, thanks to the spacious layout of each suite (rooms have separate bedrooms and living rooms). The sleek glass atrium is bustling in the morning with the complimentary breakfast buffet and in the evening during the complimentary manager's reception. A bonus for families on vacation is the location: within walking distance of Navy Pier and North Michigan Avenue. **Pros:** good value; free wine at night; short walk to clubs and other nightlife. **Cons:** long line for complimentary wine. ✉ *511 N. Columbus Dr., Near North* ☎ *312/836–5900 or 800/362–2779* 📠 *312/836–5901* ⊕ *www.chicagolakefront.embassysuites.com* 🛏 *455 suites* 🔑 *In-room: refrigerator, Internet. In-hotel: restaurant, room service, bar, pool, gym, concierge, laundry facilities, laundry service, parking (fee), no-smoking rooms* ⊟ *AE, D, DC, MC, V* 🍴*BP* ✛ *1:F4*

$ 🏠 **Flemish House of Chicago, Apartment Bed & Breakfast.** This meticulously
Fodor'sChoice kept four-story wonder is an incredible value, considering the posh zip
★ code. Each of its seven suites has a slightly different decor, but all are roomy and well appointed, with an impressive collection of antique desks, lamps, and armoires. Built in 1892, it's classic, not old, and not a single item is amiss. The rooms are converted apartments, so each has its own kitchen, stove, dishes, cookware, and utensils. With pedestal sinks and subway tile, the bathrooms are stylish and comfortable. The owners are friendly and live on-site. **Pros:** refrigerators stocked with healthy breakfast foods; complimentary use of laptops; location is ideal in terms of restaurant choices. **Cons:** the owners don't always rent rooms for a single night, though they try to be flexible. ✉ *68 E. Cedar St., Gold Coast* ☎ *312/664–9981* ⊕ *www.innchicago.com* 🛏*7 rooms* 🔑 *In-room: kitchen, refrigerator, DVD, VCR, Wi-Fi. In-hotel: no elevator, laundry facilities, public Wi-Fi, no kids under 5* ⊟ *AE, D, DC, MC, V* 🍴*CP* ✛ *1:E1*

$$$ 🏠 **Four Seasons Hotel.** At the ultrarefined Four Seasons, guest rooms
Fodor'sChoice begin on the 30th floor (the hotel sits atop the tony 900 North Michi-
★ gan Shops), so there's a distinct feeling of seclusion—and great views to boot. The rooms look elegant: 1940s French decor and spalike baths with honed Chinese marble. The property recently underwent a massive renovation. To get the most out of the experience, buy a package, like "Girls Just Wanna Have Fun," in which a handsome gent who makes custom martinis shows up at your room door. **Pros:** well-appointed and generously sized rooms; outstanding room service and housekeeping. **Cons:** clientele can be uptight, as can some staff. ✉ *120 E. Delaware Pl., Near North* ☎ *312/280–8800 or 800/332–3442* 📠 *312/280–9184* ⊕ *www.fourseasons.com* 🛏*176 rooms, 167 suites* 🔑 *In-room: refrigerator, safe, Internet, Wi-Fi. In-hotel: 2 restaurants, room service, bar, pool, gym, spa, concierge, laundry service, public Wi-Fi, parking (fee), no-smoking rooms* ⊟ *AE, D, DC, MC, V* ✛ *1:F2*

$$ 🏠 **Gold Coast Guest House Bed & Breakfast.** Set an enviable four blocks west of the Magnificent Mile, this 1873 brick town home is the ideal place to get a feel for Chicago's chi-chi side. It's on a tree-lined street dappled with preserved town houses from which well-coiffed women wearing Prada drift in and out with their terriers in tow. Sunny but cramped, the inn's biggest draw is its backyard patio that spills into a private, statuary-filled garden. **Pros:** staff is warm, welcoming, and very knowledgeable about surrounding bars and restaurants. **Cons:** spiral stairs can be troublesome for patrons with lots of luggage. ✉ *113 W. Elm St., Near North* ☎ *312/337–0361* ⊕ *www.bbchicago.com* 🛏*4*

6

When Not To Go To Chicago

Here are some considerations if you're looking for headache-free travel.

■ Many leisure travelers are fazed by Chicago's frigid winters and the somewhat rough conditions they can cause (slippery roads, delayed traffic, the very thought of schlepping around in big boots). So, while museums and performances are at their max during winter, it might not be the opportune time to travel stress-free.

■ Also be aware of the more than 1,000 conventions and trade shows scheduled throughout the year. The National Restaurant Association show in May; the Manufacturing Technology show in September; the Radiological Society of America show in late November; and the National Housewares Manufacturing show in January are among the biggest. Hotel rooms may be hard to come by—and tables at popular restaurants even harder.

■ Contact the Chicago Convention and Tourism Bureau at 877/CHICAGO (877/244–2246) for information on conventions, trade shows, and other travel concerns before you book your trip.

■ Proximity to McCormick Place, where most of Chicago's huge trade shows hunker down, is often a conventioneer's top priority, so most wind up staying in the Loop or South Loop, where hotels are just a five-minute cab ride away from the mammoth venue. In these neighborhoods accommodations tend to be older and somewhat less expensive—although there are certainly a few exceptions. Expect somewhat quiet nights in these parts; while the Loop boasts a revitalized theater district, come sundown there's a lot more revelry north of the Chicago River in the neighborhoods surrounding the Mag Mile. Vibrant Rush Street is the site of many bars, while River North has a high concentration of restaurants and nightclubs.

■ A meeting or convention in Rosemont or a tight flight schedule should be the only reasons to consider an airport hotel. Prices at these properties are a bit lower, but the O'Hare area is drab. Plus, trips from there to downtown may take an hour during rush hour, bad weather, or periods of heavy construction on the Kennedy Expressway.

---

rooms ♿ *In room: DVD, Wi-Fi. In hotel: no elevator, laundry facilities, parking (fee), no-smoking rooms, no children under age 10* ⊟AE, *D, MC, V* ⊹*1:C1*

$$ 🖼 **Homewood Suites by Hilton.** Suites here seem custom-designed for
☾ families, with sleeper sofas, separate bedrooms, and fully equipped kitchens. Free food isn't lacking; indulge in a complimentary breakfast buffet seven days a week, and an evening reception with drinks and a light meal Monday through Thursday. Another bonus? Work out for free at the Crunch Fitness facility in the basement. If that's not enough, the hotel is conveniently located so that guests are just a cab ride away from Chicago's top attractions. **Pros:** great view of skyline; heated pool; free, hot breakfast. **Cons:** bathrooms feel cramped. ⊠*40 E. Grand Ave., Near North* ☎*312/644–2222 or 800/225–5466* 🖷*312/644–7777* ⊕*www.homewoodsuiteschicago.com* ⮐*233 suites*

♻ *In-room: kitchen, refrigerator, Wi-Fi. In-hotel: room service, pool, gym, laundry facilities, parking (fee), no-smoking rooms* ▭*AE, D, DC, MC, V* ⃝|*BP* ✛*1:E4*

$ ▥ **Hotel Indigo.** Even though this hotel caters to business travelers, there is something refreshingly non-corporate about its guest rooms and lobby dressed in plucky blues and greens. The airy guest rooms have wall-to-wall photo murals (for a real vacation feel, ask for one featuring colorful sea glass). Furthering the summer-in-Cape Cod feel are the rooms' white wooden lounge chairs and hardwood floors. The hotel is just on the fringe of downtown activity—expect a 10-minute cab ride to the Loop—but, on the flip side, you'll walk to Oak Street Beach, a few blocks southeast, in no time. **Pros:** chic hotel; great value; rooms are bright and uniquely designed. **Cons:** long walk to the heart of the shopping district; elevators can be a bit noisy for some guests. ✉*1244 N. Dearborn Pkwy., Near North* ☎*312/787–4980* ⊕*www.goldcoastchicagohotel.com* ⇨*165 rooms* ♻ *In-room: Wi-Fi. In-hotel: restaurant, room service, bar, gym, spa, laundry service, concierge, public Wi-Fi, parking (fee), no-smoking rooms* ▭*AE, D, DC, MC, V* ✛*3:G4*

$$$ ▥ **InterContinental Chicago.** The Shriner greeting "Es Salamu Aleikum" ("Peace Be To God") etched on foyer columns and the marble lions throughout remind us of the building's past as the Medinah Men's Athletic Club, a private men's club. Lodging is found in two adjoining buildings. We love the contemporary air of the main building's guest rooms, featuring mahogany furniture and rich red-and-gold fabrics. The star attractions of the whole place are the junior Olympic swimming pool and a newly renovated fitness center. And be sure to check out Eno, a wine, cheese, and chocolate bar. **Pros:** you are sure to be wowed by the pool, the decor, and the view of the Magnificent Mile. **Cons:** concierge service is spotty; staff can be less than friendly. ✉*505 N. Michigan Ave., Near North* ☎*312/944–4100 or 800/628–2112* ⎙*312/944–1320* ⊕*www.icchicagohotel.com* ⇨*720 rooms, 72 suites* ♻ *In-room: refrigerator, safe, Wi-Fi. In-hotel: 2 restaurants, room service, bar, pool, gym, spa, concierge, laundry service, public Wi-Fi, parking (fee), no-smoking rooms, some pets allowed* ▭*AE, D, DC, MC, V* ✛*1:E4*

Fodor'sChoice ★ $$$ ▥ **The James Hotel.** If you don't get the hint from the bustling bar scene spilling into the lobby or the antique suitcases stacked as an art piece near the elevator, the James further announces its hipster pedigree when you enter your room. Preprogrammed alt-rock plays on the iPod-ready stereo system perched on the bar beneath the ready-to-party bottles (not minis) of vodka, whiskey, and rum. Some rooms feature not one but two flat-screen TVs, not to mention Kiehl's bath products and design-conscious furnishings like platform beds and full-length mirrors. The relatively hands-off service is fitting enough—for a party hotel. **Pros:** new and sleek with rich colors; not your typical, cookie-cutter chain. **Cons:** tiny elevators; awkward room layout. ✉*55 E. Ontario St., at Rush St., Near North* ☎*312/337–1000* ⊕*www.jameshotels.com* ⇨*291 rooms, 6 suites* ♻ *In-room: refrigerator, safe, Wi-Fi. In-hotel: restaurant, room service, bar, gym, spa, concierge, laundry service, public Wi-Fi, parking (fee), no-smoking rooms, some pets allowed* ▭*AE, D, DC, MC, V* ✛ *1:E4*

6

$ ⚑**Millennium Knickerbocker Hotel.** This 1927 hotel has had a number of identities in its time—including a 1970s stint as the Playboy Hotel and Towers under owner Hugh Hefner. Most recently, a 2008 renovation updated guest rooms with a gold, beige, plum, and espresso color palette. This luxurious feel extends to the service: guests can hang their kicks on the door at night and they'll be shined by morning. Your downtime is well spent in the Lobby Bar, which offers 50 different kinds of martinis and live jazz piano Tuesday through Saturday from 5 PM to 8 PM. **Pros:** location can't be beat; generously sized rooms; friendly front desk staff. **Cons:** service and quality of rooms are inconsistent. ✉*163 E. Walton Pl., Near North* ☎*312/751–8100 or 800/621–8140* 🖷*312/751–9205* ⊕*www.knickerbockerhotel.com* ⇆*280 rooms, 26 suites* ⚘*In-room: safe, refrigerator, Wi-Fi. In-hotel: restaurant, room service, bar, gym, concierge, laundry service, public Wi-Fi, parking (fee), no-smoking rooms* ▭*AE, D, DC, MC, V* ⊗*CP* ✛*1:F2*

$$$$ ⚑**Omni Chicago Hotel.** The only all-suites hotel on Michigan Avenue has another thing going for it: every room has a plasma TV. Large suites with French doors separate the parlor from the bedroom, giving it a residential atmosphere. The in-house 676 Restaurant & Bar, features northern Italian and American cuisine with views overlooking Michigan Avenue. Good choice for extended stays or visitors traveling with kids—young travelers receive a backpack filled with games and books to keep, and a goodie bag upon check-in. **Pros:** modern, comfortable rooms with spacious sitting area, desk, and bar. **Cons:** hotel can be too noisy for some. ✉*676 N. Michigan Ave., Near North* ☎*312/944–6664 or 800/843–6664* 🖷*312/266–3015* ⊕*www.omnichicago.com* ⇆*347 suites* ⚘*In-room: safe, DVD, Internet, Wi-Fi. In-hotel: restaurant, room service, bar, pool, gym, concierge, laundry service, parking (fee), no-smoking rooms, some pets allowed* ▭*AE, D, DC, MC, V* ✛*1:E3*

$$$$ ⚑**Park Hyatt Chicago.** The 67-story Park Hyatt, which dominates the
Fodor'sChoice   skyline high above the old Water Tower, outdoes its grand-hotel neigh-
★   bors by going all-out with extras. Splash out on one of their enormous suites and you'll discover TVs over the bathtubs and motion-sensor lights in the closets. Not much here has been overlooked. For a price there are plenty more extravagances to be had, including a butler-drawn candlelit bath. The beautifully designed public spaces feature a world-class collection of sculpture and painting, including works by Gerhardt Richter and Isamu Noguchi. The sweeping views from the pool and spa look out to the horizon over Lake Michigan. **Pros:** marble bath and soaking tub; great view of downtown. **Cons:** hotel lobby can be noisy. ✉*800 N. Michigan Ave., Near North* ☎*312/335–1234 or 800/778–7477* 🖷*312/239–4000* ⊕*www.parkchicago.hyatt.com* ⇆*198 rooms, 13 suites* ⚘*In-room: safe, refrigerator, DVD, Internet, Wi-Fi. In-hotel: restaurant, room service, bar, pool, gym, spa, concierge, laundry service, parking (fee), no-smoking rooms* ▭*AE, D, DC, MC, V* ✛1:E3*

$$$$ ⚑**Peninsula Chicago.** On weekend nights the Peninsula's soaring lobby
Fodor'sChoice   lounge becomes a chocolate fantasia, centered on an overflowing choco-
★   late buffet. The hotel, committed to keeping its guests well fed and well rested, is also home to one of the city's most creative restaurants

LODGING ALTERNATIVES

APARTMENT RENTALS

Furnished rentals can save you money, especially if you're traveling with a group. Home-exchange directories sometimes list rentals as well as exchanges.

Rental apartments are available in the Loop for temporary business lodging.

Hideaways International ✉767 Islington St., Portsmouth, NH 03801 ☎603/430–4433 or 800/843–4433 🖷603/430–4444 ⊕www.hideaways. com; annual membership $145.

BED-AND-BREAKFASTS

Chicago Bed & Breakfast Association ☎773/394–2000 or 800/375–7084 🖷773/394–2002 ⊕www.chicago-bed-breakfast.com

HOME EXCHANGES

HomeLink International ✉Box 47747, Tampa, FL 33647 ☎813/975–9825 or 800/638–3841 🖷813/910–8144 ⊕www.homelink. org; $110 yearly for a listing, online access, and catalog; $70 without catalog. **Intervac U.S.** ✉ 30 Corte San Fernando Tiburon, CA 94920 ☎800/756–4663 🖷415/435–7440 ⊕www.intervacus.com; $125 yearly for a listing, online access, and a catalog; $65 without catalog.

HOSTELS

No matter what your age, you can save on lodging costs by staying at hostels. In some 4,500 locations in more than 70 countries around the world, **Hostelling International (HI)**, the umbrella group for a number of national youth-hostel associations, offers single-sex, dorm-style beds and, at many hostels, rooms for couples and family accommodations. Membership in any HI national hostel association, open to travelers of all ages, allows you to stay in HI-affiliated hostels at member rates; one-year membership is about $28 for adults (C$35 for a two-year minimum membership in Canada, £14 in the United Kingdom, A$52 in Australia, and NZ$40 in New Zealand); hostels charge about $10–$30 per night. Members have priority if the hostel is full; they're also eligible for discounts around the world, even on rail and bus travel in some countries.

ORGANIZATIONS

Hostelling International—USA, ✉8401 Colesville Rd., Suite 600, Silver Spring, MD 20910 ☎301/495–1240 🖷301/495–6697 ⊕www.hiusa.org.

6

(Avenues), along with a lavish and popular afternoon tea. One of only three branches in the United States of the venerable Hong Kong–based Peninsula chain, it features comfortable rooms with plush pillow-top beds, Wi-Fi, and state-of-the-art bedside consoles that control both the TV and the "do not disturb" light. The rooftop lap pool is enclosed in a Zen aerie offering stunning views over the city. Make time to enjoy the property's award-winning spa. **Pros:** top-notch bath products; separate shower and bath. **Cons:** in-house dining options are not the best for families with children. ✉*108 E. Superior St., Near North* ☎*312/337–2888 or 866/288–8889* 🖷*312/751–2888* ⊕*www.chicago. peninsula.com* ⮡*339 rooms, 83 suites* ⟐*In-room: refrigerator, safe, Internet, Wi-Fi. In-hotel: 4 restaurants, room service, bar, pool, gym,* *spa, concierge, laundry service, parking (fee), no-smoking rooms, some pets allowed* ⊟*AE, D, DC, MC, V* ✛*1:E3*

$$ 🔲**Raffaello Hotel.** It's hard to tell what kind of crowd this hotel will attract, given its complete renovation (it was formerly the Raphael Hotel)—but the steps-from-Michigan Avenue location is working in its favor. Don't dither in the lobby; it's small and—with just a small check-in desk, a few chairs, and little else—there's not much excitement there. Guest rooms are spacious and comfortable. Dressed in varying shades of a neutral hay color, they have modern-looking bathrooms with rain showers and excellent city views (ask for a room facing west for a close-up look at the John Hancock Building). **Pros:** rooms are comfortable and elegant. **Cons:** overly stringent cancellation policy (cancellations must be received at least 72 hours prior to arrival). ✉*201 E. Delaware Pl., Near North* ☎*888/560–4977* ⊕*chicagoraffaello.com* ⟲*90 rooms, 75 suites* ⚒*In-room: kitchen, refrigerator, DVD, Wi-Fi. In-hotel: restaurant, room service, gym, laundry service, concierge, public Wi-Fi, airport shuttle, parking (fee), no-smoking rooms* ⊟*AE, D, MC, V* ✛*1:F2*

$$$$ 🔲**Ritz-Carlton Chicago.** Perched over Water Tower Place, Michigan

Fodor's Choice   Avenue's best-known shopping mall, the Ritz-Carlton specializes in

★   showering guests' with attention. Amenities aren't wanting: rooms are spacious, with walk-in closets and separate dressing areas. A fitness center, indoor pool, and spa services are available to guests looking for respite from their busy days. The hotel goes out of its way to cater to families with children, providing complimentary use of items such as cribs, children's DVDs, books, and toys, to name a few. The two-story, flower-filled greenhouse lobby serves afternoon tea, and the Café's chef, Mark Payne, has earned a top-notch reputation. A recent multimillion-dollar renovation left the rooms with clean lines and amber and blue topaz hues. **Pros:** guests feel pampered; great stay for families with small children. **Cons:** lobby feels worn and dated. ✉*160 E. Pearson St., Near North* ☎*312/266–1000, 800/621–6906 outside Illinois* 🖨*312/266–1194* ⊕*www.fourseasons.com/chicagorc* ⟲*435 rooms, 91 suites* ⚒*In-room: refrigerator, safe, DVD (some), Wi-Fi. In-hotel: 2 restaurants, room service, bar, pool, gym, spa, concierge, laundry service, public Internet, public Wi-Fi, parking (fee), no-smoking rooms, some pets allowed* ⊟*AE, D, DC, MC, V* ✛ *1:E2*

$$ 🔲**Sheraton Chicago Hotel and Towers.** Enormous and ideally situated, this hotel calls out to families with its generously sized rooms and a large pool. Bustling, it attracts numerous executives and caters to all with its six restaurants and bars. The rooms—rennovated in 2007—are typical of a big chain, but the beds are divine. You can't get closer to the heart of Chicago; it's walking distance from shopping and a reasonable cab ride away from major museums. Well appointed yet casual, the site is close to a popular bowling alley/movie theater, great for a family getaway. **Pros:** just a short walk from Michigan Avenue and Navy Pier but with all that's inside you might not need to leave. **Cons:** this is a place for families and businesspeople; not necessarily a romantic weekend. ✉*301 East North Water Street , Near North* ☎*312/464–1000* ⊕*www.sheratonchicago.com* ⟲*1169 rooms, 40 suites In-room: safe, kitchen (some), refrigerator, TV, Internet, Wi-Fi. In-hotel: 6 restaurants,* room service, bars, pool, gym, spa, laundry service, Internet terminal, Wi-Fi, parking (fee), some pets allowed ⊟AE, D, DC, MC, V ✛1:G5

$$$$ 🏨**Sofitel Chicago Water Tower.** A

Fodor'sChoice wonder of modern architecture,

★ this French-owned gem is a prism-shaped structure that juts over the street and widens as it rises. Design sensibility shines in guest rooms,

too, with honey maplewood fur-nishings, Barcelona chairs, and marble bathrooms bedecked with bam-boos (think feng shui). The sophisticated Cafe des Architectes is notable for its 30-minute executive lunch, while Le Bar is a homey den of sorts. **Pros:** modern decor; great ambience. **Cons:** the place is so sleek that some guests have a hard time finding the light switches. ⊠*20 E. Chestnut St., Near North* ☎*312/324–4000 or 877/813–7700* 🖷*312/324–4026* ⊕*www.sofitel.com* 🛏*382 rooms, 33 suites* ⌂*In-room: safe, Internet, Wi-Fi. In-hotel: restaurant, room service, bars, gym, concierge, laundry service, parking (fee), no-smoking rooms, some pets allowed* ⊟*AE, D, DC, MC, V* ✛*1:D2*

$$$ 🏨**Sutton Place Hotel.** Talk about art in unexpected places: the largest single collection of original Robert Mapplethorpe floral photographs graces the walls in rooms and common spaces at this hotel. Rooms—decorated in calming sage and neutral tones—have sound-resistant walls, down duvets, and three phones. Splurge for a loft suite, with terraces overlooking bustling Rush Street. Rande Gerber (Cindy Craw-ford's husband) owns the Mexx Kitchen at the Whiskey, serving sea-sonal selections for breakfast, a modern Mexican lunch, and dinner. **Pros:** great location; soothing color scheme; seasonal outdoor seating at restaurant. **Cons:** some guests have complained of low water pres-sure and haphazard housekeeping. ⊠*21 E. Bellevue Pl., Near North* ☎*312/266–2100 or 800/606–8188* 🖷*312/266–2141* ⊕*www.sutton place.com* 🛏*206 rooms, 40 suites* ⌂*In-room: safe, Wi-Fi. In-hotel: restaurant, room service, bar, gym, concierge, laundry service, public Internet, parking (fee), no-smoking rooms, some pets allowed* ⊟*AE, D, DC, MC, V* ✛*1:D1*

$$$$ 🏨**Talbott.** The Talbott is a European-style boutique hotel with a mul-tilingual staff. In 2006 guest rooms were renovated with new carpets, drapes, and custom furniture, making the moderate-size lodgings even more appealing. Another bonus? Free Wi-Fi is available throughout the hotel, and guests get free admission to the nearby gym. **Pros:** hotel has an updated look; staff goes out of their way to please. **Cons:** rooms can be too dark and too noisy for some. ⊠*20 E. Delaware Pl., Near North* ☎*312/944–4970 or 800/825–2688* 🖷*312/944–7241* ⊕*www.talbott hotel.com* 🛏*120 rooms, 29 suites* ⌂*In-room: safe, Wi-Fi. In-hotel: restaurant, room service, bar, concierge, laundry service, parking (fee), no-smoking rooms, no pets allowed* ⊟*AE, D, DC, MC, V* ✛*1:D2*

6

$$ ⌂ **Tremont.** Just off North Michigan Avenue, this hotel's restaurant, Mike Ditka's, gets infinitely more attention than the rooms do. Standard guest rooms—with a cream-color theme—are on the small side, but offer all the essential amenities. Need more space? Book one of the suites, which are equipped with kitchens. Complimentary use of the fitness center is a plus for guests looking to keep up with their workout regimen even if they're on vacation. **Pros:** great location; good value. **Cons:** rooms need to be updated and cleaned; valet parking is pricey ⊠ *100 E. Chestnut St., Near North* ☎ *312/751–1900 or 800/621–8133* 🖷 *312/751–8691* ⊕ *www.tremontchicago.com* ⇶ *118 rooms, 12 suites* ♨ *In-room: refrigerators (some), safe, Wi-Fi. In-hotel: restaurant, bar, concierge, laundry service, public Internet, parking (fee), no-smoking rooms* ▭ *AE, D, DC, MC, V* ✛ *1:E2*

$$ ⌂ **W Chicago Lakeshore.** Once a dreary Days Inn, this place has undergone a complete renovation that transformed it into a sleek, high-energy hotel—and the only one in Chicago directly overlooking Lake Michigan. The lobby is part lounge, part club scene, with velvety couches and DJs on weekends. The hotel's "whatever, whenever" desk—its version of a concierge service—is on call 24 hours a day. Pamper yourself at the Bliss Chicago Spa, located on the eighth floor, where hotel guests can get priority booking for their spa treatments. For those who have a hard time leaving their pets at home, the W Chicago Lakeshore allows guests to bring their furry friends. **Pros:** cool, hip vibe; guest rooms feel like swank lounges. **Cons:** service not commensurate with the price. ⊠ *644 N. Lake Shore Dr., Near North* ☎ *312/943–9200 or 877/946–8357* 🖷 *312/255–4411* ⊕ *www.whotels.com/lakeshore* ⇶ *525 rooms, 27 suites* ♨ *In-room: safe, DVD, Internet, Wi-Fi. In-hotel: restaurant, room service, bar, pool, gym, spa, concierge, laundry service, public Wi-Fi, parking (fee), no-smoking rooms, some pets allowed* ▭ *AE, D, DC, MC, V* ✛ *1:G4*

Fodor's Choice ★

$$$$ ⌂ **Westin Michigan Avenue.** The lobby of the Westin reminds us of an airport hangar—long, narrow, and full of folks tapping away on laptops. Location-wise, the hotel scores big, as major malls and flagship shops are within steps of the hotel's front door. Rooms are furnished with specially designed Simmons Heavenly beds with quilted mattresses—that guests have raved about and even purchased—as well as foam, feather, and rolled pillows. The lobby restaurant, the Grill on the Alley, is a steak house with a clubby atmosphere. **Pros:** guests love the "heavenly" beds, the proximity to area attractions, and the ever-present cabs. **Cons:** gym is a bit cramped; rooms are a bit small; elevators too slow. ⊠ *909 N. Michigan Ave., Near North* ☎ *312/943–7200 or 800/937–8461* 🖷 *312/397–5580* ⊕ *www.westin.com/michiganave* ⇶ *728 rooms, 23 suites* ♨ *In-room: safe, Internet, Wi-Fi. In-hotel: restaurant, room service, bar, gym, concierge, laundry service, public Wi-Fi, parking (fee), some pets allowed* ▭ *AE, D, DC, MC, V* ✛ *1:E2*

$$ ⌂ **Whitehall Hotel.** There's a woodland-lodge feel in this hotel's lobby, where oil paintings of hunting dogs and horses hang in gilt frames. The recently renovated Old World–style rooms, many with four-poster beds, include modern luxuries such as marble bathrooms and broadband. Fornetto Mei is a pan-Italian dining concept—with standout pizza from a

wood-burning oven—that deserves more attention than it gets. The Whitehall hotel also features key amenities such as a 24-hour business center and fitness facilities. Animal lovers take notice: the hotel is pet-friendly. **Pros:** hotel has a 1920s-era charm and an old-school style. **Cons:** rooms could use an update: wallpaper is faded and peeling in spots. ⊠*105 E. Delaware Pl., Near North* ☎*312/944–6300 or 800/948–4255* 🖶*312/944–8552* ⊕*www.thewhitehallhotel.com* ⇆*214 rooms, 8 suites* ♨*In-room: safe, Internet. In-hotel: restaurant, room service, bar, gym, concierge, laundry service, public Wi-Fi, parking (fee), no-smoking rooms* ▭*AE, D, DC, MC, V* ✛*1:E2*

RIVER NORTH

Aside from the concentration of independently owned galleries, commerce around these parts tends to be of a national-chain nature (note the Hard Rock Cafe and Red Lobster). The same can be said of the hotels. But while boutique-lodging charm is harder to find, good prices are not; you'll find plenty of competitive rates from familiar names.

🏨**Affinia Chicago.** In an often overlooked section of Chicago just east of Michigan Ave., This hotel offers an outstanding outdoor bar with an enviable view of the city. The rooms are modern and homey, with a green, gray, and earth-tone palette. Check out the pillow menu and Affinia Experience BYOB Kit, which includes a guide to the city's favorite BYOB restaurants, a wine carrier, a picnic blanket, and discounts to local wine vendors. Another kit caters to yoga and Pilates lovers. This place loves kids and pets and offers amenities to both. They also have Aveda bath products. **Pros:** bars and restaurants steps away; excellent customer service; some pillows have built-in iPod speakers. **Cons:** exterior of the building is nondescript, and you might need a map to navigate the neighborhood on foot. ⊠*166 East Superior Street, Streeterville* ☎*312/787–6000* ⊕*www.affinia.com* ⇆*154 rooms, 61 suites* ♨*In-room: safe, refrigerator, TV, Internet, Wi-Fi. In-hotel: restaurant, room service, 2 bar, gym, laundry service, parking (fee), some pets allowed* ▭*AE, D, DC, MC, V* ✛*1:F3*

$$ 🏨**Amalfi Hotel Chicago.** With popular magazines on the desks and well-worn books on the shelves, this well-situated hot spot is aiming for a residential feel. Check out the complimentary reception every night from 5:30 to 7 PM for free drinks, Italian beer, and antipasti, among other treats. And unlike other hotels that serve their continental breakfast in the lobby, this one offers its breakfast on every floor. The clientele is eclectic and laid-back; the reception brings everyone together. Surrounded by both upscale restaurants and famous chains—including Harry Caray's—there's no shortage of nightlife. **Pros:** Aveda products available. **Cons:** some guests note that the bedding looks and feels worn. ⊠*20 W. Kinzie St., River North* ☎*312/395–9000*

6

⊕*amalfihotelchicago.com* ⤴*210 rooms, 5 suites* ⬧*In-room: safe, refrigerator, DVD, Wi-Fi. In-hotel: restaurant, room service, bar, gym, laundry service, concierge, public Internet, public Wi-Fi, parking (fee), some pets allowed* ▭*AE, D, DC, MC, V* ✛*1:D5*

$ **Best Western River North.** Partially housed in a turn-of-the-last-cen-
Ⓢ tury freezer building, this hotel retains a loft-like air. The somewhat
forgettable lobby decor is offset by large and reasonably priced guest
rooms featuring black-and-white tiled bathrooms. Parking is free, a
cost-saving rarity downtown. Families convene at the on-site Pizzeria
Ora for Chicago-style deep-dish pies. **Pros:** excellent service; great location; free parking—an extremely rare find in Chicago. **Cons:** creaking
floors have irked some guests, especially around bedtime; rooms could
use a fresher look. ⊠*125 W. Ohio St., River North* ☎*312/467–0800 or
800/727–0800* ⊟*312/467–1665* ⊕*www.rivernorthhotel.com* ⤴*125
rooms, 25 suites* ⬧*In-room: safe, refrigerator (some), Wi-Fi. In-hotel:
restaurant, room service, bar, pool, gym, public Wi-Fi, parking (no fee),
no-smoking rooms* ▭*AE, D, DC, MC, V* ✛*1:D4*

$$$ **Courtyard by Marriott/Magnificent Mile.** Visitors will love the location,
the modern, bustling lobby, and the reasonably priced rooms. Stylish
with black granite and track lighting, the hotel is modern but not cold or
pretentious. The rooms are modest—with muted beige walls and white
linens—but efficient. Expect lots of tourists. The double queen room
sleeps five with a sofa bed, so it's great for families. Parents take notice:
there is no lifeguard at the indoor pool. The restaurant, Viand, offers
fine American cuisine in a dark but lively atmosphere with an attrac-
tive bar. **Pros:** great location, right in the heart of the shopping district.
Cons: pool is on the small side; the sink is located outside the bathroom.
⊠*165 E. Ontario, River North* ☎*312/573–0800* ⊕*www.courtyard
chicago.com* ⤴*283 rooms, 23 suites* ⬧*In-room: refrigerator (some),
Internet, Wi-Fi. In-hotel: restaurant, room service, bar, pool, gym, laun-
dry facilities, laundry service, concierge, public Internet, public Wi-Fi,
parking (fee), some pets allowed* ▭*AE, D, DC, MC, V* ✛*1:F4*

$$ **Dana Hotel and Spa.** Posh and über comfy, this chic new hot spot
has crushed velvet couches, hardwood floors, elegant wood furniture,
and floor-to-ceiling windows. Hipsters love the bar upstairs—it has
incredible views and is dotted with tasteful photos of tatooed beauties.
While the public spaces lean toward the under-35 set, the rooms will
appeal to any age group. Newly built, the hotel makes creative use of
recycled goods; the spa's flooring is made of crushed beer bottles but
looks like high-end marble. Air travelers will love at the downstairs
kiosks that allow airline passengers to print out their tickets from the
hotel lobby. No joke. **Pros:** the honor bar offers reasonably priced snacks
and bottles of wine for under $20. **Cons:** some say the upstairs bar,
which attracts a crowd, can make the lobby cramped at night. ⊠*660
North State Street, River North* ☎*888/301–7952 or 312/202–6000*
⊕*danahotelandspa.com* ⬧*In-room: safe, refrigerator, TV, Internet,
Wi-Fi. In-hotel: restaurant, room service, bars, gym, spa, laundry service, Internet terminal, Wi-Fi, parking (fee), some pets allowed* ▭*AE,
D, DC, MC, V* ✛*1:D3*

$$$ **Embassy Suites Downtown.** The suites are arranged around an 11-story, plant-filled atrium lobby, where bubbling fountains keep noise levels relatively high. Bright rooms use space efficiently, with sensible separate living rooms with a pullout sofa, four-person dining table, and extra television. A 24-hour business center, complimentary full breakfast each morning, and cocktails each evening are especially appealing to business travelers. The indoor pool and fitness center are a plus, as is the renowned onsite restaurant, Osteria Via Stato. **Pros:** great cocktail hour; hotel is just three blocks away from the Magnificent Mile. **Cons:** paid Internet ($9.95 a day or $44.95 for five days). ⊠*600 N. State St., River North* ☎*312/943–3800 or 800/362–2779* ☏*312/943–7629* ⊕*www.embassysuiteschicago.com* ⮞*367 suites* ⌂*In-room: refrigerator, Wi-Fi. In-hotel: restaurant, room service, bar, pool, gym, concierge, laundry facilities, laundry service, parking (fee), no-smoking rooms* ⊟*AE, D, DC, MC, V* ⦿*BP* ✛*1:D4*

$$$ **Hotel 71.** Just blocks away from the Wrigley Building and Tribune Tower—both architectural marvels—this recently renovated property offers delightfully rare views of the heart of downtown, fantastic in daytime and even better at night. There are also lovely views of the Chicago River. Sea urchin–shaped lighting fixtures set a dramatic and elegant tone in the lobby. The rooms are bright yet romantic, a rich mix of greens, browns, and creams. The location is prime, steps away from Grade A restaurants and bars. Rooms service is prompt and reasonably priced. **Pros:** great service; beautiful views. **Cons:** the cleaning service is super friendly, but a tad loud; maids like to knock early in the morning, so don't forget your do-not-disturb sign. ⊠*71 E. Wacker Drive, River North* ☎*312/346–7100* ⊕*www.hotel71.com* ⮞*273 rooms, 24 suites* ⌂*In-room: safe (some), refrigerator (some), DVD (some), TV, Internet (some), Wi-Fi (some). In-hotel: room service, bar, gym, laundry service, Internet terminal, Wi-Fi, parking (fee), some pets allowed* ⊟*AE, D, DC, MC, V* ✛*1:E5*

$ **Hotel Cass, Holiday Inn Express.** The Hotel Cass is a true boutique hotel, and bears no resemblance to the chain. The crisp, white lobby is sparse and elegant, and the dramatic red hallway is offset with a touch of humor; it's lined with several austere portraits of chickens. The rooms are simple, bright, and cheerful, with light-color walls and green headboards that nearly reach the ceiling. The subway-style tile in the bathroom harks back to the 1920s. The rooms are modern and warm, and the in-room artwork includes photos of 1950s fashion icons. **Pros:** stellar location; family-friendly; close to several notable art galleries. **Cons:** some guest rooms and bathrooms can be on the small side. ⊠*640 N. Wabash Ave., River North* ☎*312/265–3370* ⊕*www.casshotel.com* ⮞*172 rooms, 3, suites* ⌂*In-room: safe, Internet, Wi-Fi. In-hotel: room service, laundry service, public Internet, public Wi-Fi, airport shuttle, parking (fee)* ⊟*AE, D, DC, MC, V* ✛*3:H6*

$$ **Hotel Sax Chicago.** Visitors to Chicago would be hard-pressed to find a more chic or tech-savvy place than the Hotel Sax. Stark white walls, adorned with appropriately risqué artwork, make the scented lobby feel ultra swank. In the rooms, modern furniture is chunky and ornate, and mismatched colors and patterns somehow look fabulous together.

Fodor'sChoice ★

6

A high-tech game room leaves guests weak in the knees. Eager-to-please staff will download your favorite record if they don't have it already, then pipe it in while you play Guitar Hero. **Pros:** no need to leave the hotel for nightlife, thanks to the Crimson lounge; the House of Blues is right next door. **Cons:** scented lobby is a bit much for some; rooms and hallways can be too dim. ⊠ *333 N. Dearborn St., River North* ☎ *312/245–0333* ⊕ *www.hotelsaxchicago.com* 🛏 *334 rooms, 19 suites* ♿ *In-room: safe, Internet, Wi-Fi. In-hotel: 6 restaurants, room service, 6 bars, gym, laundry service, concierge, public Internet, public Wi-Fi, parking (fee), some pets allowed* ⊟ *AE, D, DC, MC, V* ✛ *1:D5*

$$$
Fodor'sChoice
★

Trump International Hotel & Tower. With some of the best views in Chicago, the Trump International Hotel & Tower has attracted a crowd of power brokers, business travelers, and women in fur coats. The elegant guest rooms have muted gray walls, cream-colored couches, and chocolate-brown furniture; each room has its own kitchen with granite counter tops and cupboards stocked with top-of-the-line cookware, as well as a TV inside the bathroom mirror. Guests need not venture any further than Sixteen to enjoy fine dining. The full-service spa is immense. **Pros:** impeccable service; lavish amenities **Cons:** may be too decadent for some; $25 bottled water (for sale) in each room. ⊠ *401 N. Wabash Ave., North Loop* ☎ *312/588–8000* ⊕ *www.trumpchicagohotel.com* 🛏 *218 rooms, 121 suites* ♿ *In-room: safe, kitchen, refrigerator, DVD, Internet, Wi-Fi. In-hotel: restaurant, room service, 2 bars, pool, gym, spa, laundry service, concierge, public Internet, public Wi-Fi, parking (fee), some pets allowed* ⊟ *AE, D, DC, MC, V* ❚❂❙ *CP* ✛ *3:H6*

$$$

Westin Chicago River North. Gym rats don't need to hoof it to the on-site fitness center, thanks to four Westin Workout Guest Rooms that come equipped with either a bicycle or a treadmill. Standard rooms—some with views of the Chicago River—have all the basics, including high-speed Internet. Nab a Deluxe Room for more square footage. This elegant hotel is centrally located near the premier shopping destination, Michigan Avenue, as well as top Chicago attractions, which makes it an ideal stay for first-time visitors. **Pros:** polite staff; the "heavenly bed" is nothing less than heavenly. **Cons:** fee for use of the fitness center; no pool. ⊠ *320 N. Dearborn St., River North* ☎ *312/744–1900 or 887/866–9216* 🖷 *312/527–2650* ⊕ *www.westinchicago.com* 🛏 *407 rooms, 17 suites* ♿ *In-room: Internet, Wi-Fi. In-hotel: 2 restaurants, room service, bar, gym, spa, concierge, laundry service, parking (fee), some pets allowed* ⊟ *AE, D, DC, MC, V* ✛ *1:D5*

SOUTH LOOP

Rapid gentrification, most apparent in the new restaurants popping up along South Michigan Avenue, has made this area increasingly popular. A hotel boom has not occurred here yet, so lodging choices are limited to a few old and reliable standards. Many hotels offer package deals with the nearby Museum Campus.

$$$
Fodor'sChoice
★

The Blackstone. A six-year renovation has restored this once faded building to its original splendor. The lobby, with its gold-trimmed walls and ultramodern flower arrangements, is an unusual mix of old and new. The guest rooms are simple and elegant, with striking bold colors—a stunning combination of gold, red, black, and white—and the ballroomwith its ornate carvings is otherworldly. The service is exceptional; visitors are warmly greeted within seconds. Ask about the hotel's storied past; both presidents and mob bosses have stayed here. **Pros:** new owners spared no expense in this beautifully redone space. **Cons:** decor can be a bit too ornate. ⊠*636 S. Michigan Ave., South Loop* ☎*312/447–0955* ⊕*www.marriott.com/hotels/travel/chirh-the-black stone-a-renaissance-hotel* ⌑*328 rooms, 4 suites* ⎘*In-room: safe, refrigerator, Internet, Wi-Fi. In-hotel: restaurant, room service, 2 bars, gym, laundry service, concierge, executive floor, public Internet, public Wi-Fi, parking (fee)* ⊟*AE, D, DC, MC, V* ⍒❘*EP* ✛*4:G3*

$ ⚘ Fodor's Choice ★
Essex Inn. Don't judge this hotel on appearance alone: the nondescript, plain-brick tower containing small, boxlike guest rooms is actually one of the city's most accessible and family-friendly. Along with being a five-minute walk from the Museum Campus, it offers package deals with popular attractions such as the Shedd Aquarium and Sears Tower. That said, you might not want to leave the hotel; its huge fourth-floor pool is open year-round (note to anxious parents: a lifeguard is always on duty) and is surrounded by sliding-glass doors that open to views of Grant Park and Lake Michigan. **Pros:** good value; pool complete with a lifeguard. **Cons:** rooms can be drafty during winter months; staff can be slow to address complaints. ⊠*800 S. Michigan Ave., South Loop* ☎*312/939/2800 or 800/621–6909* ⊕*essexinn.com* ⌑*254 rooms* ⎘*In room: refrigerator (some), Wi-Fi. In hotel: restaurant, room service, pool, gym, laundry service, public Internet, parking (fee), no-smoking rooms* ⊟*AE, D, DC, MC, V* ✛*4:G3*

$$$
Hilton Chicago. On a busy day the lobby of this Hilton might be mistaken for a terminal at O'Hare Airport; it's a bustling convention hotel, but one that retains its distinguished 1920s heritage in a Renaissance-inspired entrance hall and gold-and-gilt grand ballroom. We're fans of its gym, which, at 28,000 square feet, includes an indoor track and swimming pool. Tip for families: Ask for a room with two double beds and two baths (if you nab one with a view of Lake Michigan and the Museum Campus, all the better). **Pros:** spacious rooms, proximity to the museum district; well-appointed public spaces. **Cons:** a hike to the main shopping area on the Magnificent Mile; a fee for use of the fitness area. ⊠*720 S. Michigan Ave., South Loop* ☎*312/922–4400 or 800/445–8667* 🖷*312/922–5240* ⊕*www.hiltonchicagosales.com* ⌑*1,477 rooms, 67 suites* ⎘*In-room: Wi-Fi. In-hotel: 3 restaurants, room service, bar, pool, gym, concierge, laundry service, parking (fee), no-smoking rooms, some pets allowed* ⊟*AE, D, DC, MC, V* ✛*4:G3*

$$$ ⚘
Holiday Inn & Suites Downtown Chicago. Thanks to its proximity to the financial district, this hotel welcomes hordes of business travelers. But leisure seekers have an added incentive to visit in the summer months: the rooftop pool. Guests appreciate the accessibility of this hotel: not only is it near Chicago's main attractions, transportation is provided to both Midway Airport and O'Hare International Airport directly from the hotel (with a fee). The on-site Aurelio's, part of a popular pizza chain, serves breakfast, lunch, and dinner. **Pros:** staff goes

6

out of their way to be helpful; convenient on-site washing machines and dryers. **Cons:** the lobby can get quite crowded; bathrooms are on the small side. ✉*506 W. Harrison St., South Loop* ☎*312/957–9100* 🖨*312/957–0474* ⊕*www.hidowntown.com* 📧*145 rooms, 27 suites* 🗝*In-room: refrigerator (some), Wi Fi. In-hotel: restaurant, room service, bar, pool, gym, laundry facilities, laundry service, parking (fee), no-smoking rooms* 🖃*AE, D, DC, MC, V* ✛*4:E3*

WESTERN SUBURBS

$$$ 🍴**Lynfred Winery Bed & Breakfast.** Something of an anomaly amid the strip malls and big restaurant chains in nearby Schaumburg, located 45 minutes northwest of downtown Chicago, this B&B feels like a quaint country inn—one with surprising gourmet leanings. Each of its four generously sized suites has a heated bathroom floor and is decorated in the style of a different country (the French Suite has a gilded mirror and Louis IV–style chairs). The adjoining wine cellar and tasting room is where you'll try inexpensive yet tasty cabernets, aged in barrels on-site. All stays include a cellar tour and a full breakfast cooked by a Culinary Institute of America grad. **Pros:** affordable wine tastings; well-appointed rooms. **Cons:** not every wine is a hit; some guests feel that the rooms are overpriced. ✉*15 S. Roselle Rd., Western Suburbs* ☎*630/529–9463* ⊕*lynfredwinery.com* 📧*4 rooms* 🗝*In room: refrigerator, DVD, Wi-Fi. In hotel: room service, laundry facilities, laundry service, parking (no fee), no guests under 21, no-smoking rooms* 🖃*AE, D, MC, V* ✛*4:A1*

Shopping

7

WORD OF MOUTH

"Everyone shops on Michigan Avenue, but you can hit some of the other areas of the city. Oak Street between Michigan and Rush is home to exclusive boutiques such as Hermes, Prada, Halston and Barney's New York. Even if you can't buy anything, it's fun to look. You could also head to the area around Armitage and Halsted."
—Citylights

SHOPPING PLANNER

Itineraries for the Obsessed

If art is your thing, head to River North and the West Loop, which are quick cab rides from each other and loaded with fabulous galleries.

If you're looking to head home with funky fashions, go to Bucktown and Wicker Park. Must-hits include **p. 45** (*1643 N. Damen Ave., 773/862–4523*) for women's styles; **G Boutique** for va-va-va-voom lingerie (*2131 N. Damen Ave., 773/235–1234*); and **shebang** (*1616 N. Damen Ave., 773/486–3800*) for pretty accessories.

Need to buy some things for the little ones in your life? Hit Lincoln Park's **Stinky Pants** (*844 W. Armitage Ave., 773/281–4002*) and **LMNOP** (*2574 N. Lincoln Ave., 773/975–4055*). Find treats for tiny feet at **Piggy Toes** (*2205 N. Halsted St., 773/281–5583*). For stuff for the home, best bets are **Bellini** (*1800 N. Clybourn, 312/981–6301*) and the **Land of Nod** (*900 W. North Ave., 312/475–9903*) for stylish bedding, bath items, books, and toys.

Cold-Weather Considerations

Visiting during winter or on one of Chicago's chilly days? Don't let the cold keep you from scoring some serious stash. Take a cue from weather-savvy local shoppers, who hit indoor urban malls like Water Tower Place and 900 North Michigan on the Mag Mile when the winds whip up.

If you're willing to brave the elements, dress wisely. The weather can change on a dime here, so wear layers that are easy to peel off and carry—something that'll make dressing-room acrobatics go quicker, too. We're talking warm undershirt, long-sleeved shirt, sweater or warm jacket, and windbreaker—substitute heavy winter coat for that last one if you're visiting in the dead of winter, along with the necessary accoutrements (scarf, hat, gloves). Happily, you'll find plenty of places along the way for a hot cocoa, coffee, or tea if the cold is getting the best of you.

Getting Around

Second only in size to that of New York City, the public transportation system in Chicago serves roughly 1.5 million riders a day and can get you to the city's main shopping drags with relative ease. With so many riders, it can get pretty crowded during weekday rush hours. Improvement and repair projects can cause delays on many train lines, so plan accordingly.

For both the bus and train (called the El, for the elevated tracks that run around the Loop) fares are $2.25 when using cash, $2 with a transit card.

If you plan on riding frequently, buy a transit card at any El station vending machine or at many grocery and drug stores (rides are $2.25). Bus and train rides cost $2 with a transit card, and transfers on both the bus and El cost an additional 25 cents; no transfers are given when paying with cash.

Some of the neighborhoods we mention here are easy to walk between, like the Mag Mile and River North, and parts of Lincoln Park and Lakeview, but it's best to consult a map to determine whether the distances you're planning to travel warrant wheels.

Chicago Hours

Keep these timing tips in mind as you plan out your day:

Most stores keep traditional retail hours, opening around 10 AM and closing at 6 or 7 PM, though different neighborhood styles and street traffic can dictate otherwise. In Bucktown and Wicker Park, for example, many shops don't open until 11 AM or noon, and may stay open later in the evening.

Count on mall stores to keep later hours, usually until 7 or 8 PM. Most are open (with shorter hours than other days) on Sunday.

If there's a particular boutique you want to visit, call ahead. Simply flip through this chapter and you'll find all the contact information you'll need.

Pamper Your Pet

Chicago is a pet-lover's city, and it's filled with fun places to shop for them. Check out the **Down Town Dog** (Macy's, 111 N. State St., 312/782–4575), a delightful boutique within Macy's that's stocked with everything for the urban pooch (and kitty).

In Bucktown, **Red Dog House** (2031 N. Damen Ave., 773/227–7341) keeps pace with the fashionable 'hood by selling spa products (such as paw balm), high-end treats (biscotti for pups), and sculptural bowls and beds. If your dog comes along for the trip, there are some retail stores that let well-behaved pups on leashes do a little browsing.

Our favorite: **Neiman Marcus** (737 N. Michigan Ave., 312/642–5900), where pedigree types can peruse Burberry carriers and other fancy items.

Word of Mouth

"I would not miss taking a walk or a bike ride along the lakefront path (my favorite is to do this on Sunday morning, maybe before breakfast?). You might also enjoy the CAF architectural river cruise, which is relaxing and informative (and Chicago architecture is, needless to see, fabulous)."
—dmlove

"Highly, highly recommend the Segway tour. My husband never wants to turn his in at the end. The route is incredibly scenic and riding the Segways is great fun."
—djkbooks

The other neighborhoods which I would recommend considering are Wicker Park/Bucktown and Lincoln Square. They each have interesting shopping options and a number of good places to eat. In addition, Lincoln Square has the Old Town School of Folk Music, which has a fine family-oriented schedule but isn't dumbed-down entertainment for adults.
—exiledprincess

Updated by
Heidi Moore

A POTENT CONCENTRATION OF FAMOUS retailers around Michigan Avenue and neighborhoods bursting with one-of-a-kind shops combine to make Chicago a shopper's city. Michigan Avenue's world-class Magnificent Mile lures thousands of avid shoppers every week. How often can you find Neiman Marcus, Macy's, Nordstrom, Saks Fifth Avenue, Lord & Taylor, and Barneys New York within walking distance of one another? Neighborhood shopping areas, like fun-but-sophisticated Lincoln Park or the hipster haven of Bucktown/Wicker Park, have singular stores for specialty interests, whether Prairie Style furniture, cowboy boots, or outsider art. Those averse to paying retail won't have to venture far to unearth bargains on everything from fine jewelry to business attire. When it comes to shopping, this is one city that has it all.

Be forewarned that a gulp-inducing 10.25% sales tax is added to all purchases in the city except groceries and prescription drugs. Neighborhood shops on the North Side, especially those in Bucktown and Wicker Park, tend to open late—around 11 or noon. Most stores, particularly those on North Michigan Avenue and the North Side, are open on Sunday, although this varies by type of business; where applicable, more information is provided at the beginning of each area or category.

THE LOOP AND SOUTH LOOP

This area—named for the elevated train track that encircles it—is the heart of Chicago's business and financial district. Two department stores that long defined shopping here, Marshall Field's and Carson Pirie Scott, departed from **State Street** in early 2007, a double hit for the stretch that has been striving to regain the stature it had when it was immortalized as "State Street, that great street." Carson's is empty for the time being, while Macy's has taken over the Marshall Field's building. State Street is more enticing for shoppers than it was in the 1980s and early 1990s, particularly for those interested in discount department stores, but it's still a far cry from the shopping mecca that is the Mag Mile. The blocks surrounding the intersection of Wabash Avenue and Madison Street are designated as Jewelers Row; five high-rises cater to the wholesale trade, but many showrooms sell to the public at prices 25% to 50% below retail. Despite the preponderance of working moms who spend their weekday lunch hours shopping in the area, the Loop lacks a strong presence of retail for kids, and some of the discount chains are even pulling their children's lines from Loop outposts. Not all Loop stores maintain street-level visibility: several gems are tucked away on upper floors of office buildings.

Department stores and major chains are generally open on Sunday. Smaller stores are likely to be closed on Sunday and keep limited Saturday hours. Loop workers tend to start their day early, so many stores keep pace by opening by 8:30 and closing at 5 or 6.

DEPARTMENT STORES

Filene's Basement. Patience can pay off at Filene's, where shoppers flip through racks of discounted clothing for a great find or two. Women can do well at either the State Street or Michigan Avenue location, but men will find a superior selection of designer names at State Street.

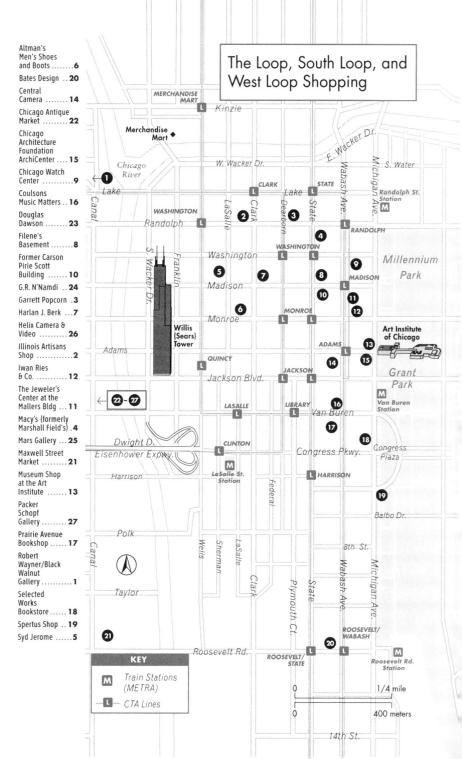

The Loop, South Loop, and West Loop Shopping

MERCHANDISE MART

Merchandise Mart ◆

Kinzie

E. Wacker Dr.

S. Water

Chicago River

W. Wacker Dr.

Randolph St. Station

Chicago

Lake

Canal

S. Wacker Dr.

Franklin

CLARK

State

Wabash Ave.

Michigan Ave.

WASHINGTON

Randolph

Washington

Willis
(Sears)
Tower

Madison

Monroe

Adams

QUINCY

Jackson Blvd.

LASALLE

LIBRARY

Van Buren

Dwight D.
Eisenhower Expwy.

CLINTON

Congress Pkwy.

LaSalle St.
Station

Harrison

HARRISON

Polk

Balbo Dr.

Canal

8th St.

Taylor

Wells

Sherman

LaSalle

Clark

Federal

Plymouth Ct.

State

Wabash Ave.

Michigan Ave.

ROOSEVELT/
WABASH

Roosevelt Rd.

ROOSEVELT/
STATE

Roosevelt Rd.
Station

14th St.

RANDOLPH

Millennium
Park

WASHINGTON

MADISON

MONROE

Art Institute
of Chicago

Grant
Park

Van Buren
Station

Congress
Plaza

Museum Shop

KEY

M Train Stations
(METRA)

L CTA Lines

0   1/4 mile

0   400 meters

Watch newspaper ads midweek for special shipments. ✉*1 N. State St., Loop* ☎*312/553–1055* ✉*830 N. Michigan Ave., Magnificent Mile* ☎*312/482–8918.*

★ **Macy's.** In the fall of 2006 Marshall Field's, Chicago's most famous— and perpetually struggling—department store, became a Macy's. Some of the higher-end designers Field's carried are gone from the racks, but overall the store remains the same, still standing as a glorious reminder of how grand department stores used to be. Founder Marshall Field's motto was "Give the lady what she wants!" And for many years both ladies and gentlemen had been able to find everything from furs to personalized stationery on one of the store's nine levels. The ground floor and lower level are fashioned in the model of European department stores to include leased boutiques. These stores-within-the-store include national companies like Yahoo!, selling Internet service and computer equipment, and an Yves St. Laurent accessories boutique, as well as local retailers like Merz Apothecary, a pharmacy that opened on the North Side of Chicago in 1875 and specializes in homeopathic remedies. You can still buy Field's famous Frango mints (though they're no longer made locally), and the Walnut Room restaurant on the 7th floor is still a magical place to dine at Christmas. And, the famous Tiffany Dome—designed in 1907 by Louis Comfort Tiffany—is visible from the fifth floor. ✉*111 N. State St., Loop* ☎*312/781–1000* ✉*Water Tower Place, 835 N. Michigan Ave., Magnificent Mile* ☎*312/335–7700.*

SPECIALTY STORES

BOOKS AND MUSIC **Coulsons Music Matters.** Musicians come here to find sheet music that suits their style—whether it's jazz, classical, pop, or just about anything else. You'll also find handy accessories like piano lights and metronomes. ✉*75 E. Van Buren St., Loop* ☎*312/461–1989.*

Prairie Avenue Bookshop. Massive tables amid architectural artifacts in the Prairie Style interior give browsers room to peruse nearly 20,000 new, rare, and out-of-print titles on architecture, interior design, and urban planning. ✉*418 S. Wabash Ave., Loop* ☎*312/922–8311.*

Selected Works Bookstore. This charming used bookstore relocated from a warrenlike basement in Wrigleyville to a bright, sunny shop on the second floor of the Fine Arts Building. Inside you'll find an intriguing, though somewhat chaotic, selection of used books and sheet music watched over by the proprietor's friendly cat. ✉*410 S. Michigan Ave., Suite 210, Loop* ☎*312/447–0068.*

CAMERAS
Fodor'sChoice
★ **Central Camera.** This century-old, third-generation-owned store is a Loop institution, stacked to the rafters with cameras and darkroom equipment at competitive prices. ✉*230 S. Wabash Ave., Loop* ☎*312/427–5580.*

CLOTHING AND SHOES **Altman's Men's Shoes and Boots.** Price tags are still written by hand at this 75-year-old institution, which has 27 stockrooms holding 50,000 pairs of men's shoes in sizes from 5 to 19 and in widths from AAAA to EEE. You can find anything from Timberland and Tony Lama boots to Allen-Edmonds and Alden oxfords, all at a decent discount. ✉*120 W. Monroe St., Loop* ☎*312/332–0667.*

Bates Design. Barbara Bates has been designing upscale fashions with a distinct urban edge since 1986 for a who's-who client list that includes

Oprah Winfrey, Michael Jordan, Will Smith, and Mary J. Blige. But she's still invested in her community; her eponymous foundation donates custom prom dresses and tuxedos to disadvantaged inner-city teens set to graduate from high school. This new studio showcases her couture and traditional labels. ⊠*1130 S. Wabash Ave., Suite 407, South Loop* ☎*312/427–0284.*

Syd Jerome. Board of Trade types who like special attention and snazzy designers come to this legendary clothier for Giorgio Armani, Ermenegildo Zegna, and on-the-spot custom alterations. Home and office consultations are available. ⊠*2 N. LaSalle St., Loop* ☎*312/346–0333.*

DISCOUNT **Chicago Watch Center.** This large street-side booth in the Wabash Jew-
JEWELRY AND elers Mall has one of the city's most outstanding inventories of used
WATCHES luxury watches. ⊠*Wabash Jewelers Mall, 21 N. Wabash Ave., Loop* ☎*312/609–0003.*

The Jeweler's Center at the Mallers Building. The largest concentration of wholesale and retail jewelers in the Midwest has been housed in this building since 1921, and is open to the general public. Roughly 190 retailers span 13 floors, offering all kinds of jewelry, watches, and related repairs and services. ⊠*5 S. Wabash Ave., Loop* ☎*312/424–2664.*

MUSEUM **Museum Shop at the Art Institute of Chicago.** Museum reproductions in the
STORES form of jewelry, posters, and Frank Lloyd Wright–inspired decorative accessories, as well as books and toys, fill the Art Institute's gift shop. If you're keen on one of the museum's current big exhibits, chances are you'll find some nifty souvenirs to take away. ⊠*111 S. Michigan Ave., Loop* ☎*312/443–3583.*

Spertus Shop. Come here for all your modern Jewish must-haves, like Moses action figures and Jonathan Adler yarmulkes. There's also more traditional holiday ware, books, and music. The shop's inside the Spertus Institute of Jewish Studies. ⊠*610 S. Michigan Ave., Loop* ☎*312/322–1740.*

SOUVENIRS **Chicago Architecture Foundation ArchiCenter Shop & Tour Center.** Daniel
OF CHICAGO Burnham's 1904 Santa Fe Building is a fitting home for the Chicago
Fodor'sChoice Architecture Foundation. Chock-full of architecture-related books,
★ home accessories, and everything and anything related to Frank Lloyd Wright, the store is also the place to sign up for one of the foundation's acclaimed tours conducted on foot or by bus, bicycle, and river cruise. ⊠*224 S. Michigan Ave., Loop* ☎*312/922–3432.*

★ **Garrett Popcorn.** Bring home a tub of Chicago's famous popcorn instead of a giant pencil or T-shirt, and you'll score major points. The lines can be long, but trust us—this stuff is worth the wait. ⊠*26 W. Randolph St., Loop* ☎*312/201–0455* ⊠*4 E. Madison St., Loop* ☎*312/263–8087* ⊠*2 W. Jackson Blvd., Loop* ☎*312/360–1108* ⊠*500 W. Madison St., Citicorp Center, 2nd fl., Loop* ☎*312/337–7214.*

Illinois Artisans Shop. This store run by the Illinois State Museum culls the best jewelry, ceramics, glass, and dolls from craftspeople around the state and sells them at very reasonable prices. There are also exhibits on anything from quilting to Celtic design. ⊠*James R. Thompson Center, 100 W. Randolph St., Suite 2–100, Loop* ☎*312/814–5321* ⊙*Closed weekends.*

7

SPECIALTY **Harlan J. Berk.** Travel back to antiquity amid this wondrous trove of
STOPS classical Greek, Roman, and Byzantine coinage and artifacts. Don't
miss the gallery rooms in the back. ⊠*31 N. Clark St., Loop* ☎*312/ 609–0016.*

★ **Iwan Ries and Co.** Iwan Ries did not just jump on the cigar bandwagon;
the family-owned store has been around since 1857. Cigar smokers are
welcome to light up in the smoking area, which also displays antique
pipes. ■TIP→**Almost 100 brands of cigars are available, as are 10,000 or so pipes, deluxe Elie Bleu humidors, and all manner of smoking accessories.** ⊠*19 S. Wabash Ave., 2nd fl., Loop* ☎*312/372–1457.*

WEST LOOP

Art aficionados and gallery owners are taking a new direction in Chicago. After years of doing business in River North and along Michigan Avenue, their new credo is to go west—specifically, to the West Loop, an area just west of downtown marked by Halsted Street to the east, Fulton Market (still a busy meat-packing center) to the north, Ogden Avenue to the west, and Roosevelt Avenue to the south. Large former warehouses and loft spaces coupled with more reasonable rents have led many galleries from more established neighborhoods to join what was once a sparse number of experimental artists and dealers here. Most are clustered around the northern section of the neighborhood.

ART GALLERIES

Douglas Dawson. Douglas Dawson has 8,000 square feet of space plus a sculpture garden in his West Loop space to showcase ancient and historic art from Africa, Oceania, and the Americas. ⊠*400 N. Morgan St., West Loop* ☎*312/226–7975.*

G.R. N'Namdi. This gallery represents contemporary painters and sculptors, with an emphasis on African-American and Latin American artists. ⊠*110 N. Peoria St., West Loop* ☎*312/563–9240.*

Mars Gallery. A neighborhood pioneer that showcases contemporary pop and outsider artwork, Mars Gallery shows work by Peter Mars and other well-known locals like Kevin Luthardt. ⊠*1139 W. Fulton Market, West Loop* ☎*312/226–7808.*

Packer Schopf Gallery. Browse through an extensive collection of vintage photography and contemporary art with a special emphasis on folk and outsider pieces at this gallery run by well-known local owners Aron Packer and William Schopf. ⊠*942 W. Lake St., West Loop* ☎*312/226–8984.*

Robert Wayner/Black Walnut Gallery. The gallery has a selection of beautiful handcrafted wood furniture, sculpture, and art as well as stunning and affordable ($30 to $5,000) contemporary art. ⊠*220 N. Aberdeen, West Loop* ☎*312/286–2307.*

CAMERAS AND ELECTRONICS

Helix Camera & Video. Professional photographers buy and rent camera and darkroom equipment at this eight-story warehouse on Racine Avenue just west of Greektown (1½ mi west of the Loop). A good selection of used equipment is available. Underwater photography equipment is a specialty. ⊠*310 S. Racine Ave., West Loop* ☎*312/421–6000.*

NOTABLE MARKETS

Fodor's Choice
★ **Chicago Antique Market.** This indoor–outdoor flea market is similar to the ones you might find in London and Paris. On the last Sunday of the month in season more than 200 stalls line Randolph Street selling furniture, jewelry, books, and more. ■TIP→ **The vibe is more funky fashions and vintage treasures than tube socks and refurbished vacuums.** There's also an Indie Designer Fashion Market, showcasing one-of-a-kind wearables by up-and-coming local designers. Children under 12 get in free. ⊠*Randolph St. between Ogden Ave. and Ada St., West Loop* ☎*312/666–1200* 🔄*$10* ⊙*May–Oct., last Sun. of month.*

Maxwell Street Market. A legendary outdoor bazaar that is part of the cultural landscape of the city, the Maxwell Street Market was closed by the city of Chicago amid much controversy in the 1990s. Soon after, it reopened in its current location as the New Maxwell Street Market, where it remains a popular spot, particularly for Latino immigrants, to buy and sell wares. The finds aren't so fabulous, but the atmosphere sure is fun: live blues and stalls selling Mexican street food keep things lively. ⊠*Intersection of Canal St. and Roosevelt Rd., West Loop* ☎*312/745–4676* 🔄*Free* ⊙*Sun. 7 AM–3 PM.*

> ### ONE-OF-KIND SOUVENIRS
>
> **Chicago Architecture Foundation ArchiCenter Shop & Tour Center** (*224 S. Michigan Ave., Loop, 312/922—3432*) is chock-full of treasures to remind you of the city's glorious architecture.
>
> **Garrett Popcorn** (*26 W. Randolph St., Loop, 312/2010511*) lures people off the street with its mouthwatering aromas.
>
> **City of Chicago Store** (*163 E. Pearson St., Near North, 312/742—8811*) makes you forget the snow globes and lets you bring home something really authentic—like an old city parking meter.

NEAR NORTH

The Near North section of Chicago encompasses the Gold Coast, which is as swanky as its name suggests. Filled with exclusive apartment buildings, luxury hotels, and top-notch restaurants, it also has some of the best shopping in the city. This is where you'll find the Magnificent Mile, Chicago's most famous shopping strip, as well as a bevy of significant shopping streets in the surrounding area. Check out the boutiques on Rush Street, which offers something for everyone—from young hipsters to ladies who lunch. Along the big avenues like Chicago and Ohio, you'll find hyper-sized versions of familiar fare.

SPECIALTY STORES

BOOKS, MUSIC AND ART
Europa Books. Europa is the place for foreign-language books, newspapers, and magazines. This well-stocked bookstore carries French, Spanish, German, and Italian titles, and is known for its selection of Latin American literature. ⊠*832 N. State St., Near North* ☎*312/335–9677.*

Jazz Record Mart. Billing itself as the world's largest jazz record store, this "mart" sells tens of thousands of new and used titles on CD, vinyl, and cassette. You'll also find a broad selection of world music. A vast,

Near North and
River North Shopping

7

in-depth selection of jazz and blues and knowledgeable sales staff make the store a must for music lovers. Sometimes you can catch a live performance here on a Saturday afternoon. ⊠ *27 E. Illinois St., Near North* ☎ *312/222–1467.*

Museum of Contemporary Art Store and Bookstore. This outstanding museum gift shop has out-of-the-ordinary decorative accessories, tableware, and jewelry, as well as a superb collection of books on modern and contemporary art. The shop has its own street-level entrance. ⊠ *220 E. Chicago Ave., Near North* ☎ *312/397–4000* ⊗ *Closed Mon.*

FOR KIDS **American Girl Place.** American Girl attracts little girls from just about everywhere with their signature dolls in tow. There's easily a day's worth of activities here—shop at the boutique, take in a live musical revue, and have lunch or afternoon tea at the café, where dolls can partake in the meal from their own "sassy seats." ⚠ **Brace yourself for long lines just to get into the store during high shopping seasons.** ⊠ *835 N. Michigan Ave., Near North* ☎ *877/247–5223.*

Madison and Friends. Mini Mag Mile shoppers get their own high-end shopping experience at this boutique, which stocks labels like Hannah Banana and Les Tout Petits in newborn through junior sizes. They also carry top-of-the-line strollers and accessories. Adults can shop in the Denim Lounge downstairs, where the latest styles from Miss Sixty, True Religion, and other of-the-moment brands are available. ⊠ *43 E. Oak St., Near North* ☎ *312/642–6403.*

CLOTHING **Adidas Originals Chicago.** Old-school sneakers and hip urban fashions
AND SHOES for a fresh generation of fans are the draw here. ⊠ *923 N. Rush St., Near North* ☎ *312/932–0651.*

The Daisy Shop. Gently worn new and vintage couture clothing is the draw at this high-end consignment shop. Knowledgeable staffers guide you through the collection, which features fashion's heaviest hitters as well as a well-edited selection of bags, pearls, and other accessories— all offered at a relative bargain. ⊠ *67 E. Oak St., 6th fl., Near North* ☎ *312/943–8880.*

Ikram. A household name in chichi Gold Coast high-rises, this 4,000-square-foot store named for owner Ikram Goldman carries an assortment of new and old fashion icons, from Alexander McQueen and Jean Paul Gaultier to Narciso Rodriguez and Zac Posen. There's also a carefully edited selection of vintage designs. ⊠ *873 N. Rush St., Near North* ☎ *312/587–1000.*

CLOTHING **Jake.** The motto here is "fashion without victims," and the own-
FOR MEN AND ers have taken heed to stock clothes for both sexes by up-and-com-
WOMEN ing designers you don't see elsewhere. This shop has been a favorite
★ from the moment it opened its doors. ⊠ *939 N. Rush St., Near North* ☎ *312/664–5553.*

Londo Mondo. A great selection of swimwear for buff beach-ready bodies is here. You can also find workout and yoga gear and men's and women's in-line skates. ⊠ *1100 N. Dearborn St., Near North* ☎ *312/751–2794* ⊠ *2148 N. Halsted St., Lincoln Park* ☎ *773/327–2218.*

FOR THE HOME **Jonathan Adler.** Design guru Adler's store is chock-full of his signature fun, funky pottery and home furnishings, all arranged in a series of small living spaces. ✉*676 Wabash Ave., Near North* ☎*312/274–9920.*

Quatrine. The washable upholstered and slipcovered furniture for dining rooms, living rooms, and bedrooms here looks decidedly chic and not at all what you'd consider child- or pet-friendly. ✉*670 N. Wabash Ave., Near North* ☎*312/649–1700.*

Room & Board. Straightforward yet stylish pieces with a modern sensibility blend quality craftsmanship and materials with affordable pricing. ✉*55 E. Ohio St., Near North* ☎*312/222–0970.*

SOUVENIRS
OF CHICAGO
Fodor's Choice
★

City of Chicago Store. Nab unusual souvenirs of the city here—anything from a street sign to a real parking meter. It's also a good source for guidebooks, posters, and T-shirts. ✉*Chicago Waterworks Visitor Information Center, 163 E. Pearson St., Near North* ☎*312/742–8811.*

SPOTLIGHT: NAVY PIER

Extending more than ½ mi onto Lake Michigan from 600 East Grand Avenue, Navy Pier treats you to spectacular views of the skyline, especially from a jumbo Ferris wheel set in slow motion. Stores and carts gear their wares to families and tourists, and most don't merit a special trip. But if you're out there, check out **Oh Yes Chicago!** for souvenirs and the **Chicago Children's Museum Store** for educational kids' toys. Many stores are open late into the evening, especially in summer.

RIVER NORTH

7

Contained by the Chicago River on the south and west, Clark Street on the east, and Oak Street on the north, River North is home to art galleries, high-end antiques shops, home-furnishings stores, and a few clothing boutiques. The biggest news in this neighborhood is the resurrection of Tree Studios, part of a controversial restoration project to a building originally designed as an artists' colony. On the verge of demolition a few years ago, the building is again housing retail and tenants involved in the arts, although they are no longer permitted to live here. Most of the businesses in River North have a distinctive style that fits in with this art-minded area. Strangely, it's also a wildly popular entertainment district; touristy theme restaurants such as Ed Debevic's and Rainforest Café peddle logo merchandise as aggressively as burgers.

MERCHANDISE MART

This massive marketplace between Wells and North Orleans streets just north of the Chicago River is more notable for its Art Deco design than its shopping. Much of the building is reserved for the design trade, meaning that only interior-design professionals have access to its wares. However, the first two floors have been turned into retail with the unveiling of LuxeHome, a group of 24 high-end kitchen, bath, and building showrooms that are open to the public as well as the design trade. Tenants include de Giulio kitchen design, Waterworks, and Christopher Peacock Cabinetry. The Chopping Block, a local culinary school with a loyal fan base, has a spacious location here. The Mart is usually closed on Sunday, and stores keep relatively short Saturday hours.

SPECIALTY STORES

ANTIQUES **Antiquarians Building.** Five floors of dealers in Asian and European
AND antiques display their wares; some examples of modernism and Art
COLLECTIBLES Deco are thrown in for good measure. ⊠*159 W. Kinzie St., River
North* ☎*312/527–0533.*

Christa's, Ltd. Chests, cabinets, tables, and bureaus are stacked three and
four high, creating narrow aisles that are precarious to negotiate but
make for adventurous exploring. Look in, over, and under each and
every piece to assess the gems stashed in every possible crevice. ⊠*217
W. Illinois St., River North* ☎*312/222–2520.*

Evanstonia Antique Gallery. Dealer Ziggy Osak has a rich collection of
fine 19th-century English and continental antiques that are prized for
being as functional as they are striking. ⊠*120 W. Kinzie St., River
North* ☎*312/222–0102.*

Jay Robert's Antique Warehouse. Jay Robert's has enough antique merchandise to fill a 50,000-square-foot showroom on his own. He specializes
in 18th- and 19th-century European pieces, and has many large-scale
armoires, dining sets, sideboards, fireplace mantels, and clocks. ⊠*149
W. Kinzie St., River North* ☎*312/222–0167.*

P.O.S.H. It's hard to resist the charming displays of piled-up, never-been-
used, vintage hotel and restaurant china here. There's also an impressive selection of silver gravy boats, creamers, and flatware that bear the
marks of ocean liners and private clubs. ⊠*Tree Studios, 613 N. State
St., River North* ☎*312/280–1602.*

Rita Bucheit, Ltd. Devoted to the streamlined Biedermeier aesthetic, this
shop carries choice furniture and accessories from the period along with
Art Deco and modern pieces that are perfect complements to the style.
⊠*449 N. Wells St., River North* ☎*312/527–4080.*

ART GALLERIES The contemporary art scene continues to thrive in River North, despite
losing some of its residents to a slightly lower-rent warehouse district
in the nearby West Loop and a burgeoning gallery scene in Pilsen,
southwest of the Loop. The neighborhood is chock-full of galleries,
most open Tuesday through Saturday. ■**TIP➔Every Saturday morning
at 11, the Art Dealers Association of Chicago offers complimentary gallery
tours.** Groups meet at the Starbucks at 750 North Franklin Street and
are guided each week by a different gallery owner or director from the
area. For more information, and to check holiday weekend schedules,
call ☎*312/649–0065* or go to ⊕*www.chicagoartdealers.org.*

Alan Koppel Gallery. An eclectic mix of works by modern masters and
contemporary artists is balanced by a selection of French and Italian
Modernist furniture from the 1920s to 1960s. ⊠*210 W. Chicago Ave.,
River North* ☎*312/640–0730.*

Ann Nathan Gallery. The specialty here is contemporary paintings, but
the gallery also showcases sculpture and singular artist-made furniture.
⊠*212 W. Superior St., River North* ☎*312/664–6622.*

Byron Roche. Contemporary paintings and drawings, many by Chicago
artists, are exhibited here. ⊠*750 N. Franklin St., Ste. 210, River North*
☎*312/654–0144.*

Continued on page 261

THE MAGNIFICENT MILE: A SHOPPER'S SHANGRI-LA

One mile. Nearly 500 shops. Four vertical malls.
Art galleries, haute couture, bargains, and boutiques.
Does it get any better than this?

We've got news for shopaholics who consider the Midwest nothing but flyover country: If you haven't shopped Chicago's Magnificent Mile, dare we say, you simply haven't shopped.

With four lavish malls and more than 460 stores along the stretch of Michigan Avenue that runs from the Chicago River to Oak Street, the Mag Mile is one of the best shopping strips the world over. (Swanky Oak Street is also considered part of the Mag Mile, though neighboring streets technically are not. Shops on those streets are listed in this chapter under "Near North.")

Chanel, Hermès, Gucci, and Armani are just a few of the legendary fashion houses with fabulous boutiques here. Other notables like Anne Fontaine, Kate Spade, and Prada also have Mag Mile outposts, recognizing the everybody-who's-anybody importance of the address.

Shoppers with down-to-earth budgets will find there's plenty on the Mag Mile as well, with national chains making an extra effort at their multi-level megastores here. But the Mag Mile is much more than a paradise for clothes horses, with stores for techies, furniture fiends, sports fans, art collectors, and almost anyone else with money to spend.

Following is a selective guide to stores in the area. Hours generally run from 10 AM to 7 or 8 PM Monday through Saturday, with shorter hours on Sunday.

Bellevue Pl.

Jil Sander · Palazzo Chasalla Hermès

Kate Spade ·

Prada · Ultimo

1000 E. Oak St. E. Lake Shore Dr.

Barneys · Bravco Tod's · Chanel
New York Beauty Colletti
Centre Gallery

Jimmy E. Walton St.
Choo **900 North** • Louis Vuitton
Michigan Shops • Anne
(with Bloomingdale's) • Fontaine

900 E. Delaware Pl.

Mies van der Rohe Way
200

John Hancock
Center
Richard Gray
Gallery

E. Chestnut St.

Water Tower
Place (with
H&M • **Macy's and**
American Girl
E. Pearson St. **Place)**

Water Tower • City of Chicago
Store

Giorgio Armani •

800 Chicago Ave.

Polo/Ralph Lauren •

Neiman Marcus

E. Superior St. Saks Fifth Avenue
• Men's Store
Chicago Place • The Disney Store
(with Saks Fifth Ave.) • Brooks Brothers

700 E. Huron St.

Clair St.

E. Erie St.

N. Wabash Ave.
N. Rush St.
N. Michigan Ave.

DEPARTMENT STORES

Barneys New York. A smaller version of the Manhattan store known for austere fashions, this one's heavy on private-label merchandise, though you'll find Donna Karan and several European designers. A Vera Wang salon caters to brides. The cosmetics and Chelsea Passage gift areas have plenty of plum choices. ⊠25 E. Oak St. ☎312/587–1700.

Bloomingdale's. Chicago's Bloomie's is built in an airy style that is part Prairie School, part postmodern

(quite unlike its New York City sibling), giving you plenty of elbow room to sift through its selection of designer labels. The new Space on 5 has trendier fashions. ⊠900 North Michigan Shops ☎312/440–4460.

The Disney Store. This Mecca to the Mouse has everything little Disney disciples need for a fix: giant monitors playing Walt's classics, plus a plethora of plush toys, videos, games, and other goodies. ⊠717 N. Michigan Ave. ☎312/654–9208.

Neiman Marcus. Prices may be high, but they're matched by the level of taste. The selection of designer clothing and accessories is outstanding, and the gourmet top-floor food area tempts with hard-to-find delicacies and impeccable hostess gifts. ⊠737 N. Michigan Ave. ☎312/642–5900.

Nordstrom. This is a lovely department store with a killer shoe department. Note the Nordstrom Spa on the third floor. ⊠The Shops at North Bridge, 520 N. Michigan Ave. ☎312/464–1515.

Saks Fifth Avenue. The smaller, less-crowded cousin of the New York flagship doesn't scrimp on its selection of designer clothes. A men's specialty store is directly across the street. ⊠Chicago Place, 700 N. Michigan Ave. ☎312/944–6500 ⊠Men's Store, 717 N. Michigan Ave. ☎312/944–6500.

CLOTHING FOR WOMEN

Anne Fontaine Paris. The French designer's famous takes on the classic white shirt sport hefty price tags, thanks to her attention to detail. ⌧ 909 N. Michigan Ave. ☎ 312/943–0401.

Chanel Boutique. Ensconced in the Drake Hotel, this shop carries the complete line of Chanel products, including ready-to-wear, fragrances, and cosmetics. ⌧ 935 N. Michigan Ave. ☎ 312/787–5500.

Palazzo. Chic urban brides trust Jane and Saeed Hamidi for their clean-lined bridal collection. ⌧ 49 E. Oak St. ☎ 312/337–6940.

Ultimo. Check out the well-edited selection of designer goods from such names as John Galliano, Michael Kors, Chloe, and Manolo Blahnik. Oprah is a customer! ⌧ 116 E. Oak St. ☎ 312/787–1171.

BEAUTY-A-GO-GO

Bravco Beauty Centre. Need a hard-to-find shampoo, an ionic hair dryer, or simply a jar of Vaseline? Bravco is the place for all this and more. Cash or check only. ⌧ 43 E. Oak St. ☎ 312/943–4305.

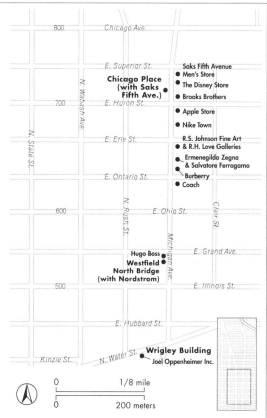

CLOTHING FOR MEN

Ermenegildo Zegna. The sportswear, softly tailored business attire, and dress clothes of this Italian great are gathered all under one roof. ⌧ 645 N. Michigan Ave. ☎ 312/587–9660.

Hugo BOSS. Men will find modern, well-cut suits with attention to tailoring, as well as other signature Boss clothing and accessories here. ⌧ Westfield North Bridge, 520 N. Michigan Ave. ☎ 312/321–0700.

Saks Fifth Avenue Men's Store. Spread over 30,000 square feet and three levels, Saks is the city's leading retailer for menswear. ⌧ 717 N. Michigan Ave. ☎ 312/944–6500 or 888/643–7257.

7

IN FOCUS THE MAGNIFICENT MILE

ALL THINGS OLIVE

Ta-Ze. This olive-centric shop carries 40 types of Turkish olive oil—all single estate, cold pressed, and first pressed—as well as beauty products made from olive oil and all manner of gourmet products that make great gifts for foodies. Sample anything before you buy. ⊠520 N. Michigan, Shops at 106 North Bridge, 3rd. fl. ☎312/527–2576.

CLOTHING FOR MEN & WOMEN

Brooks Brothers. The bastion of ready-to-wear conservative fashion still sells boatloads of their classic 1837 navy blazer. But this one-stop shop for oxfords and khakis also sneaks in the occasional bold color. ⊠713 N. Michigan Ave. ☎312/915–0060.

Burberry. The label once favored by the conservatively well-dressed is now hot with young fashionistas, who can't get enough of the label's signature plaid on everything from bikinis to baby gear. ⊠633 N. Michigan Ave. ☎312/787–2500.

Chasalla. Chasalla isn't for the timid—the bold, sexy clothes and accessories of European couture houses such as Dolce & Gabbana, Gianni Versace, and Hugo Boss are the norm here. ⊠106 E. Oak St. ☎312/640–1940.

Giorgio Armani. An airy, two-floor space displays Armani's discreetly luxurious clothes and accessories, including the top-priced Black Label line. ⊠800 N. Michigan Ave. ☎312/751–2244.

Gucci. Though the prices aren't for the faint of heart, there are plenty of pieces here that will last a lifetime. ⊠900 North Michigan Shops ☎312/664–5504.

H&M. Bargain-savvy fashionistas around the world love the cheap-n-chic styles on offer; the constant crowds at the Mag Mile store prove Chicagoans are no different. ⊠840 N. Michigan Ave. ☎312/640–0060.

Hermès of Paris. The well-heeled and very well-paid shop here for suits, signature scarves, and leather accessories. ⊠110 E. Oak St. ☎312/787–8175.

Jil Sander. This line has captured the devotion of the fashion flock for its minimalist designs and impeccable tailoring. Prices are at the upper end of the designer range. ⊠48 E. Oak St. ☎312/335–0006.

Mark Shale. Here you'll find two floors filled with stylish suits and separates from an international array of designers. ⊠900 North Michigan Shops ☎312/440–0720.

Prada. The store has a spare, cool look that matches its modern inventory of clothing, shoes, and bags. In fact, unless you're a Miuccia devotee, the three-story shop can seem almost bare. ⊠30 E. Oak St. ☎312/951–1113.

Polo/Ralph Lauren. Manor house meets mass marketing. The upper-crust chic covers men's, women's, and children's clothes and housewares. Fabrics are often enticing (suede, silk, cashmere), but expect to pay a pretty penny. ⊠750 N. Michigan Ave. ☎312/280–1655.

TECH STUFF

Apple Store. It's a multilevel fantasyland for Mac users, complete with the full range of products—from computers to iPods to digital cameras. There's an Internet café where PC fans can get a glimpse of life on the other side. ⊠679 N. Michigan Ave. ☎312/981–4104.

SHOES & ACCESSORIES

Coach. Well-designed leather goods, in the form of purses, smart shoes, briefcases, and cell phone and PDA holders, are Coach's specialty. ⊠625 N. Michigan Ave. ☎312/587–3167 ⊠900 North Michigan Shops ☎312/440–1777.

Jimmy Choo. These are the heels that have celebs and stylish women the world over drooling. Break out the plastic. ⊠63 Oak St. ☎312/255–1170.

Kate Spade. The goddess of handbags has filled her two-floor boutique in the middle of Oak Street with adorable shoes, pajamas, small leather goods, men's accessories from the Jack Spade line, and, of course, her to-die-for purses. ⊠56 E. Oak St. ☎312/654–8853.

Louis Vuitton. Here you have it all under one roof—the coveted purses, leather goods, and luggage bearing the beloved logo, plus men's and women's shoes and jewelry. ⊠919 N. Michigan Ave. ☎312/944–2010.

Salvatore Ferragamo. The shoes have been the classic choice of the well-heeled for generations, but it's the handbags, with a fresh, contemporary sensibility, that are generating excitement of late. ⊠645 N. Michigan Ave. ☎312/397–0464.

Tod's. Choose from a wide selection of the signature handbags and driving moccasins that made Tod's famous, as well as newer additions to the line, including high heels. ⊠ 121 E. Oak St. ☎312/943–0070 or 800/457–8637.

GET SPORTY

Niketown. This is one of Chicago's top tourist attractions. Many visitors—including professional athletes—stop here to take in the sports memorabilia, road test a pair of sneakers, or watch the inspirational videos. ⊠669 N. Michigan Ave. ☎312/642–6363.

ART GALLERIES

Colletti Gallery. Fine antique posters, a serious collection of European ceramics and glass, and an eclectic selection of furniture transport you to the late 19th century. ⊠ 67 E. Oak St. ☎312/664–6767.

Joel Oppenheimer, Inc. Established in 1969, this gallery in the Wrigley Building has an amazing collection of Audubon prints and specializes in antique natural-history pieces. ⊠410 N. Michigan Ave. ☎312/642–5300.

R. H. Love Galleries. For three decades, this gallery has specialized in museum-quality American art from the colonial period to the early 20th century. ⊠645 N. Michigan Ave., 2nd fl. entrance on Erie St., ste. 200 ☎312/640–1300.

R. S. Johnson Fine Art. More than 50 museums can be counted among the clients of R. S. Johnson, a Mag Mile resident for 50 years. The family-run gallery sells old masters along with art by modernists like Pablo Picasso, Edgar Degas, and Goya.

⊠645 N. Michigan Ave., 2nd fl. entrance on Erie St. ☎312/943–1661.

Richard Gray Gallery. This gallery lures serious collectors with pieces by modern masters such as David Hockney and Roy Lichtenstein. ⊠John Hancock Center, 875 N. Michigan Ave., Suite 2503 ☎312/642–8877.

NOT LIKE THE ONE BACK HOME

On the Mag Mile, everything seems bigger and better—even chain stores, which make an extra effort in this larger-than-life atmosphere. Here are our favorites:

Banana Republic ⊠744 N. Michigan Ave. ☎312/642–0020.

Crate&Barrel ⊠646 N. Michigan Ave. ☎312/787–5900.

The Gap ⊠555 N. Michigan Ave. ☎312/494–8580.

Victoria's Secret ⊠830 N. Michigan Ave. ☎312/664–2711.

Williams-Sonoma ⊠900 North Michigan Shops ☎312/587–8080.

MIGHTY VERTICAL MALLS

Forget all your preconceived notions about malls being suburban wastelands. Four decidedly upscale urban malls dot the Mag Mile.

The toniest of the four is 900 North Michigan, with a dazzling list of tenants, plus live weekend piano serenades. A more casual but no less entertaining shopping mecca is just blocks away at Water Tower Place. Fuel up there with a snack from **Wow Bao**, which sells steamed meat and vegetable buns that are *delish*.

Check out the beautiful views from Chicago Place's airy top-floor food court. The newest kid on the block is Westfield North Bridge, which opened in 2000.

Chicago Place. Saks Fifth Avenue is the big tenant here, and there's also a multilevel Ann Taylor. Other shops include Love from Chicago, Time-Us and Tall Girl. ⊠700 N. Michigan Ave. ☎312/642–4811.

900 North Michigan Shops. There's a ritzy feel to the mall that houses the Chicago branch of Bloomingdale's along with dozens of boutiques and specialty stores, such as Gucci, Coach, Lalique, and Fogal. ⊠900 N. Michigan Ave. ☎312/915–3916.

Water Tower Place. The Ritz-Carlton Hotel sits atop this mall, which contains branches of Macy's and American Girl Place, as well as seven floors of shops. The more unusual spots here include Teavana (a modern tea shop) and Jacadi (children's wear). **Foodlife**, a step above usual mall food-court fare, is a fantastic spot for a quick bite. ⊠835 N. Michigan Ave. ☎312/440–3165.

The Shops at North Bridge. The big draw here is Nordstrom. Chains like Sephora and Ann Taylor Loft share space with specialty stores like Vosges Haut-Chocolat, a local chocolatier with an international following. The third floor is for tots, with a LEGO Store, a play area, and Oilily Kids. ⊠ 520 N. Michigan Ave. ☎ 312/327–2300.

THE ANNUAL LIGHTS FESTIVAL

Chicago's holiday season officially kicks off every year at the end of November with the **Magnificent Mile Lights Festival**, a weekend-long event consisting of family-friendly activities that packs the shopping strip to the gills. Music, ice-carving contests, and stage shows kick off the celebration, which culminates in a parade and the illumination of more than one million lights along Michigan Avenue. Neighborhood stores keep late hours to accommodate the crowds. For more information, check out ⊕ www.themagnificentmile.com.

Carl Hammer Gallery. Lee Godie, Henry Darger, and Jordan Mozer are among the outsider and self-taught artists whose work is shown at this gallery. ⊠*740 N. Wells St., River North* ☎*312/266–8512.*

Catherine Edelman Gallery. This gallery of contemporary photography explores the work of emerging, mixed-media, photo-based artists such as Maria Martinez-Canes and Jack Spencer. ⊠*300 W. Superior St., River North* ☎*312/266–2350.*

Habatat. Collectors of fine studio art glass are drawn here by luminaries such as Dale Chihuly. ⊠*222 W. Superior St., River North* ☎*312/ 440–0288.*

Primitive Art Works. Find ethnic and tribal art, including textiles, furniture, and jewelry, at this longtime Chicago favorite gallery. ⊠*130 N. Jefferson St., River North* ☎*312/575–9600.*

Stephen Daiter Gallery. This space showcases stunning 20th-century European and American photography, particularly avant-garde photojournalism. A separate contemporary gallery highlights work by younger artists pushing the boundaries of contemporary photography. ⊠*311 W. Superior St., River North* ☎*312/787–3350.*

ART SUPPLIES AND BOOKS **Abraham Lincoln Book Shop.** The shop owner here buys, sells, and appraises books, paintings, documents, and other paraphernalia associated with American military and political history. It's been around since 1938. ⊠*357 W. Chicago Ave., River North* ☎*312/944–3085.*

Pearl Fine Art Supplies. Pearl is the name synonymous with the best selection of art supplies at the best prices. Paints and palettes, crafts, portfolios, tools, easels—it's all here, and it's all discounted. ⊠*225 W. Chicago Ave., River North* ☎*312/915–0200.*

CHEAP CHOCOLATE **Blommer Chocolate Outlet Store.** "Why do parts of River North smell like freshly baked brownies?" is a question you hear fairly often. The oh-so-sweet reason: it's near the Blommer Chocolate Factory, which has been making wholesale chocolates here since 1939. More important, the retail outlet store is also here, so you can snap up your Blommer chocolates and candies at a discount—a handy tip to know when those smells give you a case of the munchies. ⊠*600 W. Kinzie St., at N. Jefferson St., River North* ☎*312/492–1336.*

CLOTHING FOR WOMEN **Betsey Johnson.** All of the bold designer's signature fun and over-the-top styles are here. ⊠*835 N. Michigan Ave., Water Tower Place, River North* ☎*312/280–6964.*

Blake. A no-nonsense boutique without pomp, circumstance, or even signage, Blake displays clean-lined clothes in a pristine setting. You'll find designers like Dries van Noten and Balenciaga, and shoes and accessories of a similar subtle elegance. ⊠*212 W. Chicago Ave., River North* ☎*312/202–0047.*

Clever Alice. This women's boutique carries a well-chosen inventory of fashion from local designers like Alice in Oz and Veronica Martin Riley, plus other avant-garde labels like Kitchen Orange and Metalicus. ⊠*1920 N. Damen, River North* ☎*773/276–2444.*

FOR THE HOME Fodor'sChoice ★ **Bloomingdale's Home & Furniture Store.** The Medinah Temple once occupied this space, and Bloomie's kept the historically significant exterior intact but gutted the inside to create its first stand-alone furnishings store in Chicago. Naturally, it's stocked to the rafters with everything you need to eat, sleep, and relax in your home in high style. ✉*600 N. Wabash Ave., Near North* ☎*312/324–7500.*

Cambium. A particularly expansive line of kitchen fittings and accoutrements is one of many temptations at this home-furnishings store. ✉*113–119 W. Hubbard St., River North* ☎*312/832–9920.*

★ **The Chopping Block.** New and seasoned chefs appreciate an expertly edited selection of pots and pans, bakeware, gadgets, and ingredients here. The intimate cooking classes are hugely popular and taught by a fun, knowledgeable staff. (Students get 10% off store merchandise.) The Lincoln Square location has a wine shop. ✉*Merchandise Mart Plaza, Suite 107, River North* ☎*312/644–6360* ✉*4747 N. Lincoln Ave., Lincoln Square* ☎*773/472–6700.*

Design Within Reach. This showroom in the historic Tree Studios building is one of the home-furnishings chain's largest. Inside you'll find several floors of furnishings—from lounge designs and workspace furniture to lighting and accessories—all reflecting the store's focus on classic modern design at affordable prices. ✉*1574 N. Kingsbury, River North* ☎*312/482–8661.*

Golden Triangle. This is a must-stop shop for anyone enamored of the East-meets-West aesthetic. There are 11,000 square feet of choice pieces, including antique Chinese and British colonial Raj furniture from Burma, Asian accessories, and idiosyncratic pieces from Thailand. ✉*330 N. Clark St., River North* ☎*312/755–1266.*

Lightology. This 20,000-square-foot showroom of modern light designs is an essential stop for designers and architects, not to mention passersby drawn to the striking designs visible from the windows. It's the brainchild of Greg Kay, who started out as a roller-disco lighting designer in the 1970s and made a name for himself in Chicago with Tech Lighting, a contemporary design gallery. ✉*215 W. Chicago Ave., River North* ☎*312/944–1000.*

Luminaire. The city's largest showroom of international contemporary furniture includes pieces by Philippe Starck, Antonio Citterio, Alberta Meda, and Shiro Kuromata. Sleek kitchen designs are from Italian manufacturer Bofi, and a large home accessories section has equally edgy offerings from Alessi, Zani & Zani, Rosenthal, and Mono. ✉*301 W. Superior St., River North* ☎*312/664–9582.*

Manifesto. In a huge, street-level space, one of the largest design ateliers in the city showcases work by furniture designer (and owner) Richard Gorman, plus contemporary furniture from Armani Casa (Giorgio Armani's furniture line) and streamlined Finnish accessories. ✉*755 N. Wells St., River North* ☎*312/664–0733.*

Orange Skin. The go-to resource for modern furniture, lighting, and accessories in Chicago carries pieces by Minotti, Alessi, Michael Graves, and Tisettanta. A recent move from Wicker Park to a bi-level space means a bigger inventory of goodies to choose from. ✉*223 W. Erie St., Ste. 1NW, River North* ☎*312/335–1033.*

★ **Sawbridge Studios.** Sawbridge Studios displays custom handcrafted furniture by about 40 American artisans. The specialties include Frank Lloyd Wright reproductions, newly designed pieces with an Arts and

Crafts or Shaker aesthetic, and contemporary pottery. ⊠*153 W. Ohio St., River North* ☎*312/828–0055.*

GIFTS **Pops for Champagne.** Choose from well-chosen group of bubbly plus assorted accoutrements at the retail shop of this popular champagne bar. ⊠*605 N. State St., River North* ☎*312/266–7676.*

JEWELRY AND ACCESSORIES **June Blaker.** Chicago retail veteran June Blaker returns to the scene with this standout shop displaying her own jewelry line as well as an eclectic assortment of accessories, bags, clothing, and leather goods by designers such as Comme des Garçons and Brigitte Adolph. The minimalist space lets the unique merchandise take center stage. ⊠*870 N. Orleans., River North* ☎*312/751–9220.*

PAPER ★ **Paper Source.** Reams and reams of different types of paper are sold here; much of it is eclectic and expensive. Check out the custom invitation department and good selection of rubber stamps and bookbinding supplies. Ask about the classes offered. ⊠*232 W. Chicago Ave., River North* ☎*312/337–0798* ⊠*919 W. Armitage Ave., Lincoln Park* ☎*773/525–7300.*

WICKER PARK AND BUCKTOWN

Artists and musicians were the first to claim this once run-down area near the intersection of North, Damen, and Milwaukee avenues, and then, some years later, points south on and around Division Street; the trendy coffeehouses, nightclubs, and restaurants followed. Young, hip families were next, and shopping has since snowballed. Now scads of edgy clothing boutiques, art galleries, home-design ateliers, alternative-music stores, and funky kids' shops dot the area. Hipsters have been squawking about gentrification with the opening of chains like Urban Outfitters and American Apparel in the neighborhood, but this is still a one-of-a-kind shopping destination that deserves a solid chunk of time.

Many stores don't open until at least 11 AM, some shops are closed on Monday and Tuesday, and hours can be erratic. Spend a late afternoon shopping before settling in for dinner at one of the neighborhood's popular restaurants. To get here from downtown on the El, take the Blue Line toward O'Hare and exit at Damen Avenue.

SPECIALTY STORES

ACCESSORIES AND GIFTS **Paper Doll.** Doll up your gift with an unusual card and handmade wrapping paper from this Wicker Park shop, where Maude, the owners' pug, holds court on the floor. Finger puppets, candles, and other gift items are also stocked here. The popular store has newer, bigger digs a few doors down from the teeny old shop. ⊠*2048 W. Division St., Wicker Park* ☎*773/227–6950.*

Red Dog House. Finally, a place in the neighborhood to shop for hipsters' four-legged friends. This boutique has everything Fido and Kitty need to sit, stay, and live pretty, from swank sweaters to made-to-order name collars, beds, and bowls. ⊠*2031 N. Damen St., Bucktown* ☎*773/227–7341.*

RR#1 Chicago. A wood-paneled 1930s pharmacy is the setting for this charming gift shop, which stocks eclectic ideas for everyone on your

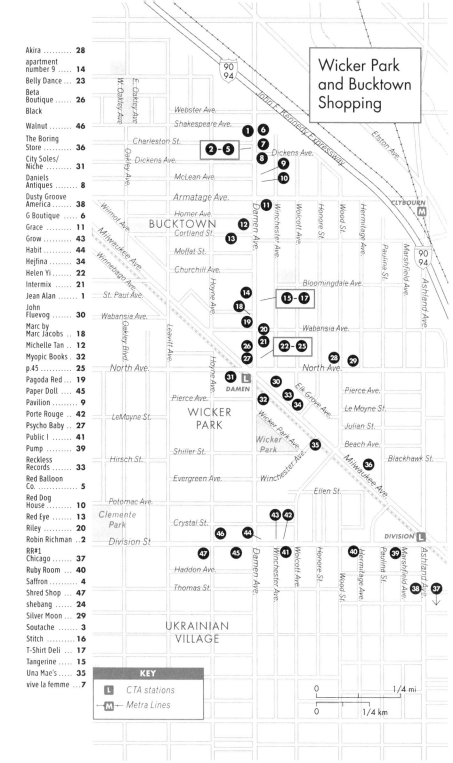

Wicker Park
and Bucktown
Shopping

KEY

🅻 CTA stations

Ⓜ Metra Lines

0 ———— 1/4 mi

0 ———— 1/4 km

list, plus a tempting array of bath and beauty product lines like Barefoot Venus and Pre de Provence. ⊠*814 N. Ashland Ave., Wicker Park* ☎*312/421–9079.*

Ruby Room. This Wicker Park spa–boutique sells an eclectic mix of bath and body products from brands like Sage Spirit, Phytologie, and Surly Girl Studios. Check out the spa services, too—everything from intuitive astrology and pet healing to brow waxing and facials. ⊠*1743–45 W. Division St., 2nd fl., Wicker Park* ☎*773/235–2323.*

shebang. Accessories junkies meet up-and-coming designers at this shop chock full of handbag, jewelry, and hat finds. Super-contemporary labels include Dutchy, Hayden-Harnett, and Alexis Bittar. ⊠*1616 N. Damen Ave., Wicker Park* ☎*773/486–3800.*

ANTIQUES AND COLLECTIBLES

Daniels Antiques. Five blocks north of the six-way Lincoln, Belmont, and Ashland intersection, this cavernous shop shelters a huge stash of Victorian and 20th-century furnishings, especially larger pieces and complete sets. ⊠*2062 N. Damen Ave., Bucktown* ☎*773/276-9600.*

Pagoda Red. Exceptionally well-priced Asian furnishings from owner Betsy Nathan's frequent overseas trips pack this open loft space. Among the treasures, you'll find Chinese deco chairs, Nepalese rugs, antique lanterns, and a rare collection of 20th-century Chinese advertising posters. ⊠*1714 N. Damen Ave., Bucktown* ☎*773/235–1188.*

Pavilion. The specialty here is French, Italian, and Scandinavian antiques, but you'll be lured in by the altogether uncommon mix of industrial and decorative furnishings, accessories, and fixtures. The eclectic selection reflects the collecting acumen of its two idiosyncratic owners, who scour Europe and the Midwest for items in the perfect state of intriguing decay. ⊠*2055 N. Damen Ave., Bucktown* ☎*773/645–0924.*

BOOKS AND MUSIC

Dusty Groove America. The retail outlet of a massive online business, Dusty Groove stocks an enormous collection of older jazz, funk, soul, and blues in both LP and CD formats. They also buy used records Monday through Saturday, from noon to 5 PM. ⊠*1120 N. Ashland Ave., Wicker Park* ☎*773/342–5800.*

★ **Myopic Books.** One of Chicago's largest used-book dealers stocks more than 80,000 titles and buys books from the public on Friday evenings and all day Saturday. ■TIP➡**A community mainstay, Myopic also hosts regular music and poetry events, and is the meeting spot for the Wicker Park Chess Club.** ⊠*1564 N. Milwaukee Ave., Wicker Park* ☎*773/862–4882.*

Reckless Records. Look for a varied selection of music at this sister store to the Lakeview flagship, including lots of rare stuff and rock paraphernalia. ⊠*1532 N. Milwaukee Ave., Bucktown* ☎*773/235–3727.*

FOR KIDS

The Boring Store. Outfit your aspiring sleuth with the necessary spy paraphernalia and secret agent supplies—such as mirror glasses, fake mustaches, and voice amplifiers—at this shop run by the nonprofit group 826CHI. Proceeds help fund the group's after-school tutoring

7

and writing programs for kids. ✉*1331 N. Milwaukee Ave., Wicker Park* ☎*773/772-8108*.

Grow. Kids can grow up green with this stock of organic cotton clothes, all-natural bath products and balms, and environmentally friendly nursery furniture. ✉*1943 W. Division St., Wicker Park* ☎*773/489–0009*.

Psycho Baby. The best-dressed urban tykes send their parents to this shop to spend a pretty penny on funky duds by designers like Imps & Elves, Rabbi's Daughters, and Paper Denim & Cloth. There's a great selection of shoes, plus toys and books, and a story hour every Monday and Wednesday for parents brave enough to tote their tykes along. ✉*1630 N. Damen Ave., Bucktown* ☎*773/772–2815*.

The Red Balloon Company. Known for its beautiful handmade children's furniture and stock of colorful Zutano infant wear, this charming store also carries a great selection of classic kids' books and toys, as well as blankets and art work that can be personalized. ✉*2060 N. Damen Ave., Bucktown* ☎*773/489–9800* ✉*5407 N. Clark St., Andersonville* ☎*773/989–8500 or 877/969–9800*.

CLOTHING FOR MEN

apartment number 9. Siblings Amy and Sarah Blessing offer sisterly advice to guys born without the metrosexual gene on what styles best suit them. Their store, named for the Tammy Wynette song, carries classic lines like Paul Smith, Marc Jacobs, and Michael Kors. ✉*1804 N. Damen Ave., Bucktown* ☎*773/395–2999*.

CLOTHING FOR MEN AND WOMEN

Akira. Young trendsetters flock to this shop for fashion-forward threads at easy-to-swallow prices. In merely five years Akira has expanded into a mini fashion empire. The flagship women's boutique shares a stretch of North Avenue with offshoot men's clothing and women's shoe stores. ✉*1814 W. North Ave., Wicker Park* ☎*773/489–0818*. ✉*1920 W. North Ave., Wicker Park* ☎*312/423–6693* ✉*1849 W. North Ave., Wicker Park* ☎*773/342–8684* . ✉*2357 N. Clark St., Lincoln Park* ☎*773/404–5826* ✉*122 S. State St., Loop* ☎*312/346–3034*.

Habit. Emerging independent designers are stocked by shop owner Lindsey Boland. As most pieces are only made in small quantities, this is where to go if you don't want anyone else wearing what you are. In-house alterations are available, and some lines, including Boland's Superficial, Inc., offer made-to-order designs. ✉*1951 W. Division St., Wicker Park* ☎*773/342–0093*.

Hejfina. This lifestyle boutique carries everything the mod Wicker Parker needs to get through the day stylishly: clothes by of-the-moment designers from across the globe, custom-made furniture from local designers, and books on modern art and architecture. The store also hosts art installations and speakers on design from time to time. ✉*1529 N. Milwaukee Ave., Wicker Park* ☎*773/772–0002*.

Intermix. Label hunters were thrilled when branches of this New York boutique opened in Lincoln Park and the Gold Coast. In 2008 a much-anticipated third outpost opened in Bucktown on Damen Avenue. The latest addition will offer the same mix of designer lines like Stella McCartney, M Missoni, Mint, and Diane von Furstenberg. ✉*1633 N. Damen Ave., Bucktown* ☎*773/292–0894* ✉*40 E. Delaware Pl.,*

Gold Coast ☎*312/640–2922* ✉*841 W. Armitage Ave., Lincoln Park* ☎*773/404–8766.*

Marc by Marc Jacobs. Neighborhood style mavens rejoiced when this store opened in Bucktown rather than on the label-conscious Mag Mile. It's a fitting locale for the fashion icon, whose whimsical, slightly offbeat designs make hipsters drool. ✉*1714 N. Damen Ave., Bucktown* ☎*773/276–2998.*

Public I. Public I prides itself on paying attention to its customers, offering plenty of helpful suggestions about which of its smart, hip, won't-find-it-down-the-street designs work best. Their inventory includes designs by How & Wen, Isda for Men, and Emerge London. ✉*1923 W. Division St., Wicker Park* ☎*773/772–9088.*

Riley. Put together a polished urban look at this clean, modern space. Men's lines run the gamut from Kenneth Cole to Jet Lag, and women can pick up cute wardrobe staples like QI cashmere sweaters and Michael Stars T-Shirts. ✉*1659 N. Damen Ave., Bucktown* ☎*773/489–0101.*

Silver Moon. Vintage wedding gowns and tuxedos are a specialty here, but you can also find less formal vintage clothing and accessories. There are also new collections from Vivienne Westwood, housewares, and custom-embellished denim for babies and small kids. ✉*1755 W. North Ave., Bucktown* ☎*773/235–5797.*

The T-Shirt Deli. Order up a made-to-order T-shirt with custom iron-on letters or throwback '70s decals. You'll get your T-shirt served up on the spot, wrapped in paper like a sandwich, and packed with a bag of chips for good measure. ✉*1739 N. Damen Ave., Bucktown* ☎*773/276–6266.*

CLOTHING FOR WOMEN

Belly Dance Maternity. The hippest moms-to-be shop here for up-to-the-minute maternity fashions by Japanese Weekend, Cadeau, and Citizens of Humanity. ✉*1647 N. Damen Ave., Bucktown* ☎*773/862–1133.*

Beta Boutique. Janice Moskoff built a following bringing occasional sample sales to young fashionistas, and now she's opened up a permanent location to hawk finds from a huge list of designers, from Cynthia Steffe to C. Ronson. The store is open Thursday to Sunday only. ✉*2016 W. Concord Pl., Bucktown* ☎*773/276–0905* ⊘*Closed Mon.–Wed.*

G Boutique. Here's an all-in-one stop for women planning for a little romance. There's beautiful lingerie from brands like Aubade and Cosabella, plus massage oils, books, videos, and toys. There's an 18-and-over admission policy. ✉*2131 N. Damen Ave., Bucktown* ☎*773/235–1234.*

Helen Yi. This loftlike, minimalist boutique stocks sophisticated styles from up-and-coming designers, including Shelly Steffee and local handbag maker Susan Fitch. ✉*1645 N. Damen Ave., Bucktown* ☎*773/252–3838.*

Michelle Tan. Local indie design star Michelle Tan's shop also serves as a working studio where she creates clothes with an emphasis on interesting textures, most in the $200 to $300 range. You'll also find pieces by other local designers, including some students. ✉*1872 N. Damen Ave., Bucktown* ☎*773/252–1888.* ★ **p. 45.** This store is a must-hit for its fashion-forward collection by a cadre of hip designers like Rebecca Taylor and Ulla Johnson. Custom-

★ **p. 45.**

> **FOR THE MOM-TO-BE**
>
> **Krista K Maternity + Baby** (*3530 N. Southport Ave., Lakeview, 773/248-4477*).
>
> **Belly Dance Maternity** (*1647 N. Damen Ave., Bucktown, 773/862-1133*).

ers from all over the city and well beyond come here for adventurous to elegant styles and prices that don't get out of hand. ✉*1643 N. Damen Ave., Bucktown* ☎*773/862–4523.*

Robin Richman. Robin Richman showcases her famous knitwear alongside designs from lesser-known European labels and local clothes designers. Chicagoland artists contribute to the shops' eclectic displays. ✉*2108 N. Damen Ave., Bucktown* ☎*773/278–6150.*

Saffron. Merchandise as indulgent and decadent as the namesake spice lures you into this Bucktown boutique. You'll find fluid, finely finished clothes made of natural fabrics, organically inspired jewelry, and lavish bath products. ✉*2064 N. Damen Ave., Bucktown* ☎*773/486–7753.*

Tangerine. Popular designers, such as Three Dots and Ashley, provide the fun, feminine clothes and accessories here. There's also a good denim selection, including styles by Joe's Jeans and Serfontaine. ✉*1719 N. Damen Ave., Bucktown* ☎*773/772–0505.*

Una Mae's. This Wicker Park favorite for vintage fashions is bursting at the seams with inventory. The bulk of the bulging stock is from the 1950s through the '80s, but there are also new lines from designers like Hot Sauce and The People Have Spoken. ✉*1528 N. Milwaukee Ave., Wicker Park* ☎*773/276–7002.*

vive la femme. The motto is "style beyond size," and the specialty is sexy, exciting clothes for women in sizes 12 to 28 from lines including Anna Scholz, Svoboda, and Z. Cavaricci. ✉*2048 N. Damen Ave., Bucktown* ☎*773/772–7429.*

GIFTS AND FOR THE HOME **Jean Alan.** The offerings at this design atelier, owned by a former feature-film set decorator, range from Victorian to mid-20th-century modern. There's always a healthy assortment of sofas and chairs recovered in eclectic fabrics, plus pillows made of unusual textiles and refurbished vintage lamps with marvelous shades. ✉*2134 N. Damen Ave., Bucktown* ☎*773/278–2345.*

Porte Rouge. Push through the red door for housewares and pretty painted tableware. Look for copper cookware from Mauviel, Spiegelau stemware, and Mariage Fréres teas. ✉*1911 W. Division St., Wicker Park* ☎*773/269–2800.*

Soutache. French for "braid," Soutache is all about the extras that make life so much more interesting: high-end trimmings and embellishments like tortoise shell-and-bamboo belt buckles and purse handles; exotic ostrich plumes; suede tassels; and reams and reams of ribbon. It's up to you how to get creative with all this fun stuff. ✉*2125 N. Damen Ave., Bucktown* ☎*773/292–9110.*

Stitch. Leather goods of every ilk—purses, travel bags, desk accessories—are the main attraction here, but you also find minimalist furniture, tabletop goods, and jewelry. ✉*1723 N. Damen Ave., Bucktown* ☎*773/782–1570.*

SHOES **City Soles/Niche.** These two shoe stores under one roof represent a version of mecca to many shoe fiends. There's a vast selection of edgy men's and women's shoes from designers like Camper and Tsubo, plus a more upscale selection of sophisticated styles from Blay, Rebecca Sanver, and others. ✉*2001 W. North Ave., Bucktown* ☎*773/489–2001* ✉*3432 N. Southport Ave., Lakeview* ☎*773/665–4233.* ✉*566 N. Damen Ave.* ☎*773/489–2001.*

Grace. Shoe fanatics are drawn to this shop's selection of hard-to-find footwear—mostly European lines such as London Sole, Hunter, and Jean-Michel Cazabat. The shop carries just one size per style, so it's unlikely you'll bump into someone wearing the same kicks. Also on display are handbags from designers like Alexis Hudson, Anya Hindmarch, and Cate Adair. ✉*1917 N. Damen Ave., Bucktown* ☎*773/384–7223.*

John Fluevog. Canadian designer Fluevog's chunky platforms and bold designs have graced the famous feet of Madonna and throngs of other loyal devotees, and they can house your toes, too, if you shop here. ✉*1539–41 N. Milwaukee Ave., Wicker Park* ☎*773/772–1983.*

Pump. High heels are in high supply here, but so are plenty of other shoe styles from well-heeled designers like Dolce Vita, Via Spiga, and Kenneth Cole. ✉*1659 W. Division St., Wicker Park* ☎*773/384–6750.*

EYEWEAR **Red Eye.** This full-service boutique stocks a wide array of specs from the likes of Anne Klein and Armani alongside stylish newcomers such as Jai Kudo, Gant, and Skago. There's even an in-house optometrist to make sure your glasses not only look good but help you look better. ✉*1869 N. Damen Ave., Wicker Park* ☎*773/782–1660.*

LINCOLN PARK AND OLD TOWN

The upscale residential neighborhood of Lincoln Park entices with its mix of distinctive boutiques and well-known national chain stores. **Armitage Avenue** between Orchard Street and Racine Avenue is a great source for of-the-moment clothing, tableware, jewelry, and gifts. There are also some good finds (lingerie, French-inspired goodies) on **Webster Avenue.** On **Halsted Street,** between Armitage Avenue and Fullerton Parkway, are chains geared to the young and thin like bebe and The Blues Jean Bar. The **Clybourn Corridor** section of this neighborhood, which runs along North Avenue and Clybourn Avenue, has become akin to a giant urban strip mall, with standbys like J. Crew (*929 W. North Ave.*) and Restoration Hardware (*938 W. North Ave.*) lining the streets. The star of the show, though, is the flagship three-story Crate&Barrel. You'll also find plenty to buy for the little ones, from children's furniture to plush and pricey clothes and gear. Just east of the Clybourn Corridor, around the intersection of **North Avenue** and **Wells Street,** you'll find the cozy, tree-lined streets of Old Town, with upscale clothiers and accessory shops. The Lincoln Park area is easily reached

Ethnic Enclaves

Chicago's ethnic neighborhoods give you the chance to shop the globe without ever leaving the city. Just southwest of the Loop is **Pilsen,** the city's largest Latino neighborhood. A walk along 18th Street between Halsted Street and Western Avenue leads you to a colorful array of bakeries, religious goods shops, and a burgeoning art-gallery district. Stretching south and east from the intersection of Cermak Road and Wentworth Avenue, **Chinatown** has shops selling Far Eastern imports, including jade and ginseng root. On the north side in **Uptown,** a heavy influx of Vietnamese and other Asian trinket shops and imported food stores around the intersection of Broadway and Argyle Street have earned the area the title of "New Chinatown." In the **Lincoln Square** neighborhood on a stretch of Lincoln Avenue between Leland and Lawrence avenues on the city's North Side, you'll still find German restaurants and stores that sell European-made health and beauty

products amid the swell of newer upscale clothing and gift boutiques attracting the hip singles and young families who now call this area home. Heading east to **Andersonville,** you'll find a slew of Swedish restaurants, bakeries, and gift shops along Clark Street between Foster and Balmoral avenues, plus specialty boutiques that sell everything from fine chocolates to eclectic home furnishings. Many non–U.S. visitors make the trek to a cluster of dingy but well-stocked electronics stores on **Devon Avenue** (between Western and Washtenaw avenues) in an Indian neighborhood on the city's Far North Side. The attraction is a chance to buy electronics that run on 220 volts. Because the United States has no value-added tax, it's often cheaper for international visitors to buy here than at home. ■TIP→ **The same stretch of Devon Avenue is also home to a cacophony of great Indian groceries, Bollywood video stores, and fabric shops where you can while away your time.**

by taking the Ravenswood (Brown Line) El to the Armitage stop, or the Howard (Red Line) El to Clybourn. To get to Old Town, take the Ravenswood (Brown Line) El to Sedgwick.

SPECIALTY STORES

ACCESSORIES **Fabrice.** The only Fabrice boutique outside of Paris stocks an abundance of French accessories: its own line of pins, necklaces, and other jewelry inspired by the gardens of Provence, plus Longchamp handbags, pretty wraps and shawls, and bath products. ⊠ *1714 N. Wells St., Old Town* ☎ *312/280–0011.*

Isabella Fine Lingerie. Lauren Amerine, a self-confessed lingerie addict who herself has inspired many obsessions among her loyal clientele, runs this high-end jewel of a shop. Look for affordable items from Cosabella and Le Mystere mixed in with more exclusive lines like Parah and Julianne, plus bridal pieces and swimwear. ⊠ *840 W. Armitage Ave., Lincoln Park* ☎ *773/281–2352.*

The Left Bank. An eclectic mix of antique-style French jewelry brings a touch of Paris chic to Chicago. There's also a beautiful selection of French-theme jewelry boxes, perfume bottles, and other accessories.

Lincoln Park and Old Town Shopping

KEY

M Train Stations (METRA)

— CTA Lines

Owner Susan Jablonski has become known for her large assortment of bridal headpieces and tiaras, and she offers wedding-planning services as well. ✉ *1155 W. Webster Ave., Lincoln Park* ☎ *773/929–7422.*

Quiltology, the Urban Quilt Space. Quilting is the new knitting for funky DIY-ers, and Colette Cogley's Lincoln Park shop stocks everything they need to keep their habit going, including designs by Amy Butler and Kaffe Fassett. Classes and workshops are available in the back-room sewing lounge, too. ✉ *2625 N. Halsted St., Lincoln Park* ☎ *773/880–5994.*

★ **1154 Lill Studio.** Creative types design their own handbags (from chic clutches to diaper totes) from tons of fabric and shape options at this super-popular shop housed in a pretty brownstone. Some limited-edition, ready-made bags are available, too. ✉ *904 W. Armitage Ave., Lincoln Park* ☎ *773/477–5455.*

BEAUTY **Aroma Workshop.** Customize lotions, massage oils, and bath salts with more than 150 essential and fragrance oils in this beauty boutique. The workshop makes its own line of facial-care products, too. ✉ *2050 N. Halsted St., Lincoln Park* ☎ *773/871–1985.*

BOOKS AND MUSIC **Different Strummer.** A sibling to the Different Strummer store in Lincoln Square, this shop within the Old Town School of Folk Music has a good ★ selection of new and used kids' instruments, plus all manner of instruments for rent. ✉ *909 W. Armitage Ave., Lincoln Park* ☎ *773/751–3410* ✉ *4544 N. Lincoln Ave., Lincoln Square* ☎ *773/751–3398.*

Gramaphone Records. Local DJs and club kids go to Gramaphone to find vintage and cutting-edge dance releases, from house to hip-hop, and hear them on the spot at one of the store's listening stations. The store also stocks DJ gear. ✉ *2843 N. Clark St., Lincoln Park* ☎ *773/472–3683.*

Powell's Bookstore. Marxism, the occult, and philosophy all have their own sections at Powell's, which focuses on used, rare, and discounted books and remainders with an intellectual bent. ✉ *2850 N. Lincoln Ave., Lincoln Park* ✉ *1501 E. 57th St., Hyde Park* ☎ *773/955–7780* ☎ *773/248–1444.*

FOR KIDS **Bellini.** Virtually everything a stylish baby will need is here, including top-of-the-line wood bedroom furniture, luxury bedding, and accessories. ✉ *800 N. Clybourn Ave., Lincoln Park* ☎ *321/981–6301.*

Camelot Children's Kingdom. This brightly colored boutique carries American and European clothing lines for babies and children (boys up to age 12, girls to size 14). Some of the brands you'll find are Little Mass and IKKS. Also on offer are cute Room Seven diaper bags and gifts. ✉ *854 Armitage, Lincoln Park* ☎ *773/525–7706.*

FOR BEAUTY-PRODUCT JUNKIES

Bravco Beauty Centre (*43 E. Oak St., Near North, 312/943–4305*) is a favorite of celebs for its expansive stock (48 types of hair extensions, anyone?), and staff who can explain the differences between them. Cash only.

Merz Apothecary (*4716 N. Lincoln Ave., Lincoln Square, 773/989–0900*) has been in business since 1875, and specializes in exclusive European lines and holistic and herbal remedies.

The Land of Nod. Crate&Barrel is a next-door neighbor (and business partner) to this quirky-cool children's furniture store. There are plenty of parent-pleasing designs, plus loads of fun accessories, toys, and a great music section, too. ✉*900 W. North Ave., Lincoln Park* ☎*312/475–9903.*

LMNOP. Tykes can get their posh on early with duds from this high-end kids' clothes shop; designers include Flora & Henri and Judith LaCroix, and sizes go up to an 8. ✉*2570 N. Lincoln Ave., Lincoln Park* ☎*773/975–4055.*

Piggy Toes. This store stocks a good (though pricey) selection of European footwear for well-heeled children. ✉*2205 N. Halsted St., Lincoln Park* ☎*773/281–5583* ✉*4548 N. Western Ave., Lincoln Square* ☎*773/878–1122.*

Stinky Pants. Parents can shop high-end kids' clothing lines like Eye Spy Baby and Lucy Sykes while their progeny entertain themselves with books and toys in the store's kid-friendly "stinky lounge." ✉*844 W. Armitage Ave., Lincoln Park* ☎*773/281–4002.*

CLOTHING
FOR MEN

Haberdash. Owner Adam Beltzman ditched his job as a lawyer to set up shop in Old Town. Tailored clothes and accessories from designers like John Varvatos, Ted Baker, and James Perse plus leather armchairs, plasma TV, and dark-wood walls make this store decidedly masculine. ✉*1350 N. Wells St., Old Town* ☎*312/440–1300.*

CLOTHING
FOR MEN AND
WOMEN

Barneys New York CO-OP. The CO-OP in Chicago has an urban-loft feel, an enormous inventory of designer denim, and lots of hip accessories. ✉*2209–11 N. Halsted St., Lincoln Park* ☎*773/248–0426.*

Guise/Chic. For men and women who want to look good without having to hit a dozen shops, Guise is the place. This one-stop shop stocks designer clothes from Theory, Earnest Sewn, J Brand jeans, and Filippa K. Separate salons offer shoeshines, haircuts, and barbershop-style shaves for men, and cut and color, hair extensions, and eyebrow shaping for women. Flat-screen televisions in the women's lounge are tuned to E!; in the men's, to sports channels. ✉*2128 N. Halsted St., Lincoln Park* ☎*773/929–6101.*

Out of the West. With an inventory that includes saddles, hats, and boots, there's a definite nod to urban cowboys at this Lincoln Park shop. But fashionistas won't feel left out either—especially if they're in the market for fancy-pants blue jeans from premium brands like Seven and Blue Cult. A tailor visits the store weekly to do custom alterations on jeans. ✉*1021 W. Armitage Ave., Lincoln Park* ☎*773/404–9378.*

Uncle Dan's. This is the place to go for camping, skiing, and general outdoorsy gear by brands like Marmot and The North Face. There's a good kids' selection, too. ✉*2440 N. Lincoln Ave., Lincoln Park* ☎*773/477–1718* ✉*3551 N. Southport Ave., Lakeview* ☎*773/348–5800.*

CLOTHING
FOR WOMEN

Art Effect. This modern-day general store stocks trendy clothes and accessories at approachable prices—think Michael Stars T-shirts, Weston Wear blouses, Orla Kiely babydoll dresses, and Me&Ro necklaces. There are also gifts and home furnishings ranging from candles and bath products to mortar-and-pestle sets and juicers. ✉*934 W. Armitage Ave., Lincoln Park* ☎*773/929–3600.*

7

Cynthia Rowley. Cynthia Rowley is a Chicago-area native, and she fills her Lincoln Park store with the exuberant, well-priced dresses, separates, and accessories that have made her so popular. ⊠*810 W. Armitage Ave., Lincoln Park* ☎*773/528–6160* ⊠*1653 N. Damen, Bucktown* ☎*773/276–9209.*

Fox's. Snap up canceled and overstocked designer clothes from the likes of Tahari and ABS at 40% to 70% discounts. New shipments come in several times a week, so there's always something new to try on. ⊠*2150 N. Halsted St., Lincoln Park* ☎*773/281–0700.*

Mint Julep. Sarah Eshaghy's keen eye for style developed a loyal following at the long-popular Tribeca on the Avenue. She's outdone herself at her new Lincoln Park boutique, chock-full of fabulous fashions from the likes of Tulle, Susanna Monaco, and Shoshanna, as well as K.Amato jewelry. The best news: more than half the inventory is priced under $100, so you can stock up without breaking the bank. ⊠*1013 W. Armitage Ave., Lincoln Park* ☎*773/296–2997* ⊠*3709 N. Southport Ave., Lakeview* ☎*773/472–6717.*

GIFTS   **Barker & Meowsky.** This "paw firm" carries great gifts for dogs, cats, and humans. There are beautiful bowls, plush beds, picture frames, treats, and even pet massage and grooming services—just the things to get tails wagging. ⊠*1003 W. Armitage Ave., Lincoln Park* ☎*773/868–0200.*

Paul Frank Store. Young fans of the designer's famous trademarked monkey, Julius, will find his likeness on stickers, slippers, and sunglasses. Scurvy, a skull and crossbones; Ellie, a pink elephant; and the designer's other kitschy characters are also well represented. ⊠*851 W. Armitage Ave., Lincoln Park* ☎*773/388–3122.*

Vosges Haut-Chocolat. Local chocolatier Katrina Markoff's exotic truffles, flavored with spices like curry and ancho chili, have fans across the globe. Her ever-expanding line of goodies now includes caramels, ice cream, chocolate tortilla chips, and even yoga wear and dresses. ⊠*951 W. Armitage Ave., Lincoln Park* ☎*773/296–9866* ⊠*520 N. Michigan Ave., Near North* ☎*312/822–9450.*

FOR THE HOME   **Bedside Manor.** Dreamland is even more inviting with these handcrafted beds and lush designer linens, many of which come in interesting jacquard weaves or are nicely trimmed and finished. ⊠*2056 N. Halsted St., Lincoln Park* ☎*773/404–2020.*

Fodor'sChoice   **CB2.** A concept store by furniture giant Crate&Barrel, CB2 got its start
★   right here in Chicago. The idea is stylish, bold basics for trendy urban abodes, all sans big-ticket price tags. ⊠*800 W. North Ave., Lincoln Park* ☎*312/787–8329.*

Crate&Barrel. There are plenty to "oohs" and "aahs" throughout the three floors of stylish home furnishings and kitchenware at Crate&Barrel's flagship location. There's plenty of free parking, and you can even take a break from your heavy-duty shopping at the top-floor café. ⊠*850 W. North Ave., Lincoln Park* ☎*312/573–9800.*

Crate&Barrel Outlet. Around the corner from the massive outpost of the flagship store, the outlet carries odds and ends from the company's housewares and kitchen lines. Look for discounts of up to 75% on out-of-season items. ⊠*1864 N. Clybourn Ave., Lincoln Park* ☎*312/787–4775.*

Unpacking Crate&Barrel

Gordon and Carole Segal saw a void in the Chicago retail market in 1962, and they set out to fill it by opening the first Crate&Barrel store in an abandoned elevator factory in the then-questionable Old Town neighborhood.

"I was doing the dishes—classic Arzberg dishes we had picked up on our Caribbean honeymoon—and I said to Carole, 'How come nobody is selling this dinnerware in Chicago?'," Gordon Segal recalls. "I think we should open a store." And, as they say, the rest is history. With "more taste than money," the Segals displayed their unique housewares en masse on the crates and barrels they were shipped in, and found a niche and a name.

At a time when gas-station give-away glasses were common kitchen table fixtures, shoppers were immediately drawn to the grocery store-style displays of contemporary merchandise at reasonable prices. As the business grew, store displays became more sophisticated and the inventory more diverse.

Before the age of home-improvement cable television shows, the Segals brought accessible design into the American home. They added the Finnish fabric line Marimekko to their inventory in the late 1960s, and the bold, colorful prints became a signature style of the era.

Carole retired to raise their family, but Gordon Segal still runs the Chicago-based company they founded together 48 years ago, now a dominant home-furnishings chain with 123 stores across the United States. Always keeping his motto, "Stay humble, stay nervous," in the back of his mind, Segal has continued to fine-tune Crate&Barrel throughout its history, creating shopping environments that engage the senses. He pays close attention to the exteriors, too, focusing on building stores with architectural merit. Stores in Illinois, Pennsylvania, and Chicago have received awards for their outstanding architectural design.

The home-furnishings industry has exploded since Crate&Barrel's humble beginnings, and Segal has kept a keen eye on what interests the buying public. In 2000 Crate&Barrel launched CB2, a new concept store aimed at a young urban market with—again—a single store on Chicago's North Side. And, so that no one in the family feels left out, in 2001 Crate&Barrel formed a partnership with Land of Nod, a quirky children's furniture catalog company. They opened one store— guess where?—on Chicago's North Side to start, and have since expanded to five locations. The Segal empire just keeps growing.

–By Judy Sutton Taylor

Jayson Home & Garden. Loaded with new and vintage European and American furnishings, this decor store carries the Mitchell Gold line. Look for oversize cupboards and armoires and decorative accessories, plus stylish garden furniture and a bevy of beautiful floral arrangements. ✉ *1885 N. Clybourn Ave., Lincoln Park* ☎ *800/472–1885.*

★ **A New Leaf.** You'll find one of the best selections of fresh flowers in town here. The breathtaking Wells Street space, designed by architect Cynthia Weese, is also stocked with singular antique and vintage furnishings and accessories as well as a mind-boggling selection of candles, vases, tiles, and pots. ✉ *1818 N. Wells St., Old Town* ☎ *312/642–8553* ✉ *1645 N. Wells St., Lincoln Park* ☎ *312/642–1576* ✉ *312 S. Dearborn St., South Loop* ☎ *312/427–9097.*

Tabula Tua. The colorful, contemporary, mix-and-match dishes and table-top accessories here are worlds away from standard formal china. Other offerings include breathtaking mosaic tables handmade to order, rustic furniture crafted from old barn wood, and sleek, polished pewter pieces. ✉ *1015 W. Armitage Ave., Lincoln Park* ☎ *773/525–3500.*

SHOES

Fodor'sChoice

★

Lori's Designer Shoes. Owner Lori Andre's obsession with shoes takes her on biannual trips to Europe to scour for styles you won't likely see at department stores. The result is an inventory that many fine-footed women consider to be the best in Chicago. Shoes by designers like Gastone Lucioli, janet & janet, and better-known ones like Franco Sarto are sold at discounts of 10% to 30% in a self-serve atmosphere. Terrific handbags, jewelry, bridal shoes, and other accessories are also available. ✉ *824 W. Armitage Ave., Lincoln Park* ☎ *773/281–5655.*

LAKEVIEW

Lakeview, a large neighborhood just north of Lincoln Park, has spawned a number of worthwhile shopping strips, including a smattering of antiques shops around Belmont and Ashland avenues. **Clark Street** between Diversey Avenue and Addison Street has myriad clothing boutiques and specialty stores such as pet boutiques and rug dealers, as well as stores filled to the gills with Chicago Cubs paraphernalia as you approach Wrigley Field at Addison. The area farther north on **Halsted Street,** between Belmont Avenue and Addison Street, is known as Boystown; here you'll find more gift shops and boutiques, many with a gay orientation, as well as vintage-clothing and antiques stores. In West Lakeview the latest hot spot is **Southport Avenue** between Belmont Avenue and Grace Street, where a recent onslaught of boutiques with a bent toward trendy upscale fashion has put it on the "must" list. **Broadway** between Diversey Avenue and Addison Street also claims its share of intriguing shops. The **Century Mall,** in a former movie palace at Clark Street, Broadway, and Diversey Parkway, houses some chain stores (Aveda, Victoria's Secret, Express), but has a tired feel compared with the rest of the area. To reach this neighborhood from downtown, take the 22 Clark Street bus at Dearborn Street or the 36 Broadway bus at State Street heading north. Or, take the Howard (Red Line) or Ravenswood (Brown Line) El north to the Belmont stop from downtown, which will drop you into the heart of Lakeview, near the intersection of Belmont and Sheffield avenues.

ANTIQUES DISTRICTS

BELMONT
AVENUE

Fans of Art Deco, kitchen collectibles, and bar gadgets can poke into the shops and malls lining Belmont Avenue, starting a bit west of Ashland Avenue and running to Western Avenue. You may have to scrounge around to unearth treasures in these stores, but the prices are some of the lowest in the city. The shops are usually open weekends, but may be closed on one or more weekdays. Call before making a special trip.

Blitz Tour: One-of-a-Kind Finds

Get ready for some serious spending—or at least some serious ogling. This itinerary is geared to the antiques lover in you; find exact addresses in the chapter's store listings.

Chicago tempts furniture buyers with antiques, collectibles, and architectural artifacts at prices that generally beat those on either coast. In fact, dealers from all over regularly troll these shops, which are clustered mostly in neighborhoods or malls, for stock to resell in their own shops. For a rundown on dealers, buy a copy of *Taylor's Guide to Antique Shops in Illinois & Southern Wisconsin* ($6), which is available in some bookstores and many antiques shops (to order, call ☎800/829–5677 or go to ⊕*www.taylorsguide.com*). Many antiques districts also publish free pamphlets that list dealers in the neighborhood; look for them in the shops.

To catch the maximum number of open dealers, it's best to tackle this route after brunch on a weekend or on a Thursday or Friday. Assuming your interest runs more toward 20th-century collectibles than Biedermeier,

this tour focuses mostly on the West Lakeview neighborhood (north of Lincoln Park and west of Wrigley Field). Take the 11 Lincoln Avenue bus or a taxi to the **Chicago Antique Centre** to browse through the wares of its 35 dealers. Keep your eyes open for other antiques and vintage-clothing shops along this stretch of Lincoln Avenue. Two superb sources for adventurous, mid-20th-century, modern furnishings and collectibles are **Urban Artifacts** and the Art Deco and Art Nouveau treasures at **Smyth son Yeats Antiques**.

There are three other compelling destinations for collectors that are short cab rides away. **Architectural Artifacts** is an amazing repository for statuary, garden ornaments, and the like. **Lincoln Antique Mall** stockpiles everything from kitchenware to furniture, mostly post-1920. There's also a huge selection of estate jewelry and photographs. Farthest north on the antiques trail is the **Broadway Antique Market**, with its excellent stash of mid-20th-century pieces that range from Art Deco and Arts and Crafts to modernism and beyond.

7

Antique Resources. Choice Georgian antiques are sold at fair prices. This is an excellent source for stately desks and dignified dining sets, but the true find is a huge trove—numbering more than 300—of antique crystal and gilt chandeliers from France. ⊠*1741 W. Belmont Ave., Lakeview* ☎*773/871–4242.*

Father Time Antiques. Father Time bills itself as the Midwest's largest restorer of vintage timepieces; it also stocks vintage Victorian and Art Deco European furniture. ⊠*2108 W. Belmont Ave., Lakeview* ☎*773/880–5599.*

LINCOLN AVENUE AND ENVIRONS A 1½-mi stretch of Lincoln Avenue is worth a visit for its funky antiques, collectibles, and vintage clothing. The shops start around the intersection of Lincoln Avenue and Diversey Parkway and continue until Irving Park Road. A car or the 11 Lincoln Avenue bus is the best way to navigate this area. To get the bus from downtown, take the Howard (Red Line) or Ravenswood (Brown Line) El to the Fullerton stop; after exiting

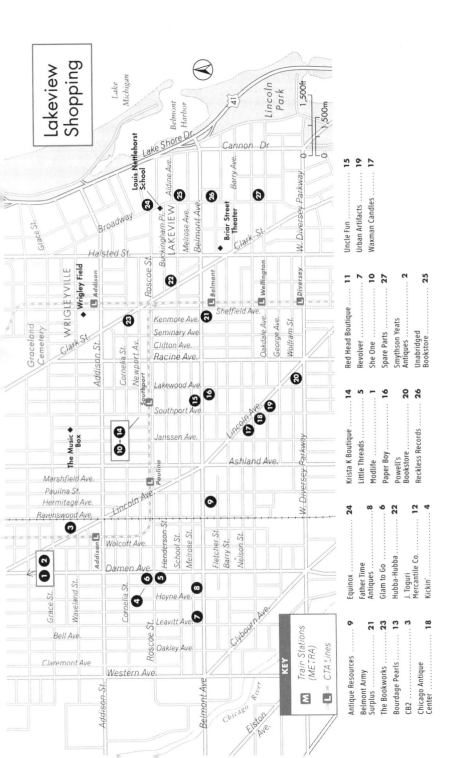

Lakeview Shopping

Antique Resources **9**	
Belmont Army Surplus **21**	
The Bookworks **23**	
Bourdage Pearls **13**	
CB2 . . . . **3**	
Chicago Antique Center **18**	

Equinox **24**	
Father Time Antiques **8**	
Glam to Go **6**	
Hubba-Hubba **22**	
J. Toguri Mercantile Co. **12**	
Kickin' **4**	

Krista K Boutique **14**	
Little Threads **5**	
Modlife **1**	
Paper Boy **16**	
Powell's Bookstore **20**	
Reckless Records **26**	

Red Head Boutique **11**	
Revolver **7**	
She One **10**	
Spare Parts **27**	
Smythson Yeats Antiques **2**	
Unabridged Bookstore **25**	

Uncle Fun **15**	
Urban Artifacts **19**	
Waxman Candles **17**	

KEY

M Train Stations (METRA)

L CTA Lines

the El station, walk ½ block east to the intersection of Fullerton and Lincoln. Then catch the 11 Lincoln Avenue bus to your stop. Most of these shops are open weekends, but may be closed early in the week.

Chicago Antique Centre. Open seven days a week, this one-stop spot houses 35 dealers on two levels, some with especially good selections of vintage dishes and jewelry. ✉ *3036 N. Lincoln Ave., Lakeview* ☎ *773/929–0200.*

Modlife. The emphasis here is on mid-20th-century finds from Herman Miller, Eames, Hans Olsen, and other well-known designers. You'll also find original abstract paintings and sculptures and overall affordable price points. ✉ *3856 N. Lincoln Ave., Lakeview* ☎ *773/868–0844.*

Smythson Yeats Antiques. An always-changing selection here includes plenty of Art Deco and Art Nouveau treasures, with an impressive selection of lamps, chandeliers, and ceramics. There are plenty of fabulous larger pieces, too—dark-wood sideboards, bookcases, and plush leather chairs. Lamp-repair service is available. ✉ *3851 N. Lincoln Ave., Lakeview* ☎ *773/244–6365.*

Urban Artifacts. A superb selection of furniture, lighting, and decorative accessories from the 1940s to the '70s emphasizes the industrial designs that are a popular theme in modern furnishings. ✉ *2928 N. Lincoln Ave., Lakeview* ☎ *773/404–1008.*

SPECIALTY STORES

BOOKSTORES **The Bookworks.** The stock here includes more than 40,000 titles, most of them used or rare. There's an emphasis on sports (for Cubs fans strolling by from nearby Wrigley Field) and contemporary fiction. Check out the vintage-vinyl-record section. The store buys used books in good condition, too. ✉ *3444 N. Clark St., Lakeview* ☎ *773/871–5318.*

Powell's Bookstore. This is one of the oldest and most reliable independent bookshops around; the strength here is the section featuring art, architecture, and photography. Also check out the impressive collection of rare books. ✉ *2850 N. Lincoln Ave., Lakeview* ☎ *773/248–1444* ✉ *828 S. Wabash Ave., South Loop* ☎ *312/341–1078* ✉ *1501 E. 57th St., Hyde Park* ☎ *773/955–7780.*

Unabridged Bookstore. For more than 20 years this independent bookshop has maintained a loyal clientele who love its vast selection and dedicated staff. Known for having one of the most extensive gay and lesbian selections in the city, it also has an impressive children's section and great magazines, too. ✉ *3251 N. Broadway, Lakeview* ☎ *773/883–9119.*

CLOTHING
FOR MEN AND
WOMEN **Belmont Army Surplus.** Puma, Diesel, and other funky brands get mixed in with fatigues, flak jackets, and even faux-fur coats in this neighborhood mainstay, which was forced to move to a new location by a CTA platform expansion project. Despite the name, don't expect too many

bargains. ⊠*855 W. Belmont Ave., Lakeview* ☎*773/549–1038* ⊠*1318 N. Milwaukee Ave., Bucktown* ☎*773/384–8448.*

Hubba-Hubba. Flowy, feminine clothes with a retro flavor mix with vintage and modern jewelry and accessories at this packed-to-the-gills shop that feels like rummaging through your best friend's closet. ⊠*3309 N. Clark St., Lakeview* ☎*773/477–1414.*

Kickin'. Hip, urban women snap up their maternity wear at this new shop. There's an emphasis on workout and yoga gear. ⊠*2142 W. Roscoe St., Lakeview* ☎*773/281–6577.*

Krista K Boutique. An inventory of must-haves for women from designers like Citizens of Humanity, Theory, and Helen Wang reflects the style of the neighborhood. The shop has become the go-to spot for the latest denim trends, too. Down the street is the maternity branch, where stylish expectant moms shop a selection that includes casual non-maternity clothes with a little extra give. ⊠*3458 N. Southport Ave., Lakeview* ☎*773/248–1967* ⊠*3530 N. Southport Ave., Lakeview* ☎*773/248–4477.*

Red Head Boutique. This colorful jewel of a shop carries a limited inventory of girly clothes with a fun and funky edge, suitable for young trendoids and cool neighborhood moms alike. Look for local labels like Doris Ruth and hard-to-find ones like Beverly & Monika. ⊠*3450 N. Southport Ave., Lakeview* ☎*773/325–9898.*

Revolver Chicago. Look effortlessly rock-star cool with threads from this menswear boutique. Video games and complimentary drinks draw in even uninspired shoppers. ⊠*2135 W. Belmont Ave., Lakeview* ☎*773/832–4866.*

She One. A plentiful assortment of bright T-shirts, oh-so-pretty dresses, and trendy jewelry dresses the stylish young urban woman. ⊠*3402 N. Southport Ave., Lakeview* ☎*773/549–9698.*

FOR THE HOME **CB2.** House-proud locals with tight budgets come to this Crate&Barrel
Fodor'sChoice offshoot for kitchenware and accessories that look great but don't break
★ the bank. ⊠*3757 N. Lincoln Ave., Lakeview* ☎*773/755–3900.*

Equinox. Equinox literally glows from within, thanks to its Tiffany-style lamps, but the true strength here is the selection of Arts and Crafts–style art tiles and reproduction pottery. ⊠*3401 N. Broadway Ave., Lakeview* ☎*773/281–9151.*

J. Toguri Mercantile Company. This warehouse-style store carries all things Asian, including tea sets, lacquerware, kimonos, hard-to-find pots, and Japanese music. ⊠*851 W. Belmont Ave., Lakeview* ☎*773/929–3500.*

FOR KIDS **Little Threads.** Junk Food, Oink Baby, and Zutano are just some of the funky kids' labels at this cute neighborhood shop. There's also a fun selection of children's reading material and even cool diaper bags for mom. ⊠*2033 W. Roscoe St., Lakeview* ☎*773/327–9310.*

GIFTS AND **Bourdage Pearls.** Sherry Bourdage sells Chinese freshwater pearls in a
GOODIES staggering array of colors and styles that range from simple and inexpensive to elaborate custom designs. ⊠*3530 N Southport Ave., Lakeview* ☎*773/244–1126.*

Glam to Go. The lotions and potions found here will help you stay soft and smelling good. There's also clothing by Language, Talla, Scrapbook, and others for getting glammed up. ⊠*2002 W. Roscoe St., Lakeview* ☎*773/525–7004.*

Spare Parts. The selection of fine leather goods here draws on a gamut of sources, including Village Tannery, Jack Spade, and local designer Susan Fitch. Jewelry, bath and body products, and home accessories round out the selection. ✉*2947 N. Broadway, Lakeview* ☎*773/525–4242.*

Uncle Fun. The astonishing and goofy inventory of new and vintage tricks, gags, party favors, and more, delight young and old—as do the reasonable prices. ∎**TIP➜ Think trendy bobble-head dolls and the Official John Travolta Picture/Postcard book.** The store is closed Monday. ✉*1338 W. Belmont Ave., Lakeview* ☎*773/477–8223.*

Waxman Candles. The candles sold here are made on the premises and come in countless shapes, colors, and scents. There's an incredible selection of holders for votives and pillars, and incense, too. ✉*3044 N. Lincoln Ave., Lakeview* ☎*773/929–3000.*

MUSIC STORE **Reckless Records.** Reckless Records ranks as one of the city's leading alternative and secondhand record stores. Besides the indie offerings, you can flip through jazz, classical, and soul recordings, or catch a live appearance by an up-and-comer passing through town. ✉*3161 N. Broadway, Lakeview* ☎*773/404–5080* ✉*1532 N. Milwaukee Ave., Wicker Park* ☎*773/235–3727* ✉*26 E. Madison St., Loop* ☎*312/795–0878.*

PAPER **Paper Boy.** A hip sensibility informs the cards, gift wrap, and invitations sold here by the people who bring you the quirky goods at Uncle Fun across the street. ✉*1351 W. Belmont Ave., Lakeview* ☎*773/388–8811.*

WORTH A SPECIAL TRIP

ANTIQUES & COLLECTIBLES

Architectural Artifacts. The selection matches the warehouse proportions here. The mammoth two-story space houses oversize garden ornaments (arbors, benches), statuary, iron grills, fixtures, and decorative tiles. Architectural fragments—marble, metal, wood, terra-cotta—hail from American and European historic buildings. ✉*4325 N. Ravenswood Ave., Ravenswood* ☎*773/348–0622.*

★ **Broadway Antique Market.** More than 75 hand-picked dealers, plus quality that is more carefully monitored than at most malls, make it worth the trek to the Broadway Antique Market, affectionately called BAM by its loyal fans. Mid-20th century is the primary emphasis, but items range from Arts and Crafts and Art Deco to Heywood-Wakefield. Display is the market's strong suit—the furniture, jewelry, and bibelots are wonderfully presented. The building itself is a prime example of Deco architecture; it's near the Thorndale stop on the Red Line. The Edgewater Antique Mall (✉*6314 N. Broadway* ☎*773/262–2525*), which specializes in 20th-century goods, is a couple of blocks north. ✉*6130 N. Broadway, Edgewater* ☎*773/743–5444.*

Lincoln Antique Mall. Dozens of dealers carrying antiques and collectibles share this large space. There's a good selection of French and mid-20th-century modern furniture, plus estate jewelry, oil paintings, and photographs, but you can find virtually anything and everything here. ✉*3115 W. Irving Park Rd., Northwest Side* ☎*773/604–4700.*

★ **Salvage One.** An enormous warehouse chock-full of stained leaded glass, garden ornaments, fireplace mantels, bathtubs, bars, and other architectural artifacts draws creative home remodelers and restaurant designers from around the country. ■ TIP➔ This is the place to hunt for all kinds of treasures, from vintage dental chairs to Paris street lamps. ⊠*1840 W. Hubbard St., Ukrainian Village* ☎*312/733–0098.*

APOTHECARY

★ **Merz Apothecary.** This old-fashioned druggist stocks all manner of homeopathic and herbal remedies, as well as a great selection of hard-to-find European toiletries, cosmetics, candles, and natural laundry products. It's closed Sunday. There's an outlet in the Macy's on State Street as well. ⊠*4716 N. Lincoln Ave., Lincoln Square* ☎*773/989–0900.*

BOOK & MUSIC STORES

Women & Children First. This feminist bookstore 6½ mi north of the Loop stocks fiction and nonfiction, periodicals, journals, small-press publications, and a strong selection of gay and lesbian titles. The children's section has a great array of books, all politically correct. ⊠*5233 N. Clark St., Andersonville* ☎*773/769–9299.*

FOR HOME AND GARDEN

A Cooler Planet. Sisters Heidi Bailey and Krista White research every item they carry in their "whole lifestyle" shop. The result is a selection of attractive, practical, and guilt-free goods made from fairly traded, organic, and sustainable materials, many of which are locally made. Displays take you from morning (natural bath products, Blue Canoe yoga wear) to night (organic cotton bedding, reclaimed-wood beds). ⊠*2211 W. Roscoe St., Roscoe Village* ☎*773/248–1110.*

Rotofugi. A toy store for grown-up kids, Rotofugi specializes in artist-created, limited-edition toys considered art (not playthings) by customers and owners alike. You'll find dozens of specialty lines from the United States, China, and Japan, like CiBoys Mini Destroyers and toys by H. Moto. The store also hosts a series of revolving gallery exhibitions. ⊠*1953 W. Chicago Ave., Ukrainian Village* ☎*312/491–9501.*

Sprout Home. If your tastes run toward modern furnishings, you'll drool over every nook and cranny of this store, which sells lines like Vessel, Pure, and Thomas Paul for your indoor life, plus unusual plants and gardening products for your outdoor one. ⊠*745 N. Damen Ave., Ukrainian Village* ☎*312/226–5950.*

HATS

Optimo Hat Co. One of the last stores of its kind, Optimo makes high-end custom straw and felt hats for men in an atmosphere that evokes 1930s and '40s haberdashery. The store also offers a complete line of hat services, from cleaning and blocking to repairs. ⊠*10215 S. Western Ave., Beverly* ☎*773/238–2999.*

WESTERN

Alcala's Western Wear. Alcala stocks more than 10,000 pairs of cowboy boots—many in exotic skins—for men, women, and children. About 2½ mi west of Michigan Avenue, it's a bit out of the way, but the amazing array of Stetson hats and rodeo gear makes this a must-see for cowboys, caballeros, and country-and-western dancers. ⊠*1733 W. Chicago Ave., Ukrainian Village* ☎*312/226–0152.*

Entertainment

WORD OF MOUTH

Then took the bus to Andy's Jazz club for dinner and music. Loved this place. We just ordered 4 small plates and shared them. They delivered them like a 4 course meal and the wait staff was great. We stayed for 2 sets and bought [the group's] CD (We never do that . . .). We had some Chicago beer (Blue Goose) and decided to splurge on a cab back to the hotel—only $6 with tip.

—Brahmama

ENTERTAINMENT PLANNER

Find out What's Going On

To find out what's happening in the Windy City, check out the following: the *Chicago Tribune*'s Metromix.com, *Time Out Chicago* magazine or Web site (⊕ *www.timeout.com/chicago*), the *Chicago Reader*, an alternative newsweekly and Web site (⊕ *www.chicagoreader.com*), and Centerstage. net, which has a calendar of music and theater events.

Getting There

Parking in North Side neighborhoods, particularly Lincoln Park and Lakeview, is increasingly scarce, even on weeknights. If you're going out in these areas, take a cab or the El. The Red, Brown, and Blue lines will get you within a few blocks of most major entertainment destinations downtown and on the North and Near Northwest sides. If you do decide to drive, use the curbside valet service available at many restaurants and clubs for about $6 to $9. If you're headed to the South Side, be cautious about public transportation late at night. It's best to drive or cab it here.

Get Tickets

You can save money on seats at **Hot Tix** (⊕ *www.hottix. org*), where unsold tickets are available, usually at half price (plus a service charge) on the day of performance; you won't know what's available until that day. On Friday, however, you can buy tickets for Saturday and Sunday. Hot Tix booths are at the Chicago Tourism Center at 72 East Randolph Street and at the Chicago Water Works Visitor Center at the southeast corner of Michigan Avenue and Pearson Street. Both Hot Tix booths are closed on Monday. Hot Tix also functions as a Ticketmaster outlet, selling advance, full-price, cash-only tickets.

You can charge full-price tickets over the phone or online at **Ticketmaster** (☎ *312/559–1212 for rock concerts and general-interest events, 312/902–1500 arts line* ⊕ *www. ticketmaster.com*).

For hot, sold-out shows, such as performances by the Chicago Symphony Orchestra or the Lyric Opera of Chicago, call a day or two before the show to see if there are any subscriber returns. Another option is to show up at the box office on concert day—a surprising number of people strike it lucky with on-the-spot tickets due to cancellations.

Small fees can have big payoffs! Many of the smaller neighborhood street festivals (there are hundreds in summer) request $5 to $10 donations upon entry, but it's often worth the expense: big-name bands are known to take the stage of even the most under-publicized festivals. For moment-to moment festival coverage, check out ⊕ *www. metromix.com*.

Don't Light Up

In January 2008 a statewide smoking ban took effect that prohibits lighting up in any public building. While most Chicagoans are breathing easier and relishing the new smoke-free scene, the throngs of smokers huddled outside nightclubs and bars may not agree, especially when temperatures drop below freezing.

Festivals

The **Chicago Humanities Festival** (☎*312/661–1028* ⊕*www.chfestival.org*), held the first two weeks of November, brings internationally renowned artists, authors, and cultural critics to various venues across the city for a series of lectures, films, and performances.

For two weeks in October the **Chicago International Film Festival** (☎*312/332–3456* ⊕*www.chicagofilmfestival. org*) screens more than 100 films, including premieres of Hollywood films, international releases, documentaries, short subjects, animation, videos, and student films. Movie stars usually make appearances at the opening events.

Grant Park Music Festival (☎*312/742–7638* ⊕*www. grantparkmusicfestival.com*), a program of the Chicago Park District, gives free concerts June through August in the spectacular new Frank Gehry–designed Jay Pritzker Pavilion in Millennium Park. Tote along dinner and make a full night of the performance by the superb Grant Park Orchestra and Chorus. Concerts are usually Wednesday, Friday, and Saturday evenings.

The annual **Pitchfork Festival** (☎*No phone* ⊕*www.pitchforkmusicfestival.com*) is a three-day concert spotlighting emerging bands. It has also drawn veterans like Sonic Youth, Public Enemy, and Yoko Ono. It's held every July in Union Park on the Near West Side.

In summer you can enjoy the Chicago Symphony at the **Ravinia Festival** (☎*847/266–5100* ⊕*www.ravinia.org*) in Highland Park, a 25-mi train trip from Chicago. The park is lovely, and lawn seats are a fun, low-cost alternative to the pavilion. Spread a blanket and enjoy music under the stars. Ravinia also draws crowds with jazz, pop, and dance concerts.

In early June the **Chicago Blues Festival** (☎*312/744–3370* ⊕*www.chicagobluesfestival.org*), the largest free blues festival in the world, rocks the city. Blues legends such as B.B. King, Koko Taylor, and Buddy Guy have all headlined the festival, and blues lovers from around the world—most notably Chuck Berry and Keith Richards—have been known to attend (and sometimes take the stage).

Labor Day weekend blasts off with the unmistakable sounds of the **Chicago Jazz Festival** (☎*312/744–3370*). Set in Grant Park, the four-day festival offers not only a prime lakefront locale, but also free performances by local, national, and international musicians and special tributes to jazz legends.

Raves and Faves

Pointe of Pride: Joffrey Ballet of Chicago

Most Wanted Tickets: Lyric Opera of Chicago

Hits Closest to Home: Steppenwolf Theatre Company

Sharpest Wits: The Second City

Hours

Live music starts around 9 PM at bars around town. If you want to guarantee a seat, arrive well before the band's scheduled start and stake out a spot.

Bars close at 2 AM Friday and 3 AM Saturday. A few dance clubs and late-night bars remain open until 4 AM or 5 AM.

Curtain calls for performances are usually at 7:30 or 8 PM.

8

Updated by
Heidi Moore

CHICAGO'S ARTS AND NIGHTLIFE SCENE is as vivacious and diverse as its neighborhoods. Sing along with a biographical musical at Black Ensemble Theater to the north or zip over to Lincoln Park's renowned Steppenwolf Theatre, where you just might run into longtime ensemble member John Malkovich. Head for the Loop, where renowned companies such as the Lyric Opera and the Joffrey Ballet hold court. And remember that this is the city that gave birth to the often-raucous "poetry slam" at the Green Mill jazz club.

Nighttime entertainment options before and after hours are infinite—as long as you're willing to explore. Sip an imported Belgian beer at Hopleaf, a cozy North Side tavern, or tap into your wild side at a downtown dance club such as Sound-Bar. And we can't forget to mention comedy: Second City has been unleashing top comedic talents, including Stephen Colbert, Mike Myers, and Tina Fey, for decades.

GREAT PERFORMANCES

If you're even mildly interested in the performing arts, Chicago has the means to put you in your seat—be it floor, mezzanine, or balcony. Just pick your preference (theater, dance, or symphony orchestra), and let Chicago's impressive body of artists do the rest. From critically acclaimed big names to fringe groups that specialize in experimental work, there truly is a performance art for everyone.

Ticket prices vary wildly, depending on whether you're seeing a high-profile group or venturing into more obscure territory. Chicago Symphony tickets range from $15 to $200, the Lyric Opera from $30 to $180 (if you can get them). Smaller choruses and orchestras charge from $10 to $30; watch the listings for free performances. Commercial theater ranges from $15 to $75; smaller experimental ensembles might charge $5, $10, or pay-what-you-can. Movie prices range from $9 for first-run houses to as low as $1.50 at some suburban second-run houses.

■TIP➜For free, live music in summer, head downtown to the classically oriented Grant Park Music Fest and the jam-packed Chicago Blues and Chicago Jazz festivals. Held at the visually stunning Millennium Park and Grant Park, they offer a cheap way to experience some of the best sights and sounds Chicago has to offer. See the Festivals section in the Planner for more information.

TOP 5 PERFORMANCES

Joffrey Ballet. Fine-tuned performances, such as the glittering production of *The Nutcracker*, make this Chicago's premier classical-dance company. Treat yourself to one of several annual performances at the Auditorium Theatre and help celebrate more than 50 seasons of superb ballet. ☎312/739–0120 ⊕*www.joffrey.com.*

Lookingglass Theatre Company. Marvel at offbeat and fantastically acrobatic performances inside the belly of the historic Chicago Water Works building. The company's physically and artistically daring works incorporate theater, dance, music, and circus arts. ☎*312/337–0665* ⊕*www.lookingglasstheatre.org.*

Fodor's Choice ★ **Steppenwolf.** The alumni roster speaks for itself: John Malkovich, Gary Sinise, Joan Allen, and Laurie Metcalf all honed their chops with this troupe. The company's trademark cutting-edge acting style and consistently successful productions have won national acclaim. ☎*312/335–1650* ⊕*www.steppenwolf.org.*

Ⓒ **Chicago Symphony Orchestra.** Two internationally celebrated conductors, two in-house award-winning composers, and more than 150 magnificent performances a year make the Chicago Symphony Orchestra a musical tour de force. The impressive annual roster offers regular concerts and special theme series including classical, chamber, and children's concerts. Tickets are sometimes scarce, but they do become available; call or check the Web site for status updates. If you buy your tickets online, click on the "Know Your Seats" section, where you can see photos of the views of the stage from different seats. ☎*312/294–3000* or 800/223–7114 ⊕*www.cso.org* � *Sept.–June.*

★ **Lyric Opera of Chicago.** The big voices of the opera world star in these top-flight productions. This is one of the top two opera companies in America today. Don't worry about understanding German or Italian; English translations are projected above the stage. All of the superb performances have sold out for more than a dozen years, and close to 90% of all Lyric tickets go to subscribers—the key to getting in is to call the Lyric in early August, when individual tickets first go on sale. ☎*312/332–2244* ⊕*www.lyricopera.org* ☉ *Sept.–Mar.*

BEAUTIFUL VOICES: HIGHLY RECOMMENDED VOCAL PERFORMANCES

From a cappella to opera, the City of Big Shoulders has some of the nation's top vocal groups. Treat the kids to a sprightly concert by the Chicago Children's Choir or hear the sacred sounds of Bella Voce reverberate from the walls of a gorgeous church. The following are our picks for the most beautiful voices in the city.

CHORAL AND CHAMBER GROUPS

Apollo Chorus of Chicago (☎*312/427–5620* ⊕*www.apollochorus.org*), formed in 1872, is one of the country's oldest oratorio societies. Don't miss the annual Handel's *Messiah* if you're here in December. Otherwise, the group performs various choral classics throughout the year at area churches.

Bella Voce (☎*312/479–1096* ⊕*www.bellavoce.org*). "Beautiful voices," indeed. Formerly known as His Majestie's Clerkes, the 20-person a cappella group performs a variety of sacred and secular music, including everything from early music to works by living composers. Concerts are often held in churches throughout the city, providing a powerful acoustical and visual accompaniment to the music. The season runs October through May.

Ⓒ A performance by the **Chicago Children's Choir** (☎*312/849–8300* ⊕*www. ccchoir.org*) is the closest thing we can imagine to hearing angels sing.

Its members—ages 8 to 18—are culled from a broad spectrum of racial, ethnic, and economic groups. Performances, selected from an international music base, take place during the holiday season and in May. Other concerts are scheduled periodically, sometimes in the Chicago Cultural Center's Preston Bradley Hall.

Take a step back in time with **Music of the Baroque** (☎*312/551–1414* ⊕*www.baroque.org*), one of the Midwest's leading music ensembles specializing in baroque and early classical music. See one of seven yearly programs at either Millennium Park's Harris Theater or one of several beautiful Chicago-area churches. Performances run from September to May.

The small but mighty **Oriana Singers** (☎*773/262–4558* ⊕*www.oriana. org*) are an outstanding a cappella sextet with an eclectic early, classical, and jazz repertoire. The close-knit traveling group performs from September to June, periodically in conjunction with Joffrey Ballet and other Chicago-area groups.

OPERA

Chicago Opera Theater (☎*312/704–8414* ⊕*www.chicagooperatheater. org*) shrugs off esoteric notions of opera, preferring to make productions that are accessible to aficionados and novices alike. The production of *Nixon in China,* a contemporary American opera detailing conversations between the former U.S. President and Henry Kissinger (among others), is a shining example of the company's open-mindedness toward the operatic canon. From innovative versions of traditional favorites to important lesser-known works, the emphasis is on both theatrical and musical aspects. Fear not—performances are sung in English, or in Italian with English supertitles projected above the stage. They're held at the Harris Theater for Music and Dance in Millennium Park.

Light Opera Works (☎*847/869–6300* ⊕*www.light-opera-works.org*) favors the satirical tones of the distinctly British Gilbert and Sullivan operettas, but takes on frothy Viennese, French, and other light operettas and American musicals from June to early January. Performances take place in Evanston, just north of the city and easily accessible by train or the El line.

HIGHLY RECOMMENDED DANCE AND THEATER TROUPES

Chicago's reputation as a dance and theatrical powerhouse stems from its impressive roster of small, independent companies that produce every type of work you could imagine, from jazz-inflected ballets to avant-garde musicals. The groups and venues listed here are known for consistently interesting work, and a few have gained national reputations. Be open-minded when you're choosing a show; even a group you've never heard of may be harboring one or two underpaid geniuses. *The Reader* carries complete dance and theater listings, plus reviews of the more avant-garde shows.

DANCE

Athenaeum Theatre (✉ *2936 N. Southport Ave., Lakeview* ☎ *773/935–6860* ⊕ *www.athenaeumtheatre.com*) hosts innovative small dance companies and local theater ensembles in a restored 1,000-seat performance space.

The Dance Center of Columbia College Chicago (✉ *1306 S. Michigan Ave., South Loop* ☎ *312/344–8300* ⊕ *www.colum.edu/dancecenter*) presents thought-provoking fare with leading national and international contemporary-dance artists.

Hubbard Street Dance Chicago (☎ *312/850–9744* ⊕ *www.hubbardstreetdance.com*), Chicago's most notable success story in dance, exudes a jazzy vitality that has made it extremely popular. The style mixes classical-ballet techniques, theatrical jazz, and contemporary dance.

Luna Negra Dance Theater (☎ *312/337–6882* ⊕ *www.lunanegra.org*) has rapidly become one of Chicago's standout dance troupes, staging highly original performances by Latino choreographers, including its Cuban-born founder and artistic director Eduardo Vilaro.

Muntu Dance Theatre of Chicago (☎ *773/602–1135* ⊕ *www.muntu.com*) showcases dynamic interpretations of contemporary and traditional African and African-American dance. Artistic director Amaniyea Payne travels to Africa to learn traditional dances and adapts them for the stage.

Trinity Irish Dance Co. (☎ *773/529–4822* ⊕ *www.trinity-dancers.com*), founded long before *Riverdance,* promotes traditional and progressive Irish dancing. In addition to the world-champion professional group, you can also catch performances by younger dancers enrolled in the Trinity Academy of Irish Dance.

THEATER

About Face Theatre (☎ *773/784–8565* ⊕ *www.aboutfacetheatre.com*) is the city's best-known gay, lesbian, bisexual, and transgender performing group, which in its short history has garnered awards for original works, world premieres, and adaptations presented in larger theaters like Steppenwolf and the Goodman.

Bailiwick Repertory Theatre (☎ *773/883–1090* ⊕ *www.bailiwick.org*) stages new and classical material at various theaters around town. Its Pride Performance series, held every summer, focuses on plays by gays and lesbians.

★ **Black Ensemble Theater** (✉ *4520 N. Beacon St., Ravenswood* ☎ *773/769–4451* ⊕ *www.blackensembletheater.org*) has a penchant for long-running musicals based on popular African-American icons. Founder and executive producer Jackie Taylor has written and directed such hits as *The Jackie Wilson Story* and *The Other Cinderella.*

★ **Chicago Shakespeare Theater** (✉ *800 E. Grand Ave., Near North* ☎ *312/595–5600* ⊕ *www.chicagoshakes.com*) devotes its considerable talents to keeping the Bard's flame alive in the Chicago area, with at least three plays a year. The best part? The Courtyard Theater, on Navy Pier, has sparkling views of the city, and seats are never farther than 30 feet from the thrust stage.

City Lit Theatre (✉*1020 W. Bryn Mawr Ave., Edgewater* ☎*773/293–3682* ⊕*www.citylit.org*) produces notable staged readings and full productions of famous literary works—by the likes of Henry James, Alice Walker, and Raymond Carver—as well as original material with a literary bent.

Collaboraction (✉*437 N. Wolcott Ave., Ukrainian Village* ☎*312/226–9633* ⊕*www.collaboraction.org*) lets actors, artists, and musicians share the stage together in an experimental free-for-all that puts the "fun" in dysfunctional. Of its several performances a year, we recommend Sketchbook—a series of 15 to 20 seven-minute-long plays—for its color and energy.

ETA Creative Arts Foundation (✉*7558 S. Chicago Ave., Grand Crossing* ☎*773/752–3955* ⊕*www.etacreativearts.org*), a South Side performing-arts center, has established a strong presence for African-American theater. In addition to showcasing new works by black playwrights, the space is home to an art gallery and a library. The best way to get here is by taxi.

Neo-Futurists (✉*5153 N. Ashland Ave., Uptown* ☎*773/275–5255* ⊕*www.neofuturists.org*) perform their long-running, late-night hit *Too Much Light Makes the Baby Go Blind* in a space—oddly enough—above a funeral home. The piece is a series of 30 ever-changing plays performed in 60 minutes; the order of the plays is chosen by the audience. In keeping with the spirit of randomness, the admission price is set by the roll of a die, plus $7.

Fodor's Choice
★ **Redmoon Theater** (☎*312/850–8440* ⊕*www.redmoon.org*) tells imaginative, almost magical stories that weave together puppetry and live action. The company's annual outdoor spectacle series stages madcap theater in unlikely places, from community parks to a lagoon. The series usually takes place in the fall, but experimental theater would be nothing if not unpredictable, so be sure to call for confirmation. Other performances are held in a West Side warehouse known as Redmoon Central.

★ **Victory Gardens Theater** (✉*2433 N. Lincoln Ave., Lincoln Park* ☎*773/871–3000* ⊕*www.victorygardens.org*) is known for its workshop productions and Chicago premieres. After buying the landmark Biograph Theater (site of John Dillinger's infamous demise) in 2006, the company stages all its productions in the impressive 299-seat proscenium-thrust house. Victory Gardens' original theater, now called the Greenhouse, hosts plays by local production companies on four stages.

AFTER DARK

Chicago's entertainment varies from loud and loose to sophisticated and sedate. You'll find classic Chicago corner bars in most neighborhoods, along with trendier alternatives like wine bars and lounges. The strains of blues and jazz provide much of the backbeat to the city's groove, and an alternative country scene is flourishing. As far as dancing is concerned, take your pick from cavernous clubs to smaller spots with DJs spinning dance tunes; there's everything from hip-hop to swing. Wicker

CINEMATHEQUE

The rowdy crowd at **Brew and View** comes for cheap flicks—both newer releases and cult faves—and beer specials. ✉ *Vic Theatre* ☎ *773/929-6713* ⊕ *www.brewview.com.*

For a change of scenery, watch current and classic films under the stars at the **Chicago Outdoor Film Festival,** which runs July through August in Grant Park on Tuesday nights. ☎ *312/742-7529.*

Facets Cinematheque shows independent and art films in its cinema and video theater. ☎ *773/281-4114* ⊕ *www.facets.org.*

Gene Siskel Film Center screens new releases from around the globe

and revivals of cinematic classics; the best part is that filmmakers often make appearances at screenings. ☎ *312/846-2600* ⊕ *www.artic. edu/webspaces/siskelfilmcenter.*

If you love old theaters, old movies, and ghosts (rumor has it the theater is haunted by the spirit of its original manager), don't miss a trip to the **Music Box Theatre.** ☎ *773/871-6604* ⊕ *www.music boxtheatre.com.*

For IMAX and OMNIMAX theaters, go to the Museum of Science and Industry (☎ *773/684-1414* ⊕ *www. msichicago.com*) or the Navy Pier (☎ *312/595-5629* ⊕ *www.navypier. com*).

Park and Bucktown have the hottest nightlife, but prime spots such as Sound-Bar and Le Passage are spread throughout the city.

The Chicago Reader (distributed midweek in bookstores, record shops, and other city establishments) is your best guide to the entertainment scene. This free weekly has comprehensive, timely listings and reviews. Another reliable weekly is *Time Out Chicago* magazine. The Friday editions of the *Chicago Tribune* and *Chicago Sun-Times* are also good sources of information. Daily updates on happenings around town are listed in the *Chicago Tribune's* sister paper, *RedEye,* or on the Web at ⊕ *www.metromix.com.*

The list of blues and jazz clubs includes several South Side locations: be cautious about transportation here late at night, because some of these neighborhoods can be unsafe. Drive your own car or ask the bartender to call you a cab.

BARS

Chicago bars—whether they're sports bars, wine bars, neighborhood bars, or even trendy bars—are surprisingly accessible. With few exceptions, snobbishness and exclusivity are not tolerated throughout the scene, so bring your ID (many places card at the door), pocket some cash, and join the party!

■ TIP➔ **If you're sticking to downtown and North Side bars, it's relatively safe to patronize public transportation. But if you're planning on staying out past midnight, we suggest taking a cab home.**

CHECK IT OUT

For complete music and theater listings, check two weeklies, *The Chicago Reader* and *TimeOut Chicago,* both published midweek; the Friday and Sunday editions of the *Chicago Tribune* and *Chicago Sun-Times*; and the monthly *Chicago* magazine.

If you're interested in Broadway-scale shows, contact the following theaters to see what's playing while you're in town.

Auditorium Theatre of Roosevelt University (☎ *312/922–2110* ⊕ *www.auditoriumtheatre.org*).

Chicago Theatre (☎ *312/462–6300* ⊕ *www.thechicagotheatre.com*).

Goodman Theatre (☎ *312/443–3800* ⊕ *www.goodman-theatre.org*).

Ford Center for the Performing Arts/Oriental Theatre (☎ *312/782–2004 or 312/902–1400* ⊕ *www.broadwayinchicago.com*).

LaSalle Bank Theatre (☎ *312/902–1400 or 312/977–1700* ⊕ *www.broadwayinchicago.com*).

For other performances, check out:

Athenaeum Theatre (☎ *773/935–6860* ⊕ *www.athenaeumtheatre.com*).

Briar Street Theatre (☎ *773/348–4000 or 800/258–3626*).

Cadillac Palace Theatre (☎ *312/977–1700* ⊕ *www.broadwayinchicago.com*).

Drury Lane Theatre Water Tower Place (☎ *312/642–2000* ⊕ *www.drurylanewatertower.com*).

Joan W. and Irving B. Harris Theater for Music and Dance (☎ *312/334–7777* ⊕ *www.harristheaterchicago.org*).

Royal George Theatre Center (☎ *312/988–9000* ⊕ *www.theroyalgeorgetheatre.com*).

Storefront Theater at Gallery 37 Center for the Arts (☎ *312/742–8497* ⊕ *www.dcatheater.org*).

Theatre Building (☎ *773/327–5252* ⊕ *www.theatrebuildingchicago.org*).

Theatre on the Lake (☎ *312/742–7994* ⊕ *www.chicagoparkdistrict.com*).

For concerts, try the following halls:

Chicago Cultural Center (☎ *312/346–3278 or 312/744–6630* ⊕ *www.cityofchicago.org*).

Mandel Hall at the University of Chicago (☎ *773/702–7300 or 773/702–8068*).

Newberry Library (☎ *312/943–9090* ⊕ *www.newberry.org*).

LOOP, SOUTH LOOP AND WEST LOOP

Sleek and sexy wine bars and lounges light up Chicago's core business district after work and on weekends. Beware: downtown bars are seldom budget-friendly (but often worth the money).

Encore (⊠ *171 W. Randolph St., Loop* ☎ *312/338–3788*) is a jazzed-up hotel lounge sandwiched between the Cadillac Palace Theatre and the Hotel Allegro. Clubby seating and a classic cocktail menu make it an appealing downtown destination for post-dinner or -theater drinks, a light bite, and conversation.

Fulton Lounge (⊠*955 W. Fulton Market, West Loop* ☎*312/942–9500*) is largely responsible for Fulton Market District's flourishing nightlife scene. The stylish lounge is all about clean-lined and understated elegance, from the slender bar right down to the low-slung swivel chairs and seasonal martinis. A sophisticated crowd mingles on the patio in summer months.

Ghost Bar (⊠*440 W. Randolph St., West Loop* ☎*312/575–9900*) is a sexy downtown space perched above the restaurant Nine. Cool and futuristic, with cushy vinyl banquettes and designer seating, the bar is white as a, well, you know what, and the muted lighting casts the fashion-conscious crowd in silhouette.

Kitty O'Shea's (⊠*Chicago Hilton and Towers, 720 S. Michigan Ave., South Loop* ☎*312/922–4400*), a handsome room in the Chicago Hilton and Towers, is an authentic Emerald Isle pub with all things Irish, including live music seven nights a week, beer, food, and bar staff.

The Tasting Room (⊠*1415 W. Randolph St., Loop* ☎*312/942–1313*) makes the short list of nightspots where Chicagoans take guests they want to impress. This two-story wine bar has a casual, loft-chic look and sweeping skyline views. More than 100 wines are poured by the glass or flight, and over 300 by the bottle. Cheese, caviar, and other light bites are the perfect complement. If you love the vintage you taste here, buy a bottle to take home at the adjacent wine shop, Randolph Wine Cellars.

Whiskey Blue (⊠*172 W. Adams St., Loop* ☎*312/782–4933*), inside the W Hotel–City Center, attracts a sophisticated crowd. The sleek, dimly lighted lounge is outfitted with leather chairs, mohair banquettes, and low-slung tables, which encourage leaning in close over an excellent martini.

NEAR NORTH AND RIVER NORTH

The famous Chicago bar scene known as **Rush Street** has faded into the mists of time, although the street has found resurgent energy with the opening of a string of upscale restaurants and outdoor cafés. For the vestiges of the old Rush Street, continue north to trendy **Division Street**, between Clark and State streets. The crowd here consists mostly of suburbanites and out-of-towners on the make. The bars are crowded and noisy. Among the better-known singles' bars are **Butch McGuire's** (⊠20 W. Division St., Near North ☎312/337–9080), the **Lodge** (⊠21 W. Division St., Near North ☎312/642–4406), and **Original Mother's** (⊠26 W. Division St., Near North ☎312/642–7251).

Reprieve from the bustling Division Street scene is only a few blocks south, in the Near North and River North neighborhoods. Hunker down in a low-key lounge or sip a hearty pint of Guinness at an authentic Irish pub. Whatever your preference, plenty of conversation-friendly bars are a brief cab ride away.

Everyone's welcome at **Citizen Bar** (⊠*364 W. Erie St., River North* ☎*312/640–1156*), a sleek space with exposed brick walls and traditional bar fare. But the real draw is the huge, multi-level outdoor area, one of the city's most coveted spots come summer.

8

CLASSIC CHICAGO SPOTS

Imbibe your way through a history lesson at these Chicago institutions.

The Omni Ambassador East's glamorous **Pump Room** (⊠ *1301 N. State Pkwy., Old Town* ☎ *312/266–0360*) is the spot for anyone interested in the Golden Age of Hollywood. Booth One alone has played host to more celebrities than Oprah Winfrey's couch, including Humphrey Bogart, Lauren Bacall, Irv "Kup" Kupcinet, and Judy Garland.

The **Green Mill** (⊠ *4802 N. Broadway, Far North Side* ☎ *773/878–5552*), opened in 1914 in Uptown, has undergone quite a few makeovers and owners (including Al Capone). We like its current incarnation: dark-wood carvings, passionate jazz, and intimate booths.

Since the 1960s, **Original Mother's** (⊠ *26 W. Division St., Near North* ☎ *312/642–7251*) has been a local favorite for cutting-edge music and dance-'til-you-drop partying. The subterranean singles' destination was immortalized by Demi Moore, Jim Belushi, and Rob Lowe in the film *About Last Night*.

Crimson Lounge (⊠ *333 N. Dearborn St., River North* ☎ *312/923–2453*), in the Hotel Sax, delivers on its name—red leather couches, red satin perches, and plush red rugs break up the wood–dominated interior. Every detail adds to the swanky atmosphere, from the ornate furnishings to the exotic scent created for the room.

Fado (⊠ *100 W. Grand Ave., River North* ☎ *312/836–0066*) uses imported wood, stone, and glass to create its Irish look. The second floor—with a bar imported from Dublin—feels more like the real thing than the first. There's expertly drawn Guinness, a fine selection of whiskeys, live music on weekends, and a menu of traditional dishes.

Hub 51 (⊠ *51 W. Hubbard St., River North* ☎ *312/828–0051*) features a vaulted, loft-like industrial space. Sip cocktails with the after-work crowd and then linger for inventive light bites or more substantial fare. Downstairs lounge space **Sub 51** serves up DJ-driven beats, but get there early or reserve a table.

Lumen (⊠ *839 W. Fulton Market, West Town* ☎ *312/733–2222*) is worth the difficulty getting here—it's in in a former meatpacking plant in the out-of-the-way warehouse district. Once inside, you'll find a clean-lined space with low-slung modular seating, sleek bamboo tables, and a stainless-steel bar. The white walls are lit by thousands of tiny lights that pulse with the music—mostly cool electronica and trip-hop beats. Best of all, there's no velvet rope or exclusionary attitude.

Motel (⊠ *600 W. Chicago Ave., River North* ☎ *312/822–2900*) has all the comforts of a real, honest-to-goodness motel bar (TVs tuned to sports, classic cocktails, and a retro color scheme), but the atmosphere is amped-up with sexy, low-rise furniture and a "room service" menu of upscale bites.

Designer Nate Berkus assembled **Rockit's** (⊠ *22 W. Hubbard St., River North* ☎ *312/645–6000*) hunter-lodge look: wood-plank-framed plasma TVs, antler chandeliers, and brown-leather booths. The crowd, much like the beer list, is diverse and tasteful, and despite the masculine vibe, there's a good mix of men and women. Dress to impress.

★ The **Signature Lounge** (✉️ *875 N. Michigan Ave., Near North* ☎312/787–9596) has no competition when it comes to views. Perched on the 96th floor of the John Hancock Center—above even the tower's observation deck—the bar offers stunning vistas of the skyline and lake for only the cost of a pricey drink. The ladies' room has an incredible south-facing view through floor-to-ceiling windows.

Swirl Wine Bar (✉️ *111 W. Hubbard St., River North* ☎312/828–9000) has a cozy, shabby-chic lounge and snob-free approach to wine that is enough to disarm even the most jaded oenophiles. Some 25 wines are available by the bottle, glass, quartino, and flight, and are thoughtfully arranged by flavor instead of region.

WICKER PARK AND BUCKTOWN

Hip cats, artists, and yuppies converge on the famed six corners of North, Milwaukee, and Damen avenues, where the cast of Real World Chicago once resided. Previously scruffy and edgy, the area is now dotted with pricey, upscale bars, though the occasional honky-tonk still survives.

California Clipper (✉️ *1002 N. California Ave., Wicker Park* ☎773/384–2547), in Humboldt Park, just to the west of Wicker Park, has a 1940s vintage look, including a curving 60-foot-long Brunswick bar and tiny booths lining the long room back-to-back like seats on a train. Alternative country acts and soul-gospel DJs are part of the eccentric musical lineup.

The Map Room (✉️ *1949 N. Hoyne Ave., Bucktown* ☎773/252–7636) might help you find your way around Chicago, if not the world. Guidebooks decorate the walls of this self-described "travelers' tavern," and the beers represent much of the world. Tuesday is international buffet night; each week brings a different country's cuisine.

Nick's Beer Garden (✉️ *1516 N. Milwaukee Ave., Wicker Park* ☎773/252–1155) is a neighborhood favorite, especially in the wee hours (it's open until 4 AM; 5 AM Sunday). Kitschy tropical decor—think palm trees, flamingos, and a surfboard—adds to the appeal.

Northside Bar & Grill (✉️ *1635 N. Damen Ave., Wicker Park* ☎773/384–3555) was one of the first anchors of the now-teeming Wicker Park nightlife scene. Arty (and sometimes slightly yuppie) types come to drink, eat, shoot pool, and see and be seen. The enclosed indoor–outdoor patio lets you get the best out of the chancy Chicago weather.

The highly stylized **Rodan** (✉️ *1530 N. Milwaukee Ave., Wicker Park* ☎773/276–7036) is a restaurant and lounge that caters mostly to the

8

young neighborhood hipsters who arrive at dinnertime (served until 11 PM) and stay put until closing. The narrow space often feels cramped, but if you can snag a spot at the bar or on a blue-suede banquette, an evening of major-league people-watching is in store. Snacks are served all night, so refuel with a pile of wasabi-tempura fries.

Silver Cloud Bar & Grill (✉*1700 N. Damen Ave., Bucktown* ☎*773/489–6212*) might be the only place in the city where you can order a champagne cocktail alongside sloppy joes and tater tots and not open yourself up to a citizen's arrest. For us, that's reason enough to go. Spacious red-leather booths, retro fringed lamps, friendly service, and an upbeat neighborhood crowd round out the good points.

★ **Sonotheque** (✉*1444 W. Chicago Ave., Wicker Park* ☎*312/226–7600*), with its tasteful, modern design and sparse, podlike seating, is one of the more visually interesting lounges in Chicago. A thoughtful Scotch list, high-profile DJs, and down-to-earth service bring heavy crowds to West Town, a few blocks south of Wicker Park, on weekends.

★ **The Violet Hour** (✉*1520 N. Damen Ave., Wicker Park* ☎*773/252–1500*) channels a Prohibition-era speakeasy—an unmarked door in the boarded-up façade leads to a mysterious, curtained hallway. Inside, twinkling crystal chandeliers cast a glow on cornflower-blue walls, and extremely high-backed blue leather chairs encourage intimate conversations. Add to that pricey but flawlessly executed cocktails and a sign discouraging cell-phone use, and it's our idea of nightlife heaven.

LINCOLN PARK

One of the most beautiful (and bustling) neighborhoods on the north side of Chicago, Lincoln Park is largely defined by the DePaul students who inhabit the area. Irish pubs and sports bars line the streets with college students, but chic wine bars attract an older, more sophisticated set.

Clybar (✉*2417 N. Clybourn Ave., Lincoln Park* ☎*773/388–1877*) is one of the few Lincoln Park bars not filled to the brim with frat boys. Inside, sophisticates of all ages gather to sip stiff drinks and carry on conversations. Booths and a roomy backroom couch are perfect for groups of four or more. Twinkling lights, dark-wood furniture, and a cherrywood fireplace add a touch of romance for those in the mood.

Delilah's (✉*2771 W. Lincoln Ave., Lincoln Park* ☎*773/472–2771*) is a rare dive bar amid Lincoln Park's tonier establishments. Dark and a bit grungy, the bar has a friendly, unpretentious vibe and a standout whisky selection (more than 300 types on offer). DJs spin punk and rockabilly.

Faith & Whiskey (✉*1365 W. Fullerton Ave., Lincoln Park* ☎*773/248–9119*) stands out among Lincoln Park bars with its hard-rock focus. Silver-framed replicas of famous guitars line the wall, along with black-and-white photos of rock stars, antler chandeliers, steer skulls and, suspended above the restrooms, twin motorcycles.

John Barleycorn (✉*658 W. Belden Ave., Lincoln Park* ☎*773/348–8899*), a historic pub with a long wooden bar, can get somewhat rowdy despite the classical music (played until 8 PM) and the art slides shown on video screens. It has a spacious summer beer garden, a good pub menu, and a wide selection of beers. There's another location: 3524 North Clark Street in Wrigleyville.

Krem (✉*1750 N. Clark St., Lincoln Park* ☎*312/932–1750*) is part subterranean lounge and part South Beach–style disco, with an all-white interior awash in blue and green lights. Leather sofas and a wall-hugging lounge bed are prime seating. A champagne bar serves up bubbly, and a menu of light bites keeps patrons from going hungry.

Webster's Wine Bar (✉*1480 W. Webster Ave., Lincoln Park* ☎*773/868–0608*), a romantic place for a date, stocks more than 500 bottles of wine—with at least 30 by the glass—as well as ports, sherries, single-malt Scotches, a few microbrews, and a menu of small tasting entrées at reasonable prices.

LAKEVIEW AND FAR NORTH SIDE

Lakeview, Uptown, and Andersonville, all on the Far North Side, have one thing in common: affordability. Unbelievable as it sounds, there are places in the city where $20 stretches beyond the price of admission and a martini. Drink deals are frequently offered at many bars.

Enter through rowdy Jack's Bar & Grill to find the serene **404 Wine Bar** (✉*2852 N. Southport Ave., Lakeview* ☎*773/404–5886*), a romantic spot filled with cozy nooks. The library-like back room has ornate chandeliers, shelves lined with books, and dramatic oxblood walls. You can grab a spot on the patio or near one of two fireplaces and enjoy a glass, flight, or bottle of wine accompanied by a cheese plate.

Gingerman Tavern (✉*3740 N. Clark St., Lakeview* ☎*773/549–2050*), up the street from Wrigley Field, deftly manages to avoid being pigeonholed as a sports bar. Folks here take their beer and billiards seriously, with three pool tables and—our favorite part—a list of more than 100 bottles of beer. New and vintage tunes crank out of the jukebox all night long.

Holiday Club (✉*4000 N. Sheridan Rd., Far North Side* ☎*773/348–9600*) bills itself as the "Swinger's mecca." Rat Pack aficionados will appreciate the 1950s decor and well-stocked CD jukebox, which has selections ranging from Dean Martin and Frank Sinatra to early punk. Down a pint of good beer (or even bad beer in cans) and scan the typical (but tasty) bar menu.

★ **Hopleaf** (✉*5148 N. Clark St., Far North Side* ☎*773/334–9851*), an anchor in the Andersonville corridor, continues the tradition of the classic Chicago bar hospitable to conversation (not a TV in sight). Pick one of the too-many-to-choose-from beers on the menu, with an emphasis on Belgian beers and regional microbrews. A menu of Belgian bar fare usurps typical bar food options. Don't miss the ale-steamed mussels and delectable skinny fries served with aioli.

Space is so limited at **Joie de Vine** (✉*1744 W. Balmoral Ave., Far North Side* ☎*773/989–6846*), the wine barely has room to breathe. Good design (and sidewalk tables in summer months) keeps things from feeling claustrophobic. Sit at the long wooden bar or opposing banquette and enjoy the real focal point of the room, a glass-brick wall lit up in multiple colors. All sorts of tasty delights, from wine (available in

BARS WITH VIEWS

Vertigo is a small price to pay for these stellar views.

Castaways (⊠ *1603 N. Lake Shore Dr., River North* ☎ *773/281–1200*) puts you so close to Lake Michigan, you might consider wearing a swimsuit. Perched atop the North Avenue Beach Boathouse, the breezy, casual bar and grill creates the perfect setup for lazy, summertime sipping.

When it comes to heights, **Signature Lounge** (⊠ *875 N. Michigan Ave., Near North* ☎ *312/787–9596*)—set on the 96th floor of the John Hancock Center—is in a category all its own. Drinks and appetizers are pricey but well worth it: the cityscape views are simply unmatched.

Glittering panoramic views of Lake Michigan and the city draw visitors worldwide to **Whiskey Sky** (⊠ *644 N. Lake Shore Dr., Near North* ☎ *312/943–9200*). The W Hotel–Lakeshore's plush, low-lit lounge also offers tasty cocktails, a cool vibe, and owner Rande Gerber's seal of approval.

flights or by the glass) to olives and cheese, are reasonably priced. Try stopping by on a weeknight when the neighborhood regulars are least likely to crowd the slender bar.

Sheffield's (⊠ *3258 N. Sheffield Ave., Lakeview* ☎ *773/281–4989*) spans the seasons with a shaded beer garden in summer and a roaring fireplace in winter. This laid-back neighborhood pub has billiards and more than 100 kinds of bottled beer that change seasonally, including regional microbrews, the bartender's "bad beer of the month"—a cheap can of beer (think PBR)—as well as 18 brands on tap.

CAFÉS

High-maintenance ("half-caff-double-foam-soy-latte-to-go") and low-maintenance ("cup 'o joe, black") coffee drinkers feel at home in the diverse range of cafés dotting the streets of Chicago's busiest North Side neighborhoods. Expect to spend anywhere from $2 to $6 (depending on your order) for a caffeinated beverage.

NEAR NORTH, WICKER PARK AND BUCKTOWN

Café Ballou's (⊠ *939 N. Western Ave., near Wicker Park* ☎ *773/342–2909*). European charm lies in details like a squishy couch, pressed-tin ceiling, and marble tables. The inviting atmosphere at this café nestled in the Ukrainian Village, near Wicker Park, is a far cry from Starbucks. Choose from a menu of international sippers that are served according to tradition, like Turkish coffee brewed on a hot plate inside a mound of sand, or Russian tea drizzled with cherry compote. The friendly owner speaks fluent Polish and Ukrainian with her customers, many of whom are local neighborhood immigrants.

Caffe de Luca (⊠ *1721 N. Damen Ave., Bucktown* ☎ *773/342–6000*) is the place to go when you crave air and light with your caffeine and calories. This sophisticated Bucktown spot hints at Tuscany with richly colored walls and a fine selection of Italian sandwiches, salads, and sorbets.

Earwax (⊠*1561 N. Milwaukee Ave., Wicker Park* ☎*773/772–4019*) is a mecca for local vegans and vegetarians looking to order scrambled tofu alongside their ordinary cup of coffee. Well-worn, comfy furniture and a quirky staff go hand-in-hand with the relaxed atmosphere and kitschy decor (colorful carnival banners adorn the walls). Stop by for coffee, sweets, or a light meal.

Third Coast Café (⊠*1260 N. Dearborn St., Near North* ☎*312/649–0730*), the oldest coffeehouse in the Gold Coast, pleases just about everyone with a full menu served until midnight seven nights a week. The inviting space combines warm woods, etched glass, and funky local art. A diverse clientele—from students and twentysomethings to retirees living nearby—comes for coffee, Sunday brunch, or late-night jazz sessions.

LAKEVIEW AND FAR NORTH SIDE

Intelligentsia (⊠*3123 N. Broadway, Lakeview* ☎*773/348–8058*) was named to invoke the pre-chain days when cafés were forums for discussion, but the long, broad farmer's tables and handsome couches are usually occupied by students and other serious types who treat the café like their office. The store does all of its own coffee roasting and sells its house blends to local restaurants.

Kopi, a Traveler's Cafe (⊠*5317 N. Clark St., Far North Side* ☎*773/989–5674*) is a study in opposites, with healthy vegetarian options as well as decadent desserts. In the Andersonville neighborhood, a 20-minute cab ride from downtown, this café has a selection of travel books, global gifts, and artfully painted tables.

The original location of **Uncommon Ground** (⊠*3800 N. Clark St., Lakeview* ☎*773/929–3680*) is roomy and inviting, with a hand-carved bar and large street-facing windows offering views of passersby. Patrons brave the wait for bowls of coffee and hot chocolate. There's also a full bar and a hearty menu. Fun perks include two fireplaces, a sidewalk café, and a steady lineup of acoustic musical acts. A hugely popular second location at 1401 West Devon Avenue on the Far Northwest Side gets bonus points for eco-friendliness, with a green roof, solar panels, and tables made from reclaimed wood.

COMEDY AND IMPROV CLUBS

Improvisation has long had a successful following in Chicago; stand-up comedy hasn't fared as well. Most comedy clubs have a cover charge ($5 to $20); many have a two-drink minimum on top of that. In the stand-up circuit, keep an eye out for performances by Steve Harvey, star of his own WB television series.

Barrel of Laughs (⊠*10345 S. Central Ave., Oaklawn* ☎*708/499–2969*), in the city's southwest suburbs (a 30-minute drive from downtown), spotlights local and national comics. The dinner package includes a meal at the adjacent Senese's restaurant and reserved seats at the show.

ComedySportz (⊠*929 W. Belmont Ave., Lakeview* ☎*773/549–8080*) specializes in "competitive improv," in which two teams vie for the audience's favor. Book a family-friendly early performance or a late-night show rife with raunchy humor. The space features cabaret-style seating and a full bar.

I.O. (✉*3541 N. Clark St., Lakeview* ☎*773/880–0199*) (formerly called ImprovOlympic) has shows with student and professional improvisation in two intimate spaces every night of the week. Team members present long-form comedic improvisations drawn on audience suggestions, including an improvised musical and a Monday-night alumni show. No drink or age minimum.

★ **Second City** (✉*1616 N. Wells St., Near North* ☎*312/337–3992*), an institution since 1959, has served as a launching pad for some of the hottest comedians around. Alumni include Dan Aykroyd and the late John Belushi. Funny, loony skit comedy is presented on two stages, with a free improv set after the show every night but Friday.

Zanies (✉*1548 N. Wells St., Near North* ☎*312/337–4027*) books outstanding national talent and is Chicago's best stand-up comedy spot. Jay Leno, Jerry Seinfeld, and Jackie Mason have all performed at this intimate venue.

DANCE CLUBS

Most clubs don't get crowded until 11 or midnight, and they remain open into the early morning hours. Cover charges range from $5 to $20. A few dance clubs have dress codes that don't allow jeans, gym shoes, or baseball caps.

To avoid the exhausting lines and cover charges at most nightclubs, chat with your hotel concierge or even your server at dinner. Admission into the VIP lounges of Chicago's hottest clubs is often a conversation-with-the-right-person away from becoming a reality.

Great news for those who like to club-hop: most of Chicago's best dance clubs (Sound-Bar, Transit, and Le Passage, to name a few) are within the Near North and River North neighborhoods, just north of downtown. The close proximity makes it relatively easy (and cheap) to cab it from one club to another. Wicker Park and Lakeview are also good 'hoods for when you feel like dancing.

Fodor'sChoice
★ **Berlin** (✉*954 W. Belmont Ave., Lakeview* ☎*773/348–4975*), a multicultural, pansexual dance club near the Belmont El station, has progressive electronic dance music and fun theme nights—Madonna and Prince are celebrated on the first and last Sunday of the month, and one Wednesday a month is devoted to disco. The crowd tends to be predominantly gay on weeknights, mixed on weekends.

Crobar—The Nightclub (✉*1543 N. Kingsbury St., Near North* ☎*312/266–1900*) has scrapped its scruffy, Goth-like decor for a sprawling South Beach makeover complete with a glass-enclosed VIP lounge and booth-lined balcony. Top DJs spin house and techno over the enormous dance floor on Wednesday, Friday, and Saturday nights.

★ **Enclave** (✉*220 W. Chicago Ave., River North* ☎*312/654-0234*) has a loftlike feel and three bars spread out on two floors. Sip a snazzy cock-

Looking for Laughs? Try Improv

Mike Myers, Tina Fey, Bill Murray, John Belushi, Dan Aykroyd, Alan Alda, Shelley Long, Ed Asner, John Candy, Andy Dick. These are just a few of the comic actors who, were they to attempt to trace their path to stardom, might credit nights spent improvising on Chicago stages.

Chicago was the birthplace of the improvisational comedy form some 50-odd years ago, and the city remains the country's primary breeding ground for this challenging art form. Performers, usually working in an ensemble, ask the audience for a suggestion, then launch into short, long, silly, serious, or surreal scenes loosely related to that original audience input.

Second City (☎ *312/337–3992*) is the anchor of Chicago improv. The revues on the company's main stage and in its smaller e.t.c. space next door are actually sketch comedy shows, but the scripts in these pre-rehearsed scenes have been developed through improvisation and there's usually a little time set aside in each show for the performers to demonstrate their quick wit. Most nights there is a free improv set after the late show, featuring cast members and invited guests (sometimes famous, sometimes not, never announced in advance). It's in **Donny's Skybox** upstairs that you're

more likely to see one of Chicago's many fledgling improv comedy troupes making their first appearance working together on freshly penned material in public.

I.O. (☎ *773/880–0199*) is the city's home to long-form improvisation. The signature piece is "The Harold," in which a team of improvisers explores a single audience suggestion throughout a series of stories and characters until they all eventually weave back together to fit with the original audience idea. At **ComedySportz Chicago** (☎ *773/549–8080*), teams of professional improvisers perform songs and scenes all based on your suggestions in an audience-interactive competition.

The itinerant group the **Annoyance Theatre** (☎ *773/561–4665*), now settled into its new home in Uptown at 4840 North Broadway, is best known for hits like *Coed Prison Sluts* and *Splatter Theatre*.

Scope out the hordes of up-and-comers at neighborhood stages such as the **Playground Theater** (☎ *773/871–3793*) at 3209 North Halsted Street. The springtime **Chicago Improv Festival** (☎ *773/935–9810*), the nation's largest festival for improvisers, has stages devoted to group, pair, and single improv, sketch comedy, and more.

8

tail and groove to remixed tunes in a grown-up nightclub complete with hardwood floors, exposed brick, and a timber-beam ceiling.

Excalibur (✉ *632 N. Dearborn St., River North* ☎ *312/266–1944*) won't win any prizes for breaking new ground, but this River North nightclub complex, carved out of the Romanesque fortress that was the original home of the Chicago Historical Society, has been going strong for years with its mix of dancing, dining, and posing. At the same address and phone number but with a separate entrance is the smaller, alternative-dance club called Vision. Deejays and music styles change all the time (as does the club's vibe), so call ahead for that night's selections.

Funky is the operative word for the **Funky Buddha Lounge** (⊠728 W. Grand Ave., Wicker Park ☎312/666–1695), with its diverse crowd, seductive dance music, and a big metal Buddha guarding the front door. It has an intimate bar and dark dance floor, where patrons groove as DJs spin dance hall, hip-hop, R&B, funk, and old-school house.

Le Passage (⊠937 N. Rush St., Near North ☎312/255–0022) feels like an underground Parisian nightclub, complete with low ceilings, dim lighting, and an entrance down a cobblestone alley. Stop in for an early-evening cocktail and plate of French-inspired cuisine and stay for late-night dancing. DJs spin house and hip-hop Thursday through Saturday. The adjacent "culinary cocktail lounge" called the Drawing Room puts the focus on top-flight wines and small plates in a plush, intimate atmosphere.

Sound-Bar (⊠226 W. Ontario St., River North ☎312/787–4480) is a labyrinth of nine bars, each with a unique design and color scheme (some even serve matching colored cocktails). Feel like dancing? Join the pulse of Chicago's best-dressed on the huge dance floor.

Spy Bar (⊠646 N. Franklin St., River North ☎312/587–8779) pulls some smooth moves. Image is everything at this subterranean spot with a brushed stainless-steel bar and exposed brick walls. The slick, stylish crowd hits the tight dance floor for house, underground, and DJ remixes.

GAY AND LESBIAN NIGHTLIFE

Chicago's gay bars appeal to mixed crowds and tastes. Most are on North Halsted Street from Belmont Avenue to Irving Park Road, an area nicknamed Boystown. Bars generally stay open until 2 AM weekends, but a few keep the lights on until 5 AM Sunday morning. The *Chicago Free Press, Windy City Times,* and *Gay Chicago* list nightspots, events, and gay and lesbian resources; all three are free and can be picked up at bookstores, bars, and some supermarkets, especially those in Boystown.

Big Chicks (⊠5024 N. Sheridan Rd., Far North Side ☎773/728–5511), in the Uptown area of the Far North Side, is a striking alternative to the Halsted strip, with a funky crowd that appreciates the owner's art collection hanging on the walls. The fun-loving staff and their self-selected eclectic music are the payoffs for the hike to get here. Special attractions include weekend dancing and free Sunday-afternoon buffets.

Charlie's (⊠3726 N. Broadway, Lakeview ☎773/871–8887), a country-and-western dance club, lets you two-step nightly to achy-breaky tunes, though dance music is played every night from about 2 AM to 4 AM. It's mostly a boots-and-denim crowd on weekends.

Circuit (⊠3641 N. Halsted St., Lakeview ☎773/325–2233), the biggest dance club in Boystown, is a stripped-down dance hall energized by flashing lights, booming sounds, and a partying crowd. Take a break in the up-front martini bar.

The **Closet** (✉3325 N. Broadway, Lakeview ☎773/477–8533) is a basic dive bar with a gay twist. This compact bar—one of the few that caters to lesbians, though it draws gay men, too—can be especially lively after 2 AM when most other bars close. Stop by Sunday afternoons when bartenders serve up what are hailed as the best Bloody Marys in town.

A gay sports bar might sound like an oxymoron, but **North End** (✉3733 N. Halsted St., Lakeview ☎773/477–7999) is a favorite spot to watch the big game or play some pool. Later at night, it has more of a typical gay bar atmosphere.

Roscoe's Tavern (✉3356 N. Halsted St., Lakeview ☎773/281–3355), in the heart of Boystown, is a longtime favorite with a mix of amenities sure to please its peppy patrons, including a jam-packed front bar, a dance floor, a pool table, an outdoor garden, and lively music. The sidewalk café serves May through September.

The video bar **Sidetrack** (✉3349 N. Halsted St., Lakeview ☎773/477–9189) is tuned into a different theme every night of the week, from show tunes on Monday to comedy on Thursday—all broadcast on TV screens that never leave your sight. The sprawling stand-and-pose bar and rooftop deck are always busy with a good-looking, professional crowd, and the vodka slushies are a house specialty.

MUSIC

COUNTRY

There are slim pickin's for country-music clubs in Chicago, even though country radio continues to draw wide audiences.

Carol's Pub (✉4659 N. Clark St., Far North Side ☎773/334–2402), in the Uptown area of the Far North Side, showcased country before it was ever cool. The house band at this urban honky-tonk plays country and country-rock tunes on weekends, and the popular karaoke night on Thursday draws all walks of life, from preppie to punk.

★ **The Hideout** (✉1354 W. Wabansia, Bucktown ☎773/227–4433), which is literally hidden away in a North Side industrial zone, has managed to make country music hip in Chicago. Players on the city's alternative country scene have adopted the friendly hole-in-the-wall, and bands ranging from the obscure to the semi-famous take the stage. The bluegrass band Devil in a Woodpile plays on Tuesday.

Horseshoe (✉4115 N. Lincoln Ave., Far Northwest Side ☎773/334–2402) brings a slice of Texas to the Midwest, along with wicked barbecue brisket and pulled pork (and some surprisingly good vegetarian versions). Live bluegrass bands or honky-tonk jukebox tunes draw displaced Southerners, whose nostalgia is drowned out by the down-home decor—think chicken-wire, scruffy floors, and horseshoe-shaped booths—and rounds of ice-cold Lone Star beer.

ECLECTIC

Clubs in this category don't limit themselves to a single type of music. Call ahead to find out what's playing.

At **Baton Show Lounge** (✉*436 N. Clark St., River North* ☎*312/644–5269*), boys will be girls. The lip-synching revues with female impersonators have catered to curious out-of-towners and bachelorette parties since 1969. Some of the regular performers, such as Chili Pepper and Mimi Marks, have become Chicago cult figures. The more the audience tips, the better the show gets, so bring your bills.

North Side stalwart **Beat Kitchen** (✉*2100 W. Belmont Ave., Lakeview* ☎*773/281–4444*) brings in the crowds because of its good sound system and local and touring rock, alternative-rock, country, and rockabilly acts. It also serves soups, salads, sandwiches, pizzas, and desserts.

Elbo Room (✉*2871 N. Lincoln Ave., Lincoln Park* ☎*773/549–5549*), a multilevel space in an elbow-shape corner building, has a basement rec-room feel. The bar plays host to talented live bands seven days a week, with a strong dose of nu-jazz, funk, soul, pop, and rock.

FitzGerald's (✉*6615 W. Roosevelt Rd., Berwyn* ☎*708/788–2118*), though a 30-minute schlep west of Chicago, draws crowds from all over the city and suburbs with its mix of folk, jazz, blues, zydeco, and rock. This early 1900s roadhouse has great sound and sight lines for its roots music.

★ **House of Blues** (✉*329 N. Dearborn St., River North* ☎*312/923–2000*), though its name implies otherwise, attracts big-name performers of all genres, from jazz, roots, blues, and gospel to alternative rock, hip-hop, world, and R&B. The interior is an elaborate cross between blues bar and ornate opera house. Its restaurant has live blues every night on a "second stage," as well as a satisfying Sunday gospel brunch. Part of the Marina City complex, the entrance is on State Street.

FOLK AND ETHNIC

★ **Old Town School of Folk Music** (✉*4544 N. Lincoln Ave., Far Northwest Side* ☎*773/728–6000*), Chicago's first and oldest folk-music school, has served as folk central in the city since it opened in 1957. This welcoming spot in Lincoln Square hosts outstanding performances by national and local acts in an intimate-feeling 420-seat concert hall boasting excellent acoustics. If you can, book a table seat next to the stage. Each summer the school sponsors the popular Chicago Folk & Roots Festival in nearby Welles Park.

The Wild Hare (✉*3530 N. Clark St., Lakeview* ☎*773/327–0868*), with a wide-open dance floor, is the place for infectious live reggae and world-beat music seven nights a week. Take a breather at the bar and sip a rum drink or a Jamaican Red Stripe beer.

JAZZ

Jazz thrives all around town. For a recorded listing of upcoming live performances, call the **Jazz Institute Hot Line** (☎*312/427–3300*).

Andy's Jazz Club (✉*11 E. Hubbard St., River North* ☎*312/642–6805*), a favorite after-work watering hole with a substantial bar menu, has live music ranging from swing jazz to bebop. In addition to the evening performances, there's a jazz program at noon on weekdays—a boon for music lovers who aren't night owls.

OUR FAVORITE DIVE BARS

Old Town Ale House (✉ *219 W. North Ave., Near North* ☎ *312/944–7020*), just a stone's throw from Second City, has attracted a diverse cast of characters since it opened in 1958, including comedy legends John Belushi and Bill Murray. With eclectic artwork, a mural of bar denizens painted in the '70s, and a lending library on-site, it's a dingy neighborhood bar unlike any other in the city—perhaps the country.

The Matchbox (✉ *770 N. Milwaukee Ave., Wicker Park* ☎ *312/666–9292*), in West Town near Wicker Park, isn't much bigger than a you-know-what, but the hodgepodge of regulars don't seem to mind. In fact, many claim it's the dark, cramped quarters (we're talking three feet wide at its narrowest) that keep them coming back. The crowd spills outside in summer, when iron rod tables dot the sidewalk.

Rainbo Club (✉ *1150 N. Damen Ave., Wicker Park* ☎ *773/489–5999*) is the unofficial meeting place for Chicago hipsters and indie rockers. Apart from the working photo booth wedged into a corner, the stripped-down hangout is pretty barren, but drinks are dirt-cheap and the bartenders are upbeat—and willing—conversationalists.

Green Dolphin Street (✉ *2200 N. Ashland Ave., Lakeview* ☎ *773/395–0066*), a stylish, upscale club and private event venue with the glamour of the 1940s (in a converted auto-body shop, no less), attracts a mostly older crowd that comes to hear tight ensembles and smooth-voiced jazz divas perform big band, bebop, Latin, and world jazz.

★ **Green Mill** (✉ *4802 N. Broadway, Far North Side* ☎ *773/878–5552*), a Chicago institution off the beaten track in not-so-trendy Uptown, has been around since 1907. Deep leather banquettes and ornate wood paneling line the walls, and a photo of Al Capone occupies a place of honor on the piano behind the bar. The jazz entertainment is both excellent and contemporary—the club launched the careers of Kurt Elling and Patricia Barber—and the Uptown Poetry Slam, a competitive poetry reading, takes center stage on Sunday.

Pops for Champagne (✉ *601 N. State St., River North* ☎ *312/266–7677*) can be found in trendy River North. The bi-level space is gloriously turned out with a champagne bar, raw bar, sidewalk café, and even a retail space called Pops Shop. Grab your (champagne) flute and head downstairs to the stylish jazz lounge for live music Tuesday through Saturday.

The owner of **Velvet Lounge** (✉ *67 E. Cermak Rd., Near South* ☎ *312/791–9050*), saxophonist Fred Anderson, has relocated his beloved institution to a cozy Near South locale, but the heart and soul of the place remain the same. Stop in for traditional and avant-garde jazz Tuesday through Saturday. Sunday is still Jam Session day.

8

ROCK

Chicago has an active rock scene with many local favorites, some of which—including Smashing Pumpkins, Wilco, and Liz Phair—have won national acclaim. Bone up on Chicago's rock scene by tuning to 91.5 FM for Chicago Public Radio's Sound Opinions, a weekly radio show hosted by *Chicago Tribune* and *Chicago Sun-Times* rock critics Greg Kot and Jim DeRogatis. The program airs Friday at 8 PM and Saturday at 11 AM.

The Abbey Pub (⊠ *3420 W. Grace St., Far North Side* ☎ *773/478–4408*), about 15 minutes northwest of downtown in the Irving Park neighborhood, showcases rock, as well as some Irish, Celtic, and country music, in a large concert hall with a separate, busy pub. By day the hall is used to show soccer and rugby games from the United Kingdom and Ireland.

Double Door (⊠ *1572 N. Milwaukee Ave., Wicker Park* ☎ *773/489–3160*) is a hotbed for music in hip Wicker Park. The large bar books up-and-coming local and national acts from rock to acid jazz. Unannounced Rolling Stones shows have been held here. The entrance is on Damen Avenue.

Empty Bottle (⊠ *1035 N. Western Ave., Wicker Park* ☎ *773/276–3600*), in the Ukrainian Village near Wicker Park, may have toys and knick-knacks around the bar (including a case of macabre baby-doll heads), but when it comes to booking rock, punk, and jazz bands from the indie scene, it's a serious place with no pretensions.

Martyrs' (⊠ *3855 N. Lincoln Ave., Far North Side* ☎ *773/404–9869*) brings local and major-label rock bands to this small, North Side neighborhood sandwiched between Lincoln Square and Roscoe Village. Music fans can see the stage from just about any corner of the bar, while the more rhythmically inclined gyrate in the large standing-room area. A mural opposite the stage memorializes late rock greats.

★ **Metro** (⊠ *3730 N. Clark St., Lakeview* ☎ *773/549–0203*) brings in progressive, nationally known artists and the cream of the local crop. A former movie palace, it's an excellent place to see live bands, whether you're moshing on the main floor or above the fray in the balcony. In the basement is **Smart Bar,** a late-night dance club that starts hopping after midnight.

Schubas Tavern (⊠ *3159 N. Southport Ave., Lakeview* ☎ *773/525–2508*) favors local and national power pop and indie rock bands. The wood-paneled back room has a laid-back atmosphere and good seating. The bar was built in 1900 by the Schlitz Brewing Company, and it still sells Schlitz beer—a bargain at about $2 a pop.

Continued on page 313

CHICAGO STILL SINGS THE BLUES

The cool, electric, urban blues are the soundtrack of the Windy City. The blues traveled up the Mississippi River with the Delta sharecroppers during the Great Migration, settled down on Maxwell Street and South Side clubs, and gave birth to such big-name talent as Muddy Waters, Howlin' Wolf, Willie Dixon, and, later, Koko Taylor. Today, you can still hear the blues in a few South Side clubs where it all began, or check out the current scene on the North Side.

THE BIRTH OF THE CHICAGO BLUES

CHESS RECORDS

Founded by Philip and Leonard Chess, Polish immigrant brothers, in 1947. For the first two years, the label was called Aristocrat.

Its famous address, 2120 S. Michigan Avenue, was the nucleus of the blues scene. Up-and-comers performed on the sidewalk out front in hopes of being discovered. Even today, locals and visitors peek through the windows of the restored studio (now the Blues Heaven Foundation) looking for glimpses of past glory.

The label's first hit record was Muddy Waters' *I Can't Be Satisfied.*

The brothers were criticized for having a paternalistic relationship with their artists. They reportedly bought Muddy Waters a car off the lot when he wasn't able to finance it himself.

The label was sold in 1969 after Leonard's death.

Did you know? When the Rolling Stones recorded the track "2120 South Michigan Avenue" (off the *12 x 5* album) at the Chess Records studio in June 1964, the young Brits were reportedly so nervous about singing in front of Willie Dixon (Buddy Guy and Muddy Waters were also hanging around the studio that day) that they literally became tongue-tied. As a result, the song is purely instrumental.

WILLIE DIXON (7/1915–1/1992)

Chess Records' leading A & R (artist and repertoire) man, bass player, and composer. Founded the Blues Heaven Foundation, Chess Records' restored office and studio. *See Blues Heaven Foundation review next page.*

Famous compositions: "Hoochie Coochie Man" (recorded by Muddy Waters), "My Babe" (recorded by Little Walter), and "Wang Dang Doodle" (recorded by Koko Taylor)

MUDDY WATERS: KING OF ELECTRIC BLUES (4/1915–4/1983)

When Muddy Waters gave his guitar an electric jolt, he didn't just revolutionize the blues. His electric guitar became a magic wand: Its jive talk (and cry) turned country-blues into city-blues, and it gave birth to rock and roll. Waters' signature sound has been firmly imprinted on nearly all subsequent musical genres.

Best known for: Riveting vocals, a swooping pompadour, and, of course, plugging in the guitar

Biggest break: Leonard Chess, one of the Chess brothers of Chess Records, let Waters record two of his own songs. The record sold out in two days, and stores issued a dictum of "one per customer"

Biggest song: "Hoochie Coochie Man"

Lyrics: *Y'know I'm here / Everybody knows I'm here / And I'm the hoochie-coochie man*

Awards: 3 Grammies, Lifetime Achievement induction into the Rock and Roll Hall of Fame

Local honor: A strip of 43rd Street in Chicago is renamed Muddy Waters Drive

HOWLIN' WOLF (6/1910–1/1976)

In 1951, at the age of 41, Wolf recorded with Sun Studios in Memphis, TN. Shortly thereafter, Sun sold Wolf's only two songs, "Moanin' At Midnight" and "How Many More Years," to Chess Records, kicking off his prolific recording career with Chess.

Most popular songs: "Backdoor Man" and "Little Red Rooster"

Instruments: Electric guitar and harmonica

Dedication to his craft: Wolf was still taking guitar lessons even a year before his death, even though he was long recognized as one of the two greatest blues musicians in the world.

8

IN FOCUS CHICAGO STILL SINGS THE BLUES

THE CHICAGO BLUES TODAY

KOKO TAYLOR:
Queen of the Blues

Blessed with neither Bessie Smith's beauty nor Billie Holiday's power of seduction, Taylor offers grit; a been-there-done-that wisdom that personified urban-blues by the 1970s.

Best known for: Slam-bang stage presence and powerhouse vocals

Big break: It wasn't until Chess Records blues producer Willie Dixon saw her singing at a South Side club one night in the early 1960s that her career really took off. Dixon reportedly said, "My God, I've never heard a woman sing the blues like you," and signed her up to record

Biggest song: "Wang Dang Doodle" sold a staggering one million copies in six weeks

Lyrics: *We gonna jump and shout 'til daylight / We gonna pitch a wang dang doodle / All night long*

Most significant hardship: Gettin' paid. Though Taylor was a star, she barely saw a penny of the profits while working with Chess Records and Willie Dixon

Awards: 25 W.C. Handy Awards (more than any other recording artist, male or female); a Grammy for *Blues Explosion,* 1984; Legend of the Year by Mayor Daley in 1993

Local honor: March 3rd is Koko Taylor Day in Chicago

Catch her act: Upcoming tour information is available at www.kokotaylor.com

BEST PLACES TO HEAR THE BLUES

Checkerboard Lounge (✉ *5201 S. Harper Ct., Hyde Park, 60615* ☎ *773/684–1472*) has reopened in Hyde Park! It was a sad day for blues fans when the world-famous Bronzeville location, owned by Buddy Guy in the 1970s and early 1980s, closed in 2003. Though the new location's in a shopping center—a far cry from its former gritty digs—it has the same diverse selection of local and big-name blues and jazz talent. Kudos on retaining some of the old picnic tables (used inside) from the first location. Note: Call ahead for information on the cover charge, which ranges from $3 to $20 depending on who's playing.

Chicago Blues Festival (☎ *312/744–3370*) There's no doubt about it; Chicago still loves to sing the blues. Each June, the city pulses with sounds from the largest free blues festival in the world, which takes place over four days and on six stages in both Grant Park and Millennium Park. The always-packed open air festival has been headlined by blues legends such as B.B. King, Koko Taylor, and Buddy Guy.

Set in an upscale part of downtown, **Blue Chicago** (✉ *536 N. Clark St., River North, 60610* ☎ *312/661–0100* ✉ *736 N. Clark St., River North, 60610* ☎ *312/642–6261*) has none of the trademark grit or edginess of the older South Side blues clubs. It does have two bars within two blocks of each

BUDDY GUY

Though he recorded his first album in 1958, Guy didn't really take off until he recorded with Vanguard in 1968 and was sent on tour with blues harmonica legend Junior Wells and the Rolling Stones.

Instrument: Electric guitar

Influenced: His stinging guitar playing had strong influences on Jimi Hendrix and Eric Clapton

Catch his act: Guy is still impressing fans with his sizzling guitar and vocals both on tour and in his Chicago-based club, Buddy Guy's Legends

Honors: 2005 inductee to the Rock and Roll Hall of Fame

DON'T MISS ACTS:

If these acts are playing when you're in town, don't miss them. For contact information for the venues mentioned below, see the club reviews on this page.

Classic slide-guitar and hard-driving blues beats mixed with jazz and even rock 'n' roll influences makes **Melvin Taylor & The Slack Band** a must-see. Call Rosa's Lounge for details. **Gloria Shannon Blues Band** plays everything from Delta blues to electric blues to Chicago blues. Catch their all-ages act every Saturday "Down in the Basement" at the Blue Chicago Store. **Billy Branch and the Sons Of Blues** frequently bring their forward-thinking sounds (steeped in blues tradition) to Rosa's Lounge and Kingston Mines, though they have been known to make rousing on-stage appearances at the Chicago Blues Festival.

---

other. Both have good sound systems, regularly book female vocalists, and attract a cosmopolitan audience that's a tad more diverse than some of the baseball-capped crowds at Lincoln Park blues clubs. We like that one cover gets you into both bars.

The **Blue Chicago Store** (✉ *534 N. Clark St., River North, 60610* ☎ *312/661–1003*) sells a variety of Blue Chicago–related souvenirs, from CDs and T-shirts to posters and books.

★ The best part about **B.L.U.E.S.** (✉ *2519 N. Halsted St., Lincoln Park, 60657* ☎ *773/528–1012*) is that there isn't a bad seat in the joint. The worst part? The crowds—arrive early if you want to score

a seat. Narrow and intimate, the jam-packed North Side club has attracted the best in local talent since it opened in 1979. Big names such as Son Seals, Otis Rush, Jimmy Johnson, and Magic Slim have all played here.

★ **Fodor's Choice** **Buddy Guy's Legends** (✉ *754 S. Wabash Ave., South Loop, 60605* ☎ *312/427–0333*) serves up Louisiana-style barbecue along with the blues. The big club has good sound, good sight lines, and pool tables if you get restless in between sets. Look for local blues acts during the week and larger-scale touring acts on weekends. Don't miss Grammy Award winning blues performer/owner Buddy Guy in January, when he performs a

A MODERN HISTORY LESSON:

The Blues Heaven Foundation (✉ *2120 S. Michigan Ave., South Loop, 60616* ☎ *312/808–1286*)

Breathe the same rarefied air as blues (and rock 'n' roll) legends Muddy Waters, Howlin' Wolf, Chuck Berry, and the Rolling Stones, all of whom recorded here. Check out the Chess brothers' private offices, the recording studio, and the back stairway used only by signed musicians. Don't miss the eerie "Life Cast Portraits" wall showcasing the plaster heads of the Chess recording artists.

Note: Make a phone reservation before stopping by—the Foundation keeps irregular hours.

inal club. Swarms of blues lovers and partying singles take in the good blues and tasty barbecue.

★ Fodor's Choice **Lee's Unleaded Blues** (✉ *7401 S. South Chicago Ave., Grand Crossing, 60619* ☎ *773/493–3477*) has been a South Side favorite since it opened in the early 1970s. Locals come decked out in their showiest threads and University of Chicago students often pop in for a round. The cramped, triangular bar may inhibit free movement, but that doesn't seem to bother the crowd that comes for powerhouse blues and jazz. Note: the club can be difficult to find if you don't know the area, so be sure to take a cab or study a map before making the trip.

month-long home stand of shows (tickets go on sale one month in advance). The club has plans to move into a new spot eventually, but for now it's staying put in its storied digs.

In 1968, **Kingston Mines** (✉ *2548 N. Halsted St., Lincoln Park, 60614* ☎ *773/ 477–4646*) went down in Chicago history as the first blues club to open on the North Side. Though it's since moved to bigger digs, it still offers the same traditional sounds and late-night hours as the orig-

★ Fodor's Choice On a given night at **Rosa's Lounge,** (✉ *3420 W. Armitage Ave., Logan Square, 60647* ☎ *773/342–0452*) near Bucktown, you'll find Tony, the owner, working the crowd, and his mother, Rosa, behind the bar. What makes the club extra special is that the duo moved here from Italy out of a pure love for the blues. Stop by and partake in Rosa's winning mixture of big-name and local talent, stiff drinks, and friendly service—the same since it opened in 1984.

PIANO BARS

Coq d'Or (✉ *140 E. Walton St., Near North* ☎ *312/932–4623*) is a dark, wood-paneled room with red-leather booths where Chicago legend Buddy Charles held court before retiring. Fine music and cocktails served in blown-glass goblets draw hotel guests as well as neighborhood regulars.

Davenport's (✉ *1383 N. Milwaukee Ave., Wicker Park* ☎ *773/278–1830*), a sophisticated cabaret booking both local and touring acts, brings a grown-up presence to the Wicker Park club scene. The piano lounge is set up for casual listening, while the cabaret room is a no-chat zone that requires your full attention—as well as reservations and a two-drink minimum.

The dueling pianists at **Howl at the Moon** (✉ *26 W. Hubbard St., Near North* ☎ *312/863–7427*) attract a rowdy crowd that delights in belting out popular tunes. Reservations aren't accepted, but party packages are available if you're willing to shell out beaucoup bucks (around $150).

★ **Pump Room** (✉ *Omni Ambassador East Hotel, 1301 N. State Pkwy., Near North* ☎ *312/266–0360*) shows off its storied past with photos of celebrities covering the walls. The bar at this restaurant has live piano music and a small dance floor that calls out for dancing cheek to cheek, especially on weekends.

Zebra Lounge (✉ *1220 N. State St., Near North* ☎ *312/642–5140*), small and funky with zebra-stripe lamps and other kitsch, attracts an interesting crowd of dressed-up and dressed-down regulars who come to sing along to the pianist on duty.

SPORTS BARS

Gamekeepers (✉ *345 W. Armitage Ave., Lincoln Park* ☎ *773/549–0400*) is full of former frat boys and sports fans. With more than 40 TVs, three projection screens, and complete satellite sports coverage, there's barely a game Gamekeepers doesn't get.

Hi-Tops (✉ *3551 N. Sheffield Ave., Lakeview* ☎ *773/348–0009*), within a ball's toss of Wrigley Field, may be the ultimate sports bar. Big-screen TVs, a lively crowd, and good bar food keep the Cubs fans coming. A dozen satellites and 65 TV monitors ensure that the place gets packed for a good game.

North Beach Chicago (✉ *1551 N. Sheffield Ave., Lincoln Park* ☎ *312/266–7842*) is all about channeling your inner child. Multiple large-screen TVs plus two sand-filled indoor volleyball courts, pool tables, four bowling lanes, a mechanical bull, and even Sumo wrestling all contribute to generalized regression.

Sluggers (✉ *3540 N. Clark St., Lakeview* ☎ *773/248–0055*) is packed after Cubs games in the nearby stadium, and the ballplayers make occasional appearances in summer. Check out the fast- and slow-pitch batting cages on the second floor, as well as the pool tables, air hockey tables, and electronic basketball.

8

UNDERSTANDING CHICAGO

CHICAGO SLANG

Like New Yorkers and New Englanders, Chicagoans put their own *unique* twist on the English language. Here's a quick primer to help you talk like a native while you're visiting.

Beef—Short for Italian beef sandwiches, a Chicago staple made of thinly sliced roast beef served on a long crusty Italian roll. Beefs are ordered "wet" (dipped in the meat juices), "hot" (with *giardiniera,* an Italian relish containing jalapeños), and/or "sweet" (with roasted sweet peppers).

Bleacher Bums—Regulars who sit in the bleachers at the "Friendly Confines" *(see below).*

The Blizzard of Oz—Nickname for Ozzie Guillen, the charismatic and often foul-mouthed manager of the 2005 World Champion Chicago White Sox.

The Boot—Short for the Denver Boot, a contraption the city uses to lock the wheels of cars with unpaid traffic and parking tickets. Often heard around town: "My car just got booted."

Brat—Short for bratwurst, a staple at sporting events and tailgating parties (pronounced "braht").

The Cell—What White Sox fans affectionately call U.S. Cellular Field, formerly known as Comiskey Park.

Cheesehead—What the locals call people from Wisconsin.

Chicagoland—Chicago and the surrounding suburbs.

The Curse—A local legend that says that a Chicago barkeep whose pet goat was denied entry into the 1945 Chicago Cubs–Detroit Tigers World Series put a curse on the team. The Cubs lost, and have not been to a World Series since. Their last championship was in 1908.

Da Bears—The Chicago Bears, of course! Variations include Da Cubs, Da White Sox, Da Bulls, and Da Blackhawks.

Da Mare—"The Mayor," pronounced like a dyed-in-the-wool native.

The Edens—Commuter term referring to I–94 as it shoots north of the city, splitting from the Kennedy Expressway.

The El—The nickname for the city's public train system, short for "elevated." Even though most of the system is aboveground, the term is used even when the train goes underground.

Friendly Confines—This means Wrigley Field, home of the Chicago Cubs. A sign inside the ballpark says WELCOME TO THE FRIENDLY CONFINES OF WRIGLEY FIELD.

Gapers—Drivers who slow down traffic to look at an accident. You'll hear about "gapers blocks" or "gapers delays" on traffic reports.

The Mag Mile—A shortened term for the "Magnificent Mile," a nickname given to the retail-heavy stretch of North Michigan Avenue between the Chicago River and Oak Street.

Pop—A soft drink, like Coca-Cola. Don't use the word "soda" here.

Reversibles—The express lanes on the Kennedy Expressway, which reverse direction depending upon the time of day.

The Riv—The hipster abbreviation for the Riviera Theater, a North Side live-music venue.

Sammitch—A sandwich, of course!

Trixies—A jabbing nickname for the young, ex-sorority types who live in and around the Lincoln Park neighborhood.

Viagra Triangle—What locals call the intersection of Clark, Dearborn, and Rush streets due to the density of bars frequented by mature gentlemen who try to pick up young ladies.

BOOKS AND MOVIES

Books

Native Chicagoan Saul Bellow set many novels in the city, most notably *Humboldt's Gift* and *The Adventures of Augie March*. Richard Wright's explosive *Native Son* and James T. Farrell's *Studs Lonigan* depict racial clashes in Chicago. The works of longtime resident Nelson Algren—*The Man with the Golden Arm, A Walk on the Wild Side*, and *Chicago: City on the Make*—show the city at its grittiest, as does playwright David Mamet's *American Buffalo*. Two series of detective novels use a present-day Chicago backdrop: Sara Paretsky's excellent V. I. Warshawski novels and the Monsignor Ryan mysteries of Andrew Greeley. Greeley has set other novels in Chicago as well, including *Lord of the Dance*. Local author Marcus Sakey set *The Blade Itself*, his debut novel about reunited crime partners, on Chicago's North and South sides. Sakey—with Paretsky and Chicago crime writers Sean Chercover, Barbara D'Amato, Michael Allen Dymmoch, Kevin Guilfoile, and Libby Hellman—are known collectively as "The Outfit."

Chicago was once the quintessential newspaper town; the play *The Front Page*, by Ben Hecht and Charles MacArthur, is set here. Local reporters have penned some excellent chronicles, including *Fabulous Chicago*, by Emmett Dedmon; and *Boss*, a portrait of the late mayor Richard J. Daley, by the late Mike Royko. For a selection of Royko's award-winning columns, check out *One More Time: The Best of Mike Royko*. Lois Wille's *Forever Open, Clear and Free* is a superb history of the fight to save Chicago's lakefront parks. Books by Studs Terkel, a great chronicler of Chicago, include *Division Street: America* and *Chicago*. Erik Larson traces two men, architect Daniel Burnham and serial killer Henry H. Holmes, through the Chicago World's Fair of 1893 in *The Devil in the White City*. *Never a City So Real* is a collection of essays by Alex Kotlowitz. Even graphic novelists have a soft spot for Chicago; one of Chicago's better-known draftsmen, Chris Ware, juxtaposes lovable-looking characters with disparaging dialogue in his graphic novel *Jimmy Corrigan: The Smartest Kid on Earth*.

Architecture buffs can choose from a number of excellent guidebooks. James Cornelius revised *Chicago on Foot*, by Ira J. Bach and Susan Wolfson; the book contains dozens of architecture-driven walking tours. Franz Schulze and Kevin Harrington edited the fourth edition of *Chicago's Famous Buildings*, a pocket guide to the city's most important landmarks and buildings. The *A. I. A. Guide to Chicago*, edited by Alice Sinkevitch, is an exhaustive source of information about local architecture. The pocket-size *Chicago: A Guide to Recent Architecture*, by Susanna Sirefman, covers everything from office buildings to the new airport terminal. For thought-provoking critiques of Chicago's major buildings, pick up *Why Architecture Matters: Lessons From Chicago*, a compilation of articles written by Chicago Tribune architecture critic Blair Kamin. Finally, David Garrad Lowe's *Lost Chicago* is a fascinating, heartbreaking history of vanished buildings.

Movies

Chicago has been the setting for films about everything from gangsters to restless suburbanites. Classic early gangster flicks include *Little Caesar* (1930), with Edward G. Robinson, and *Scarface* (1932), starring Paul Muni and George Raft. The theme is carried out on a lighter note in *The Sting* (1973), George Roy Hill's charming Scott Joplin–scored movie that stars Paul Newman and Robert Redford as suave con men. *Carrie* is the 1952 adaptation of Dreiser's novel about a country girl who loses her innocence in the city; Laurence Olivier and Jennifer Jones are the stars. Lorraine Hansberry's drama about a black Chicago family, *A Raisin in the Sun*, became a film with Sidney Poitier in 1961.

As Elwood and Jake, respectively, Dan Aykroyd and the late John Belushi brought wild energy and cool music to the screen in *The Blues Brothers* (1980). *Ordinary People*, the Oscar-winning 1980 film, starred Mary Tyler Moore in a drama about an affluent and agonized North Shore family. John Hughes directed 1986's *Ferris Bueller's Day Off*, in which Matthew Broderick and a couple of his high-school friends play hooky and tour Chicago for a day. In *About Last Night* (1986), which is based on the David Mamet play *Sexual Perversity in Chicago*, Demi Moore and Rob Lowe go through realistic modern dating games with the help (and hindrance) of hilarious friends played by Elizabeth Perkins and Jim Belushi. Brian De Palma's *The Untouchables* (1987) stars Kevin Costner as Eliot Ness and Robert De Niro as Al Capone in a gangster tale with a 1920s Chicago background. *Eight Men Out* (1988)—with John Cusack, John Mahoney, and Charlie Sheen—depicts baseball's infamous Black Sox scandal, when members of the Chicago White Sox took bribes to throw the 1919 World Series against the Cincinnati Reds.

Kurt Russell and William Baldwin play firefighter brothers in *Backdraft* (1991). In the action thriller *The Fugitive* (1993), Harrison Ford pulls off one narrow escape in Chicago's St. Patrick's Day parade. Steve James's *Hoop Dreams* (1994) is a powerful documentary about a couple of inner-city teens who dream that basketball will be their ticket out. In the romantic comedy *While You Were Sleeping* (1995), Sandra Bullock plays a CTA clerk who saves a man from death on the El. *My Best Friend's Wedding* (1997) is a romantic comedy starring Julia Roberts, who tries to break up the wedding of Dermot Mulroney and Cameron Diaz. Roberts and Mulroney dance on a boat tour in the Loop.

In *High Fidelity* (2000), John Cusack is a record-store owner struggling with his past and present romantic life. In *Save the Last Dance* (2001), suburban ballerina Julia Stiles learns hip-hop from Sean Patrick Thomas on Chicago's South Side. Second City alum Nia Vardalos adapted the screenplay for the wildly popular *My Big Fat Greek Wedding* (2002) from her one-woman play. *Chicago* (2002) razzle-dazzled its way to six Oscars, helping to bring back the movie musical. *The Road to Perdition* (2002) stars Tom Hanks and Paul Newman in a 1930s gangster drama. *Barbershop* (2002) chronicles a day in the life of a South Side barbershop. Director Robert Altman and star Neve Campbell go behind the scenes with the Joffrey Ballet of Chicago in *The Company* (2003). Will Smith visits the Lake Michigan landfill in the 2035 Chicago created in the sci-fi thriller *I, Robot* (2004). Josh Hartnett plays a young ad exec in Chicago in *Wicker Park* (2004). As a down-on-his-luck divorcé in *The Weather Man* (2004), Nicolas Cage filmed scenes in both north suburban Evanston and downtown. In *Batman Begins* (2004) Christian Bale, as Batman, is seen racing through Chicago's Lower Wacker Drive in the Batmobile. Jennifer Aniston spent some quality time in the Windy City while filming *Derailed* (2005; co-starring Clive Owen); then she was rumored to have fallen in love with Vince Vaughn while filming *The Break Up* (2006). Will Ferrell got a Golden Globe nomination for Best Actor in a Musical or Comedy for his portrayal of a regular guy whose fate is controlled by a neurotic writer in *Stranger Than Fiction* (2006), which was filmed in Chicago.

While filming his Oscar-winning performance as the Joker in the *Dark Knight* (2008), the late Heath Ledger was often spotted skateboarding around town.

Travel Smart Chicago

GETTING HERE AND AROUND

Chicago is famously known as a city of neighborhoods. The Loop is Chicago's epicenter of business, finance, and government. Neighborhoods surrounding the Loop include River North (an area populated by art galleries and high-end boutiques), Streeterville (bordered by Lake Michigan and Navy Pier), and West Loop and South Loop, both up-and-coming areas with trendy residential areas and hip dining and shopping options.

Moving north, you'll encounter the Magnificent Mile (North Michigan Avenue), which gives way to the Gold Coast, so named for its luxurious mansions, stately museums, and deluxe entertainment venues. Lincoln Park, Lakeview, Wrigleyville, Lincoln Square, and Andersonville all lie north of these areas, and each has considerable charms to explore.

Neighborhoods west of the Loop include River West, West Town, Wicker Park, and Bucktown, where of-the-moment art, shopping, dining, and nightlife venues line the streets.

Beyond South Loop lies Hyde Park, home to the University of Chicago and the Museum of Science and Industry.

Traveling between neighborhoods is a relatively sane experience, thanks to the matrix of bus and train routes managed by the Chicago Transit Authority. Driving can be harried, but taxis are normally plentiful in most parts of town.

Chicago streets generally follow a grid pattern, running north–south or east–west and radiating from a center point at State and Madison streets in the Loop. East and west street numbers go up as you move away from State Street; north and south street numbers rise as you move away from Madison Street. Each block is represented by a hundred number.

■ TIP → Ask the local tourist board about hotel and local transportation packages

that include tickets to major museum exhibits or other special events.

∎ BY AIR

To Chicago: From New York, 2 hours; from San Francisco, 4 hours; from Los Angeles, 4 hours; from Dallas, 2½ hours; from London, 7 hours; from Sydney, 17 hours.

In Chicago the general rule is to arrive at the airport two hours before an international flight; for a domestic flight, plan to arrive 90 minutes early if you're checking luggage and 60 minutes if you're not.

There are no direct flights from Chicago to Australia or New Zealand. There are several daily direct flights to the United Kingdom by British Midland, British Airways, United, and American.

Smoking policies vary from carrier to carrier. U.S. airlines prohibit smoking on all flights.

Airlines & Airports Airline and Airport Links.com (⊕ *www.airlineandairportlinks.com*) has links to many of the world's airlines and airports.

Airline Security Issues Transportation Security Administration (⊕ *www.tsa.gov*) has answers for almost every question that might come up.

AIRPORTS

The major gateway to Chicago is **O'Hare International Airport** (ORD). As one of the world's busiest airports, all major airlines pass through O'Hare. The sprawling structure is situated 19 mi from downtown, in the far northwest corner of the city. It can take anywhere from 30 to 90 minutes to travel between downtown and O'Hare, based on time of day, weather conditions, and construction on the Kennedy Expressway (Interstate 90). The Blue Line El train offers a reliable 40-minute trip between the Loop and O'Hare.

Got some time to spend before your flight? Plenty of dining and shopping options are scattered throughout O'Hare's four terminals. Chicago favorites such as the Billy Goat Tavern, Goose Island Brewing Company, Pizzeria Uno, Garrett's Popcorn, and Gold Coast Dogs can be found among the usual chain restaurants. Grab that last-minute souvenir or in-flight necessity at an array of shops, including the Chicago History Museum Society Gift Shop, the Field Museum Gift Shop, and Vosges Haut Chocolat. Or spring for a mini-massage from the Back Rub Hub. Wi-Fi is also available throughout the building.

■TIP➔ If you're stuck at O'Hare longer than you expected, the Hilton Chicago O'Hare (☎ 773/686–8000) is located within walking distance of all terminals.

Midway Airport (MDW) is situated about 11 mi southwest from downtown. Midway Airport serves Northwest, Continental, and Delta airlines along with budget carriers like Southwest, AirTran, and Frontier. Driving between Midway and downtown can take 30 to 60 minutes, depending on traffic conditions on the Stevenson Expressway (Interstate 55). The Orange Line El train runs from the Loop to Midway in about 30 minutes.

Some say the more recently renovated Midway has better dining options than O'Hare. With downtown standouts such as Harry Caray's, Manny's Deli, and Gold Coast Dogs all on-site, it's a good point. The Midway Boulevard area in the center of the building features cute shops such as Chicago Treasures and Kid's Corner. Wi-Fi is available throughout the airport.

An extended stay near Midway Airport can be spent at a number of nearby hotels, including Chicago Marriott Midway (☎ 800/228–9290), Hampton Inn

---

Midway (☎ 708/496–1900), and Hilton Garden Inn Midway (☎ 708/496–2700).

Security screenings at both airports are fairly quick (it takes about 15 to 30 minutes or less to get through security lines); however, during peak holiday travel you should arrive about two hours before your flight.

■TIP➔ Long layovers don't have to be only about sitting around or shopping. These days they can be about burning off vacation calories. Check out www.airportgyms.com for lists of health clubs that are in or near many U.S. and Canadian airports.

Airport Information Midway Airport (☎ 773/838-0600 ⊕ www.chicago-mdw.com or www.flychicago.com). **O'Hare International Airport** (☎ 773/686–2200 or 800/832–6352 ⊕ www.ohare.com or www.flychicago.com).

GROUND TRANSPORTATION

If you're traveling to or from the airport by bus or car during morning or afternoon rush hours, factor in some extra time—ground transport to or from both O'Hare and Midway airports can be slow.

BY BUS:

Shuttle buses run between O'Hare and Midway airports and to and from either airport and various points in the city. When taking an airport shuttle bus to O'Hare or Midway to catch a departing flight, be sure to allow at least 1½ hours. When going to either airport, it's a good idea to make a reservation 24 hours in advance. Though some shuttles make regular stops at the major hotels and don't require reservations, it's best to check.

Reservations are not necessary from the airports. Omega Airport Shuttle runs an hourly shuttle between the two airports for approximately $16 per person. Travel time is approximately one hour. Omega Airport Shuttle also provides an hourly service from the two airports and Hyde Park. The fare is $30 from O'Hare to Hyde Park and $17 from Midway to Hyde Park. Airport Express coaches provide service from both airports to major downtown and Near North locations and the northern suburbs. The trip downtown from O'Hare takes at least 45 minutes, depending on traffic conditions; the fare is $27, $49 round-trip. The trip downtown from Midway takes at least a half hour; the fare is $22, $39 round-trip. Call to find out times and prices for other destinations.

BY CAR:

Depending on traffic and the time of day, driving to and from O'Hare takes about an hour, and driving to and from Midway takes at least 45 minutes. From O'Hare, follow the signs to Interstate 90 east (Kennedy Expressway), which merges with Interstate 94 (Edens Expressway). Take the eastbound exit at Ohio Street for Near North locations, the Washington or Monroe Street exit for downtown. After you exit, continue east about a mile to get to Michigan Avenue. From Midway, follow the signs to Interstate 55 east, which leads to Interstate 90.

BY TAXI:

Metered taxicab service is available at both O'Hare and Midway airports. Trips to and from O'Hare may incur a $1 surcharge to compensate for changing fuel costs. Expect to pay about $40 to $45 plus tip from O'Hare to Near North and downtown locations, about $30 to $35 plus tip from Midway. Some cabs, such as Checker Taxi and Yellow Cab, participate in a shared-ride program in which each cab carries up to four individual passengers going from the airport to downtown. The cost per person—a flat fee that varies according to destination—is substantially lower than the full rate.

BY TRAIN:

Chicago Transit Authority (CTA) trains, called elevated or El trains (locals often refer to it simply as "the El"), are the cheapest way to and from the airports; they can also be the most convenient transfer. TRAINS TO CITY signs will guide you to the subway or elevated train line. In O'Hare Airport the Blue Line station is in the underground concourse between terminals. Travel time to the city is about 45 minutes. Get off at the station closest to your hotel, or from the first stop in the Loop (Washington and Dearborn streets) you can take a taxi to your hotel or change to other transit lines. At Midway Airport the Orange Line El runs to the Loop. The stop at Adams Street and Wabash Avenue is the closest to the hotels on South Michigan Avenue; for others, the simplest strategy is to get off anywhere in the Loop and hail a cab to your final destination. Train fare is $2.25, and you'll need to pay by transit card. Transit card vending machines are located in every train station. They do not give change, so only add as much as you'd like to put on your card. Pick up train brochures and system maps outside the entrances to the platforms; the "Downtown Transit Sightseeing Guide" is also helpful.

TRANSFERS BETWEEN AIRPORTS

O'Hare and Midway airports are located on opposite ends of the city, so moving between them can be a time-consuming and arduous task. Your best and cheapest move is hopping on the El. You will travel the Blue Line to the Orange Line, transferring at the Clark Street stop to get from O'Hare to Midway, reversing the trip to go from Midway to O'Hare. The entire journey should take you under 2 hours. If time is an issue, you may want to consider Coach USA Wisconsin, a shuttle bus that makes the trip between the two airports several times a day from 8:15 AM to 9:15 PM. The fare is $16 per person, one way; $29 round-trip. You can purchase tickets from the driver or in advance from the company's Web site. The trip should take you about 1 hour, depending on traffic conditions.

Taxis & Shuttles American United Cab Co. (☎773/248–7600). **Coach USA Wisconsin** (☎877/324–7767 ⊕www.coachusa.com/wisconsincoach). **Airport Express** (☎888/2THEVAN ⊕www.airportexpress.com). **Checker Taxi** (☎312/243–2537). **Flash Cab** (☎773/561–1444). **Omega Airport Shuttle** (☎773/734–6688 ⊕www.omegashuttle.com). **Yellow Cab Co.** (☎312/829–4222 ⊕www.yellowcabchicago.com).

Public Transit Information CTA (☎888/968–7282 ⊕www.transitchicago.com).

▮ BIKE TRAVEL

Mayor Daley's goal is to make Chicago the most bike-friendly city in the United States, and he's well on his way. One-hundred-twenty miles of designated bike routes run throughout the city, through historic areas, beautiful parks, and along city streets (look for the words BIKE LANE). Bicycling on busy city streets can be a challenge, and is not for the faint of heart—cars come within inches of riders, and the doors of parked cars can swing open at any time. The best bet for a scenic ride is the lakefront, which has a traffic-free 18-mi asphalt trail affording scenic views of the skyline. When your bike is unattended, always lock it; there are bike racks throughout the city. In Millennium Park at Michigan Avenue and Randolph Street (⊕www.chicagobikestation.com), there are 300 free indoor bike spaces plus showers, lockers, and bike-rental facilities offering beach cruisers, mountain and road bikes, hybrid/comfort models, tandem styles, and add-ons for kids (wagon, baby seat, etc.). Bike rentals are also readily available at Bike Chicago, which has five locations, one at Millennium Park, one at Navy Pier, one at the Riverwalk at Wacker Drive and the Chicago River, and two along the lakefront (⊕www.bikechicago.com). Bike Chicago

carries a good selection of mountain and cross bikes. Rates start at $8 per hour. The Chicago Department of Tourism publishes free route maps. Chicagoland Bicycle Federation maps cost $6.95. Maps are updated every few years. From April through October, Bobby's Bike Hike takes guests on cycling tours of Chicago. The three-hour tours begin at the Water Tower on the Magnificent Mile and cycle through historic neighborhoods, shopping areas, and the lakefront. A $30 to $35 fee includes bikes, helmets, and guides; book online for a 10 percent discount.

Information Bobby's Bike Hike (☎312/915–0995 ⊕www.bobbysbikehike.com). **Chicago Department of Tourism (CDOT)** (☎312/742–2453 ⊕egov.cityofchicago.org/Transportation) publishes free route maps. **Chicagoland Bicycle Federation** (☎312/427–3325 ⊕www.biketraffic.org).

▮ BY BOAT

Water taxis are an economical and in-the-know way to cruise parts of the Chicago River and Lake Michigan. A combination of working stiffs and tourists board these boats daily. You won't get the in-depth narrative of an architecture tour, but the views of Chicago's waterways are just as good.

Wendella Boats operates Chicago Water Taxis, which use four downtown docks (Madison Street, LaSalle Street, Michigan Avenue, and Chinatown) along the Chicago River. The entire ride takes about a half hour, and you'll get to see a good portion of the downtown part of the Chicago River. The boats operate seven days a week, April through October. You can purchase tickets at any dock or on the company's Web site.

Shoreline Water Taxis run two routes: the River Taxi cruises between the Sears Tower and Navy Pier, and the Harbor Taxi navigates Lake Michigan between Navy Pier and the Museum Campus. Water Taxis run 10 AM to 6 PM late May to early September. You can purchase

NAVIGATING CHICAGO

Chicago is a surprisingly well-ordered and manageable city. There are a few city-planning quirks, however. Streets that run on a diagonal, such as Milwaukee, Elston, and Lincoln avenues, jut and hurtle drunkenly through the city. These passageways are actually old Indian trails that followed the Chicago River. Chicago also has a proliferation of double- and even triple-decker streets, Wacker Drive being the best-known example. The uppermost level is generally used for street traffic, while the lower levels serve as thoroughfares for cutting through the city rather quickly.

The most helpful landmark to help you navigate Chicago is Lake Michigan. It will always lie on the east, as it serves as the city's only eastern border. Also, look for the Sears Tower and John Hancock Center; which reach up far enough into the sky to serve as beacons. The Sears Tower is in the Loop, and the John Hancock Center is on northern Michigan Avenue.

Chicago's public transit system blankets the city well and is fairly intuitive. Major bus lines include the 151-Sheridan, which runs along the Lakefront, the 36-Broadway, which cuts through the Gold Coast, Lincoln Park, and Lakeview, and the 125-Water Tower Express, which takes a meandering route from Union Station to Water Tower. The train system (referred to as the El, short for "elevated") is an even more comprehensive network, with eight train lines criss-crossing through the city and nearby suburbs. The most popular routes are the Blue Line, which runs from O'Hare Airport into the city through Bucktown and back out again through the Loop; the Red Line, which cuts a north–south swath through the city, crossing through Edgewater, Lakeview, Lincoln Park, the Gold Coast, the Loop, and the South Side; and the Brown Line, which travels from the Far Northwest Side through Lakeview and Lincoln Park, into the Loop, and back up north.

tickets at any dock or in advance on the company's Web site.

Information Shoreline Sightseeing (✉ *474 N. Lake Shore Dr., Suite 3511* ☎ *312/222–9328* ⊕ *www.shorelinesightseeing.com*). **Wendella Boats** (✉ *400 N. Michigan Ave. [main dock]* ☎ *312/337–1446* ⊕ *www.wendellaboats.com*).

∎ BY BUS

Greyhound has nationwide service to its main terminal in the Loop and to neighborhood stations, at the 95th Street and Dan Ryan Expressway CTA station and at the Cumberland CTA station, near O'Hare Airport. The Harrison Street terminal is far from most hotels, so plan on another bus or a cab to your hotel.

For information on bus travel within Chicago, see By Public Transportation.

Bus Information Chicago Transit Authority (☎ *888/968–7282* ⊕ *www.transitchicago.com*). **Greyhound Lines** (☎ *800/231–2222* ⊕ *www. greyhound.com*). **Main Depot** (✉ *630 W. Harrison St.* ☎ *312/408–5800*). **South Depot** (✉ *14 W. 95th St.* ☎ *312/408–5999*). **Northwest Depot (O'Hare)** (✉ *CTA Transit Building, 5800 N. Cumberland Ave.* ☎ *773/693–2474*).

∎ BY CAR

Chicago's network of buses and rapid-transit rail is extensive, and taxis and limousines are readily available (the latter often priced competitively with metered cabs), so rent a car *only* to visit the outlying suburbs that are not accessible by public transportation. Chicago traffic is often heavy, on-street parking is nearly impossible to find, parking lots are expensive, congestion creates frustrating delays, and other drivers may be impatient with those who are unfamiliar with the city and its roads. Expect snarled traffic during rush hours. In these circumstances you may find a car to be a liability rather than an asset. The Illinois Department of Transportation gives information on expressway congestion, travel times, and lane closures and directions on state roadways.

The Illinois tollways snake around the outskirts of the city. Interstate 294 runs north and south between Wisconsin and Indiana. Interstate 90 runs northwest to western Wisconsin, including Madison and Wisconsin Dells. Interstate 88 runs east–west and goes from Eisenhower to Interstate 55. Traffic on all is sometimes just as congested as on the regular expressways. Most toll gates are unmanned, so bring lots of change if you don't have an I-Pass, which are sometimes included with rental cars. Even though tolls are double without the I-Pass, it's not cost effective to purchase one for a couple of days.

If you decide to rent a car, you'll have plenty of options, from the big rental chains to luxury options. The common rental agencies regularly stock new American-made models with standard amenities (air-conditioning, automatic transmission, AM/FM stereo).

Rates in Chicago begin at around $50 a day, $130 a week or $35 a weekend for an economy car with air-conditioning, automatic transmission, and unlimited mileage. This does not include the car-rental tax and other taxes totaling 18% plus a $2.75 surcharge per rental. If you rent from the airport, it's slightly more expensive because of airport taxes.

GASOLINE
Gas stations are lessnumerous in downtown Chicago than in the outlying neighborhoods and suburbs. Filling up is about 50 cents higher per gallon downtown, when you can find a station. Expect to pay anywhere between $2 and $3 per gallon of gas (prices at time of writing). Major credit cards are accepted at all gas stations, and the majority of stations are completely self-serve.

PARKING
Most of Chicago's streets have metered parking, but during peak hours it's hard to find a spot. Most meters take quarters, buying as little as 5 minutes in high-traffic areas, up to an hour in less crowded neighborhoods. Parking lots and garages are plentiful downtown, but they're expensive. You could pay anywhere from $13 for the day in a municipal lot to $24 for three hours in a private lot. Some neighborhoods, such as the area of Lakeview known as Wrigleyville, enforce restricted parking (especially strict on game nights) and will tow cars without permits. You won't find many public parking lots in the neighborhoods. Many major thoroughfares restrict parking during peak travel hours, generally 9 to 11 AM heading toward downtown and 4 to 6 PM heading away. Read street signs carefully to determine whether a parking spot is legal. On snow days in winter cars parked in designated "snow route areas" will be towed. There's a $30 fine plus the cost of towing the car. In sum, Chicago isn't the most car-friendly place for visitors. Unless it's a necessity, it's best to forget renting a car and use public transportation.

ROAD CONDITIONS
Chicago drivers can be reckless, zipping through red lights and breaking posted speed limits. The Loop and some residential neighborhoods such as Lincoln Park, Lakeview, and Bucktown are made up of mostly one-way streets, so be sure to read signs carefully. Check both ways after a light turns green to make sure that the cross traffic has stopped.

Rush hours are 6:30 to 9:30 AM and 4 to 7 PM, but don't be surprised if the rush starts earlier or ends later, depending on weather conditions, big events, and holiday weekends. There are always bottlenecks on the expressways, particularly where the Edens and Kennedy merge, and downtown on the Dan Ryan from 22nd Street into the Loop. Sometimes anything around the airport is rough. There are electronic signs on the expressways that post updates on the congestion. Additionally, summertime is high time for construction on highways and inner-city roads. Drive with patience.

■ TIP→ For more information about Chicago's roadways, including up-to-the-minute road conditions, check out the Illinois

Department of Transportation's Web site at www.dot.state.il.us.

ROADSIDE EMERGENCIES

Dial 911 in an emergency to reach police, fire, or ambulance services. AAA Chicago provides roadside assistance to members. Mr. Locks Emergency Locksmith & Security Service will unlock your vehicle 24 hours a day.

Emergency Services AAA Chicago (☎ 800/222-4357 [AAA-HELP]) ⊕ www.auto clubgroup.com). **Mr. Locks Emergency Locksmith & Security Service** (☎ 866/675-6257 ⊕ www.mr-locks.com).

RULES OF THE ROAD

Speed limits in Chicago vary, but on most city roads it's 35 mph. Most interstate highways, except in congested areas, have a speed limit of 55 mph. In Chicago you may turn right at a red light after stopping if there's no oncoming traffic and no posted restrictions. When in doubt, wait for the green. Cameras have been installed at certain intersections in the city to catch drivers who run red lights. There are many one-way streets in Chicago, particularly in and around the Loop, so be alert to signs and other cars. Illinois drunk-driving laws are quite strict. Anyone caught driving with a blood-alcohol content of .08 will automatically have his or her license seized and be issued a ticket, and authorities in home states will be notified. Those with Illinois drivers' licenses can have their licenses suspended for three months on the very first offense.

Passengers are required to wear seat belts. Always strap children under age eight into approved child-safety seats.

It's illegal to use hand-held cellular phones in the city, but there aren't any restrictions in the suburbs. Headlights are compulsory if you're using windshield wipers. Radar detectors are legal in Illinois.

▌ BY PUBLIC TRANSPORTATION

Chicago's extensive public transportation network includes rapid-transit trains, buses, and a commuter-rail network. The Chicago Transit Authority, or CTA, operates the rapid-transit trains (the El), city buses, and suburban buses (PACE). Metra runs the commuter rail.

The Regional Transportation Authority (RTA) for northeastern Illinois oversees and coordinates the activities of the CTA and Metra. The RTA's Web site can be a useful first stop if you are planning to combine suburban and city public transit while in Chicago. In 2008 the state passed legislation that gives seniors a free ride—literally. Seniors age 65 and older ride free on all fixed train and bus routes operated by the CTA, Metra, and Pace. Details about where to sign up and which routes are eligible are available on the RTA's Web site.

Information RTA Travel Information Center (☎ 312/836-7000 ⊕ www.rtachicago.com).

CTA: THE EL & BUSES

The Chicago Transit Authority (CTA) operates rapid-transit trains and buses. Chicago's rapid-transit train system is known as the El. Each of the eight lines has a color name as well as a route name: Blue (O'Hare–Congress–Douglas), Brown (Ravenswood), Green (Lake–Englewood–Jackson Park), Orange (Midway), Purple (Evanston), Red (Howard–Dan Ryan), Yellow (Skokie Swift), and Pink (Cermak). In general, the route names indicate the first and last stop on the train. Chicagoans refer to trains both by the color and the route name. Most, but not all, rapid-transit lines operate 24 hours; some stations are closed at night. The El, though very crowded during rush hours, is the quickest way to get around (unless you're coming from the suburbs, in which case the Metra is quicker but doesn't run as often). Trains run every 15 minutes, though during rush hour they run about every 10 minutes, and on weekends every 30 minutes. Pick up the brochure "Downtown Transit Sightseeing Guide" for hours, fares, and other pertinent information. In general, late-night CTA travel is not recommended. Note that the Red and Blue lines are subways; the rest are elevated. This means if you're heading to O'Hare and looking for the Blue Line, look for a stairway down, not up.

Fares must be paid by transit card on trains; buses accept both transit cards and cash (dollar bills or coins; no change given). Transit cards are flimsy plastic and credit-card size and can be purchased from machines at CTA train stations as well as at Jewel and Dominicks grocery stores and currency exchanges. These easy-to-use cards are inserted into the turnstiles at CTA train stations and into machines as you board CTA buses; directions are clearly posted. Use them to transfer between CTA vehicles. To transfer between the Loop's elevated lines and the subway or between rapid-transit trains and buses, you must either use a transit card with at least 25¢ stored on it, or, if you're not using a transit card, buy a transfer when you first board. If two CTA train lines meet, you can transfer for free. You can also obtain free train-to-train transfers from specially marked turnstiles at the Washington/State subway station or the State/Lake El station, or ask for a transfer card, good on downtown trains, at the ticket booth.

Buses generally stop on every other corner northbound and southbound (on State Street they stop at every corner). Eastbound and westbound buses generally stop on every corner. Buses from the Loop generally run north–south. Principal transfer points are on Michigan Avenue at the north side of Randolph Street for northbound buses, Adams Street and Wabash Avenue for westbound buses and the El, and State and Lake streets for southbound buses.

Buses are crowded during rush hour. Schedules vary depending on the time of day and route, and run every 8 to 15 minutes, though service is less frequent on weekends, very early in the morning, and late at night. Schedules are available online at www.transitchicago.com.

Pace runs suburban buses in a six-county region; these connect with the CTA and use CTA transit cards, transfers, and passes.

CTA Fares: The CTA fare structure is as follows: the basic fare for rapid-transit trains is $2.25 by transit card. The basic fare for buses is $2.25 when paying cash and $2 when using a transit card. Transfers are 25¢ when using a transit card; no transfers are issued when paying cash. Transit cards can be purchased in preset denominations of $10 or $20 at many local grocery stores, currency exchanges, and stations. You can also purchase a transit card of any denomination over $2 at any CTA stop. Transfers can be used twice within a two-hour time period. Transfers between CTA train lines are free—no transfer card is needed. Transit cards may be shared.

For $5.75 a one-day Visitor Pass offers 24 hours of unlimited CTA riding from the time you first use it. Visitor Passes are sold at hotels, museums, and other places tourists frequent, plus all transit-card booths. A three-day pass is $14, and a seven-day pass is $23.

Information CTA (⊠ *Merchandise Mart, 350 N. Wells St.* ☎ *888/968–7282* ⊕ *www.transit chicago.com*).

METRA: COMMUTER TRAINS

Metra commuter trains serve the city and surrounding suburbs. The Metra Electric railroad has a line close to Lake Michigan; its trains stop in Hyde Park. The Metra commuter rail system has 11 lines to suburbs and surrounding cities including Aurora, Elgin, Joliet, and Waukegan; one line serves the North Shore suburbs, and another has a stop at McCormick Place. Trains leave from a number of downtown terminals.

Metra trains use a fare structure based on the distance you ride. A Metra weekend pass costs $5 and is valid for rides on any of the eight operating lines all day on weekends, except for the South Shore line.

Information Metra information line
(☎ *312/322–6777* ⊕ *www.metrarail.com*).

▌BY TAXI

You can hail a cab on just about any busy street in Chicago. Hotel doormen will hail a cab for you as well. Cabs aren't all yellow anymore, but look for standard-size sedans or, in some cases, minivans. Available taxis are sometimes indicated by an illuminated rooftop light. Chicago taxis are metered, with fares beginning at $2.25 upon entering the cab and $1.80 for each additional mile or 20¢ for every 36 seconds of wait time. A charge of $1 for the first additional passenger and 50¢ is made for each additional passenger. There's no extra baggage or credit-card charge. Taxi drivers expect a 15% tip.

Taxi Companies American United Cab Co. (☎ *773/248–7600*). **Checker Taxi** (☎ *312/243–2537*). **Flash Cab** (☎ *773/561–1444* ⊕ *www.flashcab.com*). **Yellow Cab Co.** (☎ *312/829–4222* ⊕ *www.yellowcabchicago.com*).

▌BY TRAIN

Amtrak offers nationwide service to Chicago's Union Station, located at 225 South Canal Street. Some trains travel overnight, and you can sleep in your seat or book a sleeper car at an additional cost. Train schedules and payment options are available by calling Amtrak directly or consulting its Web site. Amtrak trains tend to fill up, so if you don't purchase a ticket in advance at least make a reservation.

Information Amtrak (☎ *800/872-7245* ⊕ *www.amtrak.com*).

ESSENTIALS

▌ COMMUNICATIONS

INTERNET

Chicago is more and more a wireless city, with many hotels and restaurants offering high-speed wireless access. Some hotels have a nominal fee (usually less than $10) that gets you online for 24 hours. You can also duck into places like FedEx Kinko's to check your e-mail, either on your own laptop or the available computers, but charges there can run high if you're online longer than a few minutes.

Contacts Cybercafes (⊕ www.cybercafes. com) lists over 4,000 Internet cafés worldwide. **FedEx Kinko's** (⊠ 444 N. Wells St. ☎ 312/670–4460 ⊕ www.fedexkinkos.com). **The Fixx Coffee Bar** (⊠ 3053 N. Sheffield Ave. ☎ 773/248–0841). **Intelligentsia Coffee & Tea** (⊠ 3123 N. Broadway St. ☎ 773/348–8058). **Mercury Cafe** (⊠ 1505 W. Chicago Ave. ☎ 312/455–9924). **State Restaurant & Cafe** (⊠ 935 W. Webster Ave. ☎ 773/975–8030). **Swim Cafe** (⊠ 1357 W. Chicago Ave. ☎ 312/492–8600).

▌ DAY TOURS AND GUIDES

A comprehensive collection of Chicago tours by air, water, and land can be found through **Chicago Tours** (☎ 888/881–3284 ⊕ www.chicagotours.us), a travel-reservation company offering more than 75 tours, cruises, events, and activities.

BOAT TOURS

Get a fresh perspective on Chicago by taking a water tour or cruise. Boat tour schedules vary by season; be sure to call for exact times and fares. The season usually runs from May 1 through mid-November. One cruise in particular stands out, though it's a bit more expensive than the rest: the Chicago Architecture Foundation river cruise aboard *Chicago's First Lady, Chicago's Little Lady,* or *Chicago's Fair Lady.* The CAF tour highlights more than 50 architecturally significant sights.

The cost is $28 on weekdays, $32 on weekends and holidays; reservations are recommended.

If you're looking for a maritime adventure, you can get a blast from the past on the *Windy,* a 148-foot ship modeled on old-time commercial vessels. Passengers may help the crew or take a turn at the wheel during sailing cruises of Lake Michigan. The cost is $30.

Boat Tours Chicago Architecture Foundation river cruise (☎ 312/922–3432 information, 312/902–1500 tickets ⊕ www.architecture.org). **Mercury Chicago Skyline Cruiseline** (☎ 312/332–1353 recorded information ⊕ www.mercuryskylinecruiseline.com). **Shoreline Marine** (☎ 312/222–9328 ⊕ www.shorelinesightseeing.com). **Wendella Sightseeing Boats** (⊠ 400 N. Michigan Ave. ☎ 312/337–1446 ⊕ www.wendellaboats.com). **Windy of Chicago Ltd.** (☎ 312/595–5555 ⊕ www.tallshipwindy.com).

BUS AND TROLLEY TOURS

A narrated bus or trolley tour can be a good way to orient yourself among Chicago's main sights. Tours cost roughly $20 and normally last two hours. American Sightseeing offers two routes; combined, they cover the city quite thoroughly. The double-decker buses of Chicago Motor

Coach Company tour downtown Chicago and the lakefront.

Chicago Trolley Charters schedules stops at all the downtown attractions. You can get on and off the open-air trolleys as you like; these tours vary in price, so call for details. The Chicago Architecture Foundation's bus tours often go farther afield, exploring everything from cemeteries to movie palaces.

Bus & Trolley Tours American Sightseeing (☎ 800/621–4153 ⊕ www.grayline.com). **Chicago Architecture Foundation** (Tour Center ⊠ Santa Fe Bldg., 224 S. Michigan Ave. ☎ 312/922–3432 ⊕ www.architecture.org). **Chicago Trolley Charters** (☎ 773/648–5000 ⊕ www.chicagotrolley.com).

FOREIGN-LANGUAGE TOURS

Foreign-Language Tours Chicago Tour Guides Institute, Inc. (☎ 773/276–6683 ⊕ www.chicagoguide.net).

SPECIAL-INTEREST TOURS

African-American Black Coutours (☎ 773/233–8907 ⊕ www.blackcoutours. com). **Tour Black Chicago** (☎ 773/684–9034 ⊕ www.tourblackchicago.com).

Architecture ⇨ Walking Tours.

Chocolate Accenting Chicago (☎ 312/819–5363 ⊕ www.accentingchicago.com). **Chicago Chocolate Tours** (☎ 312/929–2939 ⊕ www. chicagochocolatetours.com).

Gangsters Untouchable Tours (☎ 773/881–1195 ⊕ www.gangstertour.com).

Ghosts Chicago Supernatural Ghost Tours (☎ 708/499–0300 ⊕ www.ghosttours.com).

Historic Neighborhoods Black Metropolis Convention and Tourism Council (☎ 773/373–2842 ⊕ www.bronzevilleonline. com/bvic.htm). **Chicago Neighborhood Tours** (☎ 312/742–1190 ⊕ www.chicagoneighborhoodtours.com).

Horse & Carriage Rides Antique Coach and Carriage (☎ 773/735–9400 ⊕ www. antiquecoach-carriage.com). **Chicago Horse & Carriage Ltd.** (☎ 773/395–3950 ⊕ www.chicagocarriage.com). **Noble Horse** (☎ 312/266–7878 ⊕ www.noblehorsechicago. com).

WALKING TOURS

The Chicago Architecture Foundation has by far the largest selection of guided tours, with more than 50 itineraries covering everything from department stores to Frank Lloyd Wright's Oak Park buildings. Especially popular walking tours of the Loop are given daily throughout the year. Chicago Greeter and InstaGreeter (for last-minute weekend visits) are two free city services that match knowledgeable Chicagoans with visitors for tours of various sights and neighborhoods.

Information Chicago Architecture Foundation (Tour Centers ⊠ Santa Fe Bldg., 224 S. Michigan Ave. ☎ 312/922–3432 ⊕ www. architecture.org). **Chicago Greeter and InstaGreeter** (⊠ Chicago Office of Tourism, 78 E. Washington St. ☎ 312/744–2400 ⊕ www. chicagogreeter.com).

▮ HOURS OF OPERATION

Neighborhood business hours are generally 9 to 6 Friday through Wednesday, and 9 to 9 on Thursday. When holidays fall on a weekend, businesses usually close around four on the preceding Friday. On a Monday following a weekend holiday, retail businesses are rarely closed but regular businesses often are. Most stores close for Christmas, New Year's, and Easter Sunday.

Chicagoland museums are generally open daily 9 to 5, closing only on major holidays; some larger attractions keep later hours (until about 8 PM) one weeknight per week. A number of smaller museums keep limited hours; it's always advisable to phone ahead for details.

Most pharmacies are open regular business hours, starting as early as 8 AM. Some close as early as 5 PM, but many stay open later, anywhere from 6 to 10 PM.

Most businesses in Chicago are open 9 to 5 Monday through Saturday; many are open Sunday, too, but often with shorter hours (for example, noon to 4 or 5).

▮ MONEY

Costs in Chicago are quite reasonable compared to other large cities such as San Francisco and New York. Restaurants, events, and parking costs are markedly higher in the Loop than in any other area of the city.

ATMs are plentiful. You can find them in banks, grocery stores, and hotels, as well as at some drug stores, gas stations, and convenience stores.

Prices throughout this guide are given for adults. Substantially reduced fees are almost always available for children, students, and senior citizens.

▮ PACKING

In general, Chicago's out-and-about look is casual—jeans, a polished top, and comfortable shoes should be fine for touring around the city. The weather can change abruptly, so it's a good idea to dress in layers. Summers can be very hot and winters very cold and windy—hat, gloves, a scarf, and a warm coat are vital. Don't forget an umbrella.

For dining out, most elegant restaurants in the city require a shirt and tie for men and a dressy look for women. For mass, church, or synagogue services, people usually dress in nice slacks or skirts or dresses. Men do not always wear a suit or a sport jacket, but rarely wear jeans.

▮ RESTROOMS

Facilities are readily available in tourist areas and throughout the downtown malls, Navy Pier, and in many larger department stores. For the most part, restrooms are quite clean. Along the lakefront and in the park districts public facilities close in wintertime. Most gas stations have restrooms, though sanitation standards vary.

> **TIPS TO REMEMBER**
>
> To save money on sightseeing, buy a **Chicago CityPass** (☎ 888/330–5008 ⊕ www.citypass.com/city/chicago), which costs $69. The passes are good for nine days from the day of first use and include admission to the Field Museum, the Museum of Science and Industry, the Adler Planetarium, the Shedd Aquarium, and either the John Hancock Center Observatory or the Sears Tower Skydeck. You can buy the pass at any one of the participating attractions or on the Web site. The **Go Chicago Card** (☎ 866/628–9031 ⊕ www.gochicagocard.com) is good for more than 25 attractions and shopping, dining, and hotel discounts. The card can be purchased as a one-day or a multiday pass.

Find a Loo The Bathroom Diaries (⊕ www.thebathroomdiaries.com) is flush with unsanitized info on restrooms the world over—each one located, reviewed, and rated.

▮ SAFETY

The most common crimes in public places are pickpocketing, purse snatching, jewelry theft, and gambling scams. Men: keep your wallet in a front coat or pants pocket. Women: close your purse securely and keep it close to you. Also beware of someone jostling you and of loud arguments; these could be ploys to distract your attention while another person grabs your wallet. Leave unnecessary credit cards at home and hide valuables and jewelry from view.

Although crime on CTA buses and trains has declined, several precautions can reduce the chance of your becoming a victim: look alert and purposeful; know your route ahead of time; have your fare ready before boarding; and keep an eye on your purse or packages during the ride. Avoid taking public transit late at night.

▮TIP→**Distribute your cash, credit cards, I.D.s, and other valuables between a deep**

FOR INTERNATIONAL TRAVELERS

CURRENCY

The dollar is the basic unit of U.S. currency. It has 100 cents. Coins are the penny (1¢); the nickel (5¢), dime (10¢), quarter (25¢), half-dollar (50¢), and the rare golden $1 coin and rarer silver $1. Bills are denominated $1, $5, $10, $20, $50, and $100, all mostly green and identical in size; designs and background tints vary. A $2 bill exists but is extremely rare.

CUSTOMS

Information U.S. Customs and Border Protection (⊕ www.cbp.gov).

DRIVING

Driving in the United States is on the right. Speed limits are posted in miles per hour (usually between 55 mph and 70 mph). In small towns and on back roads limits are usually 30 mph to 40 mph. Most states require front-seat passengers to wear seat belts; children should be in the back seat and buckled up. In major cities, rush hours are 7 to 10 AM and 4 to 7 PM. Some freeways have high-occupancy vehicle (HOV) lanes, ordinarily marked with a diamond, for cars carrying two people or more.

Highways are well paved. Interstates—limited-access, multilane highways designated with an "I–" before the number—are fastest. Interstates with three-digit numbers circle urban areas, which may also have other expressways, freeways, and parkways. Limited-access highways sometimes have tolls.

Gas stations are plentiful, except in rural areas. Most stay open late (some 24 hours). Along larger highways, roadside stops with restrooms, fast-food restaurants, and sundries stores are well spaced. State police and tow trucks patrol major highways. If your car breaks down, pull onto the shoulder and wait, or have passengers wait while you walk to a roadside emergency phone (most states). On a cell phone, dial *55.

ELECTRICITY

The U.S. standard is AC, 110 volts/60 cycles. Plugs have two flat pins set parallel to each other.

EMERGENCIES

For police, fire, or ambulance, dial 911 (0 in rural areas).

HOLIDAYS

New Year's Day (Jan. 1); Martin Luther King Day (3rd Mon. in Jan.); Presidents' Day (3rd Mon. in Feb.); Memorial Day (last Mon. in May); Independence Day (July 4); Labor Day (1st Mon. in Sept.); Columbus Day (2nd Mon. in Oct.); Thanksgiving Day (4th Thurs. in Nov.); Christmas Eve and Christmas Day (Dec. 24 and 25); and New Year's Eve (Dec. 31).

MAIL

You can buy stamps and send letters and parcels in post offices. Stamp-dispensing machines can occasionally be found in airports, bus and train stations, office buildings, drugstores, convenience stores, and in ATMs. U.S. mailboxes are stout, dark-blue steel bins; pickup schedules are posted inside the bin (pull the handle). Mail parcels over a pound at a post office. A first-class letter weighing 1 ounce or less costs 42¢; each additional ounce costs 17¢. Postcards cost 27¢. Postcards or 1-ounce airmail letters to most countries cost 94¢; postcards or 1-ounce letters to Canada or Mexico cost 72¢.

To receive mail on the road, have it sent c/o General Delivery to your destination's main post office. You must pick up mail in person within 30 days with a driver's license or passport for identification.

Contacts DHL (☎ *800/225-5345* ⊕ *www.dhl.com*). **FedEx** (☎ *800/ 463-3339* ⊕ *www.fedex.com*). **Mail Boxes, Etc./The UPS Store** (☎ *800/789-4623* ⊕ *www.mbe. com*). **USPS** (⊕ *www.usps.com*).

PASSPORTS AND VISAS

Visitor visas aren't necessary for citizens of Australia, Canada, the United Kingdom, or most citizens of EU countries coming for tourism and staying for under 90 days. A visa is $100, and waiting time can be substantial. Apply for a visa at the U.S. consulate in your place of residence.

Visa Information **Destination USA** (⊕ *www.unitedstatesvisas.gov*).

PHONES

Numbers consist of a three-digit area code and a seven-digit local number. Within many local calling areas, dial just seven digits. In others, dial "1" first and all 10 digits; this is true for calling toll-free numbers—prefixed by "800," "888," "866," and "877." Dial "1" before "900" numbers, too, but know they're very expensive.

Chicago has six local area codes: 312 covers the downtown vicinity; 773 blankets the surrounding city neighborhoods. In the near west and south suburbs of Cook and Will counties, it's 708. The northern and northwestern suburbs in Cook, Lake, and Kane counties get the 847 area code, while the suburbs due west of the city have 630. Far outlying areas northwest and south of Chicago in

McHenry, Will, and Kendall counties are outfitted with the prefix 815.

For international calls, dial "011," the country code, and the number. For help, dial "0" and ask for an overseas operator. Most phone books list country codes and U.S. area codes. The country code for Australia is 61, for New Zealand 64, for the United Kingdom 44. Calling Canada is the same as calling within the United States (country code: 1).

For operator assistance, dial "0." For directory assistance, call 555-1212 or 411 (free at many public phones). To call "collect" (reverse charges), dial "0" instead of "1" before the 10-digit number.

Instructions are generally posted on pay phones. Usually you insert coins in a slot (usually 25¢–50¢ for local calls) and wait for a steady tone before dialing. On long-distance calls the operator tells you how much to insert; prepaid phone cards, widely available, can be used from any phone. Follow the directions to activate the card, then dial your number.

Cell Phones The United States has several GSM (Global System for Mobile Communications) networks, so multiband mobiles from most countries (except for Japan) work here. It's almost impossible to buy just a pay-as-you-go mobile SIM card in the U.S.—needed to avoid roaming charges—but cell phones with pay-as-you-go plans are available for well under $100. AT&T (GoPhone) and Virgin Mobile have the cheapest with national coverage.

Contacts Cingular (⊕ *www.cin gular.com*). **Virgin Mobile** (⊕ *www. virginmobileusa.com*).

front pocket, an inside jacket or vest pocket, and a hidden money pouch. Don't reach for the money pouch once you're in public.

▌ TAXES

At restaurants you'll pay approximately 10% meal tax (thanks to special taxing initiatives, some parts of town are higher than others).

The hotel tax in Chicago is 15.4%, and slightly less in suburban hotels.

In Chicago a steep 10.25% state and county sales tax is added to all purchases except groceries, which have a 2% tax. Sales tax is already added into the initial price of prescription drugs.

▌ TIME

Chicago is in the central standard time zone. It's 1 hour behind New York, 2 hours ahead of Los Angeles, 6 hours behind London, and 16 hours behind Sydney.

Time Zones Timeanddate.com (⊕ *www.time anddate.com/worldclock*) can help you figure out the correct time anywhere in the world.

▌ TIPPING

You should tip 15% for adequate service in restaurants and up to 20% if you feel you've been treated well. At higher-end restaurants, where there are more service personnel per table who must divide the tip, up these measures by a few percentage points. An especially helpful wine steward should be acknowledged with $2 or $3. It's not necessary to tip the maître d' unless you've been done a very special favor and you intend to visit again. Tip $1 per checked coat.

Taxi drivers, bartenders, and hairdressers expect about 15%. Bellhops and porters should get about $1 per bag; valet-parking attendants $1 or $2 (but only after they bring your car to you, not when they park it), and hotel maids about $1 to $2 per room per day of your stay. On package tours, conductors and drivers usually get about $2 to $3 per day from each group member. Concierges should get tips of $5 to $10 for special service.

▌ VISITOR INFORMATION

The Chicago Convention and Tourism Bureau is a great place to start planning your visit to the Windy City. The organization's Web site (⊕ *www.choosechicago. com*) is a veritable goldmine of information, from hotel packages to sample itineraries, event calendars, and maps. You can also call the toll-free number (☎ *877/ CHICAGO*) to speak with a travel consultant. The Mayor's Office of Special Events Web site will give you detailed instructions about getting around the city, neighborhood tours, and city-sponsored initiatives. The Illinois Bureau of Tourism offers much of the same Chicago information and is especially helpful if your travel plans will bring you outside of the downtown area. Once you're here, you can count on the visitor centers at the Chicago Cultural Center, Chicago Water Works, and Navy Pier. They are stocked with free maps, local publications, and knowledgeable staff to help you out.

Contacts Chicago Convention and Tourism Bureau (✉ *2301 S. Lake Shore Dr.* ☎ *312/567–8500 or 877/CHICAGO [877/244–2246]* ⊕ *www.choosechicago.com*). **Chicago Cultural Center** (✉ *78 E. Randolph St.,* ☎ *312/744–6630* ⊕ *egov.cityofchicago. org*). **Chicago Water Works** (✉ *163 E. Pearson,* ☎ *312/742–8811* ⊕ *www.choosechicago. com*). **Illinois Bureau of Tourism** (✉ *James R. Thompson Center, 100 W. Randolph St., Suite 3-400,* ☎ *800/2CONNECT [800/226–6632]* ⊕ *www.enjoyillinois.com*). **Mayor's Office of Special Events, General Information, and Activities** (✉ *121 N. LaSalle St., Room 806,* ☎ *312/744–3315* ⊕ *egov.cityofchicago.org*). **Navy Pier Welcome Center** (✉ *600 E. Grand Ave.* ☎ *800/595–7437 or 312/595–7437* ⊕ *www.navypier.com*).

ONLINE TRAVEL TOOLS
ALL ABOUT CHICAGO
The Chicago Convention and Tourism Bureau's site, *www.choosechicago.com*, has plenty of general tips on the city and local events, plus helpful information on convention facilities.There's also plenty of information on the City of Chicago Web site, *egov.cityofchicago.org*, from festival details to neighborhood overviews and services for visitors from the Chicago Office of Tourism.For a user-friendly introduction to the city, log on to *www.chicago.com*.

ART
For a preview of the Art Institute of Chicago, check out *www.artic.edu*.And to learn about gallery openings and art events, check out *www.chicagoartdealers.org*.

NEWSPAPERS & MAGAZINES
The Web sites of the city's daily newspapers, the *Tribune* (*www.chicagotribune.com*) and the *Sun-Times* (*www.suntimes.com/index*), are great sources for reviews and events listings.The *Chicago Reader*'s site, *www.chireader.com*, is rich in arts, entertainment, and dining reviews.*Chicago* magazine's site, *www.chicagomag.com*, carries a few Web-exclusive features along with articles from the monthly.Metromix *www.metromix.com* thoroughly covers Chicago's entertainment scene. Another good online entertainment reference is *www.timeout.com/chicago*, which gives an irreverent, in-depth look at Chicago diversions.

PUBLIC TRANSIT
To sort out the public-transit system, log on to the CTA's site at *www.transitchicago.com*.

INDEX

NOTES

NOTES

NOTES

NOTES

NOTES

NOTES

NOTES

NOTES

ABOUT OUR WRITERS

Kelly Aiglon is a Chicago-based freelance writer who enjoys sleeping in hotels—even if they're just blocks from her home. She is the editor of DailyCandy Kids Chicago and the former editor of Where Chicago Magazine, plus a contributor to the *Chicago Tribune, AAA Living,* and *Modern Luxury* magazines. She updated this edition's Museums and Architecture chapters.

Kate Leahy, *Chicago 2010*'s dining updater, is a Chicago-based journalist covering restaurant news for *Restaurants & Institutions* magazine and the coauthor of *A16 Food + Wine* (Ten Speed Press, 2008). Even though she spent five years as a line cook working in Boston, San Francisco, and the Napa Valley, she happily cedes cooking responsibilities to Chicago chefs when she goes out to eat.

Heidi Moore is a fifth-generation Chicagoan who loves exploring the city's neighborhoods, though she always comes back to the Northwest Side. A freelance writer, editor, and children's book author, Heidi has written for the *Chicago Tribune, Time Out Chicago,* and *Alaska Airlines Magazine,* among other publications. She updated this year's Neighborhoods and Entertainment chapters and the Travel Smart section.

Jo Napolitano has been a writer for 11 years. She freelanced for the *New York Times* for two and half years before working as a staff reporter for the Chicago Tribune. She is originally from Long Island, but has called Chicago her home for 8 years. Jo updated the Where to Stay chapter.

Roberta Sotonoff, a confessed travel junkie, writes to support her habit. More than 60 domestic and international newspapers, magazines, online sites, and guidebooks have published her work. One of her favorite destinations is her hometown, Chicago. This year she updated the Experience, Shopping, and Understanding chapters.